Cultura Inglesa

face2face

Intermediate Student's Book

with CD–ROM/
Audio CD

Chris Redston & Gillie Cunningham

CAMBRIDGE
UNIVERSITY PRESS

Contents

1 How do you feel?

1A Be happy!

Vocabulary weekend activities
Grammar question forms
Help with Listening questions with *you*

QUICK REVIEW ●●●

Talk to five other students. Introduce yourself and find out two things about each person. Tell the class about two people you spoke to.

Vocabulary Weekend activities

 a) Match the verbs in A to the words/phrases in B. Check in Language Summary 1 V1.1 p114.

A	B
visit	a lie-in
go	relatives
have	clubbing
meet up	a quiet night in
do	with friends
have	some gardening
tidy up	some exercise
do	the house/the flat
go	to exhibitions
chat	for a walk/a run
have	to people online
go	people round for dinner

b) Which of the things in 1a) do you: usually, often, sometimes, never do at the weekend? What other things do you do at the weekend?

c) Work in pairs. Compare ideas.

> I sometimes go to exhibitions at the weekend. Yes, so do I.

Reading

 a) Read the beginning of the article about happiness. How did the scientists make their top ten list?

b) Look at these reasons for happiness. Put them in order from 1–10 (1 = the most important).

- friends and family
- money
- being married
- helping others
- your genes
- being attractive
- growing old
- religion
- intelligence
- not wanting more than you've got

c) Work in pairs. Compare lists. Explain the order you chose.

 Turn to p113. Follow the instructions and read the rest of the article.

The secret of happiness

Many people think that being clever, rich and attractive is the best way to find happiness. But according to a recent report in *New Scientist* magazine, these things aren't as important as we think. A group of scientists reviewed hundreds of research studies from around the world and then made a list of the top ten reasons for happiness – and their list makes very surprising reading.

£1000

Listening and Grammar

 a) Look at the photos of Sarah, Greg and Jenny. What makes them happy, do you think?

b) R1.1 Listen and write two things that make each person happy.

c) Listen again. Answer these questions.

1 Who does Sarah work for? *Her father.*
2 What are her children doing at the moment?
3 What did Sarah do last Saturday?
4 How many countries has Greg been to?
5 Where did he go last year?
6 How often does he work in his garden?
7 Does Jenny usually get up early on Saturdays?
8 What did she have for breakfast last Sunday?
9 What makes her flatmate happy?

Greg

Sarah

Jenny

 Fill in the gaps in these questions with *do*, *are*, *have*, *did* or – (no auxiliary).

1 Whereabouts _do_ you live?
2 How long .... you lived there?
3 Who .... you live with?
4 Who .... gets up first in your home?
5 Why .... you studying English?
6 Who .... told you about this school?
7 .... you study here last year?
8 How many countries .... you been to in your life?
9 Which of your friends .... lives closest to you?
10 What .... you do last New Year?

Help with Listening Questions with *you*

 a) Work in pairs. How do we usually say the auxiliaries and *you* in the questions in **6**?

b) R1.2 Listen to the questions in **6**. Notice how we say *do you* /dʒə/, *have you* /həvjə/, *are you* /əjə/ and *did you* /dɪdʒə/.

 a) R1.2 P Listen again and practise.

Whereabouts do you /dʒə/ live?

TIP! ● P = pronounciation.

b) Work in pairs. Take turns to ask and answer the questions in **6**. Ask follow-up questions.

c) Tell the class three things you found out about your partner.

 Work in new pairs. Student A → p102. Student B → p107. Follow the instructions.

Help with Grammar Question forms

 a) Match questions 1–4 in **4c)** to these verb forms.

Present Simple *1*   Past Simple
Present Perfect Simple   Present Continuous

b) Write questions 2–4 from **4c)** in the table.

question word	auxiliary	subject	verb	
Who	does	Sarah	work	for?

c) Which auxiliaries do we use in the verb forms in **5a)**?

d) Look at questions 8 and 9 in **4c)**. Answer these questions.

1 Is the question word the subject or the object in these questions?
2 Why doesn't question 9 have an auxiliary?

e) Find two questions in **4c)** which have a preposition at the end.

f) Check in Language Summary 1 G1.1 p115.

Get ready ... Get it right!

a) Make a list of the top ten things you do that make you happy.

1 go out for a meal with friends
2 read in bed

b) Work in pairs. Swap lists. Write one question to ask about each thing on your partner's list.

When did you last go out for a meal with friends?
Which book are you reading at the moment?

a) Work with your partner. Take turns to ask and answer your questions. Ask follow-up questions if possible.

b) Tell the class about some of the things that make your partner happy.

1B Love it or hate it

Vocabulary likes and dislikes
Grammar positive and negative verb forms, words and phrases
Help with Listening sentence stress (1)
Review question forms

QUICK REVIEW ● ● ●
Choose a partner, but don't talk to him/her yet. Write five questions to ask your partner. Work in pairs. Take turns to ask and answer your questions. Tell the class something interesting you found out about your partner.

Vocabulary Likes and dislikes

 Match these phrases to a)–c). Check in **V1.2** p114.

> I really love ... *a)*   I really hate ...
> I don't like ... at all.   I can't stand ...
> I'm really/very/quite interested in ...
> I think ... is/are all right.
> ... really get(s) on my nerves.
> I can't bear ...   I enjoy ...
> I don't mind ...   I'm not very keen on ...
> I'm really/very/quite keen on ...
> ... drive(s) me crazy.
> I think ... is/are really boring/annoying.
> I think ... is/are great/brilliant/wonderful.

a) phrases to say you like something
b) phrases to say something is OK
c) phrases to say you don't like something

TIP! ● In these vocabulary boxes we only show the main stress in phrases.

 a) Think about how you feel about these things. Choose a different phrase from 1 for each thing.

- waiting in queues
- doing the washing-up
- buying new shoes
- going on long journeys
- getting up early
- watching reality TV

b) Work in pairs. Compare ideas. Explain why you feel like this.

Reading and Grammar

 Work in groups. Discuss these questions.

1 Have you got a mobile phone? If so, how important is it to you? If not, why haven't you got one?
2 What are the good things and bad things about mobile phones? Make two lists.

Love-hate relationships

Mobile phones

Amy

"I love my mobile. [1]I didn't get one for ages, but now I don't think I could live without one. I hardly ever call people during the day because it's quite expensive, but I text my friends all the time. My phone's also got a camera, but [2]I haven't taken many photos with it. Also I feel much safer with my mobile and never leave home without it, especially at night. The only problem is when the battery runs out or there's no signal – [3]that's happened to me once or twice, usually when [4]I'm trying to get home late at night and there are no taxis around. But [5]I don't have my mobile on all the time – when [6]I'm not feeling very sociable or talkative I just switch it off."

Amy Hansen, London

"I really hate mobile phones. None of my friends can understand why I haven't got one, but no one thinks about how annoying mobiles are to other people. Everyone always talks very loudly when they're on their mobiles and I can't bear listening to other people's conversations when I'm on the train. Also the ring tones really get on my nerves! Both of my brothers have got mobiles, but when [7]we meet up, neither of them ever switches their phone off, which drives me crazy. Last time [8]we went out for a drink together, their phones rang five times! I know I can't stop other people having them, but I don't think I'll get one."

Jeremy Fuller, Birmingham

Jeremy

4 **a)** [R1.3] **Look at the article. Read and listen to Amy and Jeremy. Which things on your lists from 3 do they talk about?**

b) Read the article again. Are these sentences true (T) or false (F)?

1 Amy phones people a lot during the day.
2 She often uses the camera on her phone.
3 She always takes her phone with her when she goes out.
4 Jeremy enjoys listening to people's phone conversations.
5 His brothers turn off their mobiles when they go out with him.

c) Who do you agree with, Amy or Jeremy? Why?

Help with Grammar Positive and negative verb forms, words and phrases

 5 **a) Match phrases 1–8 in blue in the article to these verb forms.**

Present Simple   Present Perfect Simple
Present Continuous   Past Simple

b) Find the negative form of these sentences in the article. Which verb do we usually make negative?

I think I could live without one.
I think I'll get one.

c) Find another way to say these phrases in Amy's paragraph. Which word can we use instead of *not a* and *not any*?

there isn't a signal
there aren't any taxis

d) Match these positive words to the negative words/phrases in pink in the article.

love   *hate*   everyone
always   all
usually   both

e) Check in [G1.2] **p115.**

 6 **Make these sentences negative. There is sometimes more than one possible answer.**

1 I often call my sister.
  I don't often call my sister.
2 Everyone in my family has a mobile.
3 Miranda's sent me a text.
4 I think I'll buy a new phone.
5 There's a message for you.
6 All of my friends have got mobiles.
7 Both of my sisters like texting.

 7 [R1.4] [P] **Listen and check the sentences in 6. Listen again and practise.**

I don't often call my sister.

 8 **a) Write three true sentences and three false sentences about yourself. Use the language in 5 and your own ideas.**

I've been to England three times.
I hardly ever chat to people online.

b) Work in pairs. Take turns to tell your partner your sentences. Guess which sentences are false.

Listening

 9 **a)** [R1.5] **Listen to Amy and Jeremy talking about topics 1–4. Who talks about each topic? Do they love them or hate them?**

1 cooking   3 flying
2 football on TV   4 customer service phone lines

b) Listen again. Find two reasons why each person loves or hates each topic.

Help with Listening Sentence stress (1)

● In spoken English we stress the important words.

 10 **a)** [R1.5] **Listen to the beginning of the recording again. Notice the stressed words.**

Oh, I love it, but I know a lot of people don't like it at all.
I can't understand why – it's much safer than driving.

b) Look at R1.5, p142. Listen to the first half of the recording and notice the sentence stress.

Get ready ... Get it right!

11 **Write four sentences about things you like and four sentences about things you don't like. Use the phrases from 1 and your own ideas.**

I really love watching soap operas.
I can't stand going to the dentist.

12 **a) Find one student in the class who agrees with each of your sentences. Ask follow-up questions if possible.**

I really love watching soap operas.

Yes, me too.

Which ones do you like?

b) Tell the class two things you have in common with other students.

Jorge and I both love watching soap operas.

1C The best medicine

Vocabulary adjectives to describe feelings; prepositions with adjectives
Skills Listening: How we relax; Reading: Laugh? I feel better already!
Help with Listening sentence stress (2)
Review free time activities; likes and dislikes

QUICK REVIEW ● ● ●
Write the names of five people you know. Think of two things they like doing and two things they don't like doing. Work in pairs. Take turns to tell each other about the people: *My brother Henri can't stand waiting in queues.*

Listening

1 **a)** Which of these things do you do to relax? How often do you do them? What else do you do to relax?

> watch TV   go swimming   do yoga   have a massage
> paint   go for a run   go out for a drink   meditate

b) Work in pairs. Compare your answers.

2 **a)** R1.6 Jeremy and his wife, Anne, have invited two friends, Mike and Sally, round for dinner. Listen to their conversation. What does each person do to relax?

b) Listen again. How often do they do the things that help them relax?

Help with Listening Sentence stress (2)

3 **a)** R1.6 Listen and read the beginning of the conversation. Notice the sentence stress.

SALLY   That was wonderful! I haven't had a meal like that for months.
MIKE   Yes, I didn't know you were such a good cook, Jeremy.
JEREMY   I'm glad you enjoyed it. Do you want some coffee?

b) Find examples of these parts of speech in the beginning of the conversation in 3a). Are they usually stressed (S) or unstressed (U)?

> main verbs S   positive auxiliaries   nouns
> adjectives   negative auxiliaries   pronouns

c) Look at R1.6, p142. Listen again and notice the sentence stress. Then find two examples of the stressed parts of speech in 3b) in the recording.

Vocabulary and Reading

4 **a)** Tick the words you know. Check in V1.3 p114.

> relaxed   nervous   pleased   embarrassed   annoyed
> fed up   disappointed   stressed   calm   upset   scared
> satisfied   confused   shocked   glad   frustrated   concerned

TIP! ● In these vocabulary boxes we only show the main stress in words/phrases.

b) Which words in 4a) describe negative feelings?

5 **a)** Choose six adjectives from 4a). Think of the last time you felt like this.

b) Work in pairs. Tell your partner about your adjectives.

I felt very relaxed last Sunday because I had a lie-in.

6 **a)** Look at the photo. Where are the people? What do you think they're doing?

b) Check these words/phrases with your teacher or in a dictionary.

> reduce   clap your hands
> fake   chemicals

c) Read the article and match topics a)–e) to paragraphs 1–5.

a) It worked for me – try it yourself
b) Why laughter is good for you
c) Start the day with a laugh
d) My first laughter class
e) How Laughter Clubs began

d) Read the article again. Fill in the gaps in these sentences with one or two words.

1 The first _Laughter Club_ was in Mumbai, India.
2 Children laugh _____ than adults.
3 There are _____ Laughter Clubs in the world.
4 Doctors think laughing helps people stay _____ .
5 Fake laughter is _____ for your health.
6 The reporter really _____ the class.

e) Would you like to go to a Laughter Club? Why?/Why not?

Laugh?
I feel better already!

1 Do you want to live a happier, less stressful life? Try laughing for no reason at all. That's how thousands of people start their day at Laughter Clubs around the world – and many doctors now think that having a good laugh might be one of the best ways to stay healthy.

2 The first Laughter Club was started in Mumbai, India, in 1995 by Dr Madan Kataria. "Young children laugh about 300 times a day. Adults laugh between 7 and 15 times a day," says Dr Kataria. "Everyone's naturally **good** at laughing – it's the universal language. We want people to feel **happy** with their lives." There are now more than 500 Laughter Clubs in India and over 1,300 worldwide.

3 Many doctors in the West are also **interested** in the effects of laughter on our health. According to a 5-year study at the UCLA School of Medicine in California, laughter reduces stress in the body, improves our defences against illness by about 40% and is very good for the heart.

4 So, what happens at a Laughter Club? I went along to my nearest club in south London to find out. I was quite **nervous** about it, to be honest – I wasn't **keen** on the idea of laughing with a group of strangers, and I was **worried** about looking stupid. First, our laughter teacher told us to clap our hands and say "ho ho ho, ha ha ha," while looking at each other. Apparently our bodies can't tell the difference between fake laughter and real laughter, so they still produce the same healthy chemicals.

5 Amazingly, it works. After ten minutes everybody in the room was laughing for real – and some people just couldn't stop! At the end of the class I was **surprised** by how relaxed and calm I felt. So if you're **upset** about something at work or just **fed up** with your daily routine, then start laughing. You might be very **pleased** with the results!

Help with Vocabulary Prepositions with adjectives

7 **a)** Look at the adjectives in **bold** in the article. Which preposition comes after them?

good _at_	worried ....
happy	surprised ....
interested	upset ....
nervous	fed up ....
keen	pleased ....

b) Match these prepositions to the adjectives. Sometimes there is more than one answer.

of	with	about	by	at

scared _of, by_	satisfied ....
bored	embarrassed ....
frightened	concerned ....
annoyed	angry .... something
bad	angry .... someone

c) Check in V1.4 p114.

8 **a)** Choose six adjectives from **7a)** and **7b)**. Write the name of one person you know for each adjective.

fed up – Julia

b) Work in new pairs. Tell your partner about the people. Ask follow-up questions.

> My sister Julia is fed up with her job.

> What does she do?

9 **a)** Work in groups. You are going to create a Happiness Club. Decide on these things.

- a name for the club
- the number of different rooms or areas
- activities people can do in each room/area
- music, food, drink, furniture, decoration, etc.
- any other ideas

b) Work with students from different groups. Tell them about your club. Which is the best, do you think?

1D At a barbecue

Real World question tags
Review auxiliaries; short answers; adjectives and prepositions

QUICK REVIEW ●●●

Work in pairs. Find one thing that you're both: scared of, interested in, worried about, good at, fed up with, bad at.
A *I'm scared of spiders.* **B** *Me too.*

Jack's vegetarian, _____

You work with Dave, _____

Kate went to Bristol University, _____

You haven't been to China, _____

1 a) Look at the picture. Where are the people?

b) Complete the questions in conversations A–D with these question tags.

> isn't he?   don't you?   have you?   didn't she?

c) Complete conversations A–D with these short answers.

> Yes, she did.   No, he isn't, actually.
> Yes, I do.   No, I haven't.

d) R1.7 Listen and check.

2 R1.8 Listen to the next part of conversations A–D. Choose the correct answers.

1. The woman wants Dave's *mobile number/email address*.
2. Steve's brother *wants to go/went* to Bristol University.
3. Tom *has/hasn't* been to China.
4. Jack *eats/doesn't eat* steak.

Real World Question tags

3 a) Look again at the questions in conversations A–D. Then choose the correct phrase in the rule.

- We usually use questions with question tags (*isn't he?, aren't you?*, etc.) to *check information that we think is correct/find out new information*.

b) Choose the correct words/phrases in these rules.

- We usually use the *main verb/auxiliary* in question tags.
- We only use *names/pronouns* in question tags.
- If the main part of the question is positive, the question tag is usually *positive/negative*.
- If the main part of the question is negative, the question tag is usually *positive/negative*.

c) Look at the short answers in conversations A–D. Then answer these questions.

1. Which short answers say that the information is correct?
2. Which short answer says that the information isn't correct?
3. Which word do we use to sound more polite when the information isn't correct?

d) Check in RW1.1 p115.

4 **a)** R1.9 Listen to the questions in conversations A–D again. Does the intonation on the question tag go up or down?

You work with Dave, don't you?

b) P Listen again and practise.

5 **a)** Write question tags for these sentences.

1 Your sister did law too, ... ?
2 She works for a big law firm now, ... ?
3 You're coming to my party, ... ?
4 Dave hasn't got a girlfriend, ... ?
5 You eat meat, ... ?
6 You've got a drink, ... ?
7 Tom went to school with you, ... ?
8 He isn't here today, ... ?

b) Match the questions in **5a)** to conversations A–D in the picture.

c) R1.10 Listen to the end of conversations A–D. Check your answers.

d) Listen again. Tick the information in **5a)** that is correct. Which information isn't correct?

6 **a)** Write questions with question tags to check information about six other students. For each question, think of one or two follow-up questions.

You live near the school, don't you?
Your husband's a doctor, isn't he?

b) Ask the students your questions. Is your information about them correct? Ask your follow-up questions if possible.

> You live near the school, don't you?

> Yes, I do.

> How long does it take you to get here?

c) Work in pairs. Tell your partner what you have found out about other students.

---

1 Review

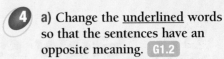 Language Summary 1, p114

1 **a)** Complete questions 1–8 with these verbs. V1.1

~~do~~	have	go to	meet up
go	tidy up	chat	visit

Last weekend did you … ?

1 ...*do*... any exercise?
2 .... clubbing?
3 .... the house/flat?
4 .... any exhibitions?
5 .... relatives?
6 .... to friends online?
7 .... a lie-in?
8 .... with friends?

b) Work in pairs. Take turns to ask and answer the questions.

2 **a)** Fill in the gaps with an auxiliary where necessary. G1.1

1 What .... you do to relax?
2 Who .... watches TV the most in your family?
3 .... you go anywhere interesting last week?
4 What .... you going to do after class?
5 How many times .... you moved house?
6 Which of your friends .... the most exercise?
7 How long .... you known your best friend?
8 .... you studying any other languages at the moment?

b) Work in groups. Take turns to ask and answer the questions. Who has similar answers to you?

3 **a)** Use these words/phrases to make sentences about entertainment, food and sport. V1.2

(not) keen on	can't stand
don't mind	enjoy	really hate
get on my nerves	drive me crazy
(not) very interested in	love

b) Work in pairs. Are any of your sentences the same?

4 **a)** Change the underlined words so that the sentences have an opposite meaning. G1.2

1 No one I know watches TV.
2 I think I'll go out tonight.
3 I hardly ever eat fish.
4 All of my friends like football.
5 I have two sisters and both of them like their jobs.
6 I always get up early at the weekend.

b) Tick the positive and negative sentences that are true for you.

c) Work in pairs. Tell your partner your sentences.

5 **a)** Choose the correct prepositions. V1.4

1 keen *in/on*
2 worried *about/of*
3 interested *of/in*
4 nervous *with/about*
5 good *at/by*
6 embarrassed *of/by*
7 scared *with/of*
8 bored *with/at*

b) Use the phrases to write three true and three false sentences about when you were a child.

When I was a child I was keen on …

c) Work in pairs. Guess which of your partner's sentences are true.

Progress Portfolio

a) Tick the things you can do in English.

- [ ] I can talk about free time activities.
- [ ] I can ask and answer questions about the past, the present and the future.
- [ ] I can talk about likes and dislikes.
- [ ] I can talk about feelings.
- [ ] I can understand a short magazine article.
- [ ] I can use question tags to check information.

b) What do you need to study again? See **CD-ROM** 1A–D.

2 We haven't got time

2A Slow down!

Vocabulary work collocations
Grammar modal verbs (1); *be able to, be allowed to, be supposed to*
Review question tags

QUICK REVIEW ● ● ●
Choose a partner, but don't talk to him/her yet. Write four things you think you know about your partner. Work in pairs. Ask questions to check your information is correct: *You studied here last year, didn't you?* Ask follow-up questions: *Where did you study before that?*

Vocabulary Work collocations

 a) Choose the correct verbs in these phrases. Check in **V2.1** p116.

1 (take)/be work home
2 be/have time to relax
3 get/work long hours
4 work/spend overtime
5 get/be a workaholic
6 meet/take deadlines
7 take/be time off work
8 have/be under pressure at work
9 leave/spend a lot of time at work
10 have/be good working conditions

b) Think of three people you know who have jobs. Choose two phrases from **1a)** for each person.

c) Work in pairs. Tell your partner about the people you chose. Which person works the hardest?

Listening and Grammar

 a) Look at the photo and the cartoon. What is the book about and what is happening in the cartoon, do you think?

b) **R2.1** Listen to the beginning of a radio programme. Two journalists, Kim and Rob, are discussing *In Praise of Slow* by Carl Honoré. Check your answers to **2a)**.

 a) Work in pairs. Try to fill in the gaps in sentences 1–6 with these countries. Use one country twice.

the USA	France	Japan	Germany	the UK

1 Some companies in _____ give their employees three days off at the weekend.
2 People in _____ spend 15% less time at work now than they did in 1980.
3 In _____ 20% of people work more than 60 hours a week.
4 60% of people in _____ said they didn't take all their paid holiday.
5 In _____ 20% of people don't take time off when they're ill.
6 In _____ they have a word that means 'death from working too hard'.

b) **R2.2** Listen to the second part of the radio programme. Check your answers to **3a)**.

4 a) **R2.2** Listen to the second part of the radio programme again. Fill in the gaps with one or two words.

1 Rob says he **must** take more time off _work_ .
2 Honoré thinks people **should** only work _____ hours a week.
3 Some French employees **are allowed to** begin their weekend at _____ on Thursday.
4 Honoré says we **ought to** spend more time relaxing with _____ .
5 People **can** get their best _____ when they're doing nothing.
6 In some American companies, employees **can** _____ whenever they want.
7 In the UK people **are supposed to** have a break every _____ .
8 Kim says that lots of people **have to** take _____ .
9 Rob says that we**'re able to** continue working when we're _____ .

b) Do you agree with Carl Honoré's ideas? Why?/Why not?

Help with Grammar Modal verbs (1); *be able to, be allowed to, be supposed to*

5 **a)** Look at the sentences in **4a)**. Then complete the rules with the verb forms in **bold**. Use the infinitive form if necessary.

- We use _be supposed to_ to say a person is expected to do something.
- We use _can_ and _____ to talk about ability or possibility.
- We use _must_ and _____ to say something is necessary.
- We use _____ and _____ to give advice.
- We use _____ and _____ to say we have permission to do something.

b) Look again at the verb forms in **bold** in **4a)**. Answer these questions.

1 Do we use the infinitive or *verb+ing* after these verb forms?
2 Which verb forms include *to*?
3 How do we make these verb forms negative?
4 How do we make questions with these verb forms?

c) Look at these sentences. Then complete the rules with *mustn't* or *don't have to*.

You **mustn't** send personal emails from the office. You can only send work emails.
You **don't have to** wear a suit to work, but you can if you want to.

- We use _____ to say something isn't necessary.
- We use _____ to say something is not allowed.

d) Check in **G2.1** p117.

6 **a)** Kim and Rob are talking after the radio programme. Read their conversation and choose the correct verb forms. Who has the best working conditions?

KIM So, do you think you ¹(should)/are allowed to relax more?

ROB Absolutely! I ²am able to/must try to slow down a bit.

KIM ³Are you able to/Should you start work when you want?

ROB ⁴I'm supposed to/I can be in the office at eight. What about you?

KIM I ⁵don't have to/mustn't be at work until ten.

ROB Lucky you. ⁶Are you allowed to/Should you work at home?

KIM Yes, we ⁷ought to/can work at home two days a week.

ROB Oh, we ⁸have to/are able to be in the office every day.

KIM Perhaps you ⁹ought to/are supposed to look for another job.

ROB Yes, maybe. Anyway, I ¹⁰have to/can go. I ¹¹mustn't/don't have to be late for my next meeting. Bye!

b) Listen and check.

c) R2.4 **P** Listen and practise the sentences in **6a)**.

Do you /dʒə/ think you should relax more?

Get ready ... Get it right!

7 Work in groups. You run a company with good working conditions. Make notes on the important things about your company. Use these ideas.

- the name of the company
- what your company does
- the number of employees
- working hours and overtime
- what employees can wear
- breaks and holidays
- any other interesting information

8 **a)** Work with students from different groups. Take turns to describe your companies. Ask questions to find out more information. Which is the best company to work for? Why?

b) Tell the class which company you think is the best to work for. Which is the most popular company in the class?

2B Ready, steady, eat

Vocabulary in the kitchen
Grammar Present Continuous and Present Simple
Review modal verbs

QUICK REVIEW ● ● ●
Think of two things you: have to do, ought to do, should do, don't have to do, are supposed to do next week. Work in pairs. Take turns to tell each other about these things. Who is going to have the busiest week?

Vocabulary In the kitchen

1 Work in groups. Discuss these questions.

1 What's your favourite meal?
2 When do you have your main meal of the day?
3 Who cooks your main meal and how long does it take to prepare?
4 Do you like cooking? Why?/Why not?

2 a) Put these words/phrases into groups 1–3. Check in **V2.2** p116.

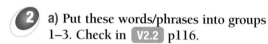

broccoli   a fridge   boil   a freezer
a red/green pepper   roast   peas
beef   bake   a cooker   a grill
lamb   grill   an oven   carrots
a microwave   a saucepan   fry
an aubergine [US: an eggplant]   heat up
a frying pan   beans   microwave
a wok   courgettes [US: zucchinis]   steam
a blender   a toaster   a rubbish bin

1 food *broccoli*
2 things in the kitchen *a fridge*
3 ways of cooking *boil*

b) Work in pairs. Answer these questions.

1 How is the food in **2a)** usually cooked in your country?
2 Which of the things in **2a)** do you both have in your kitchen?

Reading and Grammar

3 a) Look at the cartoon of Linda and her mother. What is the article about, do you think?

b) Read the article. Match headings a)–d) to paragraphs 1–4.

a) Ready meals around the world
b) How British eating habits are changing
c) Too busy to cook
d) How healthy are ready meals?

What's for dinner?

> What are you doing, Mum?

> I'm **cooking** dinner. We're having roast chicken, potatoes, broccoli and peas.

> Really? That's exactly what I'm **making**!

> CHICKEN

Linda Roberts investigates the rise in popularity of ready meals

1 Like many working people, I never actually cook anything – I just don't have the time. My mother, on the other hand, still **cooks** a full three-course meal every evening, but then she doesn't have to work any more. I usually work very long hours and now I'**m writing** a book in my spare time, so ready meals are the perfect solution – or are they?

2 According to a survey by a British market research company, we only **spend** 20 minutes cooking each day – 20 years ago it was an hour a day. One reason for this change is ready meals. Now you can heat up a delicious Indian, Thai, Chinese or Italian meal in the microwave in under four minutes. What could be easier or quicker?

3 We all know these ready meals taste delicious, but many experts now **believe** they're bad for our health because they often contain a lot of sugar, fat and salt. Health advisers say that we shouldn't eat ready meals too often and **we need** to read the labels carefully. Despite this, people who **live** in the UK spend over £1 billion a year on ready meals and the market **is growing** rapidly.

4 People in the USA and Sweden also **buy** a lot of ready meals, and they'**re becoming** more common in Germany, France and Holland. The Spanish and Italians still cook their own meals, but things are beginning to change there too. My mother will never change, though – now she'**s doing** an evening course in traditional English cooking!

4 a) Read the article again. Are sentences 1–4 true or false? Change the false ones.

1 Linda Roberts cooks a three-course meal every evening.
2 We spent more time cooking 20 years ago than we do now.
3 Health advisers say we should never eat ready meals.
4 The Spanish eat a lot of ready meals.
5 Linda doesn't think her mother will start eating ready meals.

b) Work in groups. Discuss these questions.

1 Did any of the information in the article surprise you?
2 Are ready meals popular in your country? Why?/Why not?
3 Do you ever eat ready meals at home? If so, do you like them?

Help with Grammar Present Continuous and Present Simple

 5 a) Look at the article and the cartoon again. Match the verb forms in bold to these meanings. There are two verb forms for each meaning.

● We use the **Present Continuous** for things that:

a) are happening at the moment of speaking: *'m cooking*
b) are temporary and happening around now, but maybe not at this exact moment.
c) are changing over a period of time.

● We use the **Present Simple** for:

a) habits, daily routines, things we do every day/week/year, etc.
b) things that we think are permanent, or true for a long time.
c) verbs that describe states (*have got, be, know*, etc.).

b) Look at these verbs. Do they usually describe activities (A) or states (S)? Do we usually use state verbs in the Present Continuous?

be S	watch A	talk	seem	spend	agree
eat	taste	prefer	learn	buy	own	cook
understand	want	take	remember	contain

c) How do we make the positive, negative and question forms of the Present Continuous and Present Simple?

d) Check in G2.2 p118.

 6 R2.5 P Listen and practise.

My mother still cooks a three-course meal every evening.

 7 a) Read these paragraphs. Is Linda or her mother speaking in each paragraph, do you think?

1

The ready meal I ¹_____ (cook) right now is chicken and vegetables. I ²_____ (eat) a lot of ready meals because I ³_____ (prefer) to do other things in the evening. I ⁴_____ (learn) Italian at the moment, so I often ⁵_____ (watch) Italian films in the evenings. I ⁶_____ (think) my Italian ⁷_____ (get) quite good.

2

I ⁸_____ (not understand) her. She says that she ⁹_____ (put on) weight – well, that's because she ¹⁰_____ (never eat) properly. Also she ¹¹_____ (not know) how to cook, so why ¹²_____ she _____ (study) Italian instead of going to cookery classes?

b) Put the verbs in brackets in the Present Simple or Present Continuous.

 8 a) Make sentences about how eating habits in your country are changing. Use these ideas or your own.

● fast food ● supermarkets
● organic food ● food from other countries
● restaurants ● the amount people eat
● prices ● quality of food

Teenagers are eating more fast food these days.

b) Work in groups. Compare sentences. How many are the same?

Get ready ... Get it right!

 9 Make questions with *you*. Put the verbs in brackets in the Present Simple or Present Continuous.

1 *Are you feeling* (feel) hungry now?
2 _____ (usually eat) a lot of ready meals?
3 _____ (cook) every day?
4 _____ (try) to stop eating sweet things?
5 _____ (ever use) a cookery book?
6 _____ (want) to learn how to cook?
7 _____ (look) for somewhere to live?
8 _____ (do) an evening course at the moment?

 10 a) Ask other students your questions. Find one person who answers *yes* for each question. Then ask two follow-up questions.

b) Work in groups. Tell other students five things you found out about the class.

Cultura Inglesa

15

Vocabulary sleep; gradable and strong adjectives; adverbs
Skills Listening: A sleep scientist; Reading: I just can't sleep!
Help with Listening weak forms (1)
Review Present Simple and Present Continuous

VOCABULARY AND SKILLS

QUICK REVIEW ●●●
Make a list of six items of food. Work in pairs. Take turns to describe the food and say how you can cook it. Your partner guesses what it is: A *It's a type of vegetable and it's round. You can fry it, boil it or roast it.* B *Is it a potato?*

Vocabulary and Listening

1 Tick the words/phrases you know. Then check new words/phrases in **V2.3** p116.

> have a dream   fall asleep   wake up
> get (back) to sleep   snore   be fast asleep
> be wide awake   have insomnia   not sleep a wink
> have nightmares   be a light/heavy sleeper   take a nap
> doze off   have a lie-in   talk in your sleep

2 a) Choose six words/phrases from **1** that are connected to you, or people you know.

b) Work in groups. Take turns to talk about the words/phrases you chose. Ask follow-up questions if possible.

3 a) Work in pairs. Look at these sentences about sleep. Choose the correct words/phrases.

1 Tiredness causes *more/less* than 50% of all road accidents in the USA.
2 *10%/30%* of people in the UK have problems getting to sleep or staying asleep.
3 Nowadays people are sleeping *half an hour/one and a half hours* less than they did 100 years ago.
4 Teenagers need *more/less* sleep than adults.
5 We use *less/the same amount* of energy when we're asleep compared to when we're resting.
6 A thirty-minute nap at work can improve people's performance for *an hour/a few hours*.

b) **R2.6** Listen to a TV interview with a sleep scientist. Check your answers to **3a)**.

c) Listen again. Answer these questions.

1 How many British people have serious insomnia?
2 How were sleeping habits different 100 years ago?
3 Who needs the least amount of sleep?
4 What do our brains do when we're asleep?
5 What is a siesta salon?

Help with Listening Weak forms (1)

● In sentences we say many small words with a schwa /ə/ sound. These are called weak forms.

4 a) **R2.7** Listen to the strong and weak forms of these words. Do we usually say these words in their strong or weak forms?

	strong	weak		strong	weak
do	/duː/	/də/	of	/ɒv/	/əv/
you	/juː/	/jə/	and	/ænd/	/ən/
at	/æt/	/ət/	to	/tuː/	/tə/
for	/fɔː/	/fə/	can	/kæn/	/kən/

b) Match the words in **4a)** to these parts of speech.

1 auxiliary *do*   3 preposition
2 pronoun   4 connecting word

c) Look at these sentences from the beginning of the interview. Which words do we hear as weak forms?

(Do) people (you) know have problems sleeping at night? Or maybe you just can't get to sleep yourself. For many people, insomnia is a way of life and not being able to get to sleep isn't just annoying – it can also be very dangerous.

d) **R2.6** Listen and check. Are weak forms ever stressed?

e) Look at R2.6, p143. Listen to the interview again. Notice the weak forms and sentence stress.

Reading and Vocabulary

5 a) Work in groups. Tell other students what you do when you can't get to sleep. Which is the most unusual method of getting to sleep?

b) Read the article. Why does Emma have insomnia? What has she tried to do to get a good night's sleep?

6 a) Read the article again. Answer these questions.

1 How much sleep did Emma get last night?
2 What happens on a typical night?
3 Why is her job very tiring?
4 Why does she have money problems?
5 Which cures for insomnia hasn't she tried? Why not?

b) Work in pairs. What advice would you give Emma?

I just can't sleep!

Emma talks about how her stressful life has made getting a good night's sleep impossible.

Last night I was fast asleep by 11 p.m., but I woke up again at 1 a.m. Even though I was exhausted when I went to bed, I was suddenly wide awake and it was impossible to get back to sleep again. So I just lay there watching the clock change from three to four to five without sleeping a wink – it was very frustrating. Finally, I got up at 6.15 and went off to work feeling terrible. That's a typical night for me. I've had insomnia for so long I'm amazed that anyone else actually sleeps through the night. And when this goes on for too many nights I feel really shattered.

I'm a sales manager, and I work really long hours and have to do a lot of travelling. I worry about work all the time, which makes it incredibly difficult to get to sleep. Sometimes I get home from work extremely late and when I go to bed everything is still going round my head. Money's also a huge worry for me. I borrowed a lot when I was a student and I still owe £15,000. I only get a full night's sleep once a month – but when I do I feel absolutely fantastic the next day.

I've tried nearly everything to cure my insomnia – herbal teas, yoga, meditation – you name it, I've tried it. I've also started going to the gym three times a week, but it hasn't made any difference. I have a fairly healthy diet and I don't smoke or drink coffee. I haven't tried hypnosis because it's very expensive and that would just add to my money worries. I don't want to start taking sleeping pills because I'm terrified of becoming addicted to them. Although I know it's an awful way to live, I've learned to accept that insomnia is part of my life.

Adapted from the *Evening Standard* 3/12/02

Help with Vocabulary Gradable and strong adjectives; adverbs

7 **a)** Complete the table with the strong adjectives in pink in the article.

gradable adjectives	strong adjectives
tired	_exhausted_ , ...
bad	.... , ...
good	....
big	....
difficult	....
frightened	....
surprised	....

b) Match the gradable adjectives in A to the strong adjectives in B.

A	B
tasty small cold	filthy furious delicious
hot beautiful big	delighted fascinated
interested angry	gorgeous boiling tiny
happy dirty	enormous freezing

tasty → *delicious*

c) Look at the adverbs in blue in the article. Which of these adverbs do we use with: gradable adjectives (G), strong adjectives (S)? Which adverb do we use with both types of adjective?

very G really incredibly extremely absolutely fairly

d) What other strong adjectives do you know that mean 'very good'?

e) Check in V2.4 p117.

---

8 **a)** Fill in the gaps with an adverb from 7c). Use different adverbs where possible. Then complete the sentences for you.

1 I'm usually .... exhausted after …
2 It's .... difficult for me to …
3 The last time I felt .... awful was …
4 I'm .... interested in …
5 I've got a/an .... gorgeous …
6 The last place I went to that was .... cold was …

b) Work in pairs. Take turns to say your sentences.

9 **a)** Work in groups. Write a sleep survey. Write at least six questions. Use words/phrases from 1 or your own ideas.
How many hours do you usually sleep a night?

b) Ask other students in the class. Write the answers.

c) Work in your groups. Compare answers.

d) Tell the class what you found out about other students.

2D What's the matter?

Real World showing concern, giving and responding to advice
Help with Listening intonation (1): showing concern
Review gradable and strong adjectives; Present Simple; Present Continuous

QUICK REVIEW ●●●

Write all the strong adjectives you know (*exhausted*, etc.). Work in pairs. Compare lists. What are the gradable adjectives for each one (*tired*, etc.)? Then think of one person, place or thing for each strong adjective.

1 Work in pairs. Discuss these questions.

1 Do you ever read advice columns in magazines? If so, which ones?
2 Who do you talk to when you need advice?
3 Who was the last person you gave advice to? What problem did he/she have? What did you say?

2 a) Look at the photos. What are the people talking about in each one, do you think?

b) R2.8 Listen and match conversations 1–3 to photos A–C.

(A)

(B)

(C)

3 a) Work in pairs. Tick the true sentences. Correct the false ones.

1 Lorna doesn't think her husband works hard enough.
2 Lorna has talked to her husband about the problem before.
3 Andy thinks that Lorna is spending too much on herself.
4 Robin tells Andy to take his wife out to discuss the problem.
5 Lorna's mother thinks Lorna should have a night off on her own.
6 Lorna's mother is going to babysit for them this evening.

b) R2.8 Listen again and check.

Real World Showing concern, giving and responding to advice

4 a) Write these headings in the correct places a)–c).

giving advice	responding to advice	showing concern

a) _____

Oh, dear. What's the matter?
I can see why you're upset.
Oh, how awful!
Oh, I'm sorry to hear that.
Yes, I see what you mean.
Oh, dear. What a shame.

b) _____

Have you tried talking to him about it?
Well, maybe you **should** talk to him again.
Why don't you talk to her about it?
I'd take her out for a really nice meal.
Maybe you **ought to** spend some time together.

c) _____

Well, it's worth a try, I guess.
I've tried that, but ... .
Yes, that's a good idea.
I might try that.
Yes, you could be right.

b) Which verb forms come after the phrases in **bold**?

c) Look at these ways to ask for advice. Fill in the gaps with *I* or *should*.

1 What _____ _____ do?
2 What do you think _____ _____ do?

d) Check in RW2.1 p118.

Help with Listening
Intonation (1): showing concern

5 `R2.9` Listen to the same sentences said twice. Which person shows concern, a) or b)?

1 a) (b))   4 a)   b)
2 a)   b)   5 a)   b)
3 a)   b)   6 a)   b)

6 `R2.10` `P` Listen and practise the phrases in **4a)**. Copy the intonation and sentence stress.

Oh, dear. What's the matter?

7 **a)** Use these prompts to write two conversations.

1

A   I've got a bit of a problem.
B   / dear. What / matter?
A   My girlfriend won't talk to me. What / I do?
B   Maybe / ought / write her a letter.
A   Well, / worth / try, / guess.
B   And I / send her some flowers.
A   Yes, / good idea. Thanks a lot.

2

A   Look at this plant. It's dying, isn't it?
B   Yes, / see what / mean.
A   What / think I / do?
B   / try / give / it more water?
A   Yes, / try / that, but it didn't work.
B   Well, why / put it in a bigger pot?
A   Yes, I / try that. Thanks.

b) Work in pairs. Check your answers.

c) Practise the conversations with your partner.

8 Work in groups of three. Student A → p102. Student B → p107. Student C → p112. Follow the instructions.

♪ `R2.11` Look at the song *You Can't Hurry Love* on p100. Follow the instructions.

---

1 **a)** Fill in the gaps with these verbs. Then tick the ones that are true for you or someone in your family. `V2.1`

> meet   be   work   take

1   I always _____ deadlines.
2   I _____ under pressure at work.
3   I often _____ overtime.
4   I _____ long hours.
5   I never _____ work home.
6   I _____ a workaholic.
7   I never _____ time off work.

b) Work in pairs. Compare answers.

2 **a)** Work in pairs. Complete these sentences so they are true for both of you. `G2.1`

1   We're supposed to …
2   We have to …
3   We aren't allowed to …
4   We ought to …
5   We're able to …
6   We can't …

b) Tell the class about you and your partner.

3 **a)** Work in pairs. Make a list of items of food, ways of cooking and things for the kitchen. `V2.2`

b) Work with another pair. Compare lists.

c) Tell the new pair what your favourite meals are and how you cook them.

4 **a)** Put the verbs in brackets in the correct form of the Present Simple or the Present Continuous. `G2.2`

1   _____ you _____ (know) anyone who _____ (work) abroad at the moment?
2   _____ you _____ (study) English for your work or for pleasure?
3   _____ you _____ (think) people _____ (get) more stressed these days?

4   _____ you usually _____ (arrive) late when you _____ (go) to parties?
5   _____ you _____ (read) anything interesting at the moment?
6   _____ you _____ (think) people _____ (live) longer these days?

b) Take turns to ask and answer the questions. Ask follow-up questions if possible.

5 **a)** Choose two adverbs to go with these adjectives. `V2.4`

> tasty   hot   fantastic   awful
> delicious   beautiful   difficult
> gorgeous   amazing   dirty
> wonderful   enormous

very/extremely tasty

b) Choose six phrases from **5a)** and write a sentence that is true for you.

I think Thai food is very tasty.

6 Work in pairs. Pretend you have two problems. Tell your partner about them. Try to keep each conversation going for one minute. `RW2.1`

Progress Portfolio

a) Tick the things you can do in English.

☐ I can talk about work.

☐ I can talk about things I am expected to do and have permission to do.

☐ I can describe things that are happening now or around now.

☐ I can talk about routines and things that are permanent.

☐ I can give and respond to advice.

b) What do you need to study again? `2A–D`

3 The tourist trade

3A Your holiday, my job

Vocabulary phrasal verbs (1): travel
Grammar Present Perfect Simple: experience, unfinished past and recent events
Help with Listening Present Perfect Simple or Past Simple
Review Past Simple

QUICK REVIEW ●●●
Write three problems that you, or people you know, have at the moment. Work in pairs. Take turns to tell your partner the problems and give advice.

Vocabulary
Phrasal verbs (1): travel

 a) Work in pairs. Guess the meaning of the phrasal verbs in **bold** in these sentences. Check the phrasal verbs in **V3.1** p119.

1 Have you ever **set off** very early to catch a flight?
2 What's the best way for tourists to **get around** your country?
3 Do you **bring back** souvenirs from places you've been to?
4 What's the worst problem you've ever had to **deal with** on holiday?
5 What information do you have to give the receptionist when you **check into** a hotel?
6 What's the earliest that you've had to **check out of** a hotel?
7 Have you ever had to **put up with** noisy people in a hotel?
8 Did anyone **see** you **off** when you last went on holiday?
9 Did anyone **pick** you **up** from the airport or station when you **got back**?
10 Are you **looking forward to** your next holiday?

b) Work in new pairs. Take turns to ask and answer the questions in 1a). Ask follow-up questions if possible.

> Have you ever set off very early to catch a flight?

> Yes, I have, actually.

> What time did you leave home?

Sam Edwards
Rainforest guide, Costa Rica

Marcia Brownly
Hotel manager, Cornwall, UK

Listening and Grammar

 a) **R3.1** Look at the photos of Sam and Marcia. Listen to them talking about their jobs. Answer these questions.

1 Do they like their jobs?
2 What problems do they have in their jobs?

b) Work in pairs. Who said these sentences, Sam or Marcia?

a) I've worked in two other Central American countries and I had a great time in both places.
b) We've been away together a few times, but each time there was a problem at the hotel.
c) I started working in the hotel industry 14 years ago.
d) Last month two guys set off on their own.
e) I've lived in this country for three years.
f) My husband and I have had this place since 2001.
g) I've just been to San Isidro to pick up a guest.
h) My husband's gone to see some friends off.

c) Listen again and check. Put the sentences in the order you hear them.

Help with Grammar Present Perfect Simple

3 **a)** Look at the sentences in **2b)** again. Then complete these rules with *Present Perfect Simple* (PPS) or *Past Simple* (PS). Which sentences match each rule?

- We use the _PPS_ to talk about experiences in our life up to now, but we don't say when they happened. To give more information about an experience we use the _PS_ .
- We use the _PS_ to say when something happened.
- We use the _PPS_ for something that started in the past and continues in the present.
- We use the _PPS_ for something that happened a short time ago, but we don't say exactly when.

b) Fill in the gaps for the positive and negative forms of the Present Perfect Simple with: *'s, 've, hasn't* or *past participle*. How do we make questions in the Present Perfect Simple?

I/you/we/they + _'ve_ (= *have*)/*haven't* + _past participle_

he/she/it + _'s_ (= *has*)/*hasn't*+ past participle

c) Look at sentences e)–h) in **2b)** again. What is the difference between: a) *for* and *since*? b) *been* and *gone*?

d) Which of these words/phrases can we use with the Present Perfect Simple?

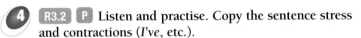

> never ✓   ago   ever ✓   recently ✓   lately ✓   before ✓   in 1997
> this week ✓   last week   just ✓   at 10 o'clock   yet ✓   already ✓

e) Look at this sentence. Then choose the correct verb form in the rule.

This is the first time we've run a hotel in a touristy place like Cornwall.

- We use the *Present Simple/Present Perfect Simple* after *this is the first time, this is the second time,* etc.

f) Check in **G3.1** p120.

4 **R3.2** **P** Listen and practise. Copy the sentence stress and contractions (*I've*, etc.).

I've worked in two other Central American countries.

Help with Listening Present Perfect Simple or Past Simple

5 **a)** **R3.3** Listen to how we say these phrases. Notice the difference.

1	I've met	I met	4	They've told	They told
2	You've had	You had	5	He's wanted	He wanted
3	We've won	We won	6	She's lived	She lived

b) **R3.4** Listen to six sentences. Are the verbs in the Present Perfect Simple or Past Simple?

6 **a)** Read about Kara and Brian's restaurant in Greece. Put the verbs in brackets in the Present Perfect Simple or Past Simple.

In the nineties we [1] *came* (come) here every year on holiday. Then in 2001 we [2]_____ (decide) to open a restaurant. We [3]_____ (live) here since then and we [4]_____ (just open) a guest house nearby. The main problem is holidays. We [5]_____ (go) to Spain twice, but our last holiday [6]_____ (be) two years ago. We [7]_____ (not have) any time off since then. My parents are here at the moment – it's the third time they [8]_____ (visit) us this year! Brian's family are arriving today too. In fact, he [9]_____ (just go) to pick them up from the airport.

b) Work in pairs. Discuss why you chose your answers for **6a)**.

c) **R3.5** Listen and check.

7 Work in pairs. Student A → p102. Student B → p107. Follow the instructions.

Get ready ... Get it right!

8 Write these places, people and things on a piece of paper. Don't write them in order.

- a friend you've known for most of your life
- someone you met on your last holiday
- something you've had for ages
- something you got for your last birthday
- a place you went to last year
- a place you've been to this year

9 **a)** Work in pairs. Swap papers. Take turns to ask and answer questions about the places, people and things on your partner's paper.

b) Tell the class two things you found out about your partner.

3B Lonely Planet

QUICK REVIEW ● ● ●
Work in pairs. Ask questions with *Have you ever ... ?* to find out five things you've done in your life that your partner hasn't done.

> **Vocabulary** phrases with *travel*, *get* and *go on*
> **Grammar** Present Perfect Continuous and Present Perfect Simple
> **Review** state and activity verbs; *for* and *since*

Vocabulary Phrases with *travel*, *get* and *go on*

1 Work in pairs. Put these words/phrases into groups 1–3. Then check in **V3.2** p119.

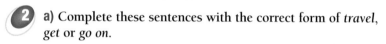

> on your own   into/out of a car   a trip   back from somewhere
> a guided tour   independently   a journey   first/economy class
> a cruise   here/there by (10.30)   separately/together   light
> on/off a bus/plane   a package holiday   a taxi home/to work

1 travel *on your own*
2 get *into/out of a car*
3 go on *a trip*

2 **a)** Complete these sentences with the correct form of *travel, get* or *go on*.

1 I *travelled* on my own quite a lot last year.
2 I usually _____ to work/school/university by 9 a.m.
3 I _____ a guided tour of a famous city last year.
4 I _____ never _____ a cruise.
5 I sometimes _____ a taxi home late at night.
6 I like _____ long journeys.
7 I usually _____ light.

b) Tick the sentences in **2a)** that are true for you.

c) Work in pairs. Compare sentences.

Reading and Grammar

3 Work in groups. Discuss these questions.

1 Do you usually take a guidebook when you go on holiday?
2 What are the advantages and disadvantages of using a guidebook in a new country?

4 **a)** Look at the photos. Who are Tony and Maureen Wheeler, do you think?

b) Read the article. Match headings 1–4 to paragraphs A–D.

1 How it all began   3 Travel guides for the world
2 Their first best-seller   4 An international company

c) Read the article again. Answer these questions.

1 Which languages does Lonely Planet publish books in?
2 Why did Tony and Maureen decide to write their first guidebook?
3 Where did they write their second guidebook?
4 How many copies has this guidebook sold?
5 How many guidebooks has Lonely Planet published?
6 What other businesses does Lonely Planet have?

The world's greatest travellers

A The most famous travellers in the world are probably Tony and Maureen Wheeler. [1]**Their company, Lonely Planet, has been publishing guidebooks for 30 years** and it sells over 5 million books a year in English. It also publishes books in Spanish, Italian and French.

B Tony and Maureen met on a park bench in London and [2]**they've been married since 1972.** After their wedding they bought an old van and travelled across Europe and Asia to Australia. They arrived in Sydney with only 27 cents in their pockets. Everyone they met asked them about their journey, so they decided to write a book about it. They wrote a 93-page guidebook called *Across Asia on the Cheap* at their kitchen table and it sold 8,000 copies in three months.

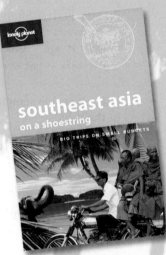

C Tony and Maureen spent the next 18 months travelling around Southeast Asia and then wrote their second guidebook, *Southeast Asia on a Shoestring*, in a Singapore hotel room. It's been a best-seller since it was first published in 1973 and has sold over a million copies.

D [3]**Lonely Planet has published over 650 guidebooks since the company began** and employs over 400 people and 150 writers. [4]**The company has also been running a website for several years**, which gets over one million visitors a day, and their television company, Lonely Planet TV, has been making programmes since 2004. "I think we've done a good thing," says Maureen, "and I still believe that travel is the best way for people to understand the world."

Tony and Maureen Wheeler

Help with Grammar Present Perfect Continuous and Present Perfect Simple

5 **a)** Look at sentences 1 and 2 in **bold** in the article. Then fill in the gaps in these rules with *Present Perfect Continuous* (PPC) or *Present Perfect Simple* (PPS).

● We usually use the .... to talk about an **activity** that started in the past and continues in the present.

● We usually use the .... to talk about a **state** that started in the past and continues in the present.

b) Fill in the gaps for the Present Perfect Continuous with *'ve, haven't, 's, hasn't, been* or *verb+ing*.

POSITIVE

I/you/we/they + ... (= *have*) + *been* + *verb+ing*
he/she/it + ... (= *has*) + *been* + ...

NEGATIVE

I/you/we/they + ... + *been* + *verb+ing*
he/she/it + ... + ... + *verb+ing*

c) Look at sentences 3 and 4 in **bold** in the article. Then choose the correct words in these rules.

● We usually use the Present Perfect *Continuous/ Simple* to say how long an activity has been happening.

● We usually use the Present Perfect *Continuous/ Simple* to say how many things are finished.

d) How do we make Present Perfect Continuous questions with *How long … ?*

e) How do we make Present Perfect Simple questions with *How many … ?*

f) Check in G3.2 p121.

6 **a)** Put the verb in brackets in the Present Perfect Continuous or the Present Perfect Simple. Use the Present Perfect Continuous where possible. Then choose *for* or *since* where necessary.

1 I *'ve been working* (work) here (for)/since two months.
2 How long .... you .... (travel) on your own?
3 Scott .... (write) books *for/since* he left university.
4 He .... (write) three books so far.
5 They .... (not play) tennis *for/since* very long.
6 I .... (know) my best friend *for/since* we were kids.
7 How long .... your sister .... (be) an actress?
8 We .... (not have) a holiday *for/since* three years.

b) Work in pairs. Compare answers. Discuss why you chose each verb form.

c) R3.6 P Listen and check. Listen again and practise. Copy the sentence stress and weak forms.

I've been /bɪn/ working here for /fə/ two months.
How long have /əv/ you been /bɪn/ travelling on your own?

7 Work in groups. Student A → p102. Student B → p107. Follow the instructions.

Get ready … Get it right!

8 **a)** Draw a timeline of your life. Write when these things happened on the line.

● you started living in your house/flat
● you first met your oldest friend
● you started learning English
● you started the job/studies you're doing now
● you first met your boyfriend/girlfriend/husband/wife
● you got your favourite possession(s)
● you bought your car/mobile phone/computer
● your own ideas

met Kathy	started living in flat	started job	
1997	2003	March	now

b) Plan what you're going to say about your timeline. Use the Present Perfect Continuous or Present Perfect Simple with *for* and *since*.

9 **a)** Work in pairs. Take turns to talk about your timeline. Ask follow-up questions if possible.

I've been living in my flat since May 2003.

Where did you live before that?

b) Work in new pairs. Tell your partner five things about the person you talked to in 9a).

Cultura Inglesa

3C Call that a holiday?

Vocabulary word formation (1): suffixes for adjectives and nouns
Skills Listening: Call that a holiday?; Reading: Holiday reviews
Help with Listening linking (1): consonant-vowel links
Review Present Perfect Simple and Present Perfect Continuous; Past Simple

QUICK REVIEW ● ● ●
Work in groups. Ask questions with *How long ... ?* to find out who has been: coming to this school the longest, learning English the longest, working in the same job the longest, living in the same house the longest.

Listening

1 Work in pairs. Discuss these questions.

1 Which holidays can you remember from your childhood?
2 What was the best, or worst, holiday you've ever had?
3 Have you or anyone you know ever had an unusual holiday? If so, why was it unusual?

2 Read about a TV programme and answer these questions.

1 What is the programme about?
2 How many holidays are in the programme?
3 Which holiday sounds the most interesting, do you think?

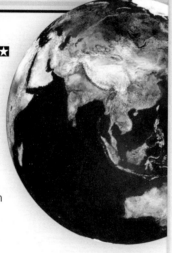

TOP TV this week

Call that a holiday?
Tuesday 6.45 p.m. ITV5 ★★★★

This fascinating new holiday programme follows the adventures of four people who have chosen to go on a holiday with a difference. So if you've ever wanted to travel across Africa in a Jeep, go on a cycling tour of China, work on an organic farm in Australia, or go on a South African cosmetic surgery and safari holiday, then this is the programme for you. Package holidays will never be the same again!

Presented by Judith Gardner.

3 a) **R3.7** Listen to part of the TV programme. Which holidays are Alan and Emily going on? Why did they choose these holidays?

b) Listen again. Tick the true sentences. Correct the false ones.

1 Alan is going on holiday next week.
2 He's been working in advertising for thirteen years.
3 He's going on a safari before the operation.
4 He's looking forward to seeing a lion.
5 Emily works for a women's magazine.
6 She's flying to Australia next weekend.
7 She never goes on package holidays.
8 She's worried about the work she'll have to do.

c) Work in pairs. Check your answers.

Help with Listening
Linking (1): consonant-vowel links

● We usually link words that end in a consonant sound with words that start with a vowel sound.

4 a) **R3.7** Listen to the beginning of the TV programme again. Notice the consonant-vowel links.

JUDITH   So let's meet our first holidaymaker. Hello there, can you tell us a bit about yourself?

ALAN   Hi, Judith. My name's Alan Marsh. I'm in my fifties and I work in advertising.

JUDITH   And which of our holidays are you going on?

b) Look at R3.7, p145. Listen again and notice the linking.

Reading and Vocabulary

5 Alan and Emily wrote reviews on their holidays for the TV programme's website. Work in two groups. Group A, read about Alan's holiday. Group B, read about Emily's holiday. Answer these questions.

1 How long did he/she stay?
2 What was the accommodation like?
3 What did he/she do during the holiday?
4 What was the best thing about the holiday?
5 What was the most difficult part of the holiday?
6 Would he/she go on the same holiday again?

6 a) Work with a student from the other group. Take turns to ask and answer the questions in 5.

b) **R3.8** Read and listen to the two holiday reviews. Check your partner's answers.

Holiday reviews

Alan's holiday

My holiday began when I arrived at the medical centre in Cape Town. I had my operation the next day and it went very well, I'm glad to say. However, I had to spend the next five days inside, which is quite **difficult** when you're on holiday. But you need to be **patient** – you can't just sit in the sun after having a facelift. The second week I just relaxed by the pool. In the third week I went on safari, which was definitely the best thing about the holiday. We saw lots of lions and other wild animals, but we were never in any **danger**. We stayed in a guest house in the jungle, which was extremely **comfortable**. The staff were very **kind** and helpful, and it was fantastic being surrounded by **nature**. I'd definitely come back again and I'm sure this kind of holiday will increase in **popularity** as more people worry about their **health** and appearance.

Emily's holiday

My holiday on an organic farm in New South Wales in Australia was hard work, but very enjoyable. The couple who ran the farm were fantastic, and I was amazed by their **kindness** and **patience**. We worked five hours a day, six days a week. At first I had a lot of **difficulty** doing what they asked because I wasn't very strong. However, I soon got stronger and by the end of my two weeks there I felt incredibly fit and **healthy**. The best thing about the holiday was the people I met there, who were from all over the world, and it also felt great to eat **natural**

organic food every day. Everyone stayed in a fairly basic farmhouse, which was OK, but I missed the **comfort** of my own bed. We spent all our spare time at the beach, but I didn't go surfing because it was too **dangerous** for beginners like me. I don't know if this kind of holiday will ever become very **popular**, but I'd definitely do it again.

Help with Vocabulary Word formation (1): suffixes for adjectives and nouns

● We sometimes make adjectives from nouns, or nouns from adjectives, by adding an ending (a suffix), for example *happy → happiness*.

7 **a)** Work in pairs. Match the adjectives in pink in the reviews to the nouns in blue. Then underline the suffix in each pair of words.

difficult   difficulty

b) Write the words in the correct places in these tables.

adjective	noun	suffix
difficult	*difficulty*	*-y*
		-ce
		-ness
		-ity

noun	adjective	suffix
		-ous
		-able
		-al
		-y

c) Which words in 7b) only add the suffix? Which words have extra changes in spelling?

d) Look at the suffixes of these words. Are they adjectives (A) or nouns (N)?

knowledgeable *A*   sadness *N*   traditional   noisy
confidence   adventurous   activity   musical
possibility   honesty   fashionable   famous
touristy   importance   laziness   modesty

e) What are the nouns for the adjectives in 7d)? What are the adjectives for the nouns?

knowledgeable → knowledge   sadness → sad

f) Check in V3.3 p120.

8 Work in pairs. Take turns to test each other on the nouns and adjectives in **7**.

(tradition)   (traditional)

9 **a)** Work in new pairs. Make a list of five things that you think make a good holiday.

b) Compare lists with another pair. Choose the five best things from both lists.

c) Work in groups or with the whole class. Agree on a final list of five things.

3D A trip to India

Real World asking for and making recommendations
Review travel vocabulary

QUICK REVIEW ●●●

Work in pairs. Student A: write six adjectives that you can remember from lesson 3C. Student B: write six nouns that you can remember. Take turns to say your words and give the noun or adjective: A *patience*. B *patient*.

1 Look at the photo of Delhi, in India. Would you like to go there? Why?/Why not?

2 **a)** R3.9 Michael is going on a trip to Delhi. He is asking his friend Ellen for recommendations. Listen and tick the topics they talk about. Which two topics **don't** they talk about?

- the best time to visit
- things (not) to see in the city
- things to see outside Delhi
- dangers and problems
- getting around
- changing money
- food
- places to stay

b) Listen again. Tick the correct sentences. Change the incorrect ones.

Ellen thinks …

1 … rickshaws are the best way to get around the city.
2 … it's better to travel to other cities by bus.
3 … Michael should visit the museums in Delhi.
4 … he should go to the Red Fort in Old Delhi.
5 … he can visit the Taj Mahal and come back the same day.
6 … there's only one good restaurant in Connaught Place.

Real World Asking for and making recommendations

3 **a)** Fill in the gaps with the words in the boxes.

asking for recommendations

| good | visiting | tips | about | best |

Do you know any ¹ *good* places to stay/eat?
What's the ² _____ way to (get around)?
Is there anything else worth ³ _____ ?
What ⁴ _____ (places outside Delhi)?
Have you got any other ⁵ _____ ?

recommending things

| worth | best | definitely |
| must | recommend | |

It's probably ⁶ _____ to (use rickshaws).
I'd ⁷ _____ (the trains).
You should ⁸ _____ see (the Red Fort).
That's well ⁹ _____ seeing.
You really ¹⁰ _____ go to (Agra).

not recommending things

| bother | Don't | wouldn't | worth |

Don't ¹¹ _____ going to (the museums).
It isn't really ¹² _____ visiting.
¹³ _____ drink the water.
I ¹⁴ _____ eat anything that's sold in the street.

responding to recommendations

| useful | heard | know | sounds |

That's good to ¹⁵ _____ .
That ¹⁶ _____ good.
Thanks, that's really ¹⁷ _____ .
Yes, I've ¹⁸ _____ that before.

b) Which verb form comes after these phrases?

1 It's (well/not) worth …
2 Don't bother …
3 I'd/I wouldn't …

c) Check in RW3.1 p121.

4 R3.10 P Listen and practise the sentences in 3a).

Do you know any good places to stay?

26

5 a) Work in pairs. Use these prompts to write conversations.

1

A / know / good places to eat?
Do you know any good places to eat?

B You / definitely go / Henry's in the centre.

A What / places near the hotel?

B / recommend the Rose restaurant.

A Thanks / useful.

2

A Where / best place / stay?

B / probably best / stay in the Station Hotel.

A / got / other tips?

B I / not / carry too much money at night.

A / good / know.

3

A What / best places / visit?

B / must go to the City Art Gallery. It's amazing.

A / there anything / worth / see? What / the museums?

B Well, I / not / bother / go / the National Museum. It / not worth / visit.

A Yes / hear / before.

b) Practise the conversations with your partner.

 6 a) Work in new pairs. Choose a town, city or country you know well, but your partner doesn't know.

b) Work on your own. Decide what recommendations you can give your partner about the place you have chosen. Use the topics in 2a) or your own ideas.

c) Work with your partner. Take turns to ask for and give recommendations.

d) Which is the most interesting place, do you think? Why?

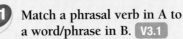 Language Summary 3, p119

 1 Match a phrasal verb in A to a word/phrase in B. V3.1

A		B	
1	set off	a)	problems
2	pick up	b)	your parents
3	get around	c)	early
4	deal with	d)	a hotel
5	check into/ out of	e)	a country

6	bring back	f)	a lot of noise
7	get back	g)	at the airport
8	put up with	h)	from Spain
9	look forward to	i)	a holiday
10	see someone off	j)	souvenirs

2 a) Use these prompts to write a conversation. Use the Present Perfect Simple or the Past Simple. G3.1

A / you ever / visit / the USA?

B Yes. I / go / there several times. I / just / get back / from Boston, actually.

A What / be / it like?

B Fantastic! I / have / a great time. / you / go / anywhere recently?

A Yes, we / go / to our holiday home in France last week.

B How long / you / have / that?

A We / have / it since the kids / be / tiny. It / belong / to my parents before us, so it / be / the family holiday home for a long time.

B / you / go / there when you / be / a child?

A Yes. Then my father / want / to sell it so I / buy / it.

b) Work in pairs. Compare answers. Then practise the conversation.

 3 a) Match two phrases to each of these verbs: *travel, get, go on*. V3.2

a guided tour   economy class
on your own   on/off a plane
a taxi   a package holiday

b) Work in pairs. Add two more phrases for each verb.

---

4 a) Tick the correct sentences. Change the incorrect ones. G3.2

1 How many emails have you ~~been sending~~ today?
   sent

2 How long have you been living in this town/city?

3 How many CDs have you been buying recently?

4 How long have you come to this school?

5 How many films have you seen this month?

6 How long have you been knowing the teacher?

b) Work in pairs. Take turns to ask and answer the questions.

5 a) Divide these words into nouns (N) and adjectives (A). V3.3

health   tourist   difficult
patience   kind   comfortable
popular   nature   danger

b) Change the nouns into adjectives and the adjectives into nouns.

c) Work in pairs. Choose three pairs of adjectives and nouns. Write a sentence for each word.

Progress Portfolio

a) Tick the things you can do in English.

☐ I can talk about past and recent events.

☐ I can talk about travel and holidays.

☐ I can ask and say how long something has been happening.

☐ I can ask how many things have been completed.

☐ I can ask for, make and respond to recommendations.

☐ I can understand a short description of someone's life.

b) What do you need to study again? ⊙ 3A–D

4 Born to be wild

Vocabulary music collocations
Grammar Past Simple and Past Continuous; *used to*
Review Present Perfect Simple

QUICK REVIEW ●●●
Think of two holiday places you have been to. Work in pairs. Take turns to ask for and give recommendations about your places. Talk about: things to see and do, food, accommodation, transport, etc.

Vocabulary Music collocations

1 Match a verb in A to a word/phrase in B. Check in **V4.1** p122.

A	B
do/play	a new album/a CD
appear	a concert/a gig
release	on TV
go to	a hit single
have	on tour
be/go	a concert/a gig/a festival
have	someone play live
see	onstage
be/go	an album/a CD in the charts

2 **a)** Write the names of three bands, musicians or singers you like. Choose phrases from 1 that you can use to talk about them.

b) Work in pairs. Talk about the bands, musicians or singers you have chosen. Use phrases from 1 in your conversations.

Reading and Grammar

3 **a)** Work in pairs. Look at the photos. What do you know about these people/bands?

b) Read the article. Fill in the gaps with the names of the people or bands in the photos.

c) **R4.1** Listen, read and check. How many did you get right? Which rider do you think is the most surprising?

Rock'n'roll Riders

★★★★★★★★★★★★★★★★★★★★★★★★★

When a band or a musician goes on tour, they have to sign a contract with the concert promoters. These contracts often include requests for things the musicians want. And these requests – or riders – are often more unusual than you might expect.

1 _____ , for example, was famous for his riders. **He always said** what size sofa he **wanted** and exactly how many flowers there should be in his dressing room. However, 2 _____ were very different. **In 1998 they were touring** in Europe and the USA for most of the year. They used to take their own furniture with them wherever they went – but they always asked the promoter for a full-size snooker table.

3 _____ is famous for being difficult. **In 2001 she went to Miami** to make a music video for charity. Her rider said that everything in her dressing room had to be white – sofas, tables, flowers, curtains, even the walls. And when 4 _____ was on tour in 2000, her contract said that the promoter had to pay $5,000 every time the phone rang in her dressing room. But perhaps the most unusual rider was from the rock star 5 _____ . He wanted everything in his hotel room covered in clear plastic.

Some food requests are also rather strange. We all know about 6 _____ and his love of food. Once, while he was staying in New York, he asked for a kitchen in his hotel suite – but it had to be exactly like his kitchen at home. And the seventies rock group 7 _____ once asked for twelve fruit pies, but not to eat. **While they were having their end-of-tour party, they threw the pies at each other** to celebrate the end of the tour!

Jennifer Lopez

Elton John

Luciano Pavarotti

The Rolling Stones

Foreigner

Cultura Inglesa

Help with Grammar Past Simple and Past Continuous

4 **a)** Look at the phrases in **bold** in the article. Match the verb forms in blue to these meanings.

- We use the **Past Simple** for:
  a) a single completed action in the past.
  b) a repeated action or habit in the past.
  c) a state in the past.
- We use the **Past Continuous** for:
  a) a longer action in the past.
  b) actions that were in progress when another (shorter) action happened.

b) Look at this sentence from the article. Answer the questions.

*While he **was staying** in New York, he **asked** for a kitchen in his hotel suite.*

1 Which action was longer?
2 Which action was shorter?
3 Which action started first?
4 Did he continue to stay in the hotel after he asked for a kitchen?

c) How do we make the positive, negative and question forms of the Past Simple and Past Continuous?

d) Check in G4.1 p123.

5 R4.2 P Listen and practise.

he asked for a kitchen in his hotel suite →
While he was staying in New York, he asked for a kitchen in his hotel suite.

6 **a)** Read about Van Halen's rider. Why was the rider important?

b) Read the text again. Choose the correct verb forms.

c) Work in pairs. Check your answers.

Help with Grammar *used to*

7 **a)** Look at these sentences. Then answer the questions.

a) They used to take their own furniture.
b) He always said what size sofa he wanted.
c) They once asked for twelve fruit pies.

1 Which sentences talk about repeated actions or habits in the past?
2 Can we use *used to* in sentences b) and c)? Why?/Why not?
3 Which verb form comes after *used to*?

b) How do we make the positive, negative and question forms of *used to*?

c) Check in G4.2 p124.

8 R4.3 P Listen and practise.
They used to /juːstə/ take their own furniture.

9 **a)** Make questions with *you* and these words. Use a form of *used to* if possible.

1 Who / be / your best friend when you were 12?
2 Where / first meet him or her?
3 / like the same music?
4 / go to gigs together?
5 / play the same sports?
6 / like the same TV programmes?
7 When / last see him or her?

b) Work in pairs. Take turns to ask and answer the questions in 9a).

Get ready ... Get it right!

10 Look at p112. Follow the instructions.

Prince

Britney Spears

The rock band Van Halen always ¹*had*/*were having* a rider in their contracts asking for bowls of M&M chocolates in their dressing room – but with all the brown ones taken out! The band ²*were including*/*included* this rider because they wanted to check if their promoters read the contract properly. If the band ³*found*/*were finding* any brown M&Ms while they ⁴*were getting*/*got* ready to go onstage, they knew that there would be problems at the gig.

For example, the following accident ⁵*happened*/*was happening* when they ⁶*were doing*/*did* a gig in Colorado. While the technicians ⁷*were putting*/*put up* the equipment, some of it ⁸*was crashing*/*crashed* to the floor. It ⁹*was costing*/*cost* $80,000 to repair the damage. Interestingly, the promoters at that gig ¹⁰*forgot*/*were forgetting* to take the brown M&Ms out of the bowls.

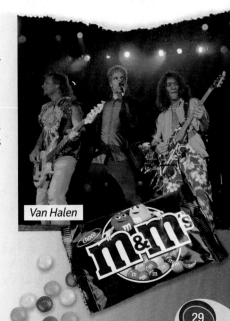
Van Halen

4B Adventurers

Vocabulary character adjectives
Grammar Past Perfect
Help with Listening Past Perfect or Past Simple
Review Past Simple

QUICK REVIEW ●●●
Write three true and three false sentences about what you were doing at different times of the day yesterday: *At 3 p.m. I was playing tennis*. Work in pairs. Swap sentences. Ask questions to find out which sentences are false: *Who were you playing tennis with?*

Vocabulary Character adjectives

 a) Tick the adjectives you know. Check in **V4.2** p122.

adventurous	talented	sensible	sensitive
brave	determined	reliable	independent
organised	stubborn	ambitious	confident
practical	generous	mean	responsible

b) Think of five people you know. Choose adjectives from 1a) to describe them. Think of reasons why you chose those adjectives.

c) Work in pairs. Tell your partner about the people you know. Who do you think is the most interesting?

Reading and Grammar

 a) Work in new pairs. Try to complete the table with the names and dates.

Famous Firsts

men	dates
~~Louis Bleriot~~	1909
Yuri Gagarin	1979 and 1982
Sir Ranulph Fiennes and Charles Burton	1961

women	dates
Valentina Tereshkova	1912
Harriet Quimby	2000 and 2002
Ann Daniels and Caroline Hamilton	1963

Who were the first people to …	fly a plane across the English Channel?	reach both the North and the South Poles?	travel in space?
men	Louis Bleriot		
dates			
women			
dates			

b) Check your answers on p141. How many did you get right?

c) Who are the women in photos A–C?

(A)

(B)

3 **a)** **R4.4** Listen to two TV producers, Beth and Luke, discussing a new TV series. Answer these questions.

1 What is Beth's new TV series about?
2 Who is the first programme about?
3 Why didn't this person become famous?

b) Listen again. Answer these questions.

1 Where did Beth get the idea for the series?
2 What did Harriet do in 1911?
3 When did she arrive in England?
4 Why didn't she fly on the Monday?
5 Did she know she was in France when she landed?
6 When and how did she die?

7 a) Put the verbs in brackets in the Past Perfect or Past Simple.

1 I _went_ (go) to the shop for some bread, but they _had sold out_ (sell out).
2 The meeting _____ (finish) by the time I _____ (get) there.
3 I _____ (invite) Tim to dinner, but he _____ (already arrange) to do something else.
4 When I _____ (get) to the airport, I realised I _____ (forget) my passport.
5 Erica _____ (ask) me to go to Spain with her, but I _____ (already book) a holiday in Italy.
6 I _____ (see) Gary Dale when I _____ (be) in town. I _____ (not see) him for ten years!

b) Work in pairs. Check your answers.

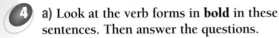

Help with Grammar Past Perfect

4 a) Look at the verb forms in **bold** in these sentences. Then answer the questions.

*I **decided** to make the series because I**'d seen** an article in the newspaper.*
*By the time she **got up** the next day, the weather **had changed**.*

1 Which action happened first in each sentence?
2 Which verbs are in the Past Simple?
3 Which verbs are in the Past Perfect?

b) Choose the correct word in the rule.

- When there is more than one action in the past, we often use the Past Perfect for the action that happened *first/second*.

c) Look at these two sentences. What is the difference in meaning?

When I turned on the TV, the programme started.
When I turned on the TV, the programme had started.

d) Fill in the gaps for the Past Perfect with *past participle*, *had* or *hadn't*.

POSITIVE
subject + _____ or 'd + past participle

NEGATIVE
subject + _____ + _____

e) Check in G4.3 p124.

5 a) R4.4 Look at R4.4, p146. Listen again and underline all the examples of the Past Perfect.

b) Work in pairs. Compare answers. How many examples did you find?

6 R4.5 P Listen and practise.

I'd seen an article in the newspaper. →
I decided to make the series because I'd seen an article in the newspaper.

Help with Listening Past Perfect or Past Simple

8 a) R4.6 Listen to these sentences. Notice the difference between the Past Perfect and the Past Simple.

1 I finished work.   I'd finished work.
2 He left home.   He'd left home.
3 They bought it.   They'd bought it.
4 Nick worked there.   Nick had worked there.

b) R4.7 Listen to six pairs of sentences. Which do you hear first: the Past Perfect (PP) or the Past Simple (PS)?

9 a) Read about the first women to walk to the North Pole. Why didn't they all reach the North Pole?

On March 1st 2002, Ann Daniels, Caroline Hamilton and Pom Oliver [1] _flew_ (fly) from England to Canada to walk to the North Pole. They [2]_____ (be) all experienced explorers and they [3]_____ (already walk) to the South Pole two years earlier. By the time they [4]_____ (leave) the UK they [5]_____ (train) for months with the British army and they [6]_____ (put on) 16 kilos in weight. However, as soon as they [7]_____ (set off) they [8]_____ (start) having problems because of bad weather and temperatures of −50°C. Pom soon [9]_____ (get) frostbite and by day 47 her feet [10]_____ (become) so painful that she couldn't continue. By the time Ann and Caroline [11]_____ (arrive) at the North Pole they [12]_____ (walk) 750 miles in 81 days. When they arrived back in England they [14]_____ (receive) a hero's welcome. No other women [15]_____ (ever walk) to both Poles before.

b) Put the verbs in brackets in the Past Simple or Past Perfect.

c) R4.8 Listen and check your answers.

Get ready ... Get it right!

10 Work in groups. Student A → p103. Student B → p108. Follow the instructions.

Vocabulary guessing meaning from context
Skills Reading: Nature's little helpers; Listening: Life in the jungle
Help with Listening linking (2): /w/, /j/ and /r/ sounds
Review Past Simple; Past Continuous; Past Perfect

QUICK REVIEW ● ● ●
Make a list of things you had done, or had learned to do, by the time you were 5, 10 and 15 years old. Work in pairs. Talk about the things on your list. Tell the class about any things that are the same: *By the time we were ten, Stephan and I had both learned to ski.*

Reading and Vocabulary

1 Work in groups. Discuss these questions.

1 Have you got a garden or a balcony where you live? If so, what's it like?
2 Have you, or people you know, ever used medicines made from plants or flowers?
3 Do you think these medicines are as good as normal medicines?

2 a) Read the article. Match pictures A–F to health problems 1–6.

1 sleep problems	4 sore throats
2 pain	5 heart problems
3 burns and cuts	6 a fever

b) Work in pairs. Compare answers.

c) Read the article again. Then change one word in these sentences to make them correct.

1 Aspirin originally came from a ~~flower~~. *tree*
2 Quinine came from a tree in India.
3 Dr Withering heard about foxglove from a patient.
4 Cleopatra used to put aloe vera on her food.
5 If you have a back problem, try taking garlic.

Help with Vocabulary Guessing meaning from context

3 a) Look at the words in pink in the article. What parts of speech are they?

b) Choose the correct meanings, a) or b). What information in the article helped you decide?

		a)	b)
1	**remedy**	a) a medicine	b) a type of plant
2	**battle**	a) a fight	b) a type of illness
3	**treat**	a) give money	b) give medical attention
4	**leaves**	a) young plants	b) the green parts of a plant
5	**heal**	a) get better	b) get worse
6	**scar**	a) a bad cold	b) a mark on your skin after a cut
7	**remarkable**	a) very unusual	b) very dangerous

c) Work in pairs. Look at the words in blue in the article. What part of speech are they? Can you guess what they mean?

d) Check in **V4.3** p122.

garlic

a foxglove

a cinchona tree

Nature's little helpers

People have been using natural medicines for thousands of years. Did you know, for example, that aspirin originally came from the bark of the willow tree? In the 5th century BC the Greek doctor, Hippocrates, gave it to his patients to stop their aches and pains.

Another natural remedy is quinine, which used to be an important drug in the battle against malaria. It comes from the bark of the cinchona tree, which grows in the Andes mountains in South America. Peruvian Indians have been using quinine for centuries to cure fevers.

In 1775 a British doctor, William Withering, was unable to treat a patient who had a serious heart problem. However, the patient made a complete recovery after taking something a local woman had given him. The woman told the doctor she'd made the remedy from purple foxgloves. This natural medicine is still given to people with heart problems because it makes your heart beat more slowly.

Many of the most effective natural remedies can be found in our homes and gardens. Put some lavender oil on your pillow at night to help you sleep. Or break open the leaves from an aloe vera plant and put the sap on your burns or cuts. This will help them to heal and might also stop you getting a scar. The Egyptian queen, Cleopatra, used this remarkable plant to keep her skin soft and young-looking.

Finally, we mustn't forget the healing power of garlic. It thins and cleans the blood, it's good for stomach problems and coughs, and it's a natural antiseptic. So, next time you have a cold, try a mixture of garlic, lemon and honey. It's magic!

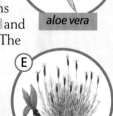
aloe vera

lavender

a willow tree

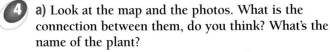

Monica   Molly   Kaz

Listening

4 a) Look at the map and the photos. What is the connection between them, do you think? What's the name of the plant?

b) [R4.9] Listen to the beginning of an interview with Monica and Kaz. Answer these questions.

1 Why were Monica and Kaz living with the Pa'Dalih people?
2 How old was their daughter, Molly?
3 What happened to Molly?

5 a) Work in pairs. Discuss these questions.

1 What do you think Monica and Kaz did next?
2 How did the Pa'Dalih people help them?

b) [R4.10] Listen to the next part of the interview. Were your answers correct?

6 a) Read this summary and correct the five mistakes.

While Monica and Kaz were living in Borneo, their daughter, Molly, got some burns on her face. The Pa'Dalih people put sap from banana leaves on her. Monica and Kaz took Molly to the nearest doctor 12 miles away. Then they took Molly to hospital. The Pa'Dalih people didn't think the doctor's medicine would leave scars.

b) [R4.10] Listen again and check.

7 a) Work in pairs. Guess the answers to these questions.

1 How did Monica and Kaz treat Molly's burns?
2 How long did the treatment last?
3 Did Molly completely recover?

b) [R4.11] Listen and check. Do you think Monica and Kaz did the right thing?

Help with Listening Linking (2): /w/, /j/ and /r/ sounds

● When a word ends in a vowel sound and the next word also starts with a vowel sound, we often link these words with a /w/, /j/ or /r/ sound.

word ends in	linking sound
/uː/ /əʊ/ /aʊ/	/w/
/ɪ/ /iː/ /aɪ/	/j/
/ə/ /ɜː/ /ɔː/ /eə/	/r/

8 a) [R4.12] Listen to these sentences from the interview. Notice the linking sounds.

The doctor wasn't happy /j/ about it, but she /j/ agreed in the /j/ end.

How /w/ often did you /w/ and Kaz have to do /w/ all of this?

No, there /r/ isn't a scar /r/ anywhere /r/ on her body.

b) [R4.11] Look at R4.11, p147. Listen to the last part of the interview again and notice the linking sounds.

9 a) Think of an interesting story about when you were a child. Choose one of these ideas or your own.

your first/last day at school   an accident
a birthday party   a sports event
the best/worst day of a holiday

b) Make notes on these things. Ask your teacher for any new vocabulary.

● where and when the story happened
● how the story started
● the main events of the story
● what happened at the end

c) Work in pairs. Take turns to tell your story. Ask questions to find out more information.

10 a) Write your story. Use the Past Simple, Past Continuous and Past Perfect.

b) Read other students' stories. Which do you like the most? Why?

It's just a game!

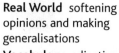

Real World softening opinions and making generalisations
Vocabulary adjectives to describe behaviour
Review character adjectives

QUICK REVIEW ● ● ●

Make a list of adjectives which describe people's character. Work in pairs and compare lists. How many of your words are different? Use the adjectives from both lists to describe people in your family.

1 Work in groups. Discuss these questions.

1 Do you, or people you know, support a football team? If so, why did you/they choose that team?

2 Have you ever been to a football match? If so, tell the group about the last match you went to.

3 Are there ever fights at football matches in your country? If so, why?

2 **a)** Tick the adjectives you know. Check new words in V4.4 p123.

> violent   arrogant   rude   polite
> noisy   loud   selfish   aggressive
> stupid   lazy   hard-working   loyal
> enthusiastic   considerate   spoilt
> patient   offensive   helpful
> bad-tempered   well-behaved

b) Work in pairs. Answer these questions.

1 Which adjectives in **2a)** have a negative meaning and which have a positive meaning?

2 Which adjectives can you use to describe football fans in your country?

3 **a)** R4.13 Listen to Ewan and Michelle talking about football fans. Choose the correct words/phrases in these sentences.

1 There were some fights at a football match last *night/weekend*.

2 Ewan thinks that *a few/most* football fans are violent.

3 Michelle thinks that *most/all* fans are loyal.

4 Michelle agrees with *everything/some of the things* Ewan says.

5 Ewan *changes/doesn't change* his opinion of football fans.

b) Listen again. Tick the adjectives in **2a)** that you hear.

Real World **Softening opinions and making generalisations**

● Sometimes English speakers soften the way they express their opinions so that they don't sound rude or offensive.

4 **a)** Match beginnings of sentences 1–6 to ends of sentences a)–f).

1 **Some of them can** be   a) just want to see a good game.
2 They **tend to** get   b) be **a bit** too enthusiastic.
3 That's **not very**   c) **quite** rude **at times**.
4 **Generally speaking,**   d) **rather** loud.
5 You get a few who **can**   e) normal behaviour.
6 **On the whole, most** fans   f) **most** people who go to matches are just loyal fans.

b) Look at the sentences in **4a)** again. Choose the correct words/phrases in these rules.

● After *tend to* we use *the infinitive/verb+ing*.

● *Rather*, *quite*, *not very* and *a bit* usually come *before/after* an adjective.

● We often put *generally speaking* and *on the whole* at the *beginning/end* of a sentence.

c) Look at these sentences. Then answer the questions.

They're stupid.   *They're not very intelligent.*

1 Which sentence is softer and more polite?

2 Do we use *not very* with a positive or a negative adjective?

d) Check in RW4.1 p124.

5 R4.14 **P** Listen and practise the sentences in **4a).**

Some of them can be quite rude at times.

6 **a)** Use the words/phrases in brackets to soften these opinions about children.

1 Children don't do very much sport. (Generally speaking; most)
Generally speaking, most children don't do very much sport.

2 They're very spoilt. (tend to; a bit)

3 They're rude to their teachers. (can; quite; at times)

4 They're very unhealthy. (Some of them; not very)

5 They watch a lot of TV. (On the whole; tend to; quite)

6 They're impatient. (Generally speaking; not very)

7 They're selfish. (Some of them; can; rather)

b) Work in pairs. Compare sentences. Do you agree with the sentences you have written? Why?/Why not?

7 **a)** Work on your own. Think of reasons why you tend to agree or disagree with these sentences.

1 Men watch too much sport.
2 Men are better at sport than women.
3 All teenagers are lazy.
4 Fast food is bad for you.
5 Pets cost a lot of money.
6 Motorbikes are dangerous.
7 There's never anything good on TV.

b) Work in groups. Discuss the sentences in **7a).** Use the language from **4a)** if possible.

1 **a)** Choose the correct words. V4.1

My brother's band has just ¹ *released/appeared* their third album. They've ² *done/had* a hit single but they haven't ³ *had/appeared* on TV. I've ⁴ *seen/been* them play live lots of times. At the moment they ⁵ *do/are* on tour and last week they ⁶ *did/play* a gig in London.

b) Work in pairs. Take turns to say a sentence. Check your partner's answers.

2 Put the verbs in brackets in the Past Simple or Past Continuous. G4.1

Once, when I ¹ _____ (be) a child I ² _____ (run) by a lake and I ³ _____ (fall) in the water. I ⁴ _____ (not know) how to swim and because I ⁵ _____ (wear) lots of clothes I ⁶ _____ (keep) going under the water. I nearly ⁷ _____ (die). Fortunately, a young man ⁸ _____ (run) around the park and he ⁹ _____ (see) me. He ¹⁰ _____ (jump) into the water and ¹¹ _____ (pull) me out.

3 **a)** Change the underlined verbs to *used to* + infinitive where possible. G4.2

My schooldays
1 I started school when I was five.
2 I got into trouble a lot.
3 I smoked.
4 I did a lot of sports.
5 I spent lots of time playing computer games.
6 I hated my last year at school.
7 I left when I was 16.

b) Write a question with *you* for each sentence in **3a).** Use *use to* + infinitive where possible.

c) Work in pairs. Take turns to ask and answer your questions.

4 **a)** Make a list of character adjectives. V4.2

b) Swap papers with another student. How many are the same?

5 Fill in the gaps with the verbs in brackets. Use the Past Simple or the Past Perfect. G4.3

1 By the time I _met_ (meet) him he _'d been_ (be) married three times.
2 I _____ (not be) tired because I _____ (already have) a few hours sleep.
3 When I got home I _____ (realise) I _____ (leave) my keys at the office.
4 After I _____ (read) the paper, I _____ (go) for a run.
5 By the time we _____ (get) home, Ben _____ (go) to bed.
6 He _____ (buy) me a book but I _____ (already read) it.

6 **a)** Soften these statements. RW4.1

1 Old people are bad-tempered. *Some old people can be a bit bad-tempered at times.*
2 Teenage boys are aggressive.
3 The cafés near here are awful.
4 The winters in this country are terrible.
5 Golf is boring.
6 Public transport in my country is unreliable.

b) Work in pairs. Compare answers. Do you agree or disagree with these sentences?

Progress Portfolio

a) Tick the things you can do in English.

☐ I can talk about music.

☐ I can tell stories about the past.

☐ I can describe people's character.

☐ I can guess the meaning of some words from the context.

☐ I can understand a radio interview.

☐ I can soften the way I express strong opinions.

b) What do you need to study again? ● 4A–D

Cultura Inglesa

5 Home truths

5A Moving house

Vocabulary homes
Grammar making comparisons: comparatives, superlatives, *much, a bit, (not) as ... as, different from*, etc.
Review adjectives to describe character and behaviour

QUICK REVIEW ●●●
Write five sentences to describe typical characteristics of your nationality: *We tend to ... , We can be rather/a bit/quite ... , Most people aren't very ... , Generally speaking, ... , On the whole, ...* Work in groups. Tell the group your sentences. Do you agree?

Vocabulary Homes

1 Work in pairs. Put these words/phrases into groups 1–3. Check in **V5.1** p125.

> a terraced house   with a nice view
> a balcony   a detached house   a loft
> a semi-detached house   in the country
> a cottage   a garage   in the suburbs
> a study   a basement   a cellar
> a three-storey house/building
> in a good/bad/rough neighbourhood
> an en-suite bathroom   a bungalow
> on the ground/first/top floor
> within walking distance of the shops
> a fitted kitchen

1 types of home
   a terraced house
2 location
   with a nice view
3 parts of a home
   a balcony

2 **a)** What are the five most important things to look for in a new home? Use the words/phrases in 1 and your own ideas.

a big garden
within walking distance of a station

b) Work in pairs. Compare lists. Choose the five most important things.

c) Work in large groups or with the whole class. Agree on a final list of five things.

Reading, Listening and Grammar

3 **a)** Read this advertisement for places to live in Manchester, England. Which do you like best? Why?

b) **R5.1** Ian and Liz are looking for a new place to live. Listen to their conversation. Which place do they both like?

4 **a)** Work in pairs. Look at these sentences. Are they about places A, B or C?

1 It's the least expensive place we've seen.
2 It seemed slightly bigger than our house.
3 It's one of the oldest houses we've seen so far.
4 It was much noisier than the other two.
5 The garden was far smaller than I expected.
6 It felt a lot more spacious.
7 It had the most amazing view.
8 It's a little further away from the city centre.
9 It's got the worst bathroom I've ever seen.
10 It's a bit less expensive than the Monton house.

b) **R5.1** Listen again and check.

SALFORD (A)

- luxury modern 2-bedroom flat
- 2 bathrooms, one en-suite
- private balcony overlooking the river
- new carpets and curtains

£230,000

Brown & Wood Estate Agents

Help with Grammar Making comparisons

5 **a)** Look at the words in blue in the sentences in **4a)**. Then answer these questions.

1 Which are comparatives?
2 Which are superlatives?
3 When do we use *-er* or *-est*?
4 When do we use *more* or *most*?
5 Which comparatives and superlatives are irregular?
6 What are the opposites of *more* and *most*?

b) Look at the words in pink in the sentences in **4a)**. Which mean: a) a big difference? b) a small difference?

c) Look at the phrases in **bold** in these sentences. Then answer the questions.

*It's **the same** size **as** ours.*
*It'll be **as** good **as** having a garden.*
*And it's very **similar to** this house.*
*It's **not as** big **as** the others.*
*It was very **different from** anything else.*

1 Which phrases mean the things we are comparing are:
   a) the same? b) nearly the same? c) not the same?
2 Do we use the adjective or its comparative form with (*not*) *as … as*?

d) Check in G5.1 p126.

ECCLES B
- 3-bedroom terraced house in quiet street
- 2 en-suite bathrooms
- new fitted kitchen
- wooden floors
- garden

£209,000

MONTON C
- spacious 4-bedroom detached house
- large kitchen/ dining room
- 2 bathrooms
- large front and back garden

£239,000

6 R5.2 P Listen and practise. Copy the weak forms.

It seemed slightly bigger than /ðən/ our house.
It was the same size as /əz/ ours.

7 Fill in the gaps with the comparative or superlative form of the adjective in brackets. Use *the* where necessary.

The **detached house** is:
1 in a much _busier_ (busy) street than the flat.
2 .... (attractive) than the terraced house.
3 .... (far) from the city centre.

The **terraced house** has got:
4 .... (few) rooms than the detached house.
5 .... (beautiful) garden in the street.
6 a .... (large) kitchen than the flat.

The **flat** is:
7 a lot .... (bright) inside than the two houses.
8 .... (modern) of the three properties.
9 in .... (fashionable) neighbourhood.

8 **a)** Rewrite these sentences with the words in brackets.

1 I'm much more confident than her. (less)
   She's much less confident than me.
2 I'm more ambitious than her. (not as … as)
3 I don't look the same as her. (different)
4 I'm a bit more stubborn than her. (less)
5 I'm not as organised as her. (more)
6 We're the same age. (as … as)
7 Her taste in music is almost the same as mine. (similar)

b) Choose a woman/girl you know well. Choose sentences from **8a)** that are true for you and her.

c) Work in pairs. Tell your partner about the woman/girl and your true sentences from **8a)**.

Get ready … Get it right!

9 Choose two houses/flats that your friends or family live in. Write six sentences to compare these homes to yours. Use these ideas or your own.

- location and size
- distance from shops/centre/station
- age and condition of house/flat
- size of rooms/balcony/garden
- type of neighbourhood

My friend Julia's house is a bit larger than mine.
My sister's flat is a lot closer to the centre.
My flat is probably the smallest.

10 **a)** Work in pairs. Take turns to tell your partner about the two houses/flats you chose and your home. Ask follow-up questions.

b) Which do you think is the best home? Why?

 Cultura Inglesa

5B A load of old junk

Vocabulary phrasal verbs (2)
Grammar the future: *will, be going to,*
Present Continuous
Help with Listening the future
Review making comparisons

Write the names of five people in your family. Think of how you can compare these people to yourself and other people in your family. Work in pairs. Take turns to tell the group about the people.

Vocabulary Phrasal verbs (2)

1 **a)** Check these words with your teacher or in a dictionary.

get rid of	keep	stuff	junk
a drawer	a cupboard	a pile	

b) Read the article. Tick the true sentences. Correct the false ones.

1 The article tells you how to get rid of rubbish.
2 You need an hour for each room.
3 You should put things in three piles.
4 Put things you don't want in a junk drawer.
5 Don't buy things if you've got something similar.

c) What do you think of the advice in the article? Do you need to do this in your home?

2 Work in pairs. Guess the meaning of the phrasal verbs in **bold** in the article. Check in V5.2 p125.

JUST GET RID OF IT!

Is your home full of stuff that you never use? If so, the time has come to get rid of all your junk and create a peaceful, relaxed atmosphere in your home.

- Give yourself at least two hours to **clear out** a room.
- Make a space on the floor and empty all the cupboards and drawers.
- **Sort out** the things you haven't used for six months and make three piles: 1) things to **give away** 2) things to **throw away** 3) things to keep.
- Put the first and second piles into separate rubbish bags and **take** them **out** of the room.
- Allow yourself one junk drawer in each room for the stuff you can't decide about.
- **Tidy up** the room and **put** everything **away**, then sit down and enjoy the calm space you have created.

And here's how to stop all your junk **coming back**.

- Before you buy anything, ask yourself: Have I got something similar? Do I need it? Where will I put it?
- When you buy something new, always **throw** something else **out**.
- **Go through** the cupboards and drawers in a different room every month and throw away anything you don't need.

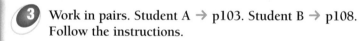

3 Work in pairs. Student A → p103. Student B → p108. Follow the instructions.

Listening and Grammar

4 **a)** Look at the picture. What are Ian and Liz doing? Why are they doing this, do you think?

b) Work in pairs. Look at the picture again. What is in piles 1–3?

c) Which pile do you think Ian and Liz are going to: give away? throw away? keep?

d) R5.3 Listen and check your answers to 4c).

5 **a)** Work in pairs. Match these sentences to things a)–e) in the picture.

1 She's picking them up tomorrow evening after work.
2 OK, I'll throw those away.
3 I'm going to sort out the rest of them at the weekend.
4 But you'll never listen to them again.
5 That old thing? It's going to break the first time he uses it!

b) R5.3 Listen again and check.

Help with Listening **The future**

7 **a)** [R5.4] Listen and write the sentences you hear. You will hear each sentence twice.

b) Listen again to sentences 1 and 2. What are the two ways we can say *going to*?

c) Match the sentences you wrote in **7a)** to the meanings in **6a)** and **6b)**.

8 [R5.5] [P] Listen again and practise.
I'm going to finish the report tonight.

9 **a)** Read the rest of Ian and Liz's conversation. What are they going to: give away? throw away? keep?

LIZ   What about this dress? Shall I keep it?
IAN   Sorry, but I don't think ¹*it's going to fit/it's fitting* you any more.
LIZ   OK, ²*I'll throw/I'm throwing* it away.
IAN   And what about your old guitar?
LIZ   Toby wants that. ³*He's coming/He'll come* to pick it up later.
IAN   Right, ⁴*I'll put/I'm going to put* it in the 'give away' pile.
LIZ   Do you want to keep your old running shoes?
IAN   Yes, ⁵*I'm starting/I'm going to start* running again soon.
LIZ   Shall we keep this mirror? ⁶*It'll look/It's looking* nice in the new house.
IAN   Yes, why not? Oh, don't forget ⁷*we're meeting/we'll meet* the estate agent at four.
LIZ   You go. ⁸*I'll finish/I'm finishing* sorting out this stuff.

b) Read the conversation again. Choose the correct verb form.

c) [R5.6] Listen and check. What does Liz do when Ian leaves?

10 **a)** Write two things you have arranged to do, two things you have planned to do and two things you will probably do in the next four weeks.

b) Work in groups. Compare lists. Who's going to have the busiest or the most interesting four weeks?

Help with Grammar **The future**

6 **a)** Look at sentences 1–3 in **5a)**. Then fill in the gaps in these rules with *will*, *be going to* or the Present Continuous.

a) We use .... when we decide to do something at the time of speaking.

b) We use .... when we already have a plan or an intention to do something.

c) We use .... when we have an arrangement with another person.

b) Look at sentences 4 and 5 in **5a)**. Choose the correct verb forms in these rules.

d) We use *will/be going to* for a prediction that is based on present evidence (we predict the future because of something we can see in the present).

e) We use *will/be going to* for a prediction that is not based on present evidence.

c) How do we make the positive, negative and question forms of *will* and *be going to*?

d) Check in [G5.2] p127.

Get ready ... Get it right!

11 Make a list of eight things in your home that you want to get rid of. Use these ideas or your own.

> CDs/records   computer games   sports equipment   DVDs/videos
> clothes   books   furniture   toys   bikes   magazines

12 **a)** Try to sell or give away your things to other students. Each person has £50 to spend. Write who agrees to buy or have each thing.

> Olga, do you want to buy my bike?   Maybe. I'll give you £15 for it.

b) Work in groups. Tell other students about the things on your list. Who made the most money?

VOCABULARY AND SKILLS

Vocabulary verb patterns (1)
Skills Reading: A furniture empire;
Listening: Shopping at IKEA;
Help with Listening fillers and
false starts
Review Past Simple and Past
Continuous

QUICK REVIEW ●●●
Work in pairs. Ask questions to find five things you're going to do next
weekend that your partner isn't going to do: A *Are you going to have a lie-in?*
B *Yes, I am./No, probably not.*

Reading and Vocabulary

1 a) Work in pairs. Look at the photos and answer these
questions.

1 What does IKEA sell?
2 Are there any IKEA stores or similar stores in your country?
3 Have you ever bought anything from these shops? If so, what
   did you buy?

b) Read the article about IKEA. Match headings a)–d) to
paragraphs 1–4.

a) Opening night problems
b) A worldwide success story
c) The beginning of flatpack
d) Why is IKEA so successful?

2 a) Read the article again. What does the article
say about these numbers and people?

a) 1943	d) Gillis Lundgren	g) 6,000
b) 365 million	e) Russell Crowe	i) 500
c) £8 billion	f) 200	h) 40

b) Work in pairs. Take turns to tell each other
about the words and numbers in 2a). Give as
much information as possible.

c) What do you think is the most interesting
thing in the article?

How to build a furniture empire IKEA

1 Since it opened its first store in 1943,
IKEA has become one of the biggest
furniture empires in the world. The
company has **made** people think
differently about the way they furnish
their homes, particularly in countries
like Germany, the UK and France. Over
365 million people worldwide spend
more than £8 billion in IKEA stores each
year and the number of customers
keeps rising. The best-selling products
are bookshelves, sofas, candles, chairs
and coat hangers, but perhaps IKEA is
most famous for its flatpack furniture.

2 Flatpack furniture was invented
by chance in 1956 by a man called Gillis
Lundgren. He lived in a Swedish town
called Almhult and worked for a small
furniture company. One day Lundgren
needed to deliver a table to a
customer, but the table **wouldn't** fit in
his car. "Let's pull off the legs and put
them underneath," said Lundgren – and
that was the moment flatpack furniture
was born. From that simple beginning,
the small furniture company became
IKEA and Lundgren became one of its
top designers.

3 The secret of IKEA's success is not just
the design, it's also the price. Flatpacks
don't take up much space, so IKEA **can**
send furniture round the world very
cheaply. Also the stores don't employ
lots of sales people to **help** you find or
carry things; it seems people **don't mind**
doing that for themselves. And most
importantly, IKEA doesn't **pay** anyone to
put the furniture together – they **let**
the customers do that. Apparently,
people **would rather** pay less and build
the furniture themselves. However, not
everyone **seems** to find this easy. When
the actor Russell Crowe was **trying** to
put together some bedroom furniture,
he got so frustrated that he attacked
the flatpack with a knife. He finally had
to **ask** someone to help him.

4 There are now over 200 IKEA stores in
more than 30 countries and every time
a new store opens it's front-page news.
In 2005, when London's fourth IKEA
opened for business at midnight, there
were 6,000 people waiting outside!
When people **began** shopping, the store
became so crowded that the manager
told the staff to close the doors. Even
though the store was only open for 40
minutes, IKEA had already sold all 500
sofas that were on special offer!

Help with Vocabulary Verb patterns (1)

 3 a) Look at the verbs in **bold** in the article. <u>Underline</u> the verb form that follows them. Then write the infinitive form of the verbs in **bold** in the table.

keep	+ verb+*ing*
need	+ infinitive with *to*
would	+ infinitive
pay	+ object + infinitive with *to*
make	+ object + infinitive

b) Write these verbs in the table in 3a). Some verbs can go in more than one place.

> enjoy   will   want   finish   prefer
> decide   love   hate   must   continue
> like   start   would like   plan   forget
> allow   should   learn   teach   could

c) Check in V5.3 p126.

 4 a) Fill in the gaps with the correct form of the verbs in brackets.

1 Do you enjoy ..*shopping*.. (shop)?
2 What was the last thing you needed .... (buy) for your home?
3 What would you like .... (get) for your home at the moment?
4 Have you ever asked someone .... (buy) something expensive for you?
5 Do you like .... (help) other people .... (choose) what to buy?
6 Do you let other people .... (buy) clothes for you?
7 Did your parents use to make you .... (wear) things you didn't like?
8 Do you prefer .... (go) out to the shops, or would you rather .... (do) your shopping on the Internet?

b) Work in pairs. Take turns to ask and answer the questions.

Listening

 5 a) R5.7 Listen to Gillian and Sue. Who likes shopping at IKEA and who doesn't? What do they agree about?

b) Listen again. Make notes on what Gillian and Sue say about these things.

Gillian
- things they sell
- personal service
- queues
- putting the furniture together

Sue
- shop assistants
- buying candles, glasses and plants
- a flat in France
- putting the furniture together

Help with Listening Fillers and false starts

- In spoken English we often use fillers (*well, you know, um*, etc.) and false starts (*I've … I've been*, etc.) to give us time to think.

 6 a) <u>Underline</u> the fillers and false starts in these sentences.

1 <u>Well</u>, <u>I've</u>, er, I've been to IKEA, er, let me think, about eight or nine times.
2 And I mean you can't argue with the prices. Everything's … well, like, everything's so cheap compared to other places.
3 You can never you know find, um, there's never anyone to help, which I find kind of annoying.
4 You see, I haven't, um, I've got no patience at all, and I just sort of stand there and get angry.

b) R5.7 Look at R5.7, p147. Listen to Gillian and notice all the fillers and false starts. Then listen to Sue and <u>underline</u> all the fillers and false starts.

 7 a) Work in pairs. Look at these questions for a shopping survey. Write three possible answers for each question. Then write two more questions of your own.

1 How often do you go shopping for pleasure?
   a) every week b) two or three times a month c) once a month or less
2 Which of these things do you enjoy shopping for the most?
3 When you're buying new clothes, which of these things is the most important?
4 Which of these places do you usually buy your food from?
5 When you go shopping, how do you usually get there and back?

b) Interview five other students. Make notes on their answers.

c) Work again with your partner. Compare the results of your surveys. Tell the class any interesting things you have found out.

 8 a) Write a short report on the results of your survey.

b) Swap reports with other students. Do you agree with their results? Why?/Why not?

Is this what you mean?

Vocabulary materials
Real World explaining what you need
Review verb patterns

QUICK REVIEW ●●●

Choose five of these phrases and write sentences about you: *I'd like, I keep, I forgot, I might, I started, I'm planning, I've decided, I often help, I usually let.* Work in pairs. Take turns to say your sentences. Ask follow-up questions.

1

a) Tick the materials you know. Then do the exercise in **V5.4** p126.

metal	plastic	paper	wool	steel	cardboard
wood	tin	rubber	glass	cotton	leather

b) Work in pairs. Write one more thing that is made of each material in 1a). Don't write them in order.

c) Swap papers with another pair. Write the correct materials next to the things on their paper.

d) Check your answers with the pair who wrote the list.

2 **a)** **R5.8** Lars is from Sweden, but now he lives in the UK. Listen to four conversations. Tick the things in photos A–G that he buys.

b) Work in pairs. Match these words to the things Lars bought.

stain remover	a charger	drawing pins	a corkscrew

c) Listen again and check.

Real World Explaining what you need

3

a) Write these headings in the correct places a)–d).

describing what something looks like	describing what something is used for
checking something is the right thing	saying you don't know the name of something

a)	b) ....
I'm sorry, I've forgotten what it's called.	It's a thing for (opening bottles of wine).
I'm sorry, I don't know the word for it.	It's stuff for (getting marks off your clothes).
I can't remember what they're called.	You use them (to put posters up on the wall).
I don't know what it's called in English.	I'm looking for (something for my mobile).
	You use it when (the batteries are dead).
c)	**d)** ....
It's a type of (liquid).	Do you mean one of these?
They're made of (metal).	Oh, you mean (stain remover).
They've got (a round top).	Is this what you're looking for?
It looks like (a black box).	

b) Look again at the phrases in 3a). Then choose the correct words in these rules.

● We often use *stuff* to talk about *countable/uncountable* nouns we don't know the name of.

● After *It's a thing for …* and *It's stuff for …* we use *the infinitive/verb+ing.*

 ● After *You use it/them …* we use *the infinitive with to/verb+ing.*

c) Check in **RW5.1** p127.

Please Pay Here

A
B
C
D
E

4 **R5.9** **P** Listen and practise the sentences in **3a)**.

I'm sorry, I've forgotten what it's called.

5 **a)** Write conversations between Lars (L) and a shop assistant (SA) from these prompts.

1

L I / look / something / mend my clothes.

SA / mean cotton? This stuff?

L No, they / make / metal. They / got / hole in the end.

SA Oh, / mean needles.

2

L It's / thing for / boil / water. / sorry, / not know / word / it.

SA / mean one / these?

L Yes, that's it. What / called / English?

SA A kettle.

3

L It's stuff / make / things smell nice. I / forget / what / called.

SA / mean perfume? Like this?

L No, you use / when / want / make / house smell better.

SA Oh, / mean air freshener.

b) Work in pairs. Compare answers. Match the things Lars bought to photos A–G.

c) Practise the conversations in **5a)** with your partner.

6 Work in new pairs. Student A → p104. Student B → p109. Follow the instructions.

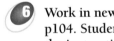 **R5.10** Look at the song *Our House* on p100. Follow the instructions.

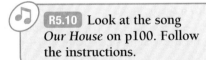

(F)

(G)

---

5 Review

Language Summary 5, p125

1 **a)** Make a list of ten words/phrases to describe types of homes, location and parts of a home. **V5.1**

a detached house

b) Write six questions with your words/phrases from **1a)**.

Do you live in a detached house?

c) Find one student who answers *yes* for each question.

2 **a)** Write the comparative and superlative forms of these adjectives. **G5.1**

> few bright amazing old
> bad busy confident organised
> cheap easy spacious far

b) Choose six adjectives. Write four true and four false sentences about you. Use these words if possible.

> slightly a lot a bit
> much a little far

I'm a lot busier than I used to be.
I'm not as organised as my sister.

c) Work in pairs. Tell your partner your sentences. Guess which sentences are false.

3 **a)** Complete the phrasal verbs with these words. **V5.2**

> put throw give
> tidy go clear

1 *throw* out the rubbish.
2 _____ up the living room.
3 _____ away clothes I don't wear any more.
4 _____ away the washing-up.
5 _____ out cupboards and drawers and _____ away things I don't want.
6 _____ away old books to friends.
7 _____ through my English notes.

b) Choose an adverb or time phrase to make the sentences in **3a)** true for you.

I throw out the rubbish once a week.

c) Work in pairs. Compare answers.

4 **a)** Write six sentences about things your friends/family have already arranged to do, planned to do or will probably do in the future. **G5.2**

I think my brother will have to look for a new job soon.

b) Work in pairs. Tell your partner your sentences. Ask follow-up questions.

5 **a)** Fill in the gaps with the correct form of the verbs in brackets. **V5.3**

I began ¹ _____ (look) for a new flat last month. I asked the estate agent ² _____ (look) for two-bedroom flats. He kept ³ _____ (show) me ones that were far too expensive, but Mum said she'd let me ⁴ _____ (borrow) some money. I don't mind ⁵ _____ (borrow) from her so I decided ⁶ _____ (buy) the first flat I'd seen.

b) Work in pairs. Compare answers.

Progress Portfolio

a) Tick the things you can do in English.

☐ I can describe homes.

☐ I can compare people and things.

☐ I can talk about future arrangements and plans.

☐ I can make predictions about the future.

☐ I can read a short newspaper article.

☐ I can describe things that I need and say what they are used for.

b) What do you need to study again? ● **5A–D**

6 Decisions and choices

6A Make up your mind

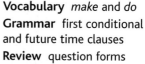
Vocabulary *make* and *do*
Grammar first conditional and future time clauses
Review question forms

QUICK REVIEW ●●●
Write a list of six things in your house. Work in pairs. Take turns to describe the things to your partner. Don't say the thing: *It's made of metal and you use it to cook eggs.* Your partner guesses what the things are: *A frying pan?*

Vocabulary *make* and *do*

 a) Do we use *make* or *do* with these phrases? Check in **V6.1** p128.

> do the cleaning   make a decision   do a course   make a mistake
> do homework   make money   make friends   do nothing   do exercise
> do the washing-up   make a noise   do the shopping   make dinner
> do some work   do the washing   do a degree   make an excuse
> make someone laugh/cry   do an exam   make up your mind
> do the housework   make progress   make a cake   do someone a favour
> make a mess of something   make an appointment

do the cleaning   make a decision

b) Work in pairs. Take turns to test each other.

> the cleaning   do the cleaning

 a) Fill in the gaps with the correct form of *make* or *do*.

Find someone who ...

... ¹ *did* someone a favour last weekend.
... has ² *done* some exercise this week.
... is good at ³ *making* people laugh.
... usually ⁴ *do* the washing-up every day.
... likes ⁵ *do* nothing at the weekend.
... usually has to ⁶ *make* dinner for other people.
... is ⁷ *doing* another course at the moment.
... has ⁸ *made* some new friends this year.
... is going to ⁹ *do* some shopping after class.
... often has to ¹⁰ *make* excuses for being late.

b) Make *yes/no* questions with *you* for the sentences in 2a).

Did you do someone a favour last weekend?
Have you done any exercise this week?

c) Ask other students your questions from 2b). Find one person who answers *yes* to each question. Ask follow-up questions if possible.

Kate

Listening and Grammar

 a) Work in groups. Discuss these questions.

1 Are you good at making decisions?
2 What was the last big decision you made?
3 How do you usually make big decisions?

b) **R6.1** Listen to Kate talking to her brother, Steve. Work in pairs. Student A, answer these questions about Kate. Student B, answer these questions about Steve.

1 Does she/he have a job at the moment? If so, what does she/he do?
2 What decision does she/he have to make?
3 What advice does she/he give to the other person?

c) Tell your partner your answers. What do you think Kate and Steve should do?

 a) Work in pairs. Who said these sentences, Kate or Steve?

1 If I start teaching again, I'll be exhausted after a year. K
2 What will you study if you go back to university? S
3 But you might have to wait until next year if you don't apply soon. S
4 But unless I do it now, I'll be too old. K
5 I'll give them a ring before they go on holiday. K
6 As soon as I make up my mind, I'll let you know. S
7 I might leave after I finish this contract. S
8 I won't tell them until I decide what to do. S
9 Well, I'll believe it when I see it! K

b) **R6.1** Listen again and check.

Steve

Help with Grammar First conditional and future time clauses

FIRST CONDITIONAL

5 **a)** Look at this sentence. Which is the main clause? Which is the *if* clause?

If I start teaching again, I'll be exhausted after a year.

b) Look again at sentences 1–3 in **4a).** Then answer questions **a)–e).**

a) Do these sentences talk about the present or the future?

b) Does the *if* clause talk about things that are possible or certain?

c) How do we make the first conditional?

d) Is the *if* clause always first in the sentence? no

e) Which word in sentence 3 means *will perhaps*? But

c) Look at sentence 4 in **4a).** Then answer these questions.

a) Which word means *if not*? Unless

b) How can you say this sentence with *if*?

d) Check in G6.1 p129.

But if I don't do it now, I'll be too old.

FUTURE TIME CLAUSES

6 **a)** Look at sentences 5–9 in **4a).** Then answer questions **a)–c).**

a) Do these sentences talk about the present or the future?

b) Which verb form do we use in the main clause?

c) Which verb form do we usually use in the clauses beginning with *before, as soon as, after, until* and *when*?

b) Check in G6.2 p129.

7 R6.2 P Listen and practise.

I'll be exhausted after a year. →
If I start teaching again, I'll be exhausted after a year.

8 Rewrite these sentences. Use the words in brackets. Change the verb forms if necessary.

1 He won't do it unless we pay him. (if)
He won't do it if we don't pay him.

2 I'll come out tonight if I don't have to work. (unless)

3 Perhaps he'll call you if he gets home in time. (might)

4 I'll have to move house unless I find a job soon. (if)

5 If Tony doesn't arrive soon, we'll go without him. (unless)

6 Perhaps I'll go away this weekend unless my friends come to visit. (might; if)

9 Fill in the gaps with the correct form of *make* or *do*.

1 He *'ll make* a decision when his boss gets back.

2 I *'ll make* dinner after I *do* the washing-up.

3 I *'ll do* some work before everyone arrives.

4 If you *make* the cleaning, I *'ll do* the shopping.

5 As soon as I *make* some progress, I'll let you know.

6 I *'ll do* my homework after this programme finishes.

7 You won't *make* any money until you *do* a business course.

8 I *'ll make* an appointment with the doctor when I have time.

9 I *'ll do* the washing if you *make* Jamie's birthday cake.

10 **a)** Complete these sentences for you.

1 As soon as I get home today, I *'ll study English.*

2 If I have any phone messages, I *'ll answer it*

3 Before I go to bed tonight, I *'ll brush my teeth.*

4 I'll be at the next class unless *I get sick*

5 After I finish this course, I *'ll do a degree.*

6 I want to study English until *I be fluent*

7 I'm going to ... this weekend unless *my car break*

8 When I retire, I think I *'ll travel*

9 I'll be very happy if *I have a baby.*

10 I might move house when *I move work.*

b) Work in pairs. Compare sentences. Are any the same?

Get ready ... Get it right!

11 Work in groups of three. Student A → p103. Student B → p108. Student C → p112. Follow the instructions.

6B Protective parents

Vocabulary reflexive pronouns
Grammar zero conditional; conditionals with imperatives and modal verbs; *in case*
Help with Listening zero or first conditional
Review *make*, *do* and *let*; first conditional; *used to*

QUICK REVIEW ●●●

Write six phrases with *make* or *do* that are connected to your life, or the lives of people you know. Work in pairs. Tell your partner why you chose these phrases. Ask follow-up questions:
A *I chose 'do an exam' because I have to do an exam next week.* **B** *What kind of exam is it?*

Reading and Grammar

 1 **Work in groups. Discuss these questions.**

1 When you were a child, what did your parents make you do? What did they let you do?
2 How do children spend their free time these days? How is this different to when you were a child?

 2 **a) Check these words with your teacher or in a dictionary.**

protect   the media
grow up   freedom

b) Read the article. Which sentence describes the article best?

1 Life for children is harder now than it used to be.
2 Parents protect their children too much these days.
3 Children don't want to play outside any more.

 3 **Read the article again. Tick the true sentences. Correct the false ones.**

1 We used to worry about our children *~~more~~* less than we do now.   F
2 Most British parents ~~let~~ *don't* their children walk to school.   F
3 Julie Benz thinks parents worry too much about their children.   T
4 Life is more ~~dangerous~~ *safe* for children now than it used to be.   F
5 Children don't spend as much time with other children as they used to.   T

The Parent Trap

As every parent knows, ¹**if you have children, you worry about them all the time.** However, it seems that these days we're worrying about our kids a lot more than we used to. Are we trying to protect our children too much and will this cause problems for them in later life?

"In the past, kids in the UK used to walk to school every day, but these days parents don't let their children go out on their own in case something bad happens to them," said Dr Andy Hallett, a childcare expert. ²**If children stay indoors all the time, they become unfit.** This means they often have health problems in later life."

The dangers of letting your kids go out by themselves are smaller than you might think. "The media makes parents worry about children's safety," says Julie Benz, a child psychologist. "But children are safer now than they have ever been. ³**If parents want their kids to grow up healthy, they shouldn't protect them so much.** Children need to make decisions themselves."

Over 27% of British children are now overweight, partly because they spend their free time playing computer games and watching TV. "I can understand why parents are concerned," says Julie Benz. ⁴**"But if kids never go outside, they can't learn to look after themselves in the real world."**

Overall, therefore, the message is clear. ⁵**If you want happy and healthy kids, give them back their freedom.**

Help with Grammar **Zero conditional; conditionals with imperatives and modal verbs; *in case***

 4 **a) Look at sentences 1 and 2 in bold in the article. These are called zero conditionals. Choose the correct words in these rules.**

● Zero conditionals talk about things that are *possible in the future*/*always true*.
● In zero conditionals both verbs are in *the Present Simple*/*a future verb form*.

b) Look at sentences 3–5 in the article. Answer these questions.

a) Which sentences have a modal verb in the main clause?   3
b) Which sentence has an imperative in the main clause?   5
c) Which verb form is in the *if* clause in each sentence?

c) Look at this sentence from the article. Then choose the correct words/phrases in the rules.

*Parents don't let their children go out on their own **in case** something bad happens to them.*

● We use *in case* to say that we are prepared for something that *might*/*is definitely going to* happen.
● *In case* and *if* have *the same*/*different* meanings.

d) Check in G6.3 **p129.**

Help with Listening Zero or first conditional

7 a) R6.4 Listen to these sentences. Notice the difference between *they* and *they'll*.

If my kids go to a friend's house, they call me.
If my kids go to a friend's house, they'll call me.

b) R6.5 Listen and write the sentences you hear. You will hear each sentence twice. Which are zero conditionals? Which are first conditionals?

Help with Vocabulary Reflexive pronouns

8 a) Look at these sentences from the article. Notice the reflexive pronouns in **bold**. Then choose the correct words/phrases in the rules.

1 They can't learn to look after **themselves**.
2 The dangers of letting your kids go out by **themselves** are smaller than you might think.
3 Children need to make decisions **themselves**.

● In sentence 1, *They* and *themselves* are *the* ~~same~~/*different* people.

● In sentence 2, *by themselves* means ~~alone~~/*with other people*.

● In sentence 3, *themselves* emphasises that children do this *with*/~~instead~~ of someone else.

b) What are the reflexive pronouns for *I*, *you* (singular), *he*, *she*, *it*, *we*, *you* (plural) and *they*?

c) Check in V6.2 p128.

5 R6.3 P Listen and practise.

you worry about them all the time →
If you have children, you worry about them all the time.

6 a) Fill in the gaps with these verb forms. Then choose *if* or *in case*.

~~feet~~	should start	need	lose	is playing
have	don't get	can't work	call	get

1 I _feel_ terrible all day *if*/~~in case~~ I _don't get_ enough sleep.
2 I usually _have_ a glass of water by the bed *if*/~~in case~~ I _get_ thirsty in the night.
3 ~~If~~/*In case* you _need_ to talk to me urgently, _call_ me on my mobile.
4 I _should start_ saving money *if*/~~in case~~ I _lose_ my job.
5 I _can't work_ *if*/~~in case~~ someone _is playing_ music.

b) Tick the sentences in 6a) that are true for you.

c) Work in pairs. Compare sentences. How many are the same?

9 Fill in the gaps with the correct reflexive pronoun.

1 I made my daughter's jumper _myself_.
2 My son likes playing by _himself_.
3 We want to educate our children _ourselves_.
4 Deborah looks after three children by _herself_.
5 I usually cut the kids' hair _myself_.
6 The party was great. All the kids enjoyed _themselves_.
7 I often go for a walk by _myself_.

Get ready ... Get it right!

10 Work in pairs. Write your top ten tips for parents.

If your children can't sleep, read them a story.
Teach your child your phone number in case they get lost.

11 a) Work with another pair. Take turns to tell each other your tips. Choose the best ten tips.

b) Compare tips with another group or with the whole class. What are the best ten tips?

Cultura Inglesa

6C Touch wood

Vocabulary synonyms
Skills Listening: The history of superstitions; Reading: Learn to be lucky
Help with Listening sentence stress (3)
Review conditionals; adjectives

QUICK REVIEW ●●●
Think about what you usually do if you: feel a bit depressed, get a cold, can't get to sleep, feel stressed, have too much work to do. Work in groups. Tell the group your ideas: *If I feel a bit depressed, I eat chocolate and watch TV!*

Vocabulary and Listening

1 a) Match these words/phrases to photos A–H.

> a black cat   a shooting star   a mirror   salt
> a ladder   wood   a lucky charm   an umbrella

b) Read about some British superstitions. Fill in the gaps with words/phrases from 1a).

British superstitions

1 If _a black cat_ walks in front of you, you'll have good luck.
2 If you walk under _a ladder_ or open _an umbrella_ in the house, you'll have bad luck.
3 If you break _a mirror_, you'll have seven years bad luck.
4 If you carry _a lucky charm_, like a rabbit's foot, it'll bring you good luck.
5 If you see _a shooting star_ in the sky, you can make a wish.
6 If you want a good thing to continue, you should touch _wood_ .
7 If you spill _salt_ on the table, you should throw it over your shoulder.

2 Work in groups. Discuss these questions.

1 Which of the British superstitions are true in your country?
2 What other superstitions do people have in your country?
3 Do you believe in any superstitions? If so, which ones?

3 a) Check these words with your teacher or in a dictionary.

> the Romans   crops   fertility   good/evil spirits

b) R6.6 Listen to Edward and Charlotte talking about superstitions. Tick the British superstitions they talk about.

c) Listen again. Complete these sentences.

1 The idea of seven years bad luck was started by _the Romans_
2 Rabbits were good luck because they had a lot of _babies_.
3 People used to believe that good spirits lived in _the trees_
4 Many years ago salt was used as a _medicine_
5 In the UK you throw salt over your _left_ shoulder.

Help with Listening Sentence stress (3)

4 a) Choose the correct words/phrases in these rules.

● We *usually*/*don't usually* stress nouns, verbs, adjectives, and negative auxiliaries.
● We *usually*/*don't usually* stress pronouns, prepositions, connecting words and positive auxiliaries.

b) Work in pairs. Look at the beginning of the conversation. Which words are stressed, do you think?

EDWARD   Charlotte, are you very superstitious?
CHARLOTTE   No, not really. Why do you ask?
EDWARD   I'm reading this absolutely fascinating book about the history of superstitions. Did you know that in the UK, people think that seeing a black cat is good luck, but in nearly every other country it's bad luck? Don't you think that's strange?

c) R6.6 Listen to the beginning of the conversation again. Check your answers. Are question words and adverbs usually stressed or unstressed?

d) Look at R6.6, p148. Listen to the rest of the conversation. Notice the sentence stress.

Reading and Vocabulary

5 **a)** Work in groups. Discuss these questions.

1 Have you ever won anything? If so, what did you win?
2 Do you think people are born lucky? Why?/Why not?

b) Check these words/phrases with your teacher or in a dictionary.

> vice versa   by chance   intuition   an optimist
> attitude   cheer yourself up   a volunteer

6 **a)** Read the article. Choose the correct answers.

1 Richard Wiseman *studies luck*/*is a very lucky person*.
2 He *thinks*/*doesn't think* some people are born lucky.
3 His research shows that people *can*/*can't* learn to be lucky.

b) Read the article again. Answer these questions.

1 Did Maureen Wilcox win the lottery?
2 How long has Dr Wiseman been studying luck?
3 Do lucky people have more new experiences than unlucky people?
4 What was the aim of Dr Wiseman's luck school?
5 How many people were luckier after going to luck school?

Learn to be lucky

Help with Vocabulary Synonyms

7 **a)** Look at the words/phrases in pink in the article. Check any words you don't know with your teacher or in a dictionary.

b) Look at the words/phrases in blue in the article. Match them to these synonyms. Write the infinitive form of the verbs.

choose	*pick*	by chance	*accidentally*
satisfied	*content*	attitude	*approach*
lucky	*fortunate*	sure	*certain*
behave	*act*	deal with	*coping with*
notice	*spot*	show	*revealed*

c) Match a word/phrase in A to a synonym in B.

A	B
concerned	chat to someone
frightened	glad
make a decision	have a go at doing
try to do	huge
talk to someone	scared
nice	make up your mind
enormous	worried
pleased	brilliant
wonderful	awful
terrible	pleasant

d) Check in **V6.3** p128.

8 Work in pairs. Take turns to test each other on the synonyms in 7b) and 7c).

9 Work in groups. Group A → p103. Group B → p108. Follow the instructions.

FOUR WAYS TO BE LUCKY

In June 1980, Maureen Wilcox became one of the US lottery's biggest losers. She chose the winning numbers for both the Rhode Island and Massachusetts lotteries. But unfortunately for her, the numbers she picked for the Rhode Island lottery were the correct ones for the Massachusetts lottery, and vice versa.

We all know lucky people – they have good relationships, successful careers and are very satisfied with their lives. But what makes them so lucky? Dr Richard Wiseman has spent ten years studying luck and has found that lucky people have a completely different approach to the world.

The results of his work revealed that people aren't born lucky. Instead, fortunate people behave in a way that creates good luck in their lives.

● They notice opportunities that happen by chance more often than unlucky people. They are also more open to meeting new people and having new experiences.
● They tend to make good decisions by listening to their intuition.
● They're optimists and are certain that the future is going to be full of good luck. This positive attitude often makes good things happen.
● They're also good at coping with bad luck and often cheer themselves up by imagining things could be worse than they are.

LUCK SCHOOL

Dr Wiseman tested his ideas by starting a luck school, where he hoped that unlucky people could learn to be lucky. 400 volunteers spent a month doing exercises to help them think and act like a lucky person. These exercises helped the volunteers spot opportunities that happen accidentally, trust their intuition more, feel sure they're going to be lucky and become better at dealing with bad luck. The results were dramatic and showed that 80% of the volunteers were now happier and more content with their lives – and most important of all, luckier.

Dr Wiseman's ideas won't help you win the lottery, but they might help you in your day-to-day life – fingers crossed!

QUICK REVIEW ●●●

Write all the pairs of synonyms you know (*sure*, *certain*, etc.) Work in pairs. Take turns to say one of your words/phrases. Your partner guesses the synonym.

1 Work in groups. Discuss these questions.

1 Have you ever been to a music festival? If so, where?
2 Which music festivals are famous in your country?
3 What problems do music festivals cause?
4 Who decides if you can have a music festival in your country?

2 a) Look at the picture of a local village meeting in the UK. Who are these people, do you think?

- the chairperson *Sarah*
- a police officer *Jim Against*
- the festival organiser *Terry Favour*
- a local resident *Felicity A*
- a local farmer *Paul F*

b) [R6.7] Listen to the beginning of the meeting. Check your answers. What is the meeting about?

3 a) [R6.8] Listen to the next part of the meeting. Who is for and who is against the festival?

b) Listen again. Tick the true sentences. Correct the false ones.

1 The festival lasts for three days. T
2 There will be 13,000 people at the festival. F
3 Terry Gibson thinks the festival will provide jobs. F
4 Most people going to the festival will pass through the village. T
5 The live music will stop at 11 p.m. F
6 Sergeant Matthews is most worried about the noise. F

c) Work in groups. Do you think Sarah Clark should give permission for the festival? Why?/Why not?

Sergeant Jim Matthews
Terry Gibson
Paul Davidson

Real World Discussion language

4 a) Fill in the gaps with the words in the boxes.

wanted	sure	absolutely
agree	true	with
opinion	think	not

point	say	just
making	interrupt	
course	ahead	

inviting people to speak

(Paul), you had something you
¹ *wanted* to say.
What's your ² *opinion* ?
What do you ³ *think* ?

ways of agreeing

That may be ⁴ *true* , but what
about ... ?
Yes, ⁵ *absolutely*
Yes, I'd agree ⁶ *with* that.

ways of disagreeing

That's ⁷ *not* true, actually.
Well, I'm not ⁸ *sure* about that.
I'm not sure I ⁹ *agree* , actually.

b) Check in [RW6.1] p129.

asking to speak

Sorry, do you mind if I ¹⁰ *interrupt* ?
Can I just ¹¹ *say* something here?
Can I make a ¹² *point* here?

allowing someone to interrupt

Sure, go ¹³ *ahead*
Yes, of ¹⁴ *course*

not allowing someone to interrupt

Can I ¹⁵ *just* finish what I
was saying?
If I could just finish ¹⁶ *making*
this point.

Felicity Richards

Sarah Clark

5 R6.9 **P** Listen and practise the sentences in **4a)**. Copy the polite intonation.

You had something you wanted to say.

6 a) Look at these sentences. Think of reasons why you agree or disagree with them.

1 Footballers get paid too much.
2 There's too much violence on TV.
3 People who live in flats shouldn't keep pets.
4 Public transport should be free.
5 Tourists destroy the places they visit.
6 Smoking shouldn't be allowed in any public places.

b) Work in groups of four. Discuss each topic for at least a minute. Use phrases from **4a)**.

> Do you think footballers get paid too much?

> Yes, I do, actually. I think that …

7 Work in groups. Group A → p104. Group B → p109. Group C → p112. Group D → p113. Follow the instructions.

6 Review
Language Summary 6, p128

1 a) Complete the sentences with the correct form of *make* or *do*. V6.1

1 Do you *make* many spelling mistakes in English?
2 When do you usually *do* your homework?
3 When was the last time you *did* an exam?
4 Do you find it difficult to *make* quick decisions?
5 Who always *makes* you laugh?
6 Are you *doing* any other courses at the moment?
7 Who has *done* you a favour recently?

b) Work in pairs. Take turns to say your sentences. Did anything surprise you?

2 a) Put the verbs in brackets in the correct form. All the sentences are about the future. G6.1 G6.2

1 When John *get* (get) home, I *'ll tell* (tell) him you called.
2 I *'ll phone* (phone) Pete before I *go* (go) home.
3 I *won't go* (not go) to the concert unless I *feel* (feel) better.
4 As soon as I *finish* (finish) this, I *'ll help* (help) you.
5 I *'ll wait* (wait) here until you *get* (get) back.

b) Work in pairs. Compare answers.

3 Work in pairs. Do sentences a) and b) have different meanings? If so, what are they? G6.3

1 a) I'll take the car if it rains.
  b) I'll take the car in case it rains.
2 a) If I go to the USA, I stay with my aunt.
  b) If I go to the USA, I'll stay with my aunt.
3 a) When he's late, he calls us.
  b) If he's late, he calls us.
4 a) If you can't do it, I might help.
  b) If you can't do it, I'll help.

4 Complete the sentence with a reflexive pronoun. V6.2

1 My parents usually go on holiday by *themselves*
2 Does she make the bread *herself* ?
3 I accidentally cut *myself* with a knife.
4 Do you clean your house *yourself* ?
5 Dan and I always cook for *ourselves* on holiday.
6 He travelled across the USA by *himself*

5 a) Write a synonym for the underlined words. Then tick the sentences that are true for you. V6.3

1 I've been *fortunate* lucky enough to travel a lot in my life.
2 I generally have a very positive *approach* attitude to life. *sure*
3 I'm never certain about what to take on holiday with me. *dealing with*
4 I'm good at coping with stress.
5 I've never chosen the right *picked* numbers in the lottery.
6 Most of my friends are content with their lives. *pleased*

b) Work in pairs. Compare sentences. How many are the same?

Progress Portfolio

a) Tick the things you can do in English.

☑ I can talk about possible and definite future events.

☑ I can talk about things that are always true.

±− I can agree and disagree with people in a discussion and give my opinion.

±− I can invite others to speak and ask others not to interrupt me.

☑ I can understand a simple conversation.

b) What do you need to study again? ● 6A–D

 Cultura Inglesa

7 Technology

7A Save, copy, delete

Vocabulary computers
Grammar ability: *be able to, manage, have no idea how, be good at*, etc.
Review discussion language; question forms

QUICK REVIEW ●●●
Decide if you agree or disagree with these sentences: a) Computer games are bad for children. b) The Internet makes people less sociable. c) People depend on computers too much. Work in groups and discuss the sentences.

Vocabulary Computers

1 **a)** Tick the words you know. Then do the exercise in V7.1 p130.

> a printer   a mouse   a monitor   a scanner
> a keyboard   a screen   speakers   a memory stick

b) Work in groups. What computer equipment do you use at school/work/home? What do you use it for?

2 **a)** Work in pairs. Fill in the gaps with these verbs. Check new words in **bold** in V7.2 p130.

> delete   log on   go   search   have   make
> close   reply to   click on   download

1 You can **save**, **copy**, **print** or _delete_ a **file** or a **document**.
2 You can **create**, **open** or _close_ a **folder**.
3 You can **get**, **send**, **forward** or _reply to_ an **email**.
4 You should _make_ a **back-up copy** of your important documents.
5 You can _log on_ by entering your **password**.
6 You can _click on_ an **icon**, **an attachment**, a **website address** or a **link** on a **web page**.
7 You can _go_ **online** and _download_ **software**, pictures or music from the Internet.
8 If you _have_ **broadband**, you can _search_ for something on the Internet very quickly.

b) Work in new pairs. Which of the things in sentences 1–8 in **2a)** have you both done in the last seven days?

Reading and Grammar

3 **a)** Do the questionnaire.

b) Work in pairs. Compare answers. How many are the same?

c) Check your answers on p141. Do you agree with the description of yourself?

How computer literate are you?

1 How old were you when you first used a computer?
   a) over 20
   b) between 10 and 19
   c) under 10

2 How long did it take you to learn how to save, copy, print and delete a file?
   a) I **was able to** learn this very quickly.
   b) I'm still **useless at** doing these things.
   c) I **could** do these things after I read the instructions.

3 How good are you at searching for information on the Internet?
   a) I **haven't got a clue how** to do this.
   b) I usually **manage** to find what I want, but not always.
   c) I'm **quite good at** doing this and I **can** always find what I want.

4 Do you know how to download software or music from the Internet?
   a) I **have no idea how** to do this.
   b) I **find this quite easy** to do.
   c) I think I **know how** to do this, but I haven't done it for a while.

5 How good are you at using new computer equipment or software?
   a) I'm **able to** use most new stuff after a very short time.
   b) I **find it difficult** to use anything new unless someone shows me.
   c) I'm **no good at** using new stuff, with or without help.

Help with Grammar Ability

4 **a)** Look at the verbs and phrases in **bold** in the questionnaire. Match them to these meanings.

- things you can do now
- things you can't do now
- ability in the past

b) Look at this sentence. Then answer the questions.

*I **managed** to download some new software, but it took me ages to find out how to do it.*

1 Did the person download the software?
2 Was it easy or difficult?

c) Look at the questionnaire again. Then complete these phrases with *infinitive*, *infinitive with to* or *verb+ing*.

1 be able to + *infinitive*
2 be useless at/quite good at + ... *verb+ing*
3 could/can + ... *verb*
4 haven't got a clue how + ... *to + verb*
5 manage + ... *to + verb*
6 have no idea how + ... *to + verb*
7 find something easy/difficult *to + verb* + ...
8 know how + ... *to + verb*

d) Which other adjectives can we use with: *be* + adjective + *at*?

be brilliant at
be hopeless at

e) Check in G7.1 p131.

5 R7.1 P Listen and practise. Copy the stress.

I was àble to /tə/ lèarn this vèry quickly.

6 **a)** Read the text. What does Bill do now?

When my father, Bill, retired a year ago, he bought himself his first ever computer. At the time he had no idea how ¹ *to use* (use) a computer and didn't even know how ² *to save* (save) a document. He couldn't ³ *type* (type) very fast and he didn't have a clue how ⁴ *to go* (go) online. So he started going to evening classes, and after a few lessons he was able to ⁵ *send* (send) emails and ⁶ *to search* (search) for things on the Internet. He even managed ⁷ *to create* (create) his own web page! His friends realised that he was good at ⁸ *working* (work) with computers and started asking him for help. He found it quite easy ⁹ *to sort out* (sort out) their problems and decided to start teaching retired people basic computer skills. Now he's working harder than he used to before he retired!

b) Put the verbs in brackets in the correct form.

c) R7.2 Listen and check your answers.

7 **a)** Write sentences about what you can and can't do on a computer. Try to use a different phrase from **4b)** for each idea.

- make back-up copies of your files
- type without looking at the keyboard
- download photos from a digital camera
- fix problems on your computer
- use a scanner
- design a web page

I haven't got a clue how to make back-up copies of my files.

b) Work in pairs. Compare sentences. What can you do that your partner can't?

Get ready ... Get it right!

8 Write four true sentences and four false sentences about other things you can and can't do. Use a different phrase from **4b)** in each sentence.

I'm quite good at playing the guitar.
I have no idea how to use a DVD player.

9 **a)** Work in pairs. Take turns to say your sentences. Your partner can ask two questions about each sentence. Then guess if your partner's sentences are true or false.

b) Tell the class two things your partner can or can't do. Which student has the most interesting or unusual ability?

Vocabulary electrical equipment
Grammar second conditional
Help with Listening first or second conditional
Review first conditional

QUICK REVIEW ●●●
Write two things on your computer that you can: save, click on, forward, download, send, create. Work in pairs. Compare answers. Which of these things have you done this week?

Vocabulary Electrical equipment

1 a) Tick the words/phrases you know. Then do the exercise in **V7.3** p130.

> a hand-held computer 9   a GPS/sat nav 7
> a dishwasher 3   a washing machine 1
> a hair dryer 2   hair straighteners 12
> a webcam 5   a hands-free phone 8
> an MP3 player 10   air conditioning 4
> central heating 11   a DVD recorder 6

b) Which of the things in 1a) have you got? Which would you like to have?

c) Work in groups. Compare answers.

2 a) Work in pairs. Put the things in 1a) in order from the most useful (1) to the least useful (12).

b) Compare answers with another pair.

Listening and Grammar

3 a) Look at the people in the photos. You are going to hear them talk about things from 1a). Which things do they talk about, do you think?

b) **R7.3** Listen and check.

c) Match these sentences to the people in the photos.

1 I'd never leave the house if I didn't have these.
2 If my car had one, life would be so much easier.
3 If we didn't have it in the office, I wouldn't get much work done.
4 I'd get one tomorrow if I had enough money.
5 If we didn't have it at home, I wouldn't get any sleep at all.
6 Would you go out in public if you looked like a clown?

d) Listen again and check. Do the people have the things they talk about?

Don

Help with Grammar Second conditional

4 a) Look at the sentences in 3c). Choose the correct words/phrases in these rules.

● We use the second conditional to talk about real/*imaginary* situations.

● The second conditional talks about *the present or the future*/the past.

● The *if* clause *is always first*/can be first or second in the sentence.

b) Look at these sentences. Then answer the questions.

If I have enough money, I'll get one for my car.
If I had enough money, I'd get one for my car.

1 Which sentence is an imaginary situation because the person doesn't have enough money? 2
2 Which sentence is a real possibility because the person might have enough money? 1

c) Fill in the gaps for the second conditional with 'd, infinitive or *Past Simple*.

if + subject + past simple , subject + 'd (= would)/wouldn't + infinitive

TIP! ● We can say *If I/he/she/it was* … or *If I/he/she/it were* … in the second conditional.

d) Fill in the gaps in these questions with *if*, *do* or *would*. What are the positive and negative short answers to question 2?

1 What would you do if you didn't have one?
2 If you didn't have one, would you get lost? yes, I would

e) Check in **G7.2** p131.

5 **R7.4** **P** Listen and practise.

if I didn't have these → I'd never leave the house if I didn't have these.

Holly

Kathy

6 **a)** Fill in the gaps with the correct form of the verbs in brackets. Then complete the sentences for you.

1 If I _won_ (win) a holiday anywhere in the world, I _would go_ (go) to …
2 If I _didn't live_ (not live) where I do, I _would_ (like) to live in ..*Paris*.
3 If I _could_ (can) change places with one person in the world, I _would choose_ (choose) …
4 If I _were_ (be) a film star, I _would like_ (like) to make a film with .*Al Pacino*.
5 If I _lived_ (live) in another country, I _would miss_ (miss) .*my mother*.
6 If I _could_ (can) talk to a famous person from history, I _would talk_ (talk) to … about …

b) Work in pairs and compare sentences. Continue the conversations if possible.

> If I won a holiday, I'd go to Africa.

> What would you do there?

> I'd go on a safari.

7 Work in new pairs. Student A → p105. Student B → p110. Follow the instructions.

---

8 **a)** **R7.5** Listen to these sentences. Notice the difference between the verb forms.

If I have some free time, I'll help you.
If I had some free time, I'd help you.

b) **R7.6** Listen to six pairs of sentences. Which do you hear first: the first conditional or the second conditional?

9 **a)** Choose the correct words in these conversations.

1
DON Oh, dear. I'll never finish this report by 5 o'clock.
JACK Sorry, ¹*I'll/I'd help* you if I ²*don't/didn't* have all this work to do. Have you asked Megan?
DON I couldn't find her.
JACK Well, if I ³*see/saw* her, ⁴*I'll/I'd* tell her to call you.

2
KATHY How do I get to your sister's place again?
BEN Surely you know the way by now!
KATHY I ⁵*won't/wouldn't* ask if I ⁶*know/knew*.
BEN Well, if I ⁷*don't/didn't* have to go to work, ⁸*I'll/I'd* take you myself. But I've got meetings all day.
KATHY Don't worry. If you just ⁹*write/wrote* the directions down for me, ¹⁰*I'll/I'd* be fine.

b) **R7.7** Listen and check your answers.

Get ready … Get it right!

10 **a)** Write these things on a piece of paper. Don't write them in order. Use the words/phrases in **1a)** or your own ideas.

- three possessions that are really important to you
- three things you don't have, but would like to have

b) Think about how your life would be different with or without these things.

If I didn't have my hand-held computer, I wouldn't be able to work on the train.
If I had a car, I'd visit my friends more often.

11 **a)** Work in pairs. Swap papers. Take turns to ask and answer questions about the things on your partner's paper.

> Have you got a hand-held computer?

> Yes, I have.

> Why is it so important to you?

> Because I travel around a lot. If I didn't have it, …

b) Tell the class two things about your partner.

Vocabulary use of articles: *a*, *an*, *the*, no article
Skills Listening: Computer viruses; Reading: Virus writers
Help with Listening weak forms (2)
Review second conditional; computers

VOCABULARY AND SKILLS

QUICK REVIEW ●●●

Decide what you would do if you: won the lottery, could speak English fluently, were the leader of your country, were ten years younger. Work in groups. Compare ideas. Which students have the same ideas as you?

Listening

 1 Work in groups. Discuss these questions.

1 How do you get computer viruses?
2 Have you, or anyone you know, ever had a computer virus? If so, what happened?

 2 a) Check these words with your teacher or in a dictionary.

> a PC   damage   crash   spread   infect   access

b) R7.8 Listen to the beginning of a lecture about computer viruses. Match the names in A to the facts in B.

A

1 John von Neumann ...
2 Frederick Cohen ...
3 Basit and Amjad Alvi ...
4 Melissa and Love Bug ...
5 Sven Jaschan ...
6 Trojan Horses ...

B

3 a) created the first ever computer virus.
1 b) predicted computer viruses in 1940.
6 c) allow other people to access your computer.
4 d) were famous viruses in 1999 and 2000.
5 e) wrote the Sasser Worm virus.
2 f) first used the word 'virus' in 1983.

c) Listen again. Answer these questions.

1 How are computer viruses similar to flu viruses?
2 Why did Basit and Amjad Alvi create the Brain virus?
3 Was the Brain virus very dangerous?
4 Where did Sven Jaschan write his virus?
5 Why was the Sasser Worm virus so dangerous?
6 If there's a Trojan Horse on your computer, what can people steal from you?

Help with Listening Weak forms (2)

● Remember: in sentences we say many small words with a schwa /ə/ sound. These are called weak forms.

 3 a) Work in pairs. How do we say the strong and weak forms of these words?

> do   you   at   for   of   and   to   can

b) R7.9 Listen and notice the difference between the strong and weak forms of these words.

	strong	weak		strong	weak
are	/ɑː/	/ə/	were	/wɜː/	/wə/
as	/æz/	/əz/	has	/hæz/	/həz/
that	/ðæt/	/ðət/	have	/hæv/	/həv/
was	/wɒz/	/wəz/	from	/frɒm/	/frəm/

c) Look at these sentences from the beginning of the lecture. Which words do we hear as weak forms?

These days, computer viruses (are) part (of) everyday life. But (as) early (as) 1940, a man called John von Neumann predicted (that) computer programmes would be able (to) make copies (of) themselves – and he (was) right. This ability (has) meant (that) people (have) been able (to) create viruses which (can) travel (from) computer (to) computer.

d) R7.8 Listen and check. Are weak forms ever stressed?

e) Look at R7.8, p150. Listen to the lecture again. Notice the sentence stress and weak forms.

Reading and Vocabulary

 4 Work in two groups. Group A, read about David L Smith. Group B, read about Onel de Guzman. Answer these questions.

1 Which country is the person from?
2 Which virus did the person create?
3 Why did the virus have that name?
4 How did the virus travel from computer to computer?
5 How much did the virus cost businesses?
6 Did the person go to prison?

 http://www.viruswriters.com/melissa

David L Smith

David L Smith created **the Melissa virus** in 1999 while he was working for **a company** in New Jersey, in **the USA**. The American computer programmer named the virus after **a dancer** he knew while he was living in **Miami**, Florida. At that time Melissa was **the worst** virus there had ever been and it crashed **email systems** around the world, including those at Microsoft and Intel. The way the virus worked was simple. As soon as it infected **a computer**, it forwarded itself to the first 50 email addresses in **the computer**'s address book. Because people thought that the emails were from friends or colleagues, they opened them immediately, which allowed the virus to infect their computers. The Melissa virus cost businesses more than $80 million in North America alone, mostly in lost work time. However, because Smith helped the police catch other virus writers, he was only sent to **prison** for 20 months.

http://www.viruswriters.com

   http://www.viruswriters.com/lovebug

Onel de Guzman

In May 2000, Onel de Guzman, **a student** from **the Philippines**, was arrested for creating **the most famous** virus in history while he was studying computing at **university**. The Love Bug virus came as **an email attachment** which said "I love you". People thought **the attachment** was a love letter, so they immediately opened it. The virus sent itself to everyone in their address book and then deleted important files on the computer's hard disk. Even when people thought they had got rid of the virus, it was clever enough to sit waiting in **an unopened file**. The virus spread around **the world** extremely quickly and after only one day about 45 million computers were infected. Love Bug did a lot of damage to **businesses** in **Asia**, Europe and the USA, and cost them over $10 billion. Fortunately for him, Onel de Guzman wasn't sent to prison because at that time there were no laws in the Philippines for computer crime.

http://www.viruswriters.com

---

5 **a)** Work with a student from the other group. Take turns to ask and answer the questions from **4**.

b) R7.10 Read and listen to both articles. Check your partner's answers are correct. Which facts do you think are the most surprising?

Help with Vocabulary
Use of articles: *a*, *an*, *the*, no article

6 **a)** Look at the words/phrases in **bold** in the article about David L Smith. Match one word/phrase to each of these rules.

- We use *a* or *an*:
a) when we don't know, or it isn't important, which one.
   a company
b) with jobs. *a dancer*
c) to talk about a person or thing for the first time. *a computer*
- We use *the*:
d) to talk about the same person or thing for the second/third/ fourth, etc. time. *the computer*
e) when there is only one (or only one in a particular place). *the Melissa virus*
f) with countries that are groups of islands or states. *the USA*
g) with superlatives. *the worst*
- We don't use an article:
h) for most towns, cities, countries and continents. *Miami*
i) to talk about people or things in general. *e-mails systems*
j) for some public places (*school*, *hospital*, etc.) when we talk about what they are used for in general. *prison*

b) Check in V7.4 p130.

7 **a)** Look at the words/phrases in **bold** in the article about Onel de Guzman. Match them to rules a)–j) in **6a)**. There is one word/phrase for each rule.
a student b)

b) Work in pairs. Compare answers.

8 Work in pairs. Student A → p105. Student B → p110. Follow the instructions.

9 **a)** Work in groups. You are going to start your own website. Choose one of these ideas or your own.

> your town/city/country   a free time activity
> a fan site for a film star/band/football team
> a TV programme   your class/school   a sport

b) Discuss what is going to be on your website. Talk about these ideas or your own. Make notes on each decision the group makes.

- the name of your website
- who you would like to visit the website
- what's on your home page (photos, links, etc.)
- how many different pages there are
- what's on each page

10 **a)** Work with students from other groups. Take turns to describe your website. Which is the best website, do you think?

b) Tell the class about the best website in your group. Which website does the whole class think is the best?

7D What's the password?

QUICK REVIEW ●●●

Make a list of all the words connected to computers that you know. Work in pairs. Who has the most words? Which words on your lists can you use together? *You can copy a document, click on an attachment … .*

> **Real World** indirect and direct questions
> **Help with Listening** intonation (2): being polite
> **Review** computers; verb forms

Simon   Carol

Ben

1 **a)** Look at the photos. Where are the people? What problems do they have, do you think?

b) **R7.11** Listen to Carol talking to people at work and then to her husband, Ben, later the same day. Tick the true sentences. Correct the false ones.

1

a) Carol has just come back from a business trip. T
b) They have changed the computers in the office. F *password*
c) Carol can't log on to her computer. T
d) The computer expert will be back around 2 p.m. F *3*

2

cinema with his friends
e) Carol's son, Tim, has gone to a friend's house. F
f) Tim has changed the password on his laptop. T
g) Carol and Ben are going to have a party soon. T
h) She called Alex Ross earlier in the day. F

2 **a)** **R7.11** Listen again. Put these questions in the order you hear them.

1

a) Could you tell me whether he'll be back soon?
b) Do you know if we asked Alex Ross to come?
c) Have you any idea where he's gone?
d) Can you tell me what his number is?
e) Do you think he's changed the password?

2

f) Will he be back soon?
g) Did we ask Alex Ross to come?
h) Where's he gone?
i) What's his number?
j) Has he changed the password?

b) Work in pairs. Compare your answers.

Real World Indirect and direct questions

3 **a)** Look at indirect questions a)–e) and direct questions f)–j) in **2a)**. Then choose the correct word in this rule.

● In more formal situations we often use *indirect/direct* questions because they sound more polite.

b) Look at questions a)–e) in **2a)**. Notice the phrases in **blue** that we use to introduce indirect questions. Then choose the correct word/phrase in these rules.

● We use *if* or *whether* in indirect questions when there *is/isn't* a question word.

● In indirect questions, *if* and *whether* are the *same/different*.

● We *use/don't use* *if* or *whether* with *Do you think … ?*.

c) Look at the phrases in **pink** in questions a)–e) in **2a)**. Then choose the correct word in the rule.

● In indirect questions, the main verb is in the *positive/question* form.

d) Check in **RW7.1** p131.

Help with Listening
Intonation (2): being polite

- We know if people are being polite by how much their voices move up and down. If their voices are flat, they often sound rude or impatient.

4 **R7.12** Listen to the same sentences said twice. Which sounds polite, a) or b)?

1 (a) b)   4 a) b)
2 a) b)   5 a) b)
3 a) b)

5 **R7.13** **P** Listen and practise. Copy the polite intonation.

Could you tell me whether he'll be back soon?

6 Put these words in order.

1 know / how / ticket machine / this / works / you / Do ?
2 idea / Have / what / wants / Jim / you / any / for his birthday?
3 whether / you / this / is / me / Can / tell / room D ?
4 think / the meeting / be / will / you / Do / Ruth / at ?
5 tell / run / how often / Could / me / the trains / you ?

7 **a)** Rewrite these direct questions as indirect questions. Use the phrases in the brackets.

1 Is there a bookshop near here? (Do you know …)
2 How do I get to the station? (Could you tell me …)
3 Should I give taxi drivers a tip? (Do you think …)
4 What time do the banks close? (Have you any idea …)
5 Where's the nearest post office? (Can you tell me …)

b) Imagine you're a tourist in the town/city you're in now. Write three more indirect questions to ask someone who lives here.

c) Work in pairs. Take turns to be the tourist. Ask the questions from 7a) and 7b).

---

1 **a)** Choose the correct words/phrases. **V7.1**

1 *delete/go* a document
2 *forward/make* an email
3 *click on/log on* an attachment
4 *print/search for* something on the Internet
5 *download/search* software
6 *print/go* online

b) Work in pairs. Check your answers. What other verbs can you use with the nouns in 1–3?

2 **a)** Make sentences about you with these phrases. **G7.1**

1 useless at
  I'm useless at singing.
2 quite good at
3 have no idea how
4 usually manage
5 was able to
6 haven't got a clue how

b) Work in pairs. Which of your partner's sentences are also true for you?

3 **a)** Fill in the missing vowels. **V7.3**

1 hAnd-hEld cOmpUtEr
2 hAIr dryEr
3 wEbcAm
4 cEntrAl hEAtIng
5 AIr cOndItIOnIng
6 hAnds-frEE phOnE
7 MP3 plAyEr
8 dIshwAshEr

b) Work in pairs. Imagine you could only have three items from 3a). Which would you choose?

4 **a)** Write second conditional sentences for these first conditional sentences. **G7.2**

1 If I can find him, I'll tell him.
2 Carla will help you if she has time.
3 If he lives with us, we'll look after him.
4 If you don't like the flat, we'll move.

---

b) Match these meanings to the first conditional sentences and the second conditional sentences you wrote in 4a).

1 a) I can't find him. *second*
  b) I'll look for him. *first*
2 a) Carla might be able to help you.
  b) Carla can't help you.
3 a) It's possible that he'll live with us.
  b) He doesn't live here.
4 a) We like the flat.
  b) We might not like the flat.

c) Work in pairs. Compare answers.

5 **a)** Change these questions into indirect questions. Use the words in brackets. **RW7.1**

1 Where's the phone? (know)
  Do you know where the phone is?
2 What time is it? (tell)
3 Does this bus go to Acton? (know/if)
4 Where's Pete gone? (any idea)
5 Should we leave now? (think)
6 What's Sally's home phone number? (can)
7 Has he changed his email address? (think)

b) Work in pairs. Compare answers.

Progress Portfolio

a) Tick the things you can do in English.

☐ I can talk about using computers.
☐ I can talk about people's past and present ability.
☐ I can name everyday electrical items.
☐ I can talk about imaginary situations.
☐ I can understand a short lecture.
☐ I can ask questions in a direct and indirect way.

b) What do you need to study again? **● 7A–D**

8 One world

8A Changing weather

Vocabulary weather
Grammar the passive
Review indirect questions; verb forms

QUICK REVIEW ●●●
Imagine you are a new student at this school. Write five indirect questions you want to ask: *Can you tell me what time the school closes?* Work in pairs. Take turns to ask and answer the questions.

www.savetheplanet.com

Vocabulary Weather

1 **a)** Work in pairs. Tick the words you know.

a storm	thunder (*trueão*)	lightning	a gale
a shower	a hurricane	fog	humid
a heat wave	a flood	a tornado	

b) Put these words in order, starting with the coldest.

hot ⁵	boiling ⁶	freezing ¹
cool ₃	warm ₄	cold/chilly ₂

c) Check new words in 1a) and your answers to 1b) in **V8.1** p132.

2 Work in groups. Discuss these questions.

1 Which countries often have really bad weather?
2 Have you ever experienced very bad weather?
3 Do you think the weather where you live has changed since you were a child? If so, how?

Reading and Grammar

3 **a)** Check these words/phrases with your teacher or in a dictionary.

atmosphere	greenhouse gases	gas	oil
coal	climate	ice cap	melt	coast

b) Read the web page of FAQs (Frequently Asked Questions) about global warming and climate change. Match questions a)–d) to paragraphs 1–4.

a) How has climate change changed the world's weather?
b) What can we do to stop global warming?
c) What is global warming?
d) How will climate change affect the world in the future?

FAQs: Global warming and climate change

1 _____ C

Heat from the sun **is held** in the Earth's atmosphere by natural greenhouse gases. These keep the planet warm and without them the average temperature would be about −18°C instead of 14°C. However, more and more heat **is being kept** in the atmosphere because of man-made greenhouse gases, particularly carbon dioxide (CO_2), which is produced by burning oil, gas and coal. This global warming is already causing changes in the weather all over the world.

2 _____ A

Since the 1970s, average global temperatures have risen by about 0.6°C and many scientists believe that more extreme weather conditions **have been caused** by climate change in recent years. For example, New Orleans **was hit** by a huge hurricane in 2005. Many people were killed and thousands were made homeless. And in the summer of 2003, 15,000 people in France died as a result of a heat wave.

3 _____ D

Experts believe that more and more places **are going to be affected** by climate change in the future. And as the ice caps at the North and South Poles melt and sea levels rise further, many towns and villages near the coast **will be flooded**. This is a frightening thought because more than half the world's population live near the coast.

4 _____ B

A lot has been written about what governments and businesses should do to slow down global warming. However, there's also a lot we can do to save energy at home. For example, always turn off TVs, DVD players and computers – machines use 70% as much electricity on stand-by as when they're being used. Many other useful tips **can be found** on public information websites.

4 a) Read the web page again. Fill in the gaps with one word.

1 Without natural greenhouse gases, the Earth would be 32°C _colder_ than it is.

2 Because the Earth is getting hotter, the _climate_ is changing.

3 A lot of people died in France in 2003 because of very _hot_ weather.

4 Sea levels are _rising_ because the polar ice caps are disappearing.

5 We can save _energy_ by turning off machines instead of leaving them on stand-by.

b) Work in groups. Discuss these questions.

1 Did any of the information in the article surprise you?

2 What other things can people do to save energy?

Help with Grammar The passive

5 a) Look at these sentences. <u>Underline</u> the subject in each sentence. What is the object of the active sentence?

active	A huge hurricane hit New Orleans.
passive	New Orleans was hit by a huge hurricane.

b) Choose the correct words in these rules.

- The object of the active sentence becomes the subject/object of the passive sentence.

- We often use the active/passive when we are more interested in what happens to someone or something than in who or what does the action.

- In passive sentences we can use 'by + the agent' to say why something happens/who or what does the action.

c) Look at the passive forms in bold in the web page. Write them in the table.

verb form	be	past participle
Present Simple	is	held
Present Continuous	is being	kept
Present Perfect Simple	have been	caused
Past Simple	was	hit
be going to	are going to be	
will	will be	flooded
can	can be	found

d) How do we make the negative form of the passive?

e) Check in G8.1 **p133.**

6 R8.1 P **Listen and practise.**

Heat from the sun is held in the Earth's atmosphere.

---

7 a) Read about Roy Sullivan. What happened to him?

The Earth ¹*hits/is hit* by lightning 8.6 million times a day. Scientists say there's a 1 in 3 million chance you ²*will hit/will be hit* by lightning, but that depends on how much time you ³*are spent/spend* outdoors. Roy Sullivan, a park ranger from Virginia, USA, ⁴*was hit/hit* by lightning seven times in his lifetime. On different occasions he ⁵*lost/was lost* his toenails, hair and eyebrows. The final lightning strike ⁶*happened/was happened* while he was fishing and he ⁷*took/was taken* to hospital with chest and stomach burns.

b) Read the text again. Choose the correct verb forms.

c) R8.2 **Listen and check.**

8 a) Look at the photo. Which city is it? What problems does this city have?

b) Put the verbs in the correct form of the passive. There is sometimes more than one possible answer.

These days, parts of Venice ¹ _are flooded_ (flood) one day in three. People believe the water will rise another 20 cms in the next 50 years. This means that Venice ²_will be flooded_ (flood) much more often. A lot of money ³_have already been collected_ (already collect) for the Save Venice Fund and many buildings ⁴_are now being repaired_ (now repair). However, more money must ⁵_be found_ (find) quickly and some people don't think the city can ⁶_be saved_ (save). Most experts agree that if important work ⁷_not be done_ (not do) soon, some of the world's most beautiful buildings ⁸_will be lost_ (lose) forever.

Get ready ... Get it right!

9 Work in groups. Group A → p106.
Group B → p111. Follow the instructions.

 **8B Recycle your rubbish**

Vocabulary containers
Grammar quantifiers: *a bit of,
too much/many, (not) enough,
plenty of,* etc.
Help with Listening quantifiers
Review weather; food

QUICK REVIEW ●●●
Write five weather words that are connected to you. Work in pairs and compare words. Tell your partner why you have chosen your five words: *I chose a storm because I saw an amazing storm last month.*

Vocabulary Containers

1 a) Match the containers in A to the things in B. Find at least two things for each container. Check in **V8.2** p132.

A	B
a bottle	milk honey tuna biscuits
a bag	sweets cat food orange juice
a tin	beer jam marmalade
a box	tomato ketchup soup
a can	chocolates potatoes
a carton	beans olive oil tissues
a jar	lemonade crisps [US: chips]
a packet	butter apple juice

b) Work in pairs. Test your partner.

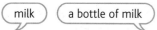

milk   *a bottle of milk*

c) Work in new pairs. What other words can you use with the containers in **1a)**?

a packet of cigarettes   *a tin of dog food*

Listening and Grammar

2 Work in groups. Discuss these questions.

1   Are there any recycling laws in your country?
2   Is there recycling where you live? If so, what do you recycle?
3   What do you throw away that you could recycle?

3 a) Look at the picture. Which things from **1a)** can you see in the kitchen?

b) **R8.3** Listen to James, Val and Pete and talking about recycling. Choose the correct answers.

1   Val and Pete *have something/don't have anything* to eat.
2   James *recycles some/doesn't recycle any* of his rubbish.
3   The UK recycles *50%/15%* of its rubbish.
4   *25%/90%* of glass in Switzerland is recycled.
5   Parts for fridges can be made from *plastic bottles/tins*.
6   James *is/isn't* going to recycle his rubbish in the future.

Pete   James   Val

4 a) R8.3 Listen again. Who says these sentences, Val, Pete or James?

1 Oh, there's a bit of pasta there too if you're hungry. *James*
2 I've found some coffee, but there's no sugar. *Val*
3 There's enough milk for two cups, but not enough for three. *Pete*
4 There are plenty of tins of cat food in the cupboard. *James*
5 Too much rubbish is just thrown away. *Val*
6 Hardly any stuff is recycled in this country. *Pete*
7 And there aren't enough recycling bins. *Val*
8 There's loads of paper and several plastic bottles. *Val*
9 There's plenty of information on it these days. *Pete*
10 Yes, too many people just don't bother. *Val*
11 I've only got a few friends who recycle things. *James*
12 We made a little progress there. *Val*

b) Work in pairs. Check your answers.

 5 a) Look at the words/phrases in pink in 4a). Are they countable nouns (C) or uncountable nouns (U)?

b) Look at the words/phrases in blue in 4a). Write them in the table.

quantity	plural countable nouns (bottles, tins, etc.)	uncountable nouns (rubbish, stuff, etc.)
nothing	not any no	not any *no*
a small quantity	not many hardly any *a few*	not much *a bit* *a little* *hardly any*
a large quantity	a lot of/lots of loads of *plenty of*	a lot of/lots of *plenty of* *loads of*
more than we want	*too many*	*too much*
less than we want	*not enough*	*not enough*
the correct quantity	enough	*enough*

c) Look at these sentences. Then choose the correct words in the rules.

I've found some coffee.   *There isn't any sugar.*
Is there any milk?   *There's a lot of stuff here.*
I haven't got many cups.   *Is there much rubbish?*

● We usually use *some/any* in positive sentences.
● We usually use *some/any* in negative sentences and questions.
● We don't usually use *a lot of/much or many* in positive sentences.

d) Check in G8.2 p132.

Help with Listening Quantifiers

 6 a) R8.4 Listen and write the sentences you hear. You will hear each sentence twice.

b) How many words are there in each sentence? Contractions (*there's*, etc.) are two words.

c) Work in pairs. Compare sentences. <u>Underline</u> the quantifiers.

 7 R8.5 P Listen again and practise. Copy the linking.

I think there's a bit of milk in the fridge.

 8 a) Choose the correct words/phrases.

1 There are *no/any* recycling bins in my street.
2 I probably drink *too much/too many* coffee.
3 I got *too many/hardly any* sleep last night.
4 I know *a few/a little* words in other languages.
5 I watched *a bit of/much* TV last night.
6 I always have *many/plenty of* time to do my homework.
7 I haven't got *enough/several* money to go on holiday.
8 I've been to *some/any* interesting places.
9 I probably eat *too much/too many* sweets.

b) Tick the sentences in 8a) that are true for you.

c) Work in pairs. Take turns to say your true sentences. Ask follow-up questions if possible.

Get ready ... Get it right!

 9 Write four good things and four bad things about the town/city you are in now. Use these ideas and your own. Use the quantifiers from 5b) in your sentences.

> recycling bins   rubbish   traffic   cycle lanes
> parks   public transport   places to park
> pollution   shops   places to go at night
> noise at night   cinemas   art galleries

There aren't enough recycling bins.
There's too much rubbish in the streets.

 10 a) Work in groups. Take turns to tell the other students your sentences. Discuss your ideas. Do you agree? Choose the two best and two worst things about this town/city.

b) Tell the class the two best and two worst things about this town/city.

8C Dangers at sea

Vocabulary word formation (2): prefixes and opposites, other prefixes and suffixes
Skills Listening: Shark attack!; Reading: Saving Jesse's arm
Help with Listening linking (3): review
Review the passive; Past Perfect; character adjectives

QUICK REVIEW ●●●
Work in pairs. Take turns to say a container. Your partner says as many things as possible that can come in that container: A *a tin*. B *soup, beans, ...* .

Listening

1 **Work in groups. Discuss these questions.**

1 When did you last go to the beach? Where was it? What did you do there?
2 Do you have a favourite beach? If so, where is it?
3 What kind of problems can people have at the beach?

2 **a)** **Check these words with your teacher or in a dictionary.**

attack	a shark
bite	oxygen

b) R8.6 **Listen to a TV news report. Answer these questions.**

1 What has happened in the USA?
2 What are dead zones?
3 What causes dead zones?
4 How many dead zones are there?

c) **Listen again. Choose the correct words.**

1 There have been *six/eight* shark attacks in the USA this year.
2 The tourist was attacked *a long way from/quite near* the beach.
3 He was bitten on the *arm/leg*.
4 The dead zone off the coast of Texas is *quite small/very big*.
5 Fifteen years ago there were *twice/half* as many dead zones as there are now.
6 The evening is a *good/bad* time to go swimming near a dead zone.
7 The Texas Wildlife Department *are/aren't* telling people to stop swimming in the sea.

Help with Listening Linking (3): review

3 **a)** **Look at this sentence from the news report. Notice the links. Then choose the correct words in the rules.**

So what turns_an_area_/r/_of the_/j/_ocean_into_/w/_a dead zone?

- We usually link words that end in a consonant sound with words that start with a *consonant/vowel* sound.
- When a word ends in a *consonant/vowel* sound and the next word also starts with a *consonant/vowel* sound, we often link these words with a /w/, /j/ or /r/ sound.

b) **Work in pairs. Look at these sentences from the beginning of the news report. Draw the links. Add extra linking sounds if necessary.**

A British tourist has been attacked by /j/ a shark off the coast of Texas, making it the eighth shark attack in the USA this year. We now go over live to Freeport for a special report from our North American correspondent, Andrew Evans. Andrew, I understand the man didn't do anything unusual to cause this attack.

c) **Look at R8.6, p151. Read the first paragraph and check your answers.**

d) R8.6 **Listen to the whole of the news report. Notice the linking.**

Reading and Vocabulary

4 **a)** **Check these words with your teacher or in a dictionary.**

conscious	estimate	strength	attach	harm	a lifeguard	a park ranger

b) **Look at the title of the article. What do you think happened to Jesse?**

c) **Read the article. Were you correct?**

Saving Jesse's Arm

Lucy Atkins describes the battle to save the life of a young boy.

At about 8 p.m. on July 6th, eight-year-old Jesse Arbogast was playing in the sea in a National Park near Pensacola, Florida. It was the end of a perfect day at the beach with his uncle and aunt. Then disaster struck. Jesse was attacked by a two-metre-long male shark, which bit off his right arm from the shoulder and also took a bite out of his leg. By the time his uncle and aunt pulled Jesse out of the water, he was unconscious and had already lost a lot of blood.

While Jesse's aunt was giving the boy the kiss of life, his uncle, Vance Flosenzier, ran into the sea and disappeared under the water. Amazingly, he managed to catch the 90-kilo shark and pull it out of the water onto the beach. Although this might sound impossible, never underestimate a man's strength when a family member's life is in danger. At that moment two park rangers arrived to help the family and one of them shot the shark four times in the head. Then he held open the shark's mouth while a volunteer firefighter reached down its throat and pulled out Jesse's arm.

A few minutes later, a helicopter took the boy and his arm to nearby Baptist Hospital, Pensacola, where Dr Ian Rogers and his team managed to reattach Jesse's arm in an eleven-hour operation. The doctors knew the operation had been a success when Jesse's fingers went pink. After such a terrible accident nobody wants to be over-optimistic, but the medical team are hopeful that Jesse will have full use of his arm in the future.

Although Jesse's story is terrifying, it would be incorrect to think that sharks are always so dangerous. Apparently this type of attack was very unusual and sharks are usually harmless to humans. "Shark attacks are uncommon," agrees JR Tomasovic, chief ranger at the Pensacola park. "You could go ten years without seeing another." However, he says that people shouldn't be irresponsible and should only swim on beaches where there are lifeguards.

Adapted from the *Guardian* 12/7/01

5 Read the article again. Tick the true sentences. Correct the false ones.

1 The shark bit off part of Jesse's arm. F
2 Jesse's uncle shot the shark. F
3 A park ranger got Jesse's arm from inside the shark. F
4 Jesse's operation took a long time. T
5 Jesse might be able to use his arm normally in the future. T

Help with Vocabulary Word formation (2): prefixes and opposites, other prefixes and suffixes

● We sometimes add prefixes (*un-*, *dis-*, etc.) or suffixes (*-ful*, *-less*, etc.) to change the meaning of a word.

6 **a)** Look at the words in blue in the article. Underline the prefixes. Then fill in the gaps in this rule.

● We often use the prefixes *un-* , *dis-* , *im*, *less* and *u* to make opposites of words.

b) Work in pairs. What are the opposites of these adjectives?

un believable	im patient	un selfish	dis honest	im considerate
im polite	dis organised	ir regular	un reliable	dis loyal	im mature
ambitious un	formal in	similar dis	sensitive in	helpful un

c) Check in **V8.3** p132.

7 **a)** Look at the words in pink in the article. Underline the prefixes and suffixes. Then complete the table with these meanings and the words in pink.

not enough	too much	without
with	do something again	

prefix/suffix	meaning	examples
under-	*not enough*	*underestimate*
re-	do sth again	re attach
over-	too much	over - optimistic
-ful	with	hopeful
-less	without	harmless

b) Which prefixes and suffixes can you use with these words? There is sometimes more than one possible answer.

under paid	re write	painful pain	over sleep	under charge
care ful	re marry	success ful	re play	use less

c) Check in **V8.4** p132.

8 **a)** You are going to tell other students about a frightening or exciting experience you have had. It can be real or imaginary. Decide what you are going to say. Use these ideas or your own.

● when and where it happened
● how the story started
● why the story was frightening or exciting
● what happened in the end

b) Work in groups. Take turns to tell your story to the group. Ask questions to find out more information. Guess whether each person's story is true or not. Were you correct?

c) Tell the class about the best story from your group.

8D Be careful!

Real World warnings and advice
Review prefixes and suffixes; *should*

QUICK REVIEW ●●●

Write eight words with prefixes or suffixes: *unconscious, useless*, etc. Work in pairs. Take turns to make sentences with your partner's words: *He was unconscious so he was taken to hospital*.

Ⓐ

Ⓑ Ⓒ

1 Work in pairs. Look at the pictures. What are the people in each picture going to do? Think of one possible danger for each situation.

2 **a)** Check these words/phrases with your teacher or in a dictionary.

> a bear   the outback   dive   cross a river   petrol
> a spare map   stay calm   a kangaroo   shiver

b) You are going to hear the people in pictures A–C asking for advice. Which conversations do you think the words in **2a)** will be in?

c) R8.7 Listen and match conversations 1–3 to pictures A–C.

d) Listen again. Answer these questions.

1 What does the park ranger think the women should take? *warm clothes*
2 What should you do if you see a bear? *make yourself bigger*
3 What should you tell people before you go into the outback? *tell people you are going there (but at night?)*
4 When do you need to be careful of kangaroos? *damage car*
5 What should you do if you see a shark? *don't move fast*
6 How often should you check your air? *2 minutes*

Real World Warnings and advice

● We give warnings when we think something might be dangerous.

3 **a)** Write these headings in the correct places a)–d).

> giving advice   responding to advice/warnings
> asking for advice   giving warnings

a) *asking for advice*

Could you give us some advice?
What should we do if we see one?
What do you think we should take with us?
Do you think it's a good idea to take some warm clothes?

b) *giving advice*

If I were you, I'd take plenty of warm clothes.
It's a good idea to take a spare map **in case** you lose one.
Don't forget to tell them when you expect to be back.
Make sure you take plenty of water.
You'd better come up immediately.

c) *giving warnings*

be careful **Watch out for** bears.
Be careful when you're crossing rivers.
Whatever you do, don't lose your partner.
Don't come up too quickly, **or else** you could be in trouble.

d) *responding to advice/warnings*

Yes, we will.
That's a good idea. I hadn't thought of that.
That's really useful, thanks.
Right, thanks. That's very helpful.

b) Look at the underlined verb forms in **3a)**. Then complete these phrases with *imperative, infinitive* or *infinitive with to*.

1 If I were you, I'd + ... *inf*
2 It's a good idea + ... *inf + to*
3 Don't forget + ... *to inf*
4 You'd better + ... *inf*
5 Whatever you do, + ... *imperative*

c) Check in RW8.1 p133.

4 [R8.8] [P] Listen and practise the sentences in 3a).

Could you give us some advice?

5 a) Fill in the gaps with a word/phrase from the box.

Don't forget   Whatever you do,
Be careful   It's a good idea
Look out for   Make sure
If I were you, I'd   Don't

Visiting the UK

1 _Don't forget_ to tell family and friends how to contact you.

2 _make sure_ you take some warm clothes.

3 _Whatever you do_ don't drive in London without an AtoZ road map.

4 _If I were you I'd_ go in May. It's really beautiful then.

5 _It's a good idea_ to book theatre tickets a long time in advance.

6 _Be careful_ when crossing the roads because they drive on the left.

7 _Don't_ go anywhere without an umbrella or else you might get wet.

8 _Look out for_ pickpockets when you're on the tube in London.

b) Work in pairs. Compare answers.

6 a) Write five warnings or pieces of advice for people visiting your country. Use phrases from 3a).

b) Work in groups. Compare sentences.

♪ [R8.9] Look at the song *Stormy Weather* on p101. Follow the instructions.

---

8 Review   Language Summary 8, p132

1 a) Find ten words for weather. [V8.1]

```
S G O W S C K P B C
H Y L P T L N G L V
U S T O O C G A L F
R H M T R H Y L F L
R O H U M I D E O O
I W B O I L I N G S
C E P C F L O O D Y
A R Z Z R Y A E J G
N F R E E Z I N G S
E I Q R E B O L I N
```

b) Work in pairs. Think of eight more words for weather.

2 Fill in the gaps with the correct form of the passive. [G8.1]

1 Towns all over the country _are being flooded_ (flood).

2 In the future many more disasters _will be caused_ (cause) by global warming.

3 Several houses _were hit_ (hit) by lightning last night.

4 Facts about climate change should _be taught_ (teach) in schools.

5 Conferences on world pollution _have been held_ (hold) every year.

6 Important laws about industrial pollution _will be introduced_ (introduce) in the next ten years.

b) Work in pairs. Compare answers.

3 a) Write a list of things that come in these containers. [V8.2]

tin   carton   packet   jar
bottle   can   bag   box

b) Work in pairs. Compare answers.

4 a) Make sentences with phrases 1–10 that are true for you. Use these words. [G8.2]

plenty of   too much/many
(not) enough   a few   a little
several   hardly any   loads of
a lot of   no   a bit of

---

1 good DVDs/videos you've seen recently
I've seen loads of good DVDs recently.
2 noise in your street
3 free time you have
4 CDs you own
5 pollution in your town/city
6 good books you've read this year
7 places to meet friends near where you live
8 photo albums you have
9 coffee you drink
10 biscuits you eat

b) Work in pairs. Compare sentences. Ask follow-up questions about your partner's sentences if possible.

5 a) Write an adjective or verb for each of these prefixes. [V8.3] [V8.4]

un-   ir-   under-   im-
in-   over-   re-   dis-

b) Work in pairs. Take turns to say an adjective or verb you wrote in 5a). Your partner says the word with a prefix.

usual → unusual

c) Work with your partner. Think of words that end in *-ful* or *-less*.

careful, careless

Progress Portfolio

a) Tick the things you can do in English.

☐ I can talk about types of weather and environmental issues.

☐ I can talk about the quantity of things.

☐ I can read a short newspaper article.

☐ I can understand a short discussion.

☐ I can give, ask for and respond to advice.

☐ I can give and respond to warnings.

b) What do you need to study again? ● 8A–D

9 Look after yourself

9A Get healthy!

Vocabulary health
Grammar relative clauses with *who*, *that*, *which*, *whose*, *where* and *when*
Review warnings and advice

QUICK REVIEW ●●●
Imagine a friend from the UK is coming to live and work in your town/city. Think of five warnings or pieces of advice to give your friend. Work in pairs. Compare sentences. What's the most important warning or piece of advice?

Reading, Listening and Grammar

1 Work in groups. Discuss these questions.

1 What do you usually eat every day?
2 Do you think you have a healthy diet? Why?/Why not?
3 How often do you eat things that you know are bad for you?
4 Has your diet changed since you were a child?

2 a) Check these words with your teacher or in a dictionary.

> a fast   a retreat   organic   toxins   digest

b) **R9.1** Read and listen to the article. Did the journalist feel healthier after doing the retreat? Why?/Why not?

3 a) Read the article again. Tick the correct sentences. Correct the false ones.

1 You only drink vegetable juice on the retreat.
2 Joanne wasn't looking forward to the experience.
3 Louise worked at the retreat centre.
4 Fasting helps your body get rid of toxins.
5 Joanne felt fine on day two of the retreat.
6 The fifth day was easier than the third day.
7 Joanne has changed her diet since the retreat.

b) Work in pairs. Discuss these questions.

1 Would you like to go on a retreat like the one in the article? Why?/Why not?
2 Do you know anyone who has done a retreat like this? If so, did they enjoy it?

Can giving up food really improve your health?
Joanne Fullerton spent a week at a retreat centre to find out.

When I arrived at the Just Juice Retreat Centre, I was feeling a bit nervous. I was going to do a seven-day fast, drinking only fresh organic fruit and vegetable juices. I'm the type of person ¹**that eats three meals a day** and can't wake up without a cappuccino, so the idea of living on juice for a week was rather terrifying.

After checking in, I was taken to the guest house ²**where everyone was staying**. Louise, the person ³**who I was sharing with**, had done the retreat four times and she looked healthier than anyone I'd ever met. According to Rachel Carr-Hill, the woman ⁴**whose fasting programme we were following**, going without food is one of the best things we can do for our health. The food ⁵**that we usually eat** contains toxins ⁶**which stay in our bodies**

and stop our digestive system working properly. When we fast, our body doesn't have to digest food, so it has time to get rid of these toxins.

The first day started with yoga at seven o'clock and then we had 'breakfast' – a big glass of carrot juice. We spent the day listening to talks about health, having massages and relaxing, with a different juice meal every three hours. On the second day I had an awful headache and felt as if I was getting a cold. Apparently this was a normal reaction because my body was starting to get rid of the toxins. On day

three my headache was much worse and this was also ⁷**when I started getting *really* hungry**. I began day-dreaming about cheeseburgers, pasta, chocolate – anything but more juice. However, by day five the hunger had gone and I felt more relaxed than I'd been for years. At the end of the retreat I'd lost 3 kilos and felt like a new woman. Now I'm much more careful about what I eat – but I still need my morning cappuccinos!

Help with Grammar
Relative clauses with *who, that, which, whose, where* and *when*

- We often use relative clauses to say which person, thing, place, etc. we are talking about.

4 **a)** Look at the relative clauses in **bold** in the article. Then fill in the gaps with *who, that, which, whose, where* and *when*.

- In relative clauses we use:
  a) _Who_ or _that_ for people.
  b) _Which_ or _that_ for things.
  c) _Where_ for places.
  d) _Whose_ for possessives.
  e) _When_ for times.

b) Look at the <u>underlined</u> relative clauses in sentences A and B. Answer the questions and choose the correct word in the rule.

A I'm the type of person <u>that eats three meals a day</u>.
B The food <u>(that) we usually eat</u> contains toxins.

1 What is the subject of *eats* in sentence A? Person
2 What is the subject of *eat* in sentence B? food

- We can leave out *who, that* or *which* when it is/isn't the subject of the relative clause.

c) Check in **G9.1** p135.

5 **a)** Fill in the gaps with *who, that, which, whose, where* or *when*.

1 Most of the food _that_ I buy is organic. ✓
2 I know lots of people _who_ are vegetarians.
3 I don't know anyone _who_ has been on a fast.
4 The food _that_ I ate last night wasn't very healthy. ✓
5 There's at least one person in my family _who_ eats meat every day.
6 In my family, we usually eat food _when_ we buy in the market.
7 I don't know anyone _whose_ lifestyle is really healthy.
8 I tend to go to restaurants _where_ they serve healthy food.
9 New Year is a time _when_ I usually eat too much.
10 I know a shop _where_ you can buy really good fruit and vegetables.

b) Look again at sentences 1–6 in **5a)**. In which of these sentences can you leave out *who, that* or *which*?

c) Tick the sentences in **5a)** that are true for you.

d) Work in groups. Compare your sentences. How many are the same?

Vocabulary Health

6 **a)** Work in pairs. Choose the correct words/phrases.

1 A surgeon/A GP is a doctor who does operations.
2 An operating theatre/A surgery is the place where you have an operation.
3 An infection/Asthma is an illness which makes it difficult for you to breathe.
4 A specialist/A prescription is a doctor who knows a lot about one area of medicine.
5 The A&E department/A ward is the part of a hospital where you go if you have an emergency.
6 An allergy/A migraine is a medical problem that some people get when they eat, breathe or touch certain things.

b) **R9.2** Listen and check. How many did you get right?

7 **a)** Fill in the gaps in these sentences with the other words/phrases from **6a)** and *who, which, that* or *where* if necessary.

1 _A migraine_ is an extremely painful headache _which_ can also make you feel sick.
2 _A ward_ is a big room with beds in a hospital _where_ patients receive medical treatment.
3 _A GP_ is a doctor _who_ gives medical treatment to people _that_ live in a particular area.
4 _A surgery_ is a building or an office _where_ you can go and ask a GP or a dentist for medical advice.
5 _A prescription_ is a piece of paper _that_ the doctor gives you so that you can get the medicine you need.
6 _An infection_ is a disease in part of your body _that_ is caused by bacteria or a virus.

b) Check in **V9.1** p134.

8 Work in pairs. Take turns to test each other on the words in **6a)** and **7a)**.

> What's a surgeon?

> It's a doctor who does operations.

Get ready ... Get it right!

9 Work in groups. Group A → p105. Group B → p110. Follow the instructions.

QUICK REVIEW ●●●
Write six words/phrases connected to health. Work in pairs.
Take turns to ask each other to describe your words/phrases:
A *What's asthma?* B *It's an illness which makes it difficult to breathe.*

Vocabulary news collocations
Grammar Present Perfect Simple active and passive for recent events
Help with Listening Present Perfect Simple active or passive
Review *just, yet, already*; relative clauses; Past Simple; health

Vocabulary News collocations

1 Work in pairs. Discuss these questions.

1 Where do you get your news from: the TV, newspapers, the radio or the Internet? Which do you prefer? Why?

2 What stories are in the news at the moment?

3 Do you ever read, watch or listen to the news in English? If so, where?

2 a) Match the verbs in A to the words/phrases in B. Check in **V9.2** p134.

A	B
accept/reject	from an illness
discover	someone to hospital
carry out	an offer
suffer	a survey
take	something new

take part	results/a report
publish	a target
protest	in a demonstration
meet	a strike
call off	against something

b) Work in pairs. Take turns to test each other on the words/phrases in 2a).

(meet)   (meet a target)

Listening and Grammar

3 a) Look at photos A–C of today's main news stories. Work in pairs. What do you think the stories are about? Use the words/phrases in 2a) or your own ideas.

b) **R9.3** Listen to the news. Put photos A–C in the same order as the news stories.

c) Listen again and fill in the gaps in the speech bubbles.

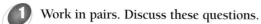

The ¹ *health service* **has failed** to meet its targets to reduce ² *waiting* times in A&E departments in NHS* hospitals.

NHS = National Health Service

We **haven't met** our targets yet, that's true, but we**'ve made** a lot of ³ *progress* . The average waiting time **has** already **been reduced** from 3½ hours to nearly ⁴ *2 1/2* hours.

Ⓐ

A new report on allergies **has** just **been published**. The report shows that allergies have become one of the ⁵ *UK* 's biggest causes of illness, with one in ⁶ *three* people now affected.

DAB digital radio

NEWS 107

The government **has** also **carried out** a survey on the ⁷ *causes* of allergies, but why **haven't** we **seen** those results yet? That survey still **hasn't been published**, although it was completed ⁸ *six* months ago.

Ⓑ

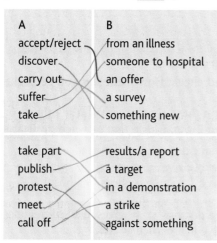

And we**'ve** just **heard** that the ⁹ *actress* Tanya Fisher **has died**. She was taken to hospital two days ago with ¹⁰ *health* problems.

Help with Listening
Present Perfect Simple active or passive

5 a) R9.4 Listen to these sentences. Notice the weak forms of *has*, *been* and *have*.

A new report on allergies has /həz/ *just been* /bɪn/ *published. The report shows that allergies have* /həv/ *become one of the UK's biggest causes of illness.*

b) R9.5 Listen to these sentences. Are the verbs in the Present Perfect Simple active or passive?

6 R9.5 P Listen again and practise.

A new survey has /həz/ *just been* /bɪn/ *published.*

7 a) Read these news stories. Put the verbs in brackets in the Present Perfect Simple active or passive.

> Over ten thousand people [1] *have taken part* (take part) in a demonstration to protest against the new increase in petrol prices. At least sixteen people [2] *have been arrested* (arrest) and one policeman [3] *has been taken* (take) to hospital.

> Monday's ambulance strike [4] *has been called off* (call off). Union leader Kevin Roberts [5] *has accepted* (accept) the government's pay offer of 8%.

> Scientists in Cambridge [6] *have found* (find) the gene that causes asthma. The gene is one of many allergy genes that [7] *has been discovered* (discover) by researchers at Cambridge University.

> Rock singer Heidi Sowter [8] *has just arrived* (just arrive) in the UK for her first-ever tour of the country. Her first album, *Perfect Ten*, [9] *has already sold* (already sell) over four million copies.

b) R9.6 Listen and check.

8 Put the words in brackets in the correct places in these sentences.

1 The strike has already lasted three weeks. (already)
2 The Prime Minister has arrived. (just)
3 The relatives haven't been told. (yet)
4 He has been questioned by the police. (already)
5 Three men have been arrested. (just)
6 Has the match finished? (yet)
7 The results haven't been published. (still)

Get ready ... Get it right!

9 Work in groups. Group A → p104. Group B → p109. Follow the instructions.

Help with Grammar Present Perfect Simple active and passive for recent events

● Remember: we use the Present Perfect Simple for giving news about things that happened in the recent past and are connected to now. We don't say exactly when these things happened.

4 a) Look at these sentences from the news stories. Then answer questions 1–4.

*The health service **has failed** to meet its targets.*
*A new report on allergies **has** just **been published**.*

1 What is the subject in each sentence?
2 Which verb form is in the Present Perfect Simple active?
3 Which verb form is in the Present Perfect Simple passive?
4 How do we make the Present Perfect Simple active and Present Perfect Simple passive?

b) Look again at the verb forms in **bold** in the speech bubbles. Which are in the Present Perfect Simple active? Which are in the Present Perfect Simple passive?

c) Look again at the speech bubbles. Find examples of *just*, *yet*, *already* and *still*. What is the difference in meaning between these words? Where do they usually go in sentences?

TIP! ● We only use *still* in negative sentences with the Present Perfect Simple: *That survey still hasn't been published.*

d) Check in G9.2 p135.

9C Faking it

QUICK REVIEW ●●●
Think of five pieces of news about yourself, your family or friends: *I've just booked a holiday. My brother has just been promoted.* Work in groups. Tell the other students your news. Ask follow-up questions if possible.

Listening

1 Work in groups. Discuss these questions.

1 When do you think it's OK to lie?
2 Do you think you're good at lying? Why?/Why not?
3 How can you tell if people are lying?

2 **a)** Check these words with your teacher or in a dictionary.

a liar	avoid	tell the truth	smile
fake	muscles	eye contact	imagination

b) Look at photos A–D. Do you think this person is lying or telling the truth in each photo?

(A)  (B)

(C)  (D)

c) R9.7 Listen to an interview with Dr Miriam Richards, an expert in body language. Check your answers to **2b)**.

3 **a)** Work in pairs. Choose the correct words/phrases in these sentences.

1 Body language can be responsible for *50%/80%* of communication.
2 Good liars often make *more/less* eye contact than usual.
3 People who are lying *often smile a lot/never smile*.
4 The *left/right* side of the brain controls the right side of the body.
5 The *left/right* side of the brain controls imagination.
6 People often cover their *mouth/nose* when they're lying.

b) R9.7 Listen again and check your answers to **3a)**.

Help with Listening British and American accents

4 **a)** R9.8 Listen to these words. Notice how British and American people say the letters in **bold** differently. You will hear the British accent first.

1 h**o**t, l**o**t, b**o**dy
2 s**aw**, t**al**k, th**ou**ght
3 **au**nt, **a**sk, c**a**n't
4 g**ir**l, f**or**ty, moth**er**
5 pa**r**ty, bette**r**, wate**r**

b) R9.9 Listen to six sentences. Which do you hear first: a British accent or an American accent?

c) R9.7 Look at R9.7, p153. Listen again and notice the difference between the interviewer's British accent and Dr Richards's American accent.

Reading and Vocabulary

5 **a)** Look at the photos in the article. What do you think is the connection between them?

b) Check these words/phrases with your teacher or in a dictionary.

a con artist	fraud	a bad cheque
a bank account	overdrawn	
the FBI	pretend	lecturer

c) Read the article. How many different jobs has Frank Abagnale Jr had? What does he do now?

6 **a)** Read the article again. Answer these questions.

1 Why was Frank Abagnale's bank account overdrawn?
2 Why did people believe he was a pilot?
3 How did he travel for free to other cities?
4 Which job was he qualified for?
5 In which two places was he arrested?
6 How long was he in prison for?

b) Work in groups. Discuss these questions.

1 How do you think Frank Abagnale Jr made so many people believe him?
2 What were the good and bad things about his lifestyle?
3 Have you seen the film *Catch Me If You Can*? If so, what did you think of it?

Catch Me If You Can

Frank Abagnale Jr is one of the most famous con artists in history. During the 1960s he made $2.5 million and was wanted for fraud in countries all over the world – and he was still only a teenager!

Frank left home at 16 and went to live in New York. He started writing bad cheques and soon his bank account was thousands of dollars overdrawn. He managed to get a pilot's uniform and a fake ID for Pan Am Airlines, then he started opening bank accounts under his new name, Frank Williams. **In spite of** his age, people believed he was a pilot because his hair was already going grey. Then Frank found out that pilots could fly for free as guests on other airlines. Every time he arrived in a new city he cashed more bad cheques. He was arrested once in Miami, but was released soon afterwards. **However**, this lucky escape made him realise he needed a change.

He moved to Atlanta and got a job as a doctor, **even though** he didn't have any medical training. Then he went to live in Louisiana, where he pretended to be a lawyer. **Although** he'd never studied law, he passed his law exams the third time he took them and then worked for a government law office. Next he became a sociology lecturer, **despite** having no teaching qualifications at all. Finally, he moved to California and returned to the lifestyle he knew best – pretending to be a pilot and writing bad cheques.

Although Frank was rich, he was lonely and unhappy. At the age of 20 he moved to France and tried to live a normal life. **However**, four months later the FBI arrested him there and he spent the next five years in prison in various different countries.

Since then Frank has changed his life completely. He now runs a successful business that gives advice to big companies on how to stop fraud, and he also gives lectures to the FBI for free. In 2002 Frank's life was made into a film called *Catch Me If You Can*, starring Leonardo DiCaprio. Frank Abagnale Jr is a millionaire again – but now he's helping the law, not breaking it.

Leonardo DiCaprio in 'Catch Me If You Can'

Help with Vocabulary Connecting words:
although, even though, despite, in spite of, however

 a) Look at this sentence. How many clauses are there? <u>Underline</u> the connecting word.

Although Frank was rich, he was lonely and unhappy.

b) Look at the words in **bold** in the article. Then choose the correct words/phrases in these rules.

- *Although*, *even though*, *despite*, *in spite of* and *however* are similar in meaning to *and/but*.
- We use *although*, *even though*, *despite* and *in spite of* to contrast *two sentences/two clauses in the same sentence*.
- We use *however* to contrast *two sentences/two clauses in the same sentence*.

c) Fill in the gaps in these rules with *although*, *even though*, *despite* or *in spite of*.

- After _____ and _____ we usually use a noun or verb+*ing*.
- After _____ and _____ we usually use a clause.

d) Check in V9.3 p134.

 Rewrite these sentences using the words in brackets. Change other words in the sentence if necessary.

1 I went out last night. I felt really tired. (despite)
  I went out last night, despite feeling really tired.
2 Robin slept really well. There was a lot of noise. (in spite of)
3 I don't get paid very much. I enjoy my job. (even though)
4 Erica was well-qualified. She didn't get the job. (however)
5 We enjoyed the concert. There weren't many people there. (even though)
6 They watched TV all night. They had to work the next day. (despite)
7 The teacher explained it twice. I still didn't understand it. (even though)

 a) Think of two things that you've done that are true and two things that are false. Write one or two words only to help you remember each thing.

b) Work in groups of four. Take turns to tell the group your things. You can ask each person one question about each thing. What is each person lying about, do you think?

c) Tell the class who was the worst liar in the group. How did you know he/she was lying? Who was the best liar in the group?

9D At the doctor's

Real World at the doctor's
Vocabulary health problems, symptoms and treatment
Review Present Perfect Continuous

QUICK REVIEW ●●●

Write all the parts of the body you know. Work in pairs. Compare lists. Who has the most words? Take turns to point to a part of the body. Your partner says the word.

1 a) Tick the words/phrases you know. Check new words/phrases in **V9.4** p134.

asthma	a runny nose	antibiotics
an allergy	a rash	wheezy	hay fever
painkillers	flu	pills	be sick
diarrhoea	a sore throat	a migraine
sneeze	a virus	a temperature
penicillin	throw up	a stomach ache
food poisoning	paracetamol
a blocked-up nose	an infection

b) Work in pairs. Put the words/phrases in **1a)** into three groups.

1 health problems   *asthma*
2 symptoms   *a runny nose*
3 treatment   *antibiotics*

c) Check your answers in **V9.4** p135.

2 a) Look at these sentences that doctors often say to patients. Fill in the gaps with these words.

problem	back	feeling	taking
look	eaten	allergic	temperature
prescription	symptoms		

1 Now, what seems to be the _problem_?
2 How long have you been _feeling_ like this?
3 Do you know if you're _allergic_ to anything?
4 What have you _eaten_ recently?
5 Come _back_ if you're not feeling better in two days.
6 Have you been _taking_ anything for them?
7 Have you got any other _symptoms_?
8 Right, let me have a _look_ at you.
9 I'm just going to take your _temperature_.
10 Here's a _____ for some painkillers.
   prescription

b) **R9.10** Listen and check your answers.

3 a) **R9.11** Listen to two conversations in a GP's surgery. What are each patient's symptoms? What does the doctor think is wrong with each patient?

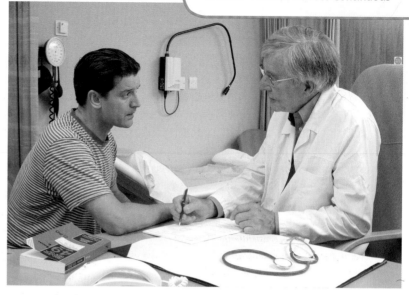

b) Listen again. Tick the true sentences. Correct the false ones.

1
a) Mr Philips isn't allergic to anything.
b) His children cooked him a meal for his ~~birthday~~ *wedding anniversary*.
c) The doctor says he shouldn't eat for a day.
d) Mr Philips has to come back and see the doctor again.

2
e) Mr Taylor has been taking paracetamol.
f) He started feeling ill two days ago.
g) The doctor tells him go to bed and rest.
h) The doctor gives him a prescription for some antibiotics. *painkiller.*

Real World At the doctor's

4 a) Match the beginnings and the ends of these sentences.

1 I'm not feeling	a) feeling very well recently.
2 I haven't been	b) getting really bad headaches.
3 I've got	c) very well.
4 My chest	d) a terrible stomach ache.
5 I keep	e) hurts.
6 I can't stop	f) to penicillin.
7 Do I need	g) sneezing.
8 I'm allergic	h) should I take them?
9 How often	i) make another appointment?
10 Do I need to	j) some antibiotics?

b) Look again at sentences 5 and 6 in **4a)**. Then choose the correct words/phrases in these rules.

● We use *I keep …* and *I can't stop …* for things that happen *once/lots of times*. We *want/don't want* these things to happen.

● After *I keep …* and *I can't stop …* we use *the infinitive/verb+ing*.

c) Check in **RW9.1** p135.

5 R9.12 P Listen and practise the sentences in **4a)**.

I'm not feeling very well.

6 Cross out the incorrect words/phrases.

1 I've been feeling *terrible/great/~~virus~~* lately.
2 I've got *asthma/a rash/~~throw up~~*.
3 I'm allergic to *cats/antibiotics/~~hay fever~~*.
4 I keep *waking up at night/~~a temperature~~/getting colds*.
5 I can't stop *coughing/being sick/~~food poisoning~~*.
6 I feel a bit *wheezy/run down/~~headache~~*.
7 You need *some painkillers/~~a migraine~~/some penicillin*.
8 I've got *a ~~sneeze~~/a runny nose/a blocked-up nose*.

7 **a)** Work in pairs. Write the first half of a conversation between a doctor and a patient. Write about the patient's symptoms only.

Hello, Mrs Jones. What seems to be the problem?
Well, I haven't been feeling very well recently. I've got ...

b) Swap papers with another pair. Write the rest of their conversation. Suggest treatment for the patient's symptoms.

c) Practise the conversation in pairs until you can remember it.

d) Work in groups of four. Take turns to role-play the conversation for the students who wrote the beginning. Do you agree with the other pair's suggestions for treatment?

8 Work in pairs. Student A → p106. Student B → p111. Follow the instructions.

9 Review
Language Summary 9, p134

1 **a)** Fill in the gaps with these words. G9.1

~~who~~ which ~~that~~
~~whose~~ ~~where~~ when

1 Coffee and chocolate are things *that* you should try to avoid.
2 A personal trainer is someone *who* helps you get fit.
3 A gym is a place *where* you can do exercise.
4 A person *whose* body is full of toxins usually feels terrible.
5 Meditation is something *which* people do to relax.
6 The Just Juice diet is one *that* cleans out toxins in the body.
7 People usually feel awful *when* they first start the diet.

b) In which sentences in **1a)** can you leave out *who*, *that* or *which*?

2 **a)** Write the words connected to health. V9.1

1 **gursrye**   s*urgery*
2 **ttpneai**   p*atient*
3 **drwa**   w*ard*
4 **tmahsa**   a*sthma*
5 **ugenosr**   s*urgeon*
6 **galleyr**   a*llergy*
7 **(A&E) dmepnartet**   d*epartment*
8 **giminera**   m*igraine*
9 **prreiptioscn**   p*rescription*

b) Work in pairs. Take turns to explain a word from **2a)**. Guess your partner's words.

The place where a GP works.

A surgery.

3 **a)** Choose the correct words/phrases. V9.2

1 *protest/reject* against something
2 *take part/carry out* in a demonstration
3 *suffer/reject* an offer
4 *meet/take* a target
5 *call off/publish* a strike
6 *meet/carry* out a survey

b) Work in pairs. Write a sentence for the phrases in **3a)**.

4 Correct any mistakes in the underlined verb forms. G9.2

a) The police [1]have ~~been~~ carried out a survey which shows that drivers don't slow down in bad weather. Hundreds of people [2]have been injured this year in accidents caused by bad weather.

b) The one-day strike by transport workers [3]has called off. The unions [4]have ~~been~~ accepted the pay offer which the government [5]has ~~been~~ increased by 2%.

c) A report [6]has published which shows that the government [7]has spent an extra £5 billion on hospitals this year. This news [8]has welcomed by doctors all over the country.

5 Complete the sentences with these words/phrases. V9.3

despite   although   in spite of
even though   however

1 _____ feeling ill, I went to work.
2 _____ I wasn't hungry, I ate a pizza.
3 She was angry. _____, she didn't show it.
4 He went out _____ being tired.
5 I was late for work, _____ I left home at 7 a.m.

Progress Portfolio

a) Tick the things you can do in English.

☐ I can explain which person, thing, place and time I'm talking about.

☐ I can talk about things that have happened in the news.

☐ I can understand the main points of news items.

☐ I can use connecting words to join sentences and clauses.

☐ I can talk about health and discuss medical problems with a doctor.

b) What do you need to study again? ● 9A–D

 Cultura Inglesa

10 Happy ever after?

10A The anniversary

Vocabulary contacting people
Grammar *was/were going to,*
was/were supposed to
Review Past Perfect

QUICK REVIEW ●●●
Write all the health problems and symptoms you know. Work in pairs.
Take turns to mime your words. Your partner guesses what the problem is.

Vocabulary Contacting people

1 Fill in the gaps with the correct form of these verbs. Check new words/phrases in **bold** in 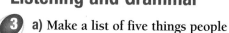 **V10.1** p136.

~~get~~ be give hear let call keep leave lose get

1 Who in your family is usually difficult to _get_ **hold of**?
2 Do you usually .... **your friends a call** on their birthdays?
3 When people .... **you messages**, do you generally .... **them back** immediately?
4 How do you usually .... **someone know** you're going to be late?
5 Have you got friends from ten years ago that you .... still **in touch with**?
6 Have you .... **touch with** everyone you knew at your first school?
7 How do you .... **in touch with** friends who live far away?
8 Is there a person you haven't .... **from** for years that you'd like to .... **in touch** with again?

2 Work in pairs. Take turns to ask and answer the questions in 1. Ask follow-up questions if possible.

Listening and Grammar

3 **a)** Make a list of five things people need for a successful marriage.

the same interests   a nice place to live

b) Work in pairs. Explain why you have chosen the things on your list. Then choose the five most important things from both lists.

c) Work in groups or with the whole class. Agree on a final list of five things.

Trevor Sheila Derek Tom Peggy Jane Brenda

a) Look at the picture of a wedding. Match these words to the people.

> the bride   the groom   the best man   the bridesmaid

b) R10.1 Listen to Peggy talking to her son, Leo, about her wedding anniversary. Then answer these questions.

1 Are Peggy and her husband going away for their anniversary?
2 What do Leo and his sister, Karen, want to do for their parents?
3 Why did they borrow some of their parents' old photos?

c) Work in pairs. Correct the five mistakes in this summary.

Peggy and her husband, Tom, have been married for thirty years. Their children, Leo and Karen, want to invite everyone who was at their parents' wedding to a party. The best man at the wedding, Derek Bradley, and his sister, Brenda, moved to Australia many years ago. Peggy knows how to get in touch with them. She's lost touch with Trevor Jones and his wife, Sheila.

d) Listen again and check.

Help with Grammar *was/were going to, was/were supposed to*

 a) Look at these sentences from Peggy and Leo's conversation. Then answer the questions.

*We **were going to** visit the Bradleys later that year, but we didn't go for some reason.*
*We **were going to** spend our anniversary in the cottage in Wales where we had our honeymoon, but it was already booked.*

1 Did Peggy and Tom plan to visit the Bradleys?
2 Did they visit them?
3 Did they plan to spend their anniversary in the cottage in Wales?
4 Are they going to spend their anniversary there?

*Tom **was supposed to** book the cottage months ago, but he forgot. I **was supposed to** call you back, wasn't I? Sorry, Leo, I was out all day.*

5 Did Tom agree to book the cottage?
6 Did he book it?
7 Did Leo expect his mother to call him back?
8 Did she call him back?

b) Fill in the gaps in these rules with *was/were going to* or *was/were supposed to*.

● We use _____ to talk about plans we made in the past which didn't happen, or won't happen in the future.

● We use _____ to talk about things we agreed to do, or other people expected us to do, but we didn't do.

c) Which verb form follows *was/were going to* and *was/were supposed to*?

d) Check in G10.1 p137.

 R10.2 P Listen and practise. Copy the stress and weak forms.

We were /wə/ going to spend our anniversary in Wales. It was /wəz/ going to be a surprise party.

 a) Match beginnings of sentences 1–7 to ends of sentences a)–g).

1 Karen had agreed to make a list of possible guests … *b)*
2 Peggy and Tom had planned to call Trevor and Sheila …
3 Leo had agreed to try and find the Bradleys' address on the Internet …
4 Karen had planned to get her parents a present on Monday …
5 Leo had decided to buy himself a new suit last week …
6 Karen had expected Leo to get in touch with Jane Lewis …
7 Leo had expected his parents to go through their old address books …

a) but his computer wasn't working.
b) but she didn't know who to invite.
c) but he lost her phone number.
d) but they couldn't find them.
e) but he didn't have enough money.
f) but they lost their phone number.
g) but she couldn't find her credit card.

b) Rewrite the sentences in 7a). Use the correct form of *was/were going to* or *was/were supposed to*.

Karen was supposed to make a list of possible guests, but she didn't know who to invite.

Get ready … Get it right!

 Write three things that you were going to do and three things you were supposed to do in the last four weeks. Think about why you didn't do these things.

visit my aunt

 a) Work in pairs. Take turns to tell each other about the things on your list. Ask follow-up questions if possible.

> I was going to visit my aunt last weekend, but I had to work instead.

> Are you going to see her this weekend?

b) Tell the class your partner's best reason for not doing one of the things on his/her list.

Vocabulary describing people
Grammar modal verbs (2): making deductions
Review contacting people; state and activity verbs

QUICK REVIEW ● ● ●

Write the names of people you know who: you haven't heard from this month, always call you back, are difficult to get hold of, you've lost touch with, left you a message on your mobile. Work in pairs. Tell your partner about these people. Ask follow-up questions if possible.

Vocabulary Describing people

1 **a)** Tick the words/phrases you know. Check new words/phrases in **V10.2** p136.

fair/dark/red/blonde/grey/dyed hair
long/short/shoulder-length hair
straight/curly/wavy hair
her hair up/in a ponytail   going bald
a moustache/a beard   a dark/light blue suit/jacket
a striped/flowery/plain tie/dress/shirt
glasses/lots of jewellery
in his/her teens/early twenties/mid-thirties/late forties

b) Work in pairs. Look at the picture of Tom and Peggy's 25th wedding anniversary party. Take turns to describe the people. Use the words/phrases in **1a)** and your own ideas. Your partner guesses who it is.

> She's got her hair up and she's wearing a red dress.

> You mean her?

Listening and Grammar

2 **a)** **R10.3** Listen and match these names to people 1–7 in the picture. Where's Peggy's husband, Tom?

Peggy *2*   Brenda   Jane   Derek
Nick   Trevor   Sheila

b) Listen again. Who said these sentences: Peggy, Karen or Leo?

1 He **could be picking** people up from the station. *Karen*
2 That **can't be** her real hair colour.
3 He **must be talking** to some guests in the other room.
4 He **may want** to be on his own for a bit.
5 It **could be** the guy that moved to New York.
6 No, that isn't Derek Bradley.
7 He **can't be having** a cigarette.
8 He **might be** in the bathroom.
9 He's practising his speech in front of the mirror.
10 He **must know** that speech by now.

c) Work in pairs. Compare answers.

Help with Grammar Modal verbs (2): making deductions

3 **a)** Look at the sentences 1–10 in 2b). Are they talking about the past, the present or the future?

b) Match sentences 1–10 in 2b) to meanings a)–e) .

The speaker …
a) knows this is definitely true. __9__
b) believes this is true. _____ _____
c) thinks this is possibly true. _1_ _____ _____ _____
d) believes this isn't true. _____ _____
e) knows this definitely isn't true. _____

c) Look at the verb forms in **bold** in 2b). Then fill in the gaps with the correct modal verbs.

● We use _____ to talk about something that we believe is true.

● We use _____ , _____ or _____ to talk about something that we think is possibly true.

● We use _____ to talk about something that we believe isn't true.

d) Which sentences in 2b) are talking about: a state? something happening now?

e) Complete these rules with *verb+ing* or *infinitive*.

● To make deductions about states we use: modal verb + _____ .

● To make deductions about something happening now we use: modal verb + *be* + _____ .

TIP! ● We don't use *can* or *mustn't* to make deductions: *It could be him.* not ~~It can be him~~. *He can't be a millionaire.* not ~~He musn't be a millionaire~~.

f) Check in G10.2 p137.

4 R10.4 P Listen and practise the sentences in 2b). *He could be picking people up from the station.*

5 Look at these sentences Karen said at the party. Choose the correct modal verb.

1 That woman *could/must* be Mum's cousin, but I'm not sure.
2 Uncle Ian isn't here yet. He *may/can't* be working late.
3 Nick *can't/must* be married yet. He's only seventeen.
4 Jane *must/can't* have dyed hair. In the wedding photo she had dark hair.
5 Sheila *can't/might* want to leave soon, she looks a bit bored.
6 Derek's just arrived from New York. He *must/can't* be feeling very tired.
7 You *must/can't* be hungry, Dad. You've just finished eating!
8 Trevor *could/must* be in the restaurant, or he *may/can't* be in the garden.

6 Fill in the gaps with the correct form of these verbs.

~~be~~	love	lose	work
need	do	know	

1 That can't _be_ the right house.
2 Joan's not here. She must _____ the shopping.
3 Paola might _____ where he lives.
4 You must _____ living in London.
5 Josh can't _____ now. His office is closed.
6 I must _____ my memory. I keep forgetting to do things.
7 We may _____ some more milk.

7 **a)** R10.5 Listen to six short recordings of sounds and voices. Write sentences with *must*, *may*, *might*, *could* or *can't* for each recording.

1 The water must be too cold.

b) Work in groups. Compare sentences. Are any the same?

c) Listen again. Compare sentences with the class.

Get ready … Get it right!

8 Look at the picture. These things all belong to people at the party. Who do you think owns each thing?

9 **a)** Work in groups. Discuss who you think each thing belongs to. Give reasons for your choices.

> I think this book could be Karen's. She might be learning to drive.

b) Look at p141. Check your answers. How many did you get right?

Vocabulary phrasal verbs (3)
Skills Reading: For better, for worse;
Listening: Prenuptial agreements
Help with Listening /t/ and /d/ at the end of words
Review describing people

VOCABULARY AND SKILLS

QUICK REVIEW ●●●

Choose three people in the class. Write sentences to describe each person. Don't write the person's name: *He's in his mid-twenties and he's got short curly hair. He's wearing a striped shirt.* Work in pairs. Take turns to say your sentences. Your partner uses *must, may, might, could* and *can't* to guess who the person is: *It might be Johann, or it could be Marcos.*

Reading and Vocabulary

1 Work in groups. Discuss these questions.

1 What do you think is the average cost of a wedding in your country?
2 Who usually pays for the wedding in your country?
3 What do they spend the money on?

2 **a)** Read the magazine article. Choose the correct words in these sentences.

1 Tony is Olivia's *third/fourth* husband.
2 Ginny *went/didn't* go to Olivia's wedding.
3 Ginny *had/hadn't* been a bridesmaid for Olivia before.
4 Olivia *has/hasn't* kept in touch with her ex-husbands.
5 *More/Fewer* people in the UK are getting married these days.

b) Read the article again. What does it say about these numbers? Did any of the numbers surprise you?

£16,000	six hours	£2,600	£15,000
459,000	286,000	53%	12%

c) Look at the phrasal verbs in **bold** in the article. Match them to their meanings 1–10. Write the infinitive of the verbs.

1 avoid doing something you don't want to do
   get out of
2 feel better after you have been unhappy or ill
3 increase or rise
4 find some information in a book or on a computer
5 tell someone some information you think they don't know or have forgotten
6 decide or arrange to do something at a later time
7 argue with someone and stop being friendly with them
8 think of an idea, or a solution to a problem
9 end a marriage or relationship
10 find something by accident

d) Check in **V10.3** p136.

It's such a special day. You only get married for the fourth time once.

For better, for worse

Ginny Bell looks at her friend's chances of having a happy marriage.

When Olivia first started going out with Tony, I thought it would never last. Two months later, she told me they were getting married. I thought she should **put** the wedding **off** for a few months until she knew Tony better. "He really is the one," Olivia told me. She'd said the same thing about her last three husbands, but I didn't like to **point** this **out** to her.

When Olivia asked me to be her bridesmaid, I tried to **get out of** the whole thing because I didn't want to see her make the same mistake again. However, I couldn't **come up with** a good excuse, so there I was again, standing outside the church wondering how much Olivia's parents had spent this time. A typical wedding costs about £16,000 and lasts six hours, so that's about £2,600 an hour. Olivia must be a very expensive daughter to have.

At the church Olivia introduced me by saying, "This is Ginny. She's been a bridesmaid at *all* my weddings." And indeed I had. I wondered how long it would be before Olivia and Tony **split up**, adding £15,000 – the average cost of a divorce – to the cost of the wedding. Fortunately, Olivia **got over** her last three divorces quickly and is still friends with all her ex-husbands.

So what are their chances of a successful marriage? The day before the wedding I **came across** a newspaper report which said that the number of divorces in the UK is still **going up**, while the number of people getting married is falling. I **looked** some figures **up** and found out that in 1971 there were 459,000 weddings in the UK, but in 2001 there were only 286,000. And as for divorce, where you live makes a huge difference. For example, the divorce rate in the UK is 53%, but in Italy it's only 12%.

When my husband and I were leaving the reception, Olivia said, "You two have never **fallen out**, have you? How can I make this marriage last?" Well, Olivia, what can I say? Move to Italy!

Help with Vocabulary Phrasal verbs (3)

 a) Read about the four types of phrasal verbs.

TYPE 1 phrasal verbs don't have an object.

*You two have never **fallen out**.*

TYPE 2 phrasal verbs always have an object. This is always after the phrasal verb.

*Olivia **got over** <u>her divorces</u> quickly.*
*Olivia **got over** <u>them</u> quickly.*

TYPE 3 phrasal verbs always have an object. If the object is a noun, you can put it in the middle or after the phrasal verb.

*I **looked** <u>some figures</u> **up**.*
*I **looked up** <u>some figures</u>.*

If the object is a pronoun, you must put it in the middle of the phrasal verb.

*I **looked** <u>them</u> **up**. not I **looked up** <u>them</u>.*

TYPE 4 phrasal verbs have three words and always have an object. The object is always after the phrasal verb.

*I tried to **get out of** <u>the whole thing</u>.*
*I tried to **get out of** <u>it</u>.*

b) Work in pairs. Look at the other phrasal verbs in **bold** in the article. Are they type 1, 2, 3 or 4?

c) Check in V10.4 p136.

 4 Work in pairs. Student A → p106. Student B → p111. Follow the instructions.

 5 Look at the words in brackets. Where can they go in these sentences? Put a tick or a cross in the gaps.

1 Katherine never got ..X.. over ..✓.. . (her divorce)
2 He always puts ...... off ...... until the last minute. (his homework)
3 You can't put ...... off ...... much longer. (it)
4 Dylan didn't want to go, but he couldn't get out ...... of .... (it)
5 Look ...... up ...... in a dictionary. (these words)
6 If you don't know the answer, look ...... up .... (it)
7 I came ...... across ...... when I was cleaning. (this)
8 The teacher pointed ...... out ...... to him. (the mistake)
9 I knew Mark was wrong, but I didn't want to point ...... out .... (it)

Boris Becker and Barbara Feltus

Steven Spielberg and Amy Irving

Listening

 a) Look at the photos. What do you know about these people? What do you think the couples have in common?

b) Check these words with your teacher or in a dictionary.

| divide up   property   legal   a guarantee   a court |

c) R10.6 Listen to a radio phone-in. Answer these questions.

1 What is a prenuptial agreement?
2 Does the lawyer think they are a good idea? Why?/Why not?

d) Listen again. Tick the true sentences. Correct the false ones.

1 Most couples usually get half of everything they own.
2 A prenuptial agreement isn't a legal guarantee in the USA.
3 Boris Becker and Barbara Feltus were married for five years.
4 Amy Irving got $10 million when she got divorced.
5 You always need a lawyer to deal with a prenuptial agreement.

Help with Listening /t/ and /d/ at the end of words

 a) Look at these sentences. Circle each *t* and *d* in **bold** you think you will hear. Cross out the ones you don't think you will hear.

PRESENTER Alison, firs(t)of all, we shoul~~d~~ star**t** with the mos**t** obvious question – wha**t** exactly is a prenuptial agreement?

ALISON Well, it's like a divorce contrac**t** couples sign before they ge**t** married. They agree how they'll divi**d**e up their property an**d** money if they ever ge**t** divorced.

b) R10.6 Listen to the beginning of the radio phone-in again. Check your answers.

c) Choose the correct word in this rule.

● We don't usually hear /t/ or /d/ sounds at the end of words when the next word starts with a *consonant/vowel* sound.

d) Look at R10.6, p155. Listen again and notice when we don't say /t/ and /d/ at the end of words.

 8 Work in groups. Discuss these questions.

1 Are prenuptial agreements a good idea? Why?/Why not?
2 If you had a prenuptial agreement, what would you include in it?

 Cultura Inglesa

10D Do you mind?

Real World asking for, giving and refusing permission
Help with Listening intonation (3): asking for permission
Review phrasal verbs

QUICK REVIEW ●●●
Make a list of eight phrasal verbs. Work in pairs and swap papers. Take turns to say a sentence for each of the phrasal verbs on your partner's list. Listen to your partner's sentences. Are they correct?

1 Work in groups. Discuss these questions.

1 When did you last stay with relatives or friends? How long did you stay?
2 Were there any problems? If so, what were they?
3 When was the last time relatives or friends came to stay with you?

2 **a)** [R10.7] Derek, Brenda and Nick Bradley are staying with Peggy and Tom after the party. Listen and fill in the gaps in these questions.

1

a) **Do you think I could** send a few .... ?
b) **Is it OK if** I borrow a couple of .... ?

2

c) **May I** download some .... onto your computer?
d) **Would you mind if I** gave my .... a call?

3

e) **Can I** make myself a .... ?
f) **Do you mind if I** do some .... ?

b) Work in pairs. Check your answers. Then match conversations 1–3 to pictures A–C.

3 **a)** Look at these responses from the conversations. Which are: giving permission? refusing permission?

1 Sorry, I don't think we have the software for that.
2 Yes, of course you can. Help yourself.
3 Sorry, I'm afraid Tom's using the computer at the moment.
4 Yes, of course it is. There are some over there you can choose from.
5 No, not at all. Go ahead.
6 Actually, I'd rather you didn't, if you don't mind.

b) Match the responses in 3a) to the questions in 2a).

c) [R10.7] Listen again and check.

Real World Asking for, giving and refusing permission

4 **a)** Look at the ways of asking for permission in **bold** in 2a). Which verb form comes after each phrase: the infinitive, Present Simple or Past Simple?

1 Do you think I could … ?
  infinitive
2 Is it OK if I … ?
  Present Simple
3 May I … ?
4 Would you mind if I … ?
5 Can I … ?
6 Do you mind if I … ?

b) Choose the correct way to give permission for these questions.

1 Can I make myself a sandwich? *Yes, of course./No, not at all.*
2 Do you mind if I make myself a sandwich? *Yes, of course./No, not at all.*

c) After which other phrase in 4a) do we say *No, not at all.* to give permission?

d) Look at the sentences that refuse permission in 3a). Answer these questions.

1 Do we usually say *no* when we refuse permission?
2 Do we usually give a reason to say why we refuse permission?
3 Which words do we use at the beginning of the sentence to be polite?

e) Check in [RW10.1] p137.

Help with Listening Intonation (3): asking for permission

5 **R10.8** Listen to the questions in 2a) said twice. Which sounds more polite, a) or b)?

1 a) (b))   4 a) b)
2 a) b)   5 a) b)
3 a) b)   6 a) b)

6 **R10.9** **P** Listen and practise the questions in 2a) and the responses in 3a). Copy the polite intonation.

Do you think I could send a few emails?

7 **a)** Put these words in order.

1 see / May / written / what / I / you've ?
2 your / use / for / I / dictionary / Can / a moment ?
3 could / borrow / Do / money / you / some / think / I ?
4 of / if / I / a photo / mind / take / you / you / Do ?
5 I / OK / CD-ROM / Is / your / if / a few days / it / borrow / for ?
6 the USA / Would / I / to call / used / if / you / your / mind / mobile ?

b) Work in pairs. Take turns to say the sentences in 7a). Decide whether to give or refuse permission. If you refuse permission, give a reason.

> May I see what you've written?
> Yes, of course. Here you are.

8 Work in pairs. Student A → p105. Student B → p110. Follow the instructions.

♪ **R10.10** Look at the song *I'm Not in Love* on p101. Follow the instructions.

1 **a)** Choose the correct verbs. Then put them in the correct form. **V10.1**

LEAH Guess what? Jim (¹*get/keep*) in touch with me yesterday.
FAY Really? I haven't (²*get/hear*) from him for years.
LEAH He's trying to (³*get/have*) hold of people we knew at university for a reunion. Have you (⁴*hear/keep*) in touch with them?
FAY No, I've (⁵*catch/lose*) touch with most of them, but I (⁶*have/be*) still in contact with Bev. I'll (⁷*make/give*) her a call.

b) Work in pairs. Compare answers. Then practise the conversation.

2 **a)** Work in pairs. Are these sentences about a personal plan, or an agreement with another person?

1 My sister's angry because I _____ babysit for her last night, but I had to work late.
2 I _____ go to the gym after work, but I was too tired.
3 Oh, sorry. I _____ phone you last night, but I didn't get home till midnight.
4 I feel awful. I _____ take my parents to the airport, but I completely forgot.
5 I _____ go to bed early, but some friends came round and stayed till 1 a.m.

b) Complete the sentences in 2a) with the correct form of *be going to* for personal plans, or *be supposed to* for agreements. **G10.1**

3 **a)** Work in pairs. Make a list of famous people you both know.

b) Take turns to describe one of the people. Your partner guesses who you are describing. **V10.2**

She's in her thirties. She's got shoulder-length blonde hair.

Cameron Diaz.

4 Complete the conversations with these verb forms. **G10.2**

| can't be   is   might be |
| must be (× 2)   isn't |

1 A Where's Jo? I've been to her office and she _____ there.
  B She _____ having lunch. She sometimes does at this time.
2 A You work in an A&E department, don't you? It _____ really hard work.
  B Yes, it often _____ .
3 A Is that Lydia?
  B It _____ her, surely! She hates doing exercise.
  A She _____ trying to get fit.

5 **a)** Write sentences asking for permission to do five things. Use these phrases. **RW10.1**

| Do you mind if I   Is it OK if I |
| Would you mind if I   May I |
| Do you think I could |

b) Work in pairs. Take turns to ask your questions from 5a). Give permission for two of your partner's requests. Politely refuse the others.

Progress Portfolio

a) Tick the things you can do in English.

☐ I can talk about contacting people.

☐ I can explain why I didn't do things I had planned to do or had agreed to do.

☐ I can describe people's appearances.

☐ I can make deductions about the present.

☐ I can understand a short radio programme.

☐ I can ask for, give and politely refuse permission to do things.

b) What do you need to study again? **● 10A–D**

My Notes

My Notes

My Notes

My Notes

My Notes

My Notes

My Notes

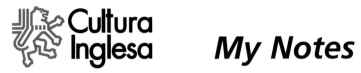

My Notes

My Notes

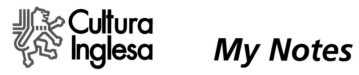

My Notes

My Notes

My Notes

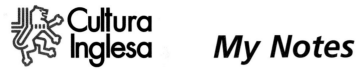

My Notes

My Notes

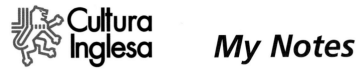

My Notes

You Can't Hurry Love 2D p19

 a) Think of three famous love songs. Do you like these songs? Why?/Why not?

b) Work in groups. Compare songs. Which song does the group think is the best/worst?

 a) `R2.11` Listen to the song. Choose the correct words/phrases.

I need love, love, to ease my ¹⟨mind⟩/life
I ²want/need to find, find someone to call mine

CHORUS
My mama said you ³mustn't/can't hurry love
No, you'll just ⁴have to/need to wait
She said love don't come ⁵easy/often
It's a ⁶game/way of give and take

You can't hurry love
No, you'll just ⁷have to/need to wait
You got to trust in a good time
No matter how ⁸much/long it takes

But how many heartaches ⁹must/can I stand
Before I ¹⁰get/find the love to let me live again
Right now the only ¹¹thing/thought that keeps me hanging on
When I feel my strength, yeah, it's ¹²nearly/almost gone
I remember …

CHORUS

How long must I wait
How much more ¹³must/can I take
Before loneliness
Will cause my heart, heart to ¹⁴ache/break?

Oh, I can't ¹⁵bear/wait to live my life alone
I grow impatient for a love to ¹⁶be/call my own
But when I feel that I, I can't ¹⁷go on/get up
These precious ¹⁸thoughts/words keep me hanging on
I remember …

CHORUS

You can't hurry love
No, you'll just have to ¹⁹stay/wait
She said trust in a good time
No matter how ²⁰much/long it takes – now break!

You know love, love don't come easy
But I keep on ²¹hoping/waiting
Anticipating for that soft voice
To ²²speak/talk to me at night
For some tender ²³arms/hands to hold me tight
I keep ²⁴hoping/waiting, ooh, keep on waiting
But it ain't easy, it ain't easy

CHORUS

b) Work in pairs. Compare answers.

 Work in pairs. Read the song again. Find three pairs of words that rhyme.

Our House 5D p43

 Work in groups. Discuss these questions.
1 Where did you grow up?
2 What was your house/flat like?
3 What did you do every day when you were a child?
4 What rules were there in your house?

 a) `R5.10` Listen to the song. Put the lines in order.

a) He can't hang around
b) Father wears his Sunday best **1**
c) Brother's got a date to keep
d) The kids are playing up downstairs
e) Mother's tired she needs a rest
f) Sister's sighing in her sleep

CHORUS

Our house, in the middle of our street (x 2)

g) Our mum she's so houseproud
h) There's always something happening
i) Our house it has a crowd **7**
j) And a mess is not allowed
k) Nothing ever slows her down
l) And it's usually quite loud

CHORUS (x 2)

m) She's the one they're going to miss
n) Mother has to iron his shirt
o) In lots of ways
p) Sees them off with a small kiss
q) Father gets up late for work **13**
r) Then she sends the kids to school

CHORUS

s) We would have such a very good time,
     such a fine time, such a happy time
t) I remember way back then,
     when everything was true and **19**
u) Then we'd say nothing would come
     between us two dreamers
v) And I remember how we'd play,
     simply waste the day away

REPEAT FIRST VERSE

CHORUS (x 2)

Our house, was our castle and our keep
Our house, in the middle of our street
Our house, that was where we used to sleep
Our house, in the middle of our street

b) Work in pairs. Compare answers.

 Work in pairs. Take turns to describe a typical day in the house/flat you live in now.

Stormy Weather   8D p67

 1 Work in groups. Discuss these questions.

1 What is your favourite/least favourite type of weather?
2 Would you like to live in a country with better weather? If so, where?
3 How does the weather affect your mood?

 2 a) R8.9 Listen to the song. Cross out the extra word in each line.

¹ Don't ~~really~~ know why
² There's no sun up in the blue sky
   stormy weather
³ Since my man and I ain't living together
⁴ Keeps raining down all the time

⁵ Life is completely bare
⁶ There's gloom and misery everywhere
   stormy weather
⁷ Just can't get my poor old self together
⁸ I'm very weary all the time, the time
⁹ So weary all the time now

¹⁰ Just when he went away
¹¹ The blues walked in here and met me
¹² If he stays away forever
¹³ Old rocking chair will probably get me

¹⁴ All I ever do is pray
¹⁵ The Lord above us will let me
¹⁶ Walk in the hot sun once more
¹⁷ Can't go on, everything I had is all gone
   stormy weather
¹⁸ Since my man and I ain't together again
¹⁹ Keeps on raining all the time (x 2)

REPEAT LINES 10–19

b) Work in pairs. Compare answers.

 3 Find words 1–5 in the song. Match them to meanings a)–e).

1	keeps	a)	tired
2	bare	b)	unhappiness
3	misery	c)	empty
4	weary	d)	continues
5	pray	e)	talk to God, often to ask for something

4 a) Write five ways you cheer yourself up when you're feeling depressed.

eat chocolate   go for a long walk

b) Work in groups. Discuss your ideas. Which ways are the most popular?

I'm Not in Love   10D p83

 1 Match words/phrases 1–8 with their meanings a)–h).

1	go through a phase	a)	stop people from seeing something
2	silly	b)	unpleasant
3	don't get me wrong	c)	don't misunderstand me
4	have got it made	d)	stupid
5	make a fuss	e)	experience a period of unusual behaviour
6	hide something		
7	nasty	f)	be successful, often without trying very hard
8	a stain	g)	a dirty mark that is difficult or impossible to remove
		h)	become very annoyed, anxious or excited, usually about something unimportant

 2 a) R10.10 Listen to the song. Fill in the gaps.

I'm not in love so don't ¹ *forget* it
It's just a silly phase I'm ² _____ through
And just ³ _____ I call you up
Don't get me wrong, don't ⁴ _____ you've got it made

I'm not in love, no no, it's because …

I like to ⁵ _____ you but then again
It doesn't mean you mean that ⁶ _____ to me
So if I call you, don't ⁷ _____ a fuss
Don't tell your friends about the ⁸ _____ of us

I'm not in love, no no, it's because …

Be quiet
Big boys don't cry (x 6)

I keep your ⁹ _____ upon the wall
It ¹⁰ _____ a nasty stain that's lying there
So don't you ask me to give it ¹¹ _____
I know you know it doesn't mean that ¹² _____ to me

I'm not in love, no no, it's because …

Ooh you'll wait a long time for me, ooh you'll wait a long time (x 2)

I'm not in love so don't ¹³ *forget* it
It's just a silly phase I'm ¹⁴ _____ through
And just ¹⁵ _____ I call you up
Don't get me wrong, don't ¹⁶ _____ you've got it made

I'm not in love (x 2)

b) Work in pairs. Compare answers.

 3 Work in groups. Discuss these questions.

1 Do you think the singer is in love? Why?/Why not?
2 How can you tell if someone is in love?
3 What would be your perfect romantic evening?

Pair and Group Work: Student/Group A

1A 10 p5

a) Work on your own. Make questions with these words.

1 from / parents / do / your / Where / come ?
Where do your parents come from?
2 do / on / Who / with / holiday / usually / go / you ?
3 like / do / on / money / spending / your / you / What ?
4 radio station / to / normally / listen / do / Which / you ?
5 you / about / friends / your / and / do / What / argue ?

b) Work with your partner. Take turns to ask and answer the questions. Ask follow-up questions if possible.

3B 7 p23

a) Work on your own. Read about Polly Kirby's job.

I've been writing guidebooks for [1] _____ years. I've written three books and now I'm working on a book about Kenya. I've been living in Africa since [2] _____ and I love it here. I've been travelling around Kenya for two weeks – I've visited [3] _____ different places so far.
At the moment I'm on a guided tour to Mount Kilimanjaro. I've wanted to climb this mountain since I arrived in Africa. We've been walking since [4] _____ and I'm absolutely exhausted. We've travelled about 15 km today and I've seen [5] _____ elephants! My guide, Shola, has been doing this job for 30 years. He's climbed Kilimanjaro [6] _____ times this year. I've only known him for three days, but we're already good friends.

b) Work with a student from group A. Make questions with *How long … ?* or *How many … ?* to complete the text. Use the Present Perfect Continuous and Present Perfect Simple.

1 How long has she been writing guidebooks?

c) Work with a student from group B. Take turns to ask and answer your questions. Fill in the gaps in the text. You start.

d) Compare your texts and check your answers.

2D 8 p19

a) Work on your own. Imagine you have this problem. Then think of one thing you've tried to do to solve the problem.

> Your brother got divorced recently and moved out of his house, so you invited him to stay for a few days. It's now six weeks later and he's still living with you. He isn't working at the moment, so he just stays at home and watches TV all day.

b) Work with students B and C. Take turns to explain your problems, show concern and give advice. Whose advice is the best, do you think?

I've got a bit of a problem.

Oh, dear. What's the matter?

Well, my brother got divorced recently …

c) Tell the class the best piece of advice you received.

3A 7 p21

a) Work on your own. Fill in the gaps with *you* and the correct form of these verbs. Use the Present Perfect Simple or Past Simple.

~~see~~	decide	have	go away
know	study	rent	speak

1 What's the best film you _'ve seen_ recently?
2 _____ to anyone in your family today?
3 _____ any DVDs last month?
4 _____ what to do this evening yet?
5 How long _____ the other students in the class?
6 _____ for the weekend last month?
7 _____ ever _____ a really bad holiday?
8 Is this the first time _____ English in a language school?

b) Work with your partner. Take turns to ask your questions. Ask follow-up questions if possible. You start.

4B 10 p31

a) Work with a student from group A. Put the verbs in brackets into the Past Simple or Past Perfect.

1 By the time Mozart _____ (be) ten years old, he _____ (write) 2, **5** or 8 symphonies.
2 John F Kennedy _____ (be) President of the USA for nearly **3**, 5 or 7 years when Lee Harvey Oswald _____ (shoot) him.
3 When the Beatles _____ (break up), they _____ (record) 137, 182 or **214** songs.
4 Michael Owen _____ (already play) for England 30, 40 or **50** times by the time he _____ (be) 23.
5 By the time Walt Disney _____ (die), he _____ (win) 15, **20** or 25 Oscars.

b) Work in a group of four with a pair from group B. Take turns to say your sentences from a). (The correct answers are in **bold**.) The students from group B choose the correct answers.

c) Which pair got more answers right?

6A 11 p45

a) Work on your own. Read about a problem you have. Think of three ways you can deal with the problem and decide what will happen if you choose each of these options.

You're doing a medical degree and you're in the third year of a five-year course. However, you have money problems. You need £3,000 to pay for next year's course, but you haven't got the money. Your parents have already lent you £3,000 and you also owe the bank £6,000.

get a part-time job → *not have enough time to study*

b) Work with a student from groups B and C. Take turns to talk about your problem and your options. Discuss what will happen if you choose each option. Your partners can also suggest other options.

If I get a part-time job, I won't have enough time to study.

Why don't you ... ?

If I do that, ...

c) Decide what to do. Does your group think you've made the right decision?

5B 3 p38

a) Work on your own. Fill in the gaps with *away*, *through*, *out* or *up*.

1 Which room in your house do you need to clear _____ ?
2 Who tidies _____ the house in your family?
3 Do you tend to keep everything or do you give things _____ ?
4 When did you last sort _____ your CD, video or DVD collection?
5 Do you put your clothes _____ before you go to bed?
6 How often do you go _____ your drawers and throw things _____ ?
7 What was the last thing you threw _____ ?

b) Work in pairs. Take turns to ask and answer the questions. Who is tidier, you or your partner?

6C 9 p49

a) Work with a student from group A. Write the correct synonym for the words in **bold**.

pleasant
1 Do you expect people you meet to be ~~nice~~ and easy to talk to?
   a) yes, always   b) sometimes   c) no, not usually

2 How **content** do you feel about your life?
   a) very   b) quite   c) not very

3 How often do you **make a decision** about something based on your intuition?
   a) usually   b) sometimes   c) hardly ever

4 When did you last **talk to** a stranger, for example in a queue or on a train?
   a) last week   b) last month
   c) more than a month ago

5 Do you ever feel **frightened** when you're going to do something new?
   a) yes, usually   b) yes, sometimes
   c) no, not usually

6 Do you think you're a **fortunate** person?
   a) yes, definitely   b) sometimes   c) no, not really

b) Work with a student from group B. Take turns to ask and answer your questions. Say the three possible answers when you ask your questions.

c) Give your partner 3 points for every a) answer, 2 points for every b) answer and 1 point for every c) answer. What is his/her score?

d) Tell your partner his/her score. Then look at p141. Who is luckier, you or your partner?

5D 6 p43

a) Work on your own. You want to buy these things. Decide how you can explain them to a shop assistant.

----------- -----------

----------- -----------

b) Work with your partner. You are a customer. Your partner is a shop assistant. Buy the things in **a)** from his/her shop. Write the English words for each thing. **Don't look at your partner's book.**

c) You are a shop assistant. Your partner is a customer. Look at these things in your shop. Listen to your partner describe the things he/she wants to buy. When you understand which thing he/she is describing, tell him/her the English word. **Don't show your partner the pictures.**

a fan   a cool bag   cotton buds

ear plugs   washing-up liquid

a pan scourer   furniture polish   a duster

d) Work in pairs. Check your answers. Did you buy the right things?

6D 7 p51

a) Last week your village was given £30,000 by the National Lottery to celebrate the village's 200th anniversary. There's going to be a meeting to decide how to spend the money. You think the village should spend the money on **improving the village park**. Work with a student from group A. Think of reasons why people should choose your idea and decide exactly what you want to spend the money on.

b) Work in groups of four with students from groups B, C and D. Discuss which idea is best. At the end of the meeting the group must decide which idea to spend the money on.

9B 9 p71

a) Work with a student from group A. Choose the correct auxiliaries in the news summary.

> Hello, here is (your name) with the news headlines.
>
> The USA ¹*has/has been* had more bad weather today. Tornadoes ²*have/have been* hit towns and cities in Texas, and hundreds of homes ³*have/have been* destroyed. Over 50 people ⁴*have/have been* injured, but so far nobody ⁵*has/has been* died.
>
> The England footballer Phil West ⁶*has just/has just been* told the media that he's getting married next year. Phil and his girlfriend, Sally, ⁷*have/have been* already decided where to have the wedding, but so far the location ⁸*has/has been* kept a secret.

b) Practise reading the news summary in **a)** to your partner from group A.

c) Work in pairs with a student from group B. Read your news summary without stopping. Your partner will answer questions in his/her book.

d) Listen to your partner's news summary. Answer these questions.

1 How many paintings have been stolen from the British Gallery?
2 Has anyone been arrested?
3 Why has the actor Gary Sanders just arrived in the UK?
4 How many people in the USA have seen the film *Last Chance*?

e) Check your answers with your partner. How many did you get right?

7B 7 p55

a) Work on your own. Fill in the gaps with the correct form of the verbs in brackets.

1 What _____ you _____ (do) if you suddenly _____ (become) incredibly rich?
2 If you _____ (not study) English, which language _____ you _____ (like) to study?
3 If you _____ (have to) sing in a karaoke bar, which song _____ you _____ (sing)?
4 How _____ your life _____ (be) different if you _____ (live) in the USA?
5 If you _____ (can) have dinner with a famous actor or actress, who _____ you _____ (choose)?

b) Work with your partner. Take turns to ask and answer your questions. Continue the conversation if possible.

> What would you do if you suddenly became incredibly rich?

> I'd leave my job and go travelling. What about you?

> I'd buy a flat in New York.

7C 8 p57

a) Work on your own. Fill in the gaps in these questions with *a, an, the* or – .

1 Have you got any friends who don't have _____ computer?
2 When did you last have _____ problem with your computer? Did you manage to solve _____ problem yourself?
3 Where's _____ best place for tourists to visit in _____ south of your country?
4 Would you prefer to go on holiday to _____ UK or _____ South Africa?
5 Which do you like best, _____ cats or _____ dogs?
6 What is/was the best thing about going to _____ school?
7 Do you know anyone who's _____ actor or _____ singer?

b) Work with your partner. Take turns to ask and answer your questions. Ask follow-up questions if possible.

9A 9 p69

a) Work with a student from group A. Write sentences to describe these words/phrases. Use *who, that, which* or *where*. Check words you don't know in a dictionary.

1 an optimist
  A person who has a positive attitude to life.
2 a garage
3 a vegetarian
4 a pillow
5 a bungalow
6 a freezer
7 an estate agent
8 an icon

b) Work with a pair from group B. Take turns to say your sentences. Guess the other pair's words. Which pair guessed the most words correctly?

10D 8 p83

a) Work on your own. Read the information about conversations 1 and 2. Decide what you want to say in each conversation.

1 You are staying with student B for a few days. Make questions to ask permission to do these things.
  - have a shower
  - phone your friend in India
  - make yourself something to eat
  - borrow his/her car tomorrow evening
  - use his/her computer to check your email
  - invite your cousin to stay the night on Saturday

2 Student B is staying with you for a few days. He/She is going to ask permission to do these things. Decide if you want to give or refuse permission. If you want to refuse permission, think of a reason why.
  - watch a DVD this evening
  - borrow £100 until next week
  - make himself/herself a cup of tea
  - stay an extra couple of days
  - give his/her sister a call
  - invite some of his/her friends to come round for dinner tomorrow

b) Work with your partner. Role-play the conversations. You start conversation 1. Your partner starts conversation 2.

c) Tell the class which things your partner refused permission for and why.

8A 9 p61

a) Work in pairs with a student from group A. Put the verbs in brackets in the correct active or passive form.

1 Do you think people _____ (take) the problem of global warming seriously enough in your country?
2 What's the best thing that individual people can _____ (do) to help the environment?
3 Do you think children _____ (teach) enough about the environment in schools these days?
4 Do you think air travel should _____ (make) more expensive to reduce the number of flights?
5 What _____ (happen) when we run out of oil?

b) Work in a group of four with a pair from group B. Take turns to ask and answer your questions. Give reasons for your answers if possible.

c) Tell the class what your group thinks about the future of the planet.

10C 4 p81

a) Work on your own. Fill in the gaps with the correct form of these phrasal verbs.

> split up   get out of   get over
> look up   put off   come up with

1 What do you think is the most common reason why couples _____ ?
2 How long does it usually take you to _____ a bad cold?
3 Are you good at _____ solutions to problems?
4 When did you last try to _____ something you didn't want to do?
5 What was the last word you _____ in a dictionary?
6 Do you usually do things immediately, or do you _____ them _____ until the last minute?

b) Work with your partner. Take turns to ask and answer your questions. Ask follow-up questions if possible.

9D 8 p75

a) Work on your own. Read the information for conversations 1 and 2. Decide what you want to say in each conversation.

1 You are a doctor. Your next patient has just moved to this town and you haven't seen him/her before. Firstly, find out a few things about him/her (job, family, etc.). Then ask what his/her symptoms are. Finally, decide on the correct treatment.

2 You are a patient. You have already seen your doctor twice this month, but he/she wasn't very helpful (last time he/she told you to take some paracetamol). Decide what your symptoms are and how long you've had them. Also decide if you've had these symptoms before.

b) Work with your partner. Role-play the conversations. You start conversation 1. Your partner starts conversation 2.

c) Tell the class about the treatment your doctor suggested. Were you happy with your doctor's advice? Why?/Why not?

Pair and Group Work: Student/Group B

1A 10 p5

a) Work on your own. Make questions with these words.

1 to / you / music / What / do / kind of / listen ?
   What kind of music do you listen to?
2 friends / and / you / What / about / your / talking / do / like ?
3 to / you / countries / want / to / Which / go / do ?
4 the / you / do / go / with / to / usually / cinema / Who ?
5 town or city / come / your / Which / best / does / from / friend ?

b) Work with your partner. Take turns to ask and answer the questions. Ask follow-up questions if possible.

3B 7 p23

a) Work on your own. Read about Polly Kirby's job.

I've been writing guidebooks for four years. I've written
a) _____ books and now I'm working on a book about Kenya. I've been living in Africa since I left university and I love it here. I've been travelling around Kenya for **b)** _____ – I've visited six different places so far. At the moment I'm on a guided tour to Mount Kilimanjaro. I've wanted to climb this mountain since **c)** _____ . We've been walking since 7 a.m. and I'm absolutely exhausted. We've travelled **d)** _____ km today and I've seen about 15 elephants! My guide, Shola, has been doing this job for **e)** _____ . He's climbed Kilimanjaro nine times this year. I've only known him for **f)** _____ , but we're already good friends.

b) Work with a student from group B. Make questions with *How long … ?* or *How many … ?* to complete the text. Use the Present Perfect Continuous and Present Perfect Simple.

a) How many books has she written?

c) Work with a student from group A. Take turns to ask and answer your questions. Fill in the gaps in the text. Your partner starts.

d) Compare your texts and check your answers.

2D 8 p19

a) Work on your own. Imagine you have this problem. Then think of one thing you've tried to do to solve the problem.

> You've got some new neighbours and they're very friendly. However, they come round to your house three or four times a day asking for help, or just to chat. They usually stay for at least half an hour each time and it's beginning to drive you crazy.

b) Work with students A and C. Take turns to explain your problems, show concern and give advice. Whose advice is the best, do you think?

I've got a bit of a problem.

Oh, dear. What's the matter?

Well, I've got some new neighbours …

c) Tell the class the best piece of advice you received.

3A 7 p21

a) Work on your own. Fill in the gaps with *you* and the correct form of these verbs. Use the Present Perfect Simple or Past Simple.

~~miss~~	have	go on	get
do	look	study	see

1 _Have you_ ever _missed_ a plane?
2 _____ anything good on TV this week?
3 _____ any long journeys lately?
4 _____ anything special with your friends or family on your last birthday?
5 How long _____ your mobile phone?
6 _____ any emails or text messages yesterday?
7 _____ at the CD-ROM for this lesson yet?
8 Is this the first time _____ the Present Perfect Simple?

b) Work with your partner. Take turns to ask your questions. Ask follow-up questions if possible. Your partner starts.

4B 10 p31

a) Work with a student from group B. Put the verbs in brackets in the Past Simple or Past Perfect.

a) When the Apollo missions _____ (stop), 6, **12** or 18 men _____ (walk) on the moon.

b) Michael Schumacher _____ (win) 5, **7** or 9 Formula One World Championships by the time he _____ (be) 36.

c) William Shakespeare _____ (write) 27, 32 or **37** plays by the time he _____ (die).

d) When Pelé _____ (retire) from football, he _____ (score) 790, 1,003 or **1,281** goals.

e) By the time Van Gogh _____ (die), he _____ (sell) **1**, 23 or 107 paintings.

b) Work in a group of four with a pair from group A. Take turns to say your sentences from a). (The correct answers are in **bold**.) The students from group A choose the correct answers.

c) Which pair got more answers right?

6A 11 p45

a) Work on your own. Read about a problem you have. Think of three ways you can deal with the problem and decide what will happen if you choose each of these options.

Yesterday you were in a department store and you saw your friend's wife, Kim, put some make-up and a skirt in her bag and walk out of the shop without paying for them. Kim and her husband are quite rich, but you know they're having problems in their marriage.

tell the police → *Kim will be arrested*

b) Work with a student from groups A and C. Take turns to talk about your problem and your options. Discuss what will happen if you choose each option. Your partners can also suggest other options.

If I tell the police, Kim will be arrested.

Why don't you ... ?

If I do that, ...

c) Decide what to do. Does your group think you've made the right decision?

5B 3 p38

a) Work on your own. Fill in the gaps with *away, through, out* or *up*.

1 Do you always put things _____ after you use them?
2 How often do you clear _____ your wardrobe?
3 When did you last tidy _____ your bedroom?
4 Do you throw _____ clothes and shoes that you never wear?
5 Who takes _____ the rubbish in your family?
6 Do you usually go _____ your homework to check for mistakes?
7 When was the last time you sorted _____ your notes from class?

b) Work in pairs. Take turns to ask and answer the questions. Who is tidier, you or your partner?

6C 9 p49

a) Work with a student from group B. Write the correct synonym for the words in **bold**.

  certain
1 How **sure** are you that your future will be positive?
  a) very b) quite c) not very

2 When was the last time something good happened to you **accidentally**?
  a) last week b) last month
  c) more than a month ago

3 What kind of **approach** to life do you have?
  a) very positive b) quite positive
  c) generally negative

4 Do you feel **worried** about the future?
  a) no, not usually b) yes, sometimes
  c) yes, most of the time

5 How good are you at **dealing with** problems in your daily life?
  a) very b) quite c) not very

6 When was the last time you **tried to do** something that you've never done before?
  a) in the last four weeks b) in the last three months
  c) more than three months ago

b) Work with a student from group A. Take turns to ask and answer your questions. Say the three possible answers when you ask your questions.

c) Give your partner 3 points for every a) answer, 2 points for every b) answer and 1 point for every c) answer. What is his/her score?

d) Tell your partner his/her score. Then look at p141. Who is luckier, you or your partner?

5D **6** p43

a) Work on your own. You want to buy these things. Decide how you can explain these things to a shop assistant.

------------------------   ------------------------

------------------------   ------------------------

b) Work with your partner. You are a shop assistant. Your partner is a customer. Look at these things in your shop. Listen to your partner describe the things he/she wants to buy. When you understand which thing he/she is describing, tell him/her the English word. **Don't show your partner the pictures.**

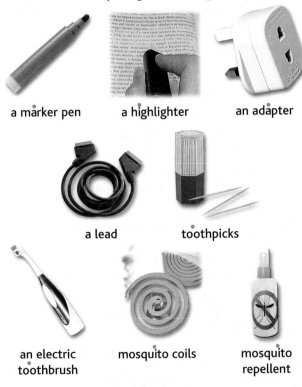

| a marker pen | a highlighter | an adapter |

| a lead | toothpicks |

| an electric toothbrush | mosquito coils | mosquito repellent |

c) You are a customer. Your partner is a shop assistant. Buy the things in **a)** from his/her shop. Write the English words for each thing. **Don't look at your partner's book.**

d) Work in pairs. Check your answers. Did you buy the right things?

6D **7** p51

a) Last week your village was given £30,000 by the National Lottery to celebrate the village's 200th anniversary. There's going to be a meeting to decide how to spend the money. You think the village should spend the money on **a 200th anniversary music festival**. Work with a student from group B. Think of reasons why people should choose your idea and decide exactly what you want to spend the money on.

b) Work in groups of four with students from groups A, C and D. Discuss which idea is best. At the end of the meeting the group must decide which idea to spend the money on.

9B **9** p71

a) Work with a student from group B. Choose the correct auxiliaries in the news summary.

Hello, here is (your name) with the news headlines.

Seventeen paintings ¹*have/have been* stolen from the British Gallery in London. The gallery's manager, Brian Lee, ²*has/has been* asked the public for help in catching the robbers. And we ³*have just/have just been* told that three men ⁴*have/have been* arrested in connection with the robbery.

The actor Gary Sanders ⁵*has just/has just been* arrived in the UK for the opening of his new film, *Last Chance*. The film has ⁶*has already/ has already been* seen by over 20 million people in the USA, and the actor ⁷*has/has been* said that it's the best film he's ever made.

b) Practise reading the news summary in **a)** to your partner from group B.

c) Work in pairs with a student from group A. Listen to your partner's news summary. Answer these questions.

1 Which part of the USA has been hit by tornadoes?
2 How many people have been injured?
3 When is the footballer Phil West getting married?
4 Do we know where the wedding will be yet?

d) Read your news summary without stopping. Your partner will answer questions in his/her book.

e) Check your answers with your partner. How many did you get right?

7B 7 p55

a) Work on your own. Fill in the gaps with the correct form of the verbs in brackets.

a) If you _____ (not be) in an English class now, where _____ you _____ (be)?

b) What _____ you _____ (do) if you _____ (find) someone's personal diary?

c) If you _____ (have to) go and live on your own for a month, which books _____ you _____ (take) with you?

d) How _____ your life _____ (change) if you suddenly _____ (become) famous?

e) If you _____ (find) someone's mobile phone in a café, what _____ you _____ (do)?

b) Work with your partner. Take turns to ask and answer your questions. Continue the conversation if possible.

> If you weren't in an English class now, where would you be?

> I'd be in the library. What about you?

> I'd probably be at home watching TV!

7C 8 p57

a) Work on your own. Fill in the gaps in these questions with *a*, *an*, *the* or – .

a) When did you last visit _____ website that was in English?

b) When did you last get _____ email with _____ photo attachment? Who or what was _____ photo of?

c) What's the worst thing about being in _____ hospital?

d) Would you prefer to go on holiday to _____ Australia or _____ USA?

e) What's _____ most expensive restaurant in _____ centre of your town or city?

f) Which do you like best, _____ Italian food or _____ Chinese food?

g) Is anyone in your family _____ doctor, _____ architect or _____ lawyer?

b) Work with your partner. Take turns to ask and answer your questions. Ask follow-up questions if possible.

9A 9 p69

a) Work with a student from group B. Write sentences to describe these words/phrases. Use *who*, *that*, *which* or *where*. Check words you don't know in a dictionary.

a) a volunteer
   A person who works but doesn't get any money.

b) a hair dryer

c) a rubbish bin

d) a detached house

e) a football fan

f) a loft

g) a microwave

h) a workaholic

b) Work with a pair from group A. Take turns to say your sentences. Guess the other pair's words. Which pair guessed the most words correctly?

10D 8 p83

a) Work on your own. Read the information about conversations 1 and 2. Decide what you want to say in each conversation.

1 Student A is staying with you for a few days. He/She is going to ask permission to do these things. Decide if you want to give or refuse permission. If you want to refuse permission, think of a reason why.

   - have a shower
   - phone his/her friend in India
   - make himself/herself something to eat
   - borrow your car tomorrow evening
   - use your computer to check his/her email
   - invite his/her cousin to stay the night on Saturday

2 You are staying with student A for a few days. Make questions to ask permission to do these things.

   - watch a DVD this evening
   - borrow £100 until next week
   - make yourself a cup of tea
   - stay an extra couple of days
   - give your sister a call
   - invite some of your friends to come round for dinner tomorrow

b) Work with your partner. Role-play the conversations. Your partner starts conversation 1. You start conversation 2.

c) Tell the class which things your partner refused permission for and why.

8A 9 p61

a) Work in pairs with a student from group B. Put the verbs in brackets in the correct active or passive form.

a) Do you think global warming _____ (take) seriously enough by governments around the world?

b) What _____ (done) in your country in the last few years to deal with climate change?

c) Which parts of your country _____ (damage) in the last few years because of climate change?

d) Do you think governments should _____ (do) more to stop people using their cars so much?

e) Do you think the problem of climate change can only _____ (solve) by governments and multinational companies?

b) Work in a group of four with a pair from group B. Take turns to ask and answer your questions. Give reasons for your answers if possible.

c) Tell the class what your group thinks about the future of the planet.

10C 4 p81

a) Work on your own. Fill in the gaps with the correct form of these phrasal verbs.

get out of   come across   get over
fall out   point out   go up

a) Have you ever tried to _____ going to a wedding or a party?

b) Have you and a close friend ever _____ ?

c) What's the best way to _____ your boyfriend or girlfriend leaving you?

d) Have prices _____ a lot in your country this year?

e) If a friend made a mistake in English, would you _____ it _____ to him/her?

f) Have you ever _____ something interesting while you were tidying up your house/flat?

b) Work with your partner. Take turns to ask and answer your questions. Ask follow-up questions if possible.

9D 8 p75

a) Work on your own. Read the information for conversations 1 and 2. Decide what you want to say in each conversation.

1   You are a patient. You've just moved to a new town and you are going to see a doctor for the first time. You have a stressful job (you're a police officer) and you've been having some health problems recently. Decide what your symptoms are and how long you've had them.

2   You are a doctor. You've already seen your next patient twice this month, but you didn't think there was anything wrong with him/her. The last time you saw him/her you told him/her to take some paracetamol. Ask the patient what his/her symptoms are. Then decide what treatment to give (if any).

b) Work with your partner. Role-play the conversations. Your partner starts conversation 1. You start conversation 2.

c) Tell the class about the treatment your doctor suggested. Were you happy with your doctor's advice? Why?/Why not?

Pair and Group Work: Student/Group C and D

2D 8 p19

a) Work on your own. Imagine you have this problem. Then think of one thing you've tried to do to solve the problem.

> Your husband/wife goes out with friends a lot in the evening. You often have to work late and he/she is usually out when you get home. You'd like him/her to stay at home more often in the evenings so you can spend some time together.

b) Work with students A and B. Take turns to explain your problems, show concern and give advice. Whose advice is the best, do you think?

> I've got a bit of a problem.

> Oh, dear. What's the matter?

> My husband/wife goes out with friends a lot ...

c) Tell the class the best piece of advice you received.

6A 11 p45

a) Work on your own. Read about a problem you have. Think of three ways you can deal with the problem and decide what will happen if you choose each of these options.

> You work for a big company that has offices all over the country. You're very good at your job and you like your colleagues, but your new boss, Kevin, never gives you any interesting work. Your old boss, Marcia, is now Kevin's manager.

look for another job → *might have to move house*

b) Work with a student from groups A and B. Take turns to talk about your problem and your options. Discuss what will happen if you choose each option. Your partners can also suggest other options.

> If I look for another job, I might have to move house.

> Why don't you ... ?

> If I do that, ...

c) Decide what to do. Does your group think you've made the right decision?

6D 7 p51

a) Last week your village was given £30,000 by the National Lottery to celebrate the village's 200th anniversary. There's going to be a meeting to decide how to spend the money. You think the village should spend the money on **a new sports centre for the village school**. Work with a student from group C. Think of reasons why people should choose your idea and decide exactly what you want to spend the money on.

b) Work in groups of four with students from groups A, B and D. Discuss which idea is best. At the end of the meeting the group must decide which idea to spend the money on.

4A 10 p21

a) Work on your own. Think of a concert you've been to that you really enjoyed. Make notes on the concert. Use these ideas.

- the band, singer, musician or orchestra you saw
- where and when the concert was
- where you were living at the time
- who you went with
- what the audience was doing during the concert
- the songs he/she/they played
- how long the concert lasted
- what you did after the concert finished
- any other interesting information

b) Work in groups. Take turns to talk about your concert. Ask questions to find out more information.

> I went to see U2 in Dublin in 2004.

> Really? What were you doing in Dublin?

> I was studying there. One of my friends ...

c) Decide which concert was the best. Tell the class about it.

1A 3 p4

a) Read the rest of the article and compare the list with your list from 2b). How many reasons are in the same order?

The top ten reasons for happiness

1 Your genes
Some people are simply born happier than others. In a study of 4,000 adult twins, differences in their genes were the main reasons for their different levels of happiness.

2 Being married
All studies show that married couples are happier than single people. Just living together without being married doesn't have the same effect.

3 Friends and family
People who have large families and lots of close friends are usually happier than people who have a lot of money but live on their own.

4 Not wanting more than you've got
People who expect to have a successful career, lots of money and the perfect relationship aren't as happy as people who accept what they've got.

5 Helping others
Studies by psychologists in different countries show that helping other people is not only good for them, it also makes you feel happier.

6 Religion
Four out of five studies show a positive link between religion and happiness. Very religious people usually live longer too.

7 Being attractive
Attractive people believe they're very happy – maybe because they also have good genes and are therefore healthier. Cosmetic surgery does not have the same effect!

8 Growing old
Studies show that old people are happy as often as young people and are unhappy less often. This is probably because they spend more time doing the things they enjoy.

9 Money
When you're poor, money can buy you some happiness. However, when people have enough money to live comfortably, more money doesn't make them happier.

10 Intelligence
Surprisingly, this has very little effect on happiness. Being able to get on well with people is much more important than how intelligent you are.

Adapted from the Daily Mail 2/10/03

b) Work in groups. Discuss these questions.

1 Whose list of reasons for happiness was closest to the list in the article?
2 Are these reasons true for people you know?
3 Do you disagree with anything in the article? If so, why?

6D 7 p51

a) Last week your village was given £30,000 by the National Lottery to celebrate the village's 200th anniversary. There's going to be a meeting to decide how to spend the money. The three ideas are: a) improving the village park, b) a 200th anniversary music festival, c) a new sports centre for the village school. You are the chairperson at the meeting. Work with a student from group D. Plan how to begin the meeting, then write two questions to ask about each idea.

b) Work in groups of four with students from groups A, B and C. You start the meeting, then ask each person to tell the group about his/her ideas. You can ask your questions when they have finished talking. Allow the group to discuss each idea, then ask the group to vote on which idea is the best. You are also allowed to vote.

c) Tell the class which idea your group chose and why you chose it.

Language Summary 1

V1.1 Weekend activities 1A ❶ p4

visit relatives	tidy up the house/flat*
go clubbing*	do some exercise
have a lie-in*	go to exhibitions
meet up with friends	chat to people online*
do some gardening	have people round for dinner
have a quiet night in	go for a walk/run

TIP! • In the Language Summaries we only show the main stress (•) in words and phrases.

*go clubbing go to clubs where there is music and dancing: *Lots of people in the UK go clubbing at the weekend.*

*have a lie-in when you stay in bed longer than usual in the morning: *I often have a lie-in on Sundays.*

*tidy up the house/flat put things back in the places where you usually keep them: *I usually tidy up the flat before I go to work.*

*chat to someone online talk to someone by sending messages to each other on the Internet: *Lots of people chat online to friends in different countries.*

TIP! • We also use *chat* or *have a chat* to mean 'talk to someone in a friendly and informal way': *He's chatting with some friends outside. I had a chat with our new neighbour.*

V1.2 Likes and dislikes 1B ❶ p6

phrases to say you like something

I really love …
I'm really/very/quite interested in …
I enjoy …
I'm really/very/quite keen on …
I think … is/are great/brilliant/ wonderful.

phrases to say something is OK

I think … is/are all right.
I don't mind …

phrases to say you don't like something

I really hate …
I don't like … at all.
I can't stand …
… really get(s) on my nerves.
I can't bear /beə/ …
I'm not very keen on …
… drive(s) me crazy.
I think … is/are really boring/ annoying.

TIPS! • *I can't stand* and *I can't bear* mean 'I hate'.
• *Great*, *brilliant* and *wonderful* all mean 'very good'.
• We can use pronouns, nouns or verb+*ing* with the phrases for likes and dislikes: *I love **it**. I can't stand **football**. **Waiting in queues** drives me crazy.*

V1.3 Adjectives to describe feelings 1C ❹ p8

relaxed /rɪˈlækst/ happy because you aren't worried about anything: *Adela felt very relaxed after her holiday in Spain.*

nervous /ˈnɜːvəs/ worried because of something that is going to happen: *I always get nervous before I speak in public.*

pleased happy about something that happened: *I'm pleased you like the present.*

embarrassed /ɪmˈbærəst/ feel stupid because of something you did or something that happened: *I felt so embarrassed when our son said he didn't like the food.*

annoyed a bit angry: *I get annoyed when I have to wait in queues.*

fed up annoyed or bored because you have done something for too long: *I'm fed up with working so hard.*

disappointed unhappy because something is not as good as you wanted it to be, or because something hasn't happened: *They were disappointed that only ten people came to their party.*

stressed worried and not able to relax: *He's very stressed about his new job.*

calm /kɑːm/ relaxed and peaceful: *I always feel very calm after doing yoga.*

upset unhappy or worried because something bad has happened: *She was very upset when she lost her job.*

scared frightened: *I'm really scared of spiders.*

satisfied pleased because something has happened in the way that you want: *She was very satisfied with her students' exam results.*

confused when you don't understand what is happening or what people are saying: *Matt was confused and didn't know what to do.*

shocked very surprised and upset: *I was shocked by the news of his death.*

glad happy and pleased: *I'm glad you enjoyed the meal.*

frustrated annoyed because things are not happening in the way that you want them to: *She felt very frustrated because people couldn't understand her.*

concerned worried: *I'm very concerned about the environment.*

TIPS! • We use *-ed* adjectives to describe how people feel: *I was very disappoint**ed** when I got my exam results.*

• We use *-ing* adjectives to describe the thing, situation, place or person that causes the feeling: *My exam results were disappoint**ing**.*

V1.4 Prepositions with adjectives 1C ❼ p9

• We often use prepositions with adjectives. The most common prepositions for these adjectives are in **bold**. Other prepositions that we can also use with these adjectives are in brackets ( ).

good **at**	scared **of** (by)
happy **with** (about)	bored **with** (by)
interested **in**	frightened **of** (by)
nervous **about**	annoyed **at** (with, by)
keen **on**	bad **at**
worried **about**	satisfied **with** (by)
surprised **by** (at)	embarrassed **by** (about)
upset **about** (by)	concerned **about** (by)
fed up **with**	angry **about** (at) something
pleased **with** (by)	angry **with** (at) someone

TIP! • After prepositions we use a noun, a pronoun or verb+*ing*.

Grammar

G1.1 Question forms 1A ④ p5

AUXILIARIES

● We usually use an auxiliary (*does, are, did, has*, etc.) to make questions.

	question word	auxiliary	subject	verb	
PRESENT SIMPLE	Who	does	Sarah	work	for?
PRESENT CONTINUOUS	What	are	her children	doing	at the moment?
PAST SIMPLE	What	did	Sarah	do	last Saturday?
PRESENT PERFECT SIMPLE	How many countries	has	Greg	been	to?

• We use the auxiliaries *do* and *does* to make questions in the Present Simple: *Who **do** you work for?*

• We use the auxiliaries *am, are* and *is* to make questions in the Present Continuous: *What **are** you looking for? What's he doing?*

• We use the auxiliaries *have* and *has* to make questions in the Present Perfect Simple: *Which countries **have** you been to?*

SUBJECT QUESTIONS

● Most questions with auxiliaries ask about the **object** of a sentence: **What** *did Jenny have for breakfast last Sunday? She had **toast and coffee**.*

● Subject questions ask about the **subject** of a sentence: **What** *makes her flatmate happy?* **Exercise** *makes her happy.*

● We don't use *do, does* or *did* in Present Simple and Past Simple subject questions: *What makes her flatmate happy?* not ~~What does make her flatmate happy?~~

● Subject questions have the same word order as positive sentences.

TIPS! • Questions with auxiliaries can also ask about a preposition + noun: **Where** *does Jenny live? She lives* **in London***.*

• We can make subject questions with *Who, What, Whose* and *Which.*

QUESTIONS WITH PREPOSITIONS

● We often put prepositions at the end of questions: *Who does Sarah work* **for***? How many countries has Greg been* **to***?*

TIP! • We don't usually put prepositions at the beginning of questions: *What are you talking about?* not ~~About what are you talking?~~

G1.2 Positive and negative verb forms, words and phrases 1B ⑤ p6

VERB FORMS

	positive	negative
PRESENT SIMPLE	we meet up	I don't have
PRESENT CONTINUOUS	I'm trying	I'm not feeling
PRESENT PERFECT SIMPLE	that's happened	I haven't taken
PAST SIMPLE	we went out	I didn't get

I DON'T THINK ...; THERE IS/ARE NO ...

● We often make negative sentences with *I don't think* ...:
I don't think I could live without one. not ~~I think I couldn't live without one.~~ *I don't think I'll get one.* not ~~I think I won't get one.~~

● We can use *no* to make negatives with *there is/there are*:
There's no signal. = There isn't a signal.
There are no taxis. = There aren't any taxis.

WORDS AND PHRASES

● Some words and phrases have a positive or negative meaning.

positive	negative		positive	negative
love	hate		everyone	no one
always	never		all	none
usually	hardly ever		both	neither

TIPS! • We can say *don't always, don't usually* and *don't often*, but not ~~don't sometimes~~, ~~don't hardly ever~~ or ~~don't never~~.

• We use plural verb forms with *both*: *Both of my brothers* **have got** *mobiles.* We use singular verb forms with *neither*: *Neither of them ever* **switches** *their phone off.*

• We don't usually use double negatives. We say: *I didn't talk to anyone.* not ~~I didn't talk to no one.~~

Real World

RW1.1 Question tags 1D ③ p10

● We usually use question tags (*isn't he?, aren't you?*, etc.) to check information that we think is correct.

● We usually use the **auxiliary** in question tags: *You work with Dave,* **don't** *you?*

● We only use **pronouns** in question tags: *Kate went to Bristol University, didn't* **she***?*

● If the main part of the question is positive, the question tag is usually **negative**: *Jack's vegetarian,* **isn't he***?*

● If the main part of the question is negative, the question tag is usually **positive**: *You haven't been to China,* **have you***?*

● We often use short answers to reply to questions with question tags (*Yes, she did. No, I haven't.*, etc.).

● When the information isn't correct, we often use *actually* after the short answer to sound more polite, then give more information: *Jack's vegetarian, isn't he? No, he isn't, actually. He just doesn't eat red meat.*

TIPS! • If the verb in the main part of the question is in the positive form of the Present Simple or Past Simple, we use *don't/doesn't* or *didn't* in the question tag: *Jim lives in the USA,* **doesn't he***? You lived in the UK,* **didn't you***?*

• We say *aren't I?* not ~~amn't I?~~: *I'm late, aren't I?*

• We use a comma (,) before question tags.

Language Summary 2

Vocabulary

V2.1 Work collocations 2A ❶ p12

take work home   meet deadlines*
have time to relax   take time off work
work long hours   be under pressure* at work
work overtime*   spend a lot of time at work
be a workaholic*   have good working conditions*

*overtime extra time that you work after your usual working hours: *I have to work overtime tonight.*
*a workaholic someone who works too much: *Chris is a real workaholic. He never does anything else.*
*a deadline the time when work must be finished: *The deadline for this report is 9 a.m. tomorrow.*
*pressure /ˈpreʃə/ difficult situations or problems that make you feel worried or unhappy: *I'm under a lot of pressure at work at the moment.*
*working conditions things which affect the quality of your job (working hours, the place you work, holidays, sick pay, etc.): *Working conditions have improved in the last fifty years.*

TIP! • We can also say *hit deadlines*: *Sally's very reliable. She always hits her deadlines.*

V2.2 In the kitchen 2B ❷ p14

FOOD

broccoli /ˈbrɒkəli/   a red/green pepper   peas /piːz/

beef   lamb /læm/   carrots

an aubergine /ˈəʊbəʒiːn/ [US: an eggplant]   beans /biːnz/   courgettes /kɔːʒets/ [US: zucchinis /zuˈkiːniːz/]

TIPS! • *Broccoli* is an uncountable noun: *I've bought some broccoli.* not ~~I've bought a broccoli.~~
• *Beef* is meat from cows. *Lamb* is meat from young sheep. Both of these words are uncountable.

THINGS IN THE KITCHEN

a fridge   a freezer   a cooker   a grill

an oven /ˈʌvən/   a microwave   a saucepan   a frying pan

a wok   a blender   a toaster   a rubbish bin

TIP! • We can say *a microwave* or *a microwave oven*.

WAYS OF COOKING

boil cook in a saucepan in water that is boiling (100°C).
roast cook chicken, lamb, potatoes, etc. in an oven.
bake cook bread, cakes, biscuits, etc. in an oven.
grill cook under a grill.
fry cook in a frying pan.
heat up make something hot that is already cooked (a ready meal, something you cooked yesterday, etc.).
microwave cook in a microwave.
steam cook with steam produced by boiling water.

TIPS! • *Roast* is also an adjective: *roast chicken, roast potatoes*, etc.
• We can also *stir fry* vegetables, meat, etc. in a wok.

V2.3 Sleep 2C ❶ p16

have a dream have stories and pictures in your head while you are sleeping: *I had a very strange dream last night.*
fall asleep start sleeping: *She fell asleep on the train home.* Also: **be asleep**.
wake up stop sleeping: *I woke up at six thirty this morning.*
get to sleep start sleeping, often with some difficulty: *It usually takes me half an hour to get to sleep.*
get back to sleep start sleeping again after you have woken up: *It took me a long time to get back to sleep.*
snore breathe in a very noisy way when you are sleeping: *Steve was snoring so loudly I couldn't get to sleep.*
be fast asleep be completely asleep: *The children were fast asleep when we got home.*
be wide awake be completely awake: *I was wide awake at 3 a.m. last night.*

have insomnia not be able to get to sleep: *Many people in the UK have insomnia.*
not sleep a wink not sleep at all (informal): *I didn't sleep a wink last night.*
have nightmares have frightening dreams: *I had a terrible nightmare last night.*
be a light/heavy sleeper be someone who wakes up easily/doesn't wake up easily: *Fiona's a very heavy sleeper – nothing can wake her up.*
take a nap have a short sleep in the day: *Charles always takes a nap after lunch.* Also: **have a nap.**
doze off fall asleep slowly, often in the day or when you don't plan to sleep: *I was so tired I dozed off in the middle of the meeting.*

V2.4 Gradable and strong adjectives; adverbs 2C 7 p17

- Strong adjectives already include the idea of *very*, for example, *exhausted* means 'very tired'.

gradable adjectives	strong adjectives
tired	exhausted /ɪgˈzɔːstɪd/, shattered
bad	terrible, awful /ˈɔːfəl/
good	fantastic
big	huge /hjuːdʒ/
difficult	impossible
frightened	terrified
surprised	amazed
tasty	delicious /dɪˈlɪʃəs/
small	tiny /ˈtaɪni/
cold	freezing
hot	boiling
beautiful	gorgeous /ˈgɔːdʒəs/
big	enormous
interested	fascinated
angry	furious /ˈfjʊəriəs/
happy	delighted
dirty	filthy /ˈfɪlθi/

- We can use *very*, *incredibly*, *extremely* and *fairly* with gradable adjectives, but not with strong adjectives: *very tired* not ~~very shattered~~; *incredibly difficult* not ~~incredibly impossible~~, etc.
- *Incredibly* and *extremely* are stronger than *very*. *Fairly* is less strong than *very*.
- We can use *absolutely* with strong adjectives, but not gradable adjectives: *absolutely terrified* not ~~absolutely frightened~~, etc.
- We can use *really* with both gradable and strong adjectives: *really tired*, *really exhausted*, etc.

TIP! • These strong adjectives all mean *very good*: *amazing*, *brilliant*, *excellent*, *fabulous*, *fantastic*, *incredible*, *marvellous*, *superb*, *terrific*, *wonderful*.

G2.1 Modal verbs (1); *be able to, be allowed to, be supposed to* 2A 5 p13

- *can, must, have to, should* and *ought to* are modal verbs.
- We use *be supposed to* to say a person is expected to do something: *In the UK people are supposed to have a break every four hours.*
- We use *can* and *be able to* to talk about ability or possibility: *People can get their best ideas when they're doing nothing. We're able to continue working when we're travelling.*
- We use *must* and *have to* to say something is necessary: *Rob says he must take more time off work. Lots of people have to take work home.*
- We use *should* and *ought to* to give advice: *People should only work 35 hours a week. We ought to spend more time relaxing.*
- We use *be allowed to* and *can* to say we have permission to do something: *Some French employees are allowed to begin their weekend at 3 p.m. on Thursday. In some American companies, employees can sleep whenever they want.*

TIPS! • We can use *have to* or *have got to* to say something is necessary: *I have to work tonight. = I've got to work tonight.* *Have got to* is very common in spoken English.
• *Must* and *have to* have very similar meanings in their positive form: *I must go now. = I have to go now.* *Have to* is more common than *must*.

POSITIVE, NEGATIVE AND QUESTION FORMS

- We use **the infinitive** after *can, must, have to, should, ought to, be able to, be allowed to* and *be supposed to*: *He must **take** …* not ~~He must taking …~~ or ~~He must to take …~~, etc.
- *Can, must, should* and *ought to* are the same for all subjects.

positive	negative	question
can go	can't go	Can I go?
must go	mustn't go	(Must I go?)
should go	shouldn't go	Should I go?
ought to go	ought not to go	(Ought I to go?)

- We make negatives and questions of *have to* by using the auxiliary *do* and *does*: *I don't have to go.; Does she have to go?*, etc.
- We make negatives and questions of *be able to, be allowed to, be supposed to* by changing the form of the verb *be*: *He isn't able to come. You aren't allowed to go in there. Are we supposed to be here tomorrow?*

TIPS! • We don't usually use *ought to* in its question form. We usually use *Do you think …* instead: *Do you think I ought to call him?*
• We usually say *Do I have to …?* instead of *Must I …?*
• We can't use *must* in the past. To say something was necessary in the past, we use *had to*: *I had to go to three meetings yesterday.*

MUSTN'T OR DON'T HAVE TO

- We use *don't have to* to say something isn't necessary: *You don't have to wear a suit to work, but you can if you want to.*
- We use *mustn't* to say something is not allowed: *You mustn't send personal emails from the office. You can only send work emails.*

TIP! • To say something wasn't necessary in the past, we use *didn't have to*: *I didn't have to get up early yesterday.* not ~~I hadn't to get up early yesterday.~~

Language Summary 2

Grammar

G2.2 Present Continuous and Present Simple

2B 5 p15

- We use the **Present Continuous** for things that:

  a) are happening at the moment of speaking: *I'm cooking dinner. That's exactly what I'm making!*

  b) are temporary and happening around now, but maybe not at this exact moment: *I'm writing a book in my spare time. She's doing an evening course in traditional English cooking!*

  c) are changing over a period of time: *The market is growing rapidly. They're becoming more common in Germany.*

- We use the **Present Simple** for:

  a) habits, daily routines, things we do every day/week/year, etc.: *My mother still cooks a full three-course meal every evening. These days we only spend 20 minutes each day cooking food.*

  b) things that we think are permanent, or true for a long time: *People who live in the UK spend over £1 billion a year. People in the USA and Sweden also buy a lot of ready meals.*

  c) verbs that describe states (*have got, be, know, think,* etc.): *Many experts now believe that they're bad for our health. We need to read the labels carefully.*

ACTIVITY AND STATE VERBS

- Activity verbs talk about activities and actions. We can use activity verbs in the Present Simple and the Present Continuous (and other continuous verb forms): *I watch TV every evening. I'm watching TV now.* Typical activity verbs are: *watch, talk, spend, eat, learn, buy, cook, take.*

- State verbs talk about states, feelings and opinions. We don't usually use state verbs in the Present Continuous (or other continuous verb forms): *I like broccoli.* not ~~I'm liking broccoli~~.

- Learn these common state verbs.

'be and have' verbs	'think and know' verbs	'like and hate' verbs	senses	other verbs
be	think	like	see	hope
have (got)	know	love	hear	seem
own	believe	hate	taste	need
belong	understand	prefer	smell	cost
	remember	want	touch	agree
	forget			weigh
	mean			contain

TIPS! • We often use *can* with verbs that describe the senses to talk about what is happening now: *I can hear a noise outside. I can't see anything.*

• Some verbs can be both activity verbs and state verbs: *I'm having dinner at the moment* (activity). *They have two dogs* (state). *What are you thinking about?* (activity). *I think football is boring* (state).

• We often use *still* with the Present Simple and Present Continuous to mean something that started in the past and continues in the present: *My mother still cooks a full three-course meal every evening. The Spanish and Italians are still cooking their own meals.*

Present Continuous

- We make the Present Continuous **positive** and **negative** with: subject + *be* + (*not*) + verb+*ing*.

  I'm (not) cooking dinner at the moment.
  You/We/They are/aren't writing a book.
  He/She/It's/isn't becoming more popular.

- We make Present Continuous **questions** with: (question word) + *am/are/is* + subject + verb+*ing*.

  What am I doing here?
  Who are you/we/they talking to?
  Is he/she/it working today?

Present Simple

- For *I/you/we/they*, the Present Simple **positive** is the same as the infinitive. For *he/she/it*, we add *-s* or *-es* to the infinitive: *he lives; she goes; it works.*

- We make the Present Simple **negative** with: subject + *don't/doesn't* + infinitive.

  I/You/We/They don't cook. He/She/It doesn't go out.

- We make Present Simple **questions** with: (question word) + *do/does* + subject + infinitive.

  Where do I/you/we/they live? Does he/she/it work?

Real World

RW2.1 Showing concern, giving and responding to advice 2D 4 p18

showing concern

Oh, dear. What's the matter?	Oh, I'm sorry to hear that.
I can see why you're upset.	Yes, I see what you mean.
Oh, how awful!	Oh, dear. What a shame.

giving advice

Have you tried talking to him about it?
Well, maybe you should talk to him again.
Why don't you talk to her about it?
I'd take her out for a really nice meal.
Maybe you ought to spend some time together.

responding to advice

Well, it's worth a try, I guess.	I might try that.
I've tried that, but	Yes, you could be right.
Yes, that's a good idea.	

- After *Have you tried ...* we use verb+*ing*: *Have you tried talking to him about it?*

- After *you should ...* , *Why don't you ...* , *I'd* (= *I would*) ... and *you ought to ...* we use the infinitive: *Well, maybe you should talk to him again.*

- We often use *What should I do?* or *What do you think I should do?* to ask for advice.

Vocabulary

V3.1 Phrasal verbs (1): travel `3A ❶ p20`

TIP! • **sb** = somebody; **sth** = something.

set off start a journey: *They set off at 5 a.m.*

get around travel to different places in the same town/city/area: *What's the cheapest way to get around?*

bring sth back (**from** a place) return from a place with something you bought there: *We brought this carpet back from Turkey.*

deal with sth do something in order to solve a problem or achieve something: *I have to deal with a lot of difficult customers as part of my job.*

check into somewhere go to the reception desk to say you have arrived and to get the key to your room: *Have you checked into the hotel yet?*

check out of somewhere go to the reception desk to pay your bill before you leave: *We checked out of the hotel early this morning.*

put up with sth accept a situation that you don't like because you can't change it: *I don't know how you put up with all this noise.*

see sb off go to the place where somebody is leaving from (for example, an airport or a station) to say goodbye to them: *My parents came to see me off at the airport.*

pick sb up go to a place where somebody is waiting and take them where they want to go: *Can you pick me up from the station?*

get back (**to/from** a place) return to a place after you have been somewhere else: *When did you get back from Brazil?*

look forward to sth feel happy and excited about something that is going to happen: *I'm really looking forward to my holiday.*

set off

see off

pick up

check into

TIPS! • We can also say *check in* and *check out* to mean 'check into/out of a hotel': *What time did you check in/out?*

• We often use verb+*ing* after *look forward to*: *I'm looking forward to **seeing** you.*

• We say *get (back) home* not ~~get (back) to/from home~~.

V3.2 Phrases with *travel, get* and *go on* `3B ❶ p24`

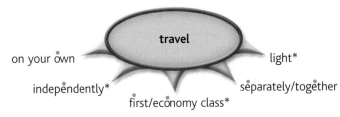

travel
on your own
independently*
first/economy class*
light*
separately/together

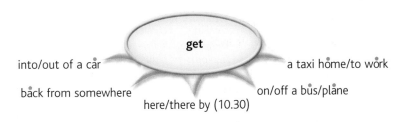

get
into/out of a car
back from somewhere
here/there by (10.30)
a taxi home/to work
on/off a bus/plane

go on
a trip*
a guided tour*
a journey*
a package holiday*
a cruise*

independently without the help of other people: *I don't like package holidays. I prefer travelling independently.*

first class the best and most expensive way to travel: *Famous people usually travel first class.*

economy class the cheapest way to travel: *I don't have much money so I always fly economy class.*

travel light travel with a very small amount of luggage: *I always travel light. I only take hand luggage.*

a trip when you go to a place for a short time and then come back: *I went on a business trip to Berlin last month.*

a guided tour /tʊə/ when you travel to lots of places in a city or country and a guide tells you about the interesting things you can see: *We're going on a guided tour of London.*

a journey /ˈdʒɜːni/ when you travel from one place to another place: *We went on a journey across Europe.*

a cruise /kruːz/ a holiday on a ship when you sail from place to place: *We're going on a Mediterranean cruise next month.*

a package /ˈpækɪdʒ/ **holiday** a holiday where everything is included in the price: *Many British people go on package holidays to Spain every summer.*

TIPS! • *Travel* is usually a verb. When we want to use a noun, we usually use *journey* or *trip*: *How was your journey/trip?* not ~~How was your travel?~~

• *Get* has many different meanings in English: *get back* = arrive back; *get a taxi* = take a taxi, etc. You can also *get on/off a train, a bike* and *a motorbike*.

• *By* + time means 'at or before': *I'll get there by 2.30.* = *I'll get there at 2.30 or earlier.*

Language Summary 3

Vocabulary

V3.3 Word formation (1): suffixes for adjectives and nouns 3C ⑦ p25

- We sometimes make adjectives from nouns, or nouns from adjectives, by adding an ending (a suffix), for example *happy* → *happi**ness***.

adjective	noun	suffix	noun	adjective	suffix
difficult	difficulty		danger	dangerous	
honest	honesty	-y	adventure	adventurous	-ous
modest	modesty		fame	famous	
patient	patience		comfort	comfortable	
confident	confidence	-ce	knowledge	knowledgeable	-able
important	importance		fashion	fashionable	
kind	kindness		nature	natural	
sad	sadness	-ness	tradition	traditional	-al
lazy	laziness		music	musical	
popular	popularity		health	healthy	
active	activity	-ity	noise	noisy	-y
tourist	touristy		possible	possibility	

TIP! • When the adjective or noun ends in *-t*, *-y* or *-e*, we sometimes have to change the spelling: *patient* → *patien**ce***, *lazy* → *lazi**ness***, *nature* → *natur**al***, etc.

Grammar

G3.1 Present Perfect Simple 3A ③ p21

- We use the **Present Perfect Simple** to talk about experiences in our life up to now, but we don't say when they happened: *I've worked in two other Central American countries. We've been away together a few times.* To give more information about an experience we use the **Past Simple**: *I had a great time in both places. Each time there was a problem back at the hotel.*

- We use the **Past Simple** to say when something happened: *I started working in the hotel industry 14 years ago. Last month two guys set off on their own.*

- We use the **Present Perfect Simple** for something that started in the past and continues in the present: *I've lived in this country for three years. My husband and I have had this place since 2001.*

- We use the **Present Perfect Simple** for something that happened a short time ago, but we don't say exactly when: *I've just been to San Isidro to pick up a guest. My husband's gone to see some friends off.*

POSITIVE AND NEGATIVE

- We make the Present Perfect Simple **positive** and **negative** with:
  I/you/we/they + *'ve* (= *have*)/*haven't* + past participle
  he/she/it + *'s* (= *has*)/*hasn't* + past participle.

  *I/You/We/They***'ve/haven't worked** in Costa Rica.
  *He/She/It***'s/hasn't been** to the USA.

QUESTIONS

- We make Present Perfect Simple **questions** with: (question word) + *have/has* + subject + past participle.

  How long **have** I/you/we/they **lived** here?
  Has he/she/it **been** there before?

FOR AND SINCE

- We use *for* with a period of time (how long): *I've lived in this country for three years.*

- We use *since* with a point in time (when something started): *My husband and I have had this place since 2001.*

TIPS! • We can also use *for* with the Past Simple: *I lived in South America for six years* (but I don't live there now).
• We don't use *during* with the Present Perfect Simple: *I've been here for a week.* not ~~I've been here during a week~~.

BEEN AND GONE

- *Go* has two past participles, *been* and *gone*.

- We use *been* to mean 'go and come back': *I've just been to San Isidro to pick up a guest* (I'm back at the place I started from now).

- We use *gone* to mean 'go, but not come back yet': *My husband's just gone to see some friends off* (he's not back yet).

ADVERBS AND TIME PHRASES

- We can use these words/phrases with the Present Perfect Simple: *never, ever, recently, lately, before, this week, just, yet, already*: *I've **never** been to Russia.*, etc.

- We must use the Past Simple with phrases that say a definite time (*ago, in 1997, last week, at 10 o'clock,* etc.): *I went there **two years ago**.* not ~~I've been there two years ago~~.

- We use *just* to say something happened a short time ago. We don't use *just* in negative sentences: *Jo's **just** phoned. Has Jo **just** phoned?* not ~~Jo hasn't just phoned~~. We put **just** before the past participle.

- We use *yet* to say something hasn't happened, but we think it will happen in the future. We don't use *yet* in positive sentences: *He hasn't finished it **yet**. Have you finished it **yet**?* not ~~I've finished it yet~~. We put **yet** at the end of the sentence or clause.

- We use *already* to say something happened some time in the past, maybe sooner than we expected. We don't use *already* in negative sentences: *We've **already** seen it. Have you **already** seen it?* but not ~~I haven't already seen it~~. We put **already** before the past participle.

- *Recently* and *lately* mean 'not long ago': *I haven't been to London **recently/lately**.*

- We use the Present Perfect Simple after *this is the first time, this is the second time,* etc.: *This is the first time we've been here.* not ~~This is the first time we are here~~.

TIP! • We also use the Present Perfect Simple with *this week/month/year,* etc. and with *this morning, this afternoon,* etc. if it is still that time of day.

Grammar

G3.2 Present Perfect Continuous and Present Perfect Simple (3B 5 p22)

- We usually use the **Present Perfect Continuous** to talk about an **activity** that started in the past and continues in the present: *Their company, Lonely Planet, has been publishing guidebooks for 30 years.*

- We usually use the **Present Perfect Simple** to talk about a **state** that started in the past and continues in the present: *They've been married since 1972.*

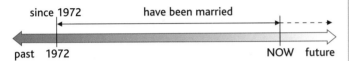

TIPS! • We often use the Present Perfect Continuous with verbs that talk about longer activities: *learn, rain, try, play, work, read, wait*, etc.: *I've been learning English for five years.*

• We don't usually use the Present Perfect Continuous with verbs that talk about short actions: *start, find, lose, break, buy, stop*, etc.: *I've started a course.* not *I've been starting a course.*

• With some verbs, both verb forms are possible: *I've lived/been living here for five years. He's worked/been working in Australia since 2003.*

PRESENT PERFECT CONTINUOUS: POSITIVE

subject	auxiliary	been	verb+*ing*	
I/You/We/They	've (= have)	been	travelling	since 1972.
He/She/It	's (= has)	been	publishing	guidebooks for 30 years.

PRESENT PERFECT CONTINUOUS: NEGATIVE

subject	auxiliary + *not*	been	verb+*ing*	
I/You/We/They	haven't	been	sleeping	well lately.
He/She/It	hasn't	been	working	for very long.

HOW LONG AND *HOW MANY*

- We usually use the **Present Perfect Continuous** to say **how long** an activity has been happening: *The company has been running a website for several years.*

- We usually use the **Present Perfect Simple** to say **how many** things are finished: *Lonely Planet has published over 650 guidebooks since the company began.*

TIPS! • We often use the Present Perfect Continuous to talk about the **activity** we have been doing: *I've been doing my homework* (we don't know if the homework is finished or not).

• We often use the Present Perfect Simple to say an activity is **finished**: *I've done my homework* (the homework is finished now).

PRESENT PERFECT CONTINUOUS: QUESTIONS WITH *HOW LONG* ... ?

How long	auxiliary	subject	*been*	verb+*ing*	
How long	have	I/you/we/they	been	waiting	here?
How long	has	he/she/it	been	publishing	books?

PRESENT PERFECT SIMPLE: QUESTIONS WITH *HOW MANY* ... ?

How many (+ noun)	auxiliary	subject	past participle
How many books	have	I/you/we/they	sold?
How many books	has	he/she/it	published?

TIP! • We can also make questions with the Present Perfect Simple and *How much* (+ noun): *How much money have you spent so far?*

Real World

RW3.1 Asking for and making recommendations (3D 3 p26)

asking for recommendations

Do you know any good places to stay/eat?
What's the best way to (get around)?
Is there anything else worth visiting?
What about (places outside Delhi)?
Have you got any other tips?

recommending things

It's probably best to (use rickshaws).
I'd recommend (the trains).
You should definitely see (the Red Fort).
That's well worth seeing.
You really must go to (Agra).

not recommending things

Don't bother going to (the museums).
It isn't really worth visiting.
Don't drink the water.
I wouldn't eat anything that's sold in the street.

responding to recommendations

That's good to know.
That sounds good.
Thanks, that's really useful.
Yes, I've heard that before.

- After *It's (well/not) worth* ... we use verb+*ing*: *That's well worth **seeing**.*

- After *Don't bother* ... we use verb+*ing*: *Don't bother **going** to the museums.*

- After *I'd/I wouldn't* ... we use the infinitive: *I'd **recommend** the trains.*

Language Summary 4

V4.1 Music collocations 4A ❶ p28

do/play a concert/a gig*
appear* on TV
release* a new album*/CD
go to a concert/a gig/a festival
have a hit single*
be/go on tour*
have an album/a CD in the charts*
see someone play live* /laɪv/
be/go onstage*

*a gig (informal) a concert (rock, pop, jazz, etc.): *I went to a brilliant gig last night.*

*appear be in a concert, film, TV programme, etc.: *The Rolling Stones have appeared on TV all over the world.*

*release make a CD, film, etc. available for the public to buy or see: *Their first album was released last week.*

*an album a collection of songs or pieces of music on a CD, record, etc.: *The Beatles' first album was called 'Please Please Me'.*

*a single a CD or record that has only one main song: *Have you heard U2's new single?*

*a hit single a single that is very successful and sells a lot of copies: *Madonna's first hit single was called 'Holiday'.*

*on tour when a band or singer is on tour, they travel from one city or country to another and play concerts in each place: *Prince is going on tour next year.*

*the charts official lists that show which singles and albums have sold the most copies each week: *REM have two singles in the charts.*

*play live /laɪv/ play in front of an audience: *Have you ever seen Van Halen play live?*

*be onstage be on a stage in a concert hall or a theatre: *What time are the band onstage?*

TIPS! • We can also use *tour* as a verb: *My favourite band are touring at the moment.*

• We can also use *live* to talk about TV programmes or sporting events that we can see at the same time as they are happening: *The World Cup final is shown live in over 160 countries.*

• We often use *a venue* /'venjuː/ to talk about a place where bands or singers play concerts: *There are lots of great venues in London.*

V4.2 Character adjectives 4B ❶ p30

Adventurous people like visiting new places and having new experiences.

Talented people have a natural ability to do something, like paint, write, play music, etc.

Sensible /'sensɪbəl/ people can make good decisions based on reasons and facts.

Sensitive people are able to understand other people's feelings and problems and help them in a way that does not upset them.

Brave people are not frightened in dangerous or difficult situations.

Determined /dɪ'tɜːmɪnd/ people want to do something very much and don't allow anything to stop them.

Reliable /rɪ'laɪəbəl/ people always do what you want or expect them to do.

Independent people don't want or need other people to do things for them.

Organised people plan things well and don't waste time.

Stubborn /'stʌbən/ people won't change their ideas or plans when other people want them to.

Ambitious /æm'bɪʃəs/ people want to be very successful or powerful.

Confident people are sure that they can do things successfully or well.

Practical people are good at planning things and dealing with problems.

Generous /'dʒenərəs/ people like giving money and presents to other people.

Mean people don't like spending money or giving things to other people.

Responsible /rɪ'spɒnsɪbəl/ people behave sensibly and can make good decisions on their own.

He's adventurous.   She's talented.   She's generous.   He's brave.

V4.3 Guessing meaning from context 4C ❸ p32

• Sometimes you can guess the meaning of a word by:
 a) deciding which part of speech it is (noun, verb, adjective, etc.).
 b) understanding the rest of the sentence and the story in general.
 c) recognising a similar word in your language, or another language you know.

1 **remedy** (noun) a medicine: *Another natural remedy is quinine.*
2 **battle** (noun) a fight: *Quinine is an important drug in the battle against malaria.*
3 **treat** (verb) give medical attention: *William Withering was unable to treat a patient.*
4 **leaves** (plural noun; singular: **leaf**) the green parts of a plant: *Pull off one of the leaves from an aloe vera plant.*
5 **heal** (verb) get better (for cuts, injuries, etc.): *This will help them heal quickly.*
6 **scar** (noun) a mark on your skin after a cut: *It might also stop you getting a scar.*
7 **remarkable** (adjective) very unusual: *Cleopatra used this remarkable plant.*

TIP! • Be careful of words/phrases that are 'false friends' in your language. For example, *sensible* in Spanish means *sensitive* (see V4.2) and *fast* in German means *almost*.

cure /kjʊə/ (verb) make someone feel better when they have an illness: *Peruvian Indians had used quinine for centuries to cure fevers.*

recovery (noun) when you feel better after an illness: *The patient made a complete recovery.*

beat (verb) when your heart beats, it makes regular movements and sounds: *It makes your heart beat more slowly.*

effective (adjective) works very well: *Many of the most effective natural remedies can be found in our gardens.*

pillow (noun) something you put your head on when you sleep: *Put some lavender oil on your pillow at night.*

sap (uncountable noun) the liquid inside plants and trees: *Put the sap on your burns or cuts.*

mixture /ˈmɪkstʃə/ (noun) a number of different things put together: *Try a mixture of garlic, lemon and honey.*

V4.4 Adjectives to describe behaviour

4D **2** p34

Violent people try to hurt or kill other people.

Arrogant people believe they are better or more important than other people.

Rude people aren't polite.

Loud people make a lot of noise.

Selfish people usually only think about themselves.

Aggressive people behave in an angry or violent way towards other people.

Stupid people are not very intelligent.

Hard-working people work very hard.

Loyal people always support their friends, etc.

Enthusiastic /ɪnˌθjuːziˈæstɪk/ people show a lot of interest and excitement about something.

Considerate people are very kind and helpful.

Spoilt people behave badly because other people always give them what they want or allow them to do what they want (often used for children).

Offensive people often upset or embarrass people by the things they say or how they behave.

Helpful people like helping other people.

Moody people are often unfriendly because they are angry and unhappy.

Bad-tempered people become annoyed or angry easily.

Well-behaved people behave in a quiet and polite way.

TIP! • *Well-behaved* is an adjective. The verb is *behave*: *Some people often don't behave very well at football matches.* The noun is *behaviour*: *That's not normal behaviour.*

Grammar

G4.1 Past Simple and Past Continuous 4A **4** p29

- We use the **Past Simple** for:

  a) a single completed action in the past: *In 2001 she **went** to Miami.*

  b) a repeated action or habit in the past: *He always **said** what size sofa he wanted.*

  c) a state in the past: *He **wanted** everything in his hotel room covered in clear plastic.*

- We use the **Past Continuous** for:

  a) a longer action in the past: *In 1998 they **were touring** in Europe and the USA for most of the year.*

  b) actions that were in progress when another (shorter) action happened: *While they **were having** their end-of-tour party, they threw the pies at each other.*

- Look at this sentence and the diagram: *While he was staying in New York, he asked for a kitchen in his hotel suite.*

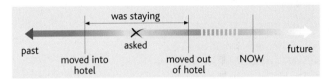

was staying = longer action (Past Continuous); *asked* = shorter action (Past Simple). Staying in the hotel started first and continued after he asked for the new kitchen.

TIPS! • We can also use the Past Continuous when the longer action is interrupted: *While we were having a picnic, it started to rain* (so we stopped having the picnic).

• We can also use the Past Continuous to talk about an activity in progress at a point of time in the past: *At four o'clock I was driving home.*

• We can use *when* or *while* with the Past Continuous: *He called me **when/while** I was waiting for the train.* We don't usually use *while* with the Past Simple: ~~*While he called me, I was waiting for a train.*~~

Past Simple

- We make the Past Simple **positive** of regular verbs by adding *-ed* or *-d* to the infinitive: *work → work**ed**, live → live**d***, etc. There are no rules for irregular verbs. There is an Irregular Verb List on p159.

  I **stayed** at home because I **didn't feel** well.

- We make the Past Simple **negative** with: subject + *didn't* + infinitive.

  He **didn't go** to work yesterday.

- We make Past Simple **questions** with: (question word) + *did* + subject + infinitive.

  What time **did** he **go** out?

Past Continuous

- We make the Past Continuous **positive** and **negative** with: subject + *was/were* + (*not*) + verb+*ing*.

  I/He/She/It **was/wasn't working** when you called.

- We make Past Continuous **questions** with: (question word) + *was/were* + subject + verb+*ing*

  What **were** you/we/they **doing** when he called?

Language Summary 4

G4.2 *used to*   4A ⑦ p29

- We can use *used to* or the Past Simple to talk about repeated actions or habits in the past: *They used to take their own furniture. He always said what size sofa he wanted.*

- We can't use *used to* to talk about one action in the past: *They once asked for twelve fruit pies.* not ~~They once used to ask for twelve fruit pies~~.

TIP! • We can only use *used to* to talk about the past. When we want to talk about habits or repeated actions in the present, we use *usually* + Present Simple: *I used to work at the weekend* (but I don't work at the weekend now). *I usually work at the weekend* (I work at the weekend now).

POSITIVE AND NEGATIVE

- We make positive and negative sentences with *used to* with:
  subject + *used to/didn't use to* + infinitive.

  He **used to be** famous.
  They **didn't use to go** on tour very often.

TIP! • *Used to* is the same for all subjects:
I/You/He/She/We/They used to live in Wales.

QUESTIONS

- We make questions with *used to* with:
  (question word) + *did* + subject + *use to* + infinitive.

  Where **did** you **use to live** when you were young?
  Did she **use to go** out a lot?

TIPS! • The short answers to *yes/no* questions with *used to* are:
Yes, I did./No, I didn't.; Yes, he did./No, he didn't., etc.
• In the negative we can use *didn't use to* or *never used to*:
I never used to go to gigs when I was young.

G4.3 **Past Perfect**   4B ④ p31

- When there is more than one action in the past, we often use the Past Perfect for the action that happened **first**.

second action (Past Simple)	first action (Past Perfect)
I **decided** to make the series	because I**'d seen** an article in the newspaper.
By the time she **got up** the next day,	the weather **had changed**.

- Compare these sentences:
  When I turned on the TV, the programme started. (First I turned on the TV, then the programme started almost immediately.)
  When I turned on the TV, the programme had started. (First the programme started, then I turned on the TV.)

TIPS! • If the order of past events is clear, we don't usually use the Past Perfect: *We had dinner, watched TV and then went to bed.*
• We don't always use the Past Perfect with *before* and *after* because the order of events is clear: *We (had) finished eating before Sally and Tony arrived. David went home after the meeting (had) finished.*

POSITIVE

- We make the Past Perfect **positive** with:
  subject + *had* or *'d* + past participle.

  The Titanic **had sunk** the day before she arrived in France.

TIP! • The Past Perfect is the same for all subjects:
I/You/He/She/It/We/They had already arrived when John got home.

NEGATIVE

- We make the Past Perfect **negative** with:
  subject + *hadn't* + past participle.

  I **hadn't heard** of any of the women before.

QUESTIONS

- We make Past Perfect **questions** with:
  (question word) + *had* + subject + past participle.

  What **had** he **done** before you met him?

TIPS! • The short answers to Past Perfect *yes/no* questions are:
Yes, I had./No, I hadn't., etc.
• We often use the Past Perfect after *realised, thought, forgot* and *remembered*: *I realised I'd only learnt about the men at school.*
• We often use *by the time, when, because, so, before, after* and *as soon as* to make sentences with the Past Perfect and Past Simple: *The party had finished by the time he arrived.*
• We use the same adverbs and time phrases with the Past Perfect as we do with the Present Perfect Simple: *Fiona had just heard the news.* For more information, see G3.1.

RW4.1 **Softening opinions and making generalisations** 4D ④ p34

- Sometimes English speakers soften the way they express their opinions so that they don't sound rude or offensive.

- We often use these phrases in **bold** to soften our opinions:
  Some of them can be **quite** rude **at times**.
  They **tend to** get **rather** loud.
  That's **not very** normal behaviour.
  Generally speaking, most people who go to matches are just loyal fans.
  You get a few who **can** be **a bit** too enthusiastic.
  On the whole, most fans just want to see a good game.

- After *tend to* we use **the infinitive**: *He tends to be a bit aggressive.*

- *Rather, quite, not very* and *a bit* usually come **before** an adjective: *They can get quite/rather/a bit noisy at times.*

- We often put *generally speaking* and *on the whole* at the **beginning** of a sentence: *Generally speaking/On the whole, most football fans aren't violent at all.*

- We often use '*not very* + positive adjective' to criticise someone or something politely: *They're not very intelligent.* (= They're stupid.) *He wasn't very polite.* (= He was rude.)

Vocabulary

V5.1 Homes 5A ❶ p36

TYPES OF HOME

a terraced /'terɪst/ house

a detached /dɪ'tætʃt/ house

a semi-detached house

a cottage /kɒtɪdʒ/

a three-storey house/building

a bungalow

LOCATION

with a nice view* in a good/bad/rough* neighbourhood*
in the country on the ground/first/top floor
in the suburbs* within walking distance of the shops

*a view the things you can see from a place (usually attractive): *The house had a lovely view of the mountains.*
*a suburb /'sʌbɜːb/ an area where people live outside the centre of a city: *They lived in a suburb of New York. People who live in the suburbs have to commute into the city.*
*rough /rʌf/ a rough area is a place where there is a lot of violence and crime: *We live in a very rough part of town.*
*neighbourhood a part of a town or city where people live: *They live in a very rich neighbourhood.*

TIPS! • In the UK *the suburbs* often have a lot of detached houses and are usually quite expensive places to live.
• We say *a three-storey building*, but we say that we live on *the first floor* not ~~the first storey~~.
• *the ground floor* [UK] = *the first floor* [US]; *the first floor* [UK] = *the second floor* [US], etc.

PARTS OF A HOME

a balcony

a loft

a garage

a study

a basement a room or area below ground level under a house or building where you can live or work: *The house also has a large basement.* Also: **a basement flat**: a flat below ground level.
a cellar /'selə/ a room under a house that is used for storing things: *We keep all our wine in the cellar.*
an en-suite /ɒn 'swiːt/ bathroom a bathroom that is directly connected to a bedroom: *All the rooms in the hotel have en-suite bathrooms.*
a fitted kitchen a kitchen where the cupboards, cooker, etc. fit exactly into the space: *Carol has spent a lot of money on her new fitted kitchen.*

V5.2 Phrasal verbs (2) 5B ❷ p38

clear sth out tidy a room, cupboard, etc. and get rid of the things in it that you don't want any more: *I'm going to clear out the garage this weekend.*

sort sth out arrange or organise things that are not in order or are untidy: *I need to sort out my English notes – I can't find anything!*

give sth away give something to someone without asking for money: *I didn't need my old TV so I gave it away.*

throw sth away or throw sth out put something in the rubbish bin that you don't want any more: *What should I do with this lamp? Throw it away/out, it's broken.*

take sth out remove something from a place: *Can you take the rubbish out for me, please?*

tidy (sth) up make a room or place tidy by putting things back in the place where you usually keep them: *I always tidy up before I go to bed.*

put sth away put something in the place where you usually keep it: *Jessie, don't leave your clothes on the floor – put them away.*

come back return to a place: *John's on holiday, but he's coming back tomorrow afternoon.*

go through sth carefully look at things to find something or to see if you want to keep them: *I went through everything in these boxes and threw away a lot of junk.*

Language Summary 5

Vocabulary

V5.3 **Verb patterns (1)** (5C **3** p41)

● When we use two verbs together, the form of the second verb usually depends on the first verb. This is called a verb pattern: *The company has **made people think** differently; the number of customers **keeps rising**; the table **wouldn't fit** in his car.*

keep don't mind begin enjoy finish prefer love hate continue like start	+ verb+*ing* (*doing*)
need seem try begin want prefer decide love hate continue like start would like plan forget learn	+ infinitive with *to* (*to do*)
would can would rather will must should could	+ infinitive (*do*)
pay ask tell help want would like allow teach	+ object + infinitive with *to* (*sb/sth to do*)
make help let	+ object + infinitive (*sb/sth do*)

TIPS! ● *Keep = continue.*

● *Let someone do something = allow someone to do something.*

● The verbs in blue in the table have more than one verb pattern. Both verb patterns have the same meaning: *I started **to write** an email. = I started **writing** an email.*

● In British English, *like/love/hate + verb+ing* is more common: *I like/love watching sport on TV.* In American English, *like/love + infinitive with to* is more common: *I like to watch sport on TV.*

V5.4 **Materials** (5D **1** p42)

Match materials 1–12 to things a)–l).

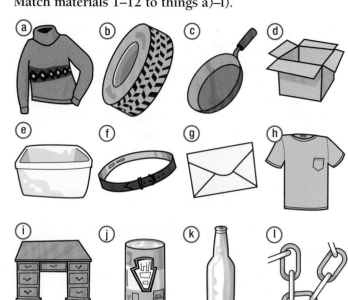

1	metal *c)*	5	steel	9	rubber
2	plastic	6	cardboard	10	glass
3	paper	7	wood	11	cotton
4	wool	8	tin	12	leather

Grammar

G5.1 **Making comparisons** (5A **5** p37)

COMPARATIVES AND SUPERLATIVES

● We use comparatives (*bigger, more expensive*, etc.) to compare two things.

● We use superlatives (*biggest, most expensive*, etc.) to compare three or more things.

1-syllable adjectives; 2-syllable adjectives ending in -y

adjective	comparative	superlative
old	old**er**	old**est**
small	small**er**	small**est**
nice	nic**er**	nic**est**
big	big**ger**	big**gest**
noisy	nois**ier**	nois**iest**

TIPS! ● When the adjective ends in -*e*, we only add -*r* or -*st*: *safe → safer, safest*.

● When the adjective ends in consonant + vowel + consonant, we double the final consonant: *thin → thinner, thinnest*.

● When a two-syllable adjective ends in -*y*, we change the -*y* to -*i* and add -*er* or -*est*: *funny → funnier, funniest*.

other 2-syllable adjectives; long adjectives

adjective	comparative	superlative
spacious	**more** spacious	**most** spacious
patient	**more** patient	**most** patient
amazing	**more** amazing	**most** amazing
expensive	**more** expensive	**most** expensive

● The adjectives *good, bad* and *far* are **irregular**: *good → better, best; bad → worse, worst; far → further/farther, furthest/ farthest.*

● The opposite of *more* is **less**: *It's a bit less expensive than the Monton house.* The opposite of *most* is **least**: *It's the least expensive place we've seen.*

● We use **much**, **far** or **a lot** before a comparative to say there's a **big** difference: *It was much/far/a lot noisier than the other two.*

● We use **slightly** /ˈslaɪtli/, **a little** or **a bit** before a comparative to say there's a **small** difference: *It seemed slightly/a little/a bit bigger than our house.*

TIPS! ● We use *the*, possessive *'s* or a possessive adjective before a superlative: *It had **the** most amazing view. He's **Peter's** best friend. This is **their** biggest room.* 'the + superlative' is the most common form.

● When we compare two things we use *than* after the comparative: *It's a bit less expensive **than** the Monton house.*

● We can also use *more* and *most* with nouns: *It's got **more rooms** than the last house. This house has got the **most space**.*

Grammar

OTHER WAYS TO MAKE COMPARISONS

- We can use **the same + (noun) + as** to say two people or things are the same: *It's the same size as ours.*

- We can also use **as + adjective + as** to say two people or things are the same: *It'll be as good as having a garden.*

- We can use **similar to + noun** to say two people or things are nearly the same: *And it's very similar to this house.*

- We can use **not as + adjective + as** to say two people or things are <u>not</u> the same: *It's not as big as the others.*

- We can also use **different from + noun** to say two people or things are <u>not</u> the same: *It was very different from anything else.*

TIP! • We can say *different from* or *different to*: *This flat is different from/to the one in Salford.*

G5.2 The future: *will, be going to,* Present Continuous   5B ❻ p39

- We use **will** when we decide to do something at the time of speaking: *OK, I'll throw those away.*

- We use **be going to** when we already have a plan or an intention to do something: *I'm going to sort out the rest of them at the weekend.*

- We use **the Present Continuous** when we have an arrangement with another person: *She's picking them up tomorrow evening after work.*

- We use **be going to** for a prediction that is based on present evidence (we predict the future because of something we can see in the present): *It's going to break the first time he uses it!*

- We use **will** for a prediction that is not based on present evidence: *But you'll never listen to them again.*

TIPS! • When we use the Present Continuous for future arrangements, we usually know exactly when the arrangements are happening. They are the kind of arrangements we can write in a diary: *I'm having dinner with Richard on Saturday.*
• We can also use *be going to* to talk about future arrangements: *What are you going to do tomorrow?*

will

POSITIVE AND NEGATIVE

- We make the **positive** and **negative** forms of *will* with: subject + 'll (= will)/won't (= will not) + infinitive.

  I'll do that for you.
  He **won't throw** that away.

TIP! • Will/won't is the same for all subjects: *I/you/he/she/it/we/they will/won't do it.*

QUESTIONS

- We make **questions** with *will* with: (question word) + *will* + subject + infinitive.

  When **will** it **be** here?
  Will it **rain** at the weekend?

TIPS! • We often use *probably* or *definitely* with *will*: *Her kids will probably/definitely like them.*
• We often use *might* to mean 'will possibly': *I might finish it this weekend.*
• We also use *will* to talk about future facts and for offers: *I'll be 45 next birthday. I'll help you clear out the study.*

be going to

POSITIVE AND NEGATIVE

- We make the **positive** and **negative** forms of *be going to* with: subject + *am/are/is* + (*not*) + *going to* + infinitive.

  I'm/I'm not going to throw that away.
  You/We/They**'re/aren't going to use** it again.
  He/She/It**'s/isn't going to sort** them out.

QUESTIONS

- We make **questions** with *be going to* with: question word + *am/are/is* + (*not*) + subject + *going to* + infinitive.

  When **am** I **going to see** you again?
  Aren't you/we/they **going to see** him?
  What**'s** he/she/it **going to do**?

TIPS! • With the verb *go*, we usually say *I'm going to the cinema.* not *I'm going to go to the cinema.* But both are correct.
• For how to make the positive, negative and question forms of the Present Continuous, see G2.2.

Real World

RW5.1 Explaining what you need   5D ❸ p42

saying you don't know the name of something

I'm sorry, I've forgotten what it's called.
I'm sorry, I don't know the word for it.
I can't remember what they're called.
I don't know what it's called in English.

describing what something is used for

It's a thing for (opening bottles of wine).
It's stuff for (getting marks off your clothes).
You use them to (put posters up on the wall).
I'm looking for (something for my mobile).
You use it when (the batteries are dead).

describing what something looks like

It's a type of (liquid).
They're made of (metal).
They've got (a round top).
It looks like (a black box).

checking something is the right thing

Do you mean one of these?
Oh, you mean (stain remover).
Is this what you're looking for?

- We often use *stuff* to talk about **uncountable** nouns we don't know the name of.

- After *It's a thing for …* and *It's stuff for …* we use **verb+ing**.

- After *You use it/them …* we use **the infinitive with** *to*.

Language Summary 6

Vocabulary

V6.1 *make* and *do* (6A ❶ p44)

make	do
a decision	the cleaning
a mistake	a course
money	homework
friends	nothing
a noise	exercise
dinner	the washing-up
an excuse*	the shopping
someone laugh/cry	some work
up your mind*	the washing
progress*	a degree
a cake	an exam
a mess of something*	the housework*
an appointment*	someone a favour*

*make an excuse give a reason to explain why you did something wrong (often used in the plural): *You need to stop making excuses and be more responsible.*

*make up your mind make a decision: *I can't make up my mind where to go on holiday.*

*make progress get closer to achieving or finishing something: *We haven't finished yet, but we're making good progress.*

*make a mess of something (informal) do something badly or make a lot of mistakes: *I really made a mess of that exam – I only got 23%.*

*make an appointment arrange a time and place to meet someone, particularly a doctor, dentist, etc.: *I've made an appointment to see the doctor.*

*do the housework do things like washing, cleaning, etc. in order to keep the house clean and tidy: *I can't stand doing the housework.*

*do someone a favour do something to help someone: *Could you do me a favour and help me with my homework?*

do the washing-up   do the washing

TIPS! • We often use *make* for 'food' words: *make breakfast, lunch, dinner, a cake, a sandwich*, etc.
• We often use *do* for 'study' words: *do homework, a degree, an exam*, etc.
• We usually use *do* for jobs connected to the house: *do the cleaning, the washing-up, the housework*, etc.
• *Do the washing-up* [UK] = *do the dishes* [US].

V6.2 Reflexive pronouns (6B ❽ p47)

• We use reflexive pronouns (*myself, yourself*, etc.) when the subject and object are the same people: ***They can't learn to look after themselves***.

• We use *by myself, yourself*, etc. to mean *alone*: *The dangers of letting your kids go out **by themselves** are smaller than you might think.*

• We also use reflexive pronouns to emphasise that we do something instead of someone else doing it for us: *Children need to make day-to-day decisions **themselves**.*

subject pronouns	reflexive pronouns	subject pronouns	reflexive pronouns
I	myself	it	itself
you (singular)	yourself	we	ourselves
he	himself	you (plural)	yourselves
she	herself	they	themselves

TIPS! • Some verbs that are reflexive in other languages aren't reflexive in English, for example *meet, relax* and *feel*.
• We can say *on my own, on your own*, etc. instead of *by myself, by yourself*, etc: *I enjoy living by myself/on my own.*
• Notice the difference between *themselves* and *each other*:

Nicky and Alice are looking at themselves.   Nicky and Alice are looking at each other.

V6.3 Synonyms (6C ❼ p49)

• We often use synonyms when we are speaking or writing so that we don't repeat words.

choose	pick	concerned	worried
satisfied	content	frightened	scared
lucky	fortunate	make a decision	make up your mind
behave	act	try to do	have a go at doing
notice	spot	talk to someone	chat to someone
by chance	accidentally	nice	pleasant
attitude	approach	enormous	huge
sure	certain	pleased	glad
deal with	cope with	wonderful	brilliant
show	reveal	terrible	awful

TIP! • Many synonyms in English have small differences in meaning or use. For example, *chat to someone* is more informal than *talk to someone*.

G6.1 First conditional 6A 5 p45

- Look at this first conditional. Notice the different clauses.

if clause (*if* + Present Simple)	main clause (*will/won't* + infinitive)
If I start teaching again,	I'll be exhausted after a year.

- The first conditional talks about the result of a possible event or situation in the **future**.

- The *if* clause talks about things that are **possible**, but not certain: *If I start teaching again, I'll be exhausted after a year* (maybe I will start teaching again). The main clause says what we think the result will be in this situation (I'm sure I will be exhausted after a year).

- We make the first conditional with:
  if + Present Simple, *will/won't* + infinitive.

- The *if* clause can be first or second in the sentence: *I'll be exhausted after a year if I start teaching again.*

- We often use *might* in the main clause to mean 'will perhaps': *But you might have to wait until next year if you don't apply soon.*

- We can use *unless* to mean 'if not' in the first conditional: *Unless I do it now, I'll be too old.* = *If I don't do it now, I'll be too old.*

G6.2 Future time clauses 6A 6 p45

- We can also use sentences with *before, as soon as, after, until* and *when* to talk about the **future**: *I'll give them a ring before they go on holiday.*

- In these sentences we use ***will/won't* + infinitive** in the main clause: *I'll believe it when I see it!*

- We use **the Present Simple** in the clauses beginning with *before, as soon as, after, until* and *when*: *I won't tell them until I decide what to do.*

TIP! • We use *when* to say we are certain that something will happen. Compare these sentences: *I'll tell Sally when I see her* (I'm certain I will see Sally). *I'll tell Sally if I see her* (maybe I will see Sally).

G6.3 Zero conditional; conditionals with modal verbs and imperatives; *in case* 6B 4 p47

ZERO CONDITIONAL

- The zero conditional talks about things that are **always true**: *If you have children, you worry about them all the time.*

- In the zero conditional both verbs are in **the Present Simple**: *If children stay indoors all the time, they become unfit.*

TIP! • *If* and *when* have the same meaning in the zero conditional: *If/When I'm worried, I don't sleep very well.*

ZERO OR FIRST CONDITIONAL

- Compare these sentences:
  If the children aren't home by five, I call the school.
  This sentence is a **zero conditional**. It talks about something that is always true.
  If the children aren't home by five, I'll call the school.
  This sentence is a **first conditional**. It talks about one specific time in the future.

CONDITIONALS WITH MODAL VERBS AND IMPERATIVES

- We can use modal verbs (*should, can*, etc.) in the main clause of conditionals: *If parents want their kids to grow up healthy, they **shouldn't** protect them so much. But if kids never go outside, they **can't** learn to look after themselves.*

- We can also use imperatives (*give, don't tell*, etc.) in the main clause of conditionals: *If you want happy and healthy kids, **give** them back their freedom. If you come home late, **don't wake** me up.*

- In these conditionals we use the Present Simple in the *if* clause: *If you **need** some help, call me.*

TIP! • We can use other modal verbs (*must, have to, might*, etc.) in these types of conditionals: *If you don't understand the instructions, you must tell me immediately.*

IN CASE

- We use *in case* to say that we are prepared for something that might happen: *Parents don't let their children go out on their own **in case** something bad happens to them. I'll take an umbrella **in case** it rains.*

- *In case* and *if* have different meanings. Compare these sentences:
  I'll buy some water in case I get thirsty.
  In this sentence the person is definitely going to buy some water, so that he/she is prepared for a time in the future when he/she might get thirsty.
  I'll buy some water if I get thirsty.
  In this sentence the person might buy some water, but only if he/she gets thirsty in the future.

Real World

RW6.1 Discussion language 6D 4 p50

inviting people to speak	asking to speak
(Paul), you had something you wanted to say. What's your opinion? What do you think?	Sorry, do you mind if I interrupt? Can I just say something here? Can I make a point here?
ways of agreeing	**allowing someone to interrupt**
That may be true, but what about … ? Yes, absolutely. Yes, I'd agree with that.	Sure, go ahead. Yes, of course.
ways of disagreeing	**not allowing someone to interrupt**
That's not true, actually. Well, I'm not sure about that. I'm not sure I agree, actually.	Can I just finish what I was saying? If I could just finish making this point.

Language Summary 7

V7.1 Computers (1) 7A ❶ p52

Match words 1–8 to the things in the picture a)–h).

1 a printer *d*
2 a mouse *h*
3 a monitor *a*
4 a scanner *c*
5 a keyboard *f*
6 a screen *b*
7 speakers *e*
8 a memory stick *g*

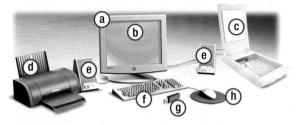

V7.2 Computers (2) 7A ❷ p52

delete remove something from a computer's memory: *I usually delete my emails after I've read them.*

a file any piece of information stored on computer: *I can't find the files I saved yesterday.*

create make something new: *How do you create a new document?*

a folder a place on a computer where you put documents, pictures, etc.: *I keep all my pictures in a separate folder.*

forward send an email, document, etc. to someone else's computer: *Could you forward me that email from the bank?*

reply (to sb/sth) answer: *Have you replied to Mrs Fisher's email?*

a back-up copy an extra copy of computer information: *Don't forget to make a back-up copy of all your work.*

log on to connect your computer to a system of computers, usually so you can start working: *I'll forward that email to you as soon as I've logged on.*

a password a secret word that allows you to use a computer: *Oh no! I've forgotten my password!*

click on press a button on the mouse in order to do something on a computer: *To go to the company's website, click on this link.*

an icon a small picture on the computer screen that you click on to make the computer do something: *This icon means 'print'.*

an attachment a document, picture, etc. that is sent with an email: *Did you read the attachment I sent you?*

a link a connection between documents or parts of the Internet: *Click on this link for more information.*

online connected to the Internet: *Are you online now?*

download to copy computer programmes, information, music, etc. into a computer's memory, especially from the Internet: *It's really easy to download music from the Internet.*

software computer programmes: *I've just downloaded some new software so that I can read Japanese websites.*

broadband [US: **ADSL**] a fast connection to the Internet that is always on: *The Internet is much faster if you have broadband.*

TIPS! • The opposite of *log on* is *log off*.

• We can say *the Net* or *the Web* instead of *the Internet*: *I found a cheap flight on the Net.*

V7.3 Electrical equipment 7B ❶ p54

Match words/phrases 1–12 with pictures a)–l).

1 a hand-held computer
2 a GPS/sat nav
3 a dishwasher
4 a washing machine
5 a hair dryer
6 hair straighteners
7 a webcam
8 a hands-free phone
9 an MP3 player
10 air conditioning
11 central heating
12 a DVD recorder

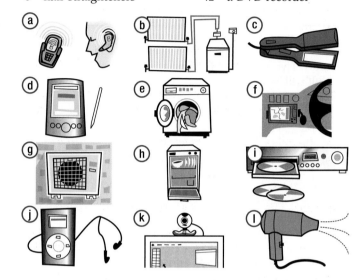

V7.4 Use of articles: *a, an, the,* no article 7C ❻ p57

● We use *a* or *an*:

a) when we don't know, or it isn't important, which one: *He was working for **a company** in New Jersey.*

b) with jobs: *He named the virus after **a dancer**.*

c) to talk about a person or thing for the first time: *As soon as it infected **a computer**, …*

● We use *the*:

d) to talk about the same person or thing for the second/third/fourth, etc. time: *… It forwarded itself to the first 50 email addresses in **the computer**'s address book.*

e) when there is only one (or only one in a particular place): *David L Smith created **the Melissa virus** in 1999.*

f) with countries that are groups of islands or states: *In **the USA**.*

g) with superlatives: *Melissa was **the worst** virus there had ever been.*

● We don't use an article:

h) for most towns, cities, countries and continents: *He was living in **Miami**, Florida.*

i) to talk about people or things in general: *It crashed **email systems** around the world.*

j) for some public places (*school, hospital, university, college, prison,* etc.) when we talk about what they are used for in general: *He was only sent to **prison** for 20 months.*

TIP! • We use *the* with public places when we talk about the building: *He's gone to **the hospital** to visit his mother.*

Grammar

G7.1 Ability · 7A ❹ p53

- We use these phrases to talk about things you can do now:
  manage to do sth: *I usually manage to find what I want.*
  be quite/very/really good at doing sth: *I'm quite good at doing this.*
  can do sth: *I can always find what I want.*
  find sth quite/very/really easy to do: *I find this quite easy to do.*
  know how to do sth: *I think I know how to do this.*
  be able to do sth: *I'm able to use most new stuff.*

- We use these phrases to talk about things you can't do now:
  be useless at doing sth: *I'm still useless at doing these things.*
  haven't/hasn't got a clue how to do sth: *I haven't got a clue how to do this.*
  have no idea how to do sth: *I have no idea how to do this.*
  find sth quite/very/really difficult to do: *I find it difficult to use anything new.*
  be no good at doing sth: *I'm no good at using new stuff.*

- We use these phrases to talk about ability in the past:
  was(n't)/were(n't) able to do sth: *I was able to learn this quickly.*
  could/couldn't do sth: *I couldn't do these things immediately.*

TIP! • We use *manage* to talk about something you are able to do, but is difficult: *I managed to download some new software, but it took me ages to find out how to do it.*

+ infinitive	+ infinitive with *to*	+ verb+*ing*
be able to could can	haven't got a clue how manage have no idea how find something easy/difficult know how	be useless at be quite/very/really good at

TIPS! • We can also say *be brilliant/great/excellent/not bad at* and *be hopeless/bad/terrible/awful/rubbish at*.

• We can also use a noun or a pronoun after *be good at, be useless at*, etc.: *Mark's really useless at **football**, but Chris is brilliant at **it**.*

• We can also use the other phrases to talk about ability in the past: *I **didn't have a clue** how to use it*, etc.

G7.2 Second conditional · 7B ❹ p54

- We use the second conditional to talk about **imaginary** situations. We often use it to talk about the opposite of what is true or real: *If my car had a GPS, life would be so much easier* (but my car doesn't have a GPS).

- The second conditional talks about **the present or the future**.

- The *if* clause **can be first or second** in the sentence.

- Compare these sentences:
  If I have enough money, I'll get one for my car.
  It's a real possibility because the person might have enough money (first conditional, see G6.1).
  If I had enough money, I'd get one for my car.
  It's an imaginary situation because the person doesn't have enough money (second conditional).

POSITIVE AND NEGATIVE

- We make the second conditional with:
  if + subject + Past Simple, subject + *'d* (= *would*)/*wouldn't* + infinitive.

  *If my car **had** one, life **would be** so much easier.*
  *If we **didn't have** it at home, I **wouldn't get** any sleep at all.*

TIPS! • We can say *If I/he/she/it was …* or *If I/he/she/it were …* in the second conditional: *If I was/were rich, I'd buy a big house.*

• We can use *could* + infinitive in the main clause of the second conditional to talk about ability: *If I had a lot of money, I could buy a new car* (= *I would be able to buy a new car*).

• We can also use *might* + infinitive in the main clause of the second conditional to mean 'would perhaps': *If I bought a GPS, I might not get lost all the time.*

QUESTIONS

- We often make questions in the second conditional with *What would you do … ?* This phrase can come at the beginning or the end of the sentence: *What would you do if you didn't have one? If you didn't have one, what would you do?*

- We can also make *yes/no* questions in the second conditional: *If you didn't have one, would you get lost?*

- The short answers to these *yes/no* questions are: *Yes, I would.* and *No, I wouldn't.* We can also say *Yes, I might.*

Real World

RW7.1 Indirect and direct questions · 7D ❸ p58

- In more formal situations we often use **indirect** questions because they sound more polite: *Could you tell me whether he'll be back soon?* sounds more polite than *Will he be back soon?*

indirect question phrase	question word or *if/whether*	main clause (positive verb form)
Could you tell me	whether	he'll be back soon?
Do you know	if	we asked Alex Ross to come?
Have you any idea	where	he's gone?
Can you tell me	what	his number is?

- We use *if* or *whether* in indirect questions when there **isn't** a question word.

- In indirect questions, *if* and *whether* are **the same**: *Do you know if/whether we asked Alex Ross to come?*

- We don't use *if* or *whether* with *Do you think … ?*: *Do you think he's changed his password?* not *Do you think if/whether he's changed his password?*

- In indirect questions, the main verb is in the **positive** form. We say: *Do you know if **we asked** Alex Ross to come?* not *Do you know if **did we ask** Alex Ross to come?*

Language Summary 8

Vocabulary

V8.1 Weather 8A ❶ p60

a storm very bad weather with lots of rain, snow, wind, etc.: *There was a terrible storm last night.*

thunder the loud noise that comes from the sky during a storm: *The thunder last night woke me up.* Also: **a thunderstorm.**

lightning a bright light in the sky caused by electricity during a storm, usually followed by thunder: *He was hit by lightning and was taken to hospital.*

a gale a very strong wind: *There will be gales in northern parts of England tonight.*

a shower a short period of rain: *It's just a shower. It'll stop soon.*

a hurricane (or **a typhoon** /ˌtaɪˈfuːn/) a violent storm with very strong winds: *Our house was damaged by a hurricane.*

fog thick cloud just above the ground or sea that makes it difficult to see: *There's often a lot of fog early in the morning.*

humid /ˈhjuːmɪd/ when the air is hot and wet: *It gets very humid in the summer.*

a heat wave a period of unusually hot weather that continues for a long time: *We had a heat wave for two weeks last summer.*

a flood /flʌd/ when a lot of water covers an area that is usually dry, especially when it rains a lot or a river becomes too full: *There are floods in many parts of India.*

a tornado [US: **a twister**] an extremely strong and dangerous wind that blows in a circle and destroys buildings: *There are often tornados in the Caribbean in the summer.*

freezing   cold/chilly   cool   warm   hot   boiling

TIPS! • The adjective for *storm* is *stormy*: *It was a very stormy night.*
• We say *thunder and lightning* not ~~lightning and thunder~~.
• The adjective for *fog* is *foggy*: *It's very foggy outside.*
• *Humid* is an adjective. The noun is *humidity*: *I can't stand the humidity here.*
• *Flood* is a noun and a verb: *The whole village was flooded.*

V8.2 Containers 8B ❶ p62

a bottle   a bag   a tin   a box

a can   a carton   a jar   a packet

COMMON COLLOCATIONS

a bottle of milk, beer, tomato ketchup, olive oil, lemonade, apple juice

a bag of sweets, potatoes, crisps [US: chips]

a tin of tuna, biscuits, cat food, soup, beans

a box of chocolates, tissues

a can of beer, lemonade

a carton of milk, orange juice, soup, apple juice

a jar of honey, jam, marmalade

a packet of biscuits, sweets, soup, tissues, beans, crisps, butter

TIPS! • We usually use *a tin* for food (*a tin of tomatoes*) and *a can* for drink (*a can of cola*).
• *Marmalade* is made from citrus fruit (oranges, etc.). *Jam* is made from soft fruit (strawberries, etc.).

V8.3 Word formation (2): prefixes and opposites 8C ❻ p65

● We often use the prefixes *un-*, *dis-*, *im-*, *in-* and *ir-* to make opposites of words.

prefix	examples
un-	unconscious, unusual, uncommon, unbelievable, unselfish, unreliable, unambitious, unhelpful
dis-	disappear, dishonest, disorganised, disloyal, dissimilar
im-	impossible, impatient, impolite, immature
in-	incorrect, inconsiderate, informal, insensitive
ir-	irresponsible, irregular

TIPS! • We can use these prefixes to make opposites of adjectives and verbs: *unconscious*, *dishonest* (adjectives); *undo*, *disappear* (verbs).
• Adjectives beginning with *p* usually take the prefix *im-*: *patient* → *impatient*.
• Adjectives beginning with *r* usually take the prefix *ir-*: *responsible* → *irresponsible*.

V8.4 Word formation (2): other prefixes and suffixes 8C ❼ p65

● We often use other prefixes and suffixes to change the meaning of words.

prefix/suffix	meaning	examples
under-	not enough	underestimate, underpaid, undercharge, underuse
re-	do something again	reattach, repaid, rewrite, recharge, remarry, replay, reuse
over-	too much	over-optimistic, overpaid, oversleep, overcharge, overuse
-ful	with	hopeful, painful, careful, successful, playful, useful
-less	without	harmless, painless, sleepless, careless, useless

TIP! • The opposite of *successful* is *unsuccessful*.

Grammar

G8.1 The passive (8A ⑤ p61)

	subject	verb	object
active	A huge hurricane	**hit**	New Orleans.

	subject	verb	*by + agent*
passive	New Orleans	**was hit**	by a huge hurricane.

- The object of the active sentence becomes the **subject** of the passive sentence.
- We often use the **passive** when we are more interested in what happened to someone or something than in who or what did the action.
- In passive sentences we can use '*by* + the agent' to say who or what does the action: *More and more places are going to be affected by climate change in the future.*
- We make the passive with: subject + *be* + past participle.

verb form	*be*	past participle
Present Simple	am/are/is	held
Present Continuous	am/are/is being	kept
Present Perfect Simple	have/has been	caused
Past Simple	was/were	hit
be going to	am/are/is going to be	affected
will	will be	flooded
can	can be	found

- We make negative passive sentences by making the verb form of *be* negative: *it **isn't** held, they **aren't** being kept, it **hasn't been** caused, it **wasn't** hit*, etc.

TIPS! • We can use other modal verbs (*could, must, should, might*, etc.) in passive verb forms: *Many people could be made homeless.*
• We only use '*by* + the agent' when it is important or unusual information. We don't use it when it is clear from the context: *Twelve people were arrested by the police.*

G8.2 Quantifiers (8B ⑤ p63)

quantity	plural countable nouns (*bottles, tins*, etc.)	uncountable nouns (*rubbish, stuff*, etc.)
nothing	not any no	not any no
a small quantity	not many hardly any several a few	not much a bit of hardly any a little
a large quantity	a lot of/lots of loads of plenty of	a lot of/lots of loads of plenty of
more than we want	too much	too many
less than we want	not enough	not enough
the correct quantity	enough	enough

TIP! • *Not many, hardly any* and *not much* have a negative meaning. *Several, a few, a bit of* and *a little* have a positive meaning. *Several* is usually more than *a few*.

SOME, ANY, MUCH, MANY

- We usually use *some* in positive sentences: *I've found some coffee.*
- We usually use *any* in negative sentences and questions: *There isn't any sugar. Is there any milk?*
- We don't usually use *much* or *many* in positive sentences: *There's a lot of stuff here.* not ~~There's much stuff here.~~ *I've got lots of cups.* not ~~I've got many cups.~~

TIPS! • We use *some* and *any* with plural countable nouns (*biscuits, beans*, etc.) and uncountable nouns (*pasta, milk*, etc.).
• We often use *some* in questions with *Would you like … ?*: *Would you like some coffee?*

Real World

RW8.1 Warnings and advice (8D ③ p66)

- We give warnings when we think something might be dangerous.

asking for advice

Could you give us some advice?
What should we do if we see one?
What do you think we should take with us?
Do you think it's a good idea to take some warm clothes?

giving advice

If I were you, I'd take plenty of warm clothes.
It's a good idea to take a spare map **in case** you lose one.
Don't forget to tell them when you expect to be back.
Make sure you take plenty of water.
You'd better come up immediately.

giving warnings

Watch out for bears.
Be careful when you're crossing rivers.
Whatever you do, don't lose your partner.
Don't come up too quickly, **or else** you could be in trouble.

responding to advice/warnings

Yes, we will.
That's a good idea. I hadn't thought of that.
That's really useful, thanks.
Right, thanks. That's very helpful.

- After *If I were you, I'd …* and *You'd better …* we use the **infinitive**: *If I were you, I'd **take** plenty of warm clothes. You'd better **come up** immediately.*
- After *It's a good idea …* and *Don't forget …* we use the **infinitive with to**: *It's a good idea **to take** a spare map. Don't forget **to tell** them when you expect to be back.*
- After *Whatever you do …* we use the **imperative** (usually the negative imperative): *Whatever you do, **don't lose** your partner.*

TIPS! • After *Be careful* we can also use *of* + noun: *Be careful of pickpockets.*
• *You'd better = You had better.*

Language Summary 9

Vocabulary

V9.1 Health (9A 6 7 p69)

A **surgeon** /'sɜːdʒən/ is a doctor who does operations.
An **operating theatre** is the place where you have an operation.
Asthma /'æsmə/ is an illness which makes it difficult for you to breathe.
A **specialist** is a doctor who knows a lot about one area of medicine.
The **A&E department** is the part of a hospital where you go if you have an emergency
An **allergy** /'ælədʒi/ is a medical problem that some people get when they eat, breathe or touch certain things.
A **migraine** is an extremely painful headache *that/which* can also make you feel sick.
A **ward** is a big room with beds in a hospital *where* patients receive medical treatment.
A **surgery** /'sɜːdʒəri/ is a building or an office *where* you can go and ask a GP or a dentist for medical advice.
A **GP** is a doctor *who/that* gives medical treatment to people *who/that* live in a particular area.
A **prescription** is a piece of paper *that/which* the doctor gives you so that you can get the medicine you need.
An **infection** is a disease in part of your body *that/which* is caused by bacteria or a virus.

TIPS! • We can also say that we are *allergic* /ə'lɜːdʒɪk/ *to* something: *My sister is allergic to eggs.*
• *A GP = a general practitioner.*

V9.2 News collocations (9B 2 p70)

accept/reject* an offer
discover something new
carry out* a survey
suffer from* an illness
take someone to hospital

take part* in a demonstration*
publish results/a report
protest against something*
meet a target*
call off* a strike*

*reject not accept: *The workers rejected the pay offer.*
*carry out do something that someone told you to do, or you agreed to do: *They carried out a survey on childhood asthma.*
*suffer (from sth) to have an illness or other health problem that gives you pain: *Ben suffers from migraines.*
*take part (in sth) be involved in something with other people: *Leaders from six countries took part in today's meeting.*
*a demonstration when a group of people stand or walk somewhere to show that they disagree with or support something: *30,000 people took part in today's demonstration.*
*protest (against sth) say or show that you disagree with something: *A large crowd were protesting against the war.*
*a target something you want to achieve: *The company met its sales target for the year.*
*call sth off cancel something that was planned: *The match was called off because of bad weather.*
*a strike a period of time when people don't go to work because they want more money, better working conditions, etc.: *The postal workers' strike is now in its fifth day.*

V9.3 Connecting words: *although, even though, despite, in spite of, however* (9C 7 p73)

● We often use connecting words to join two clauses.

connecting word	first clause	second clause
Although	Frank was rich,	he was lonely and unhappy.

● *Although* /ɔːl'ðəʊ/, *even though* /ðəʊ/, *despite*, *in spite of* and *however* are similar in meaning to **but**.
● We use *although, even though, despite* and *in spite of* to contrast **two clauses in the same sentence**: *Although/Even though he was rich, Frank was lonely and unhappy. He became a sociology lecturer, despite/in spite of having no teaching qualifications at all.*
● We use *however* to contrast **two sentences**: *He was arrested once in Miami, but was released soon afterwards. However, this lucky escape made him realise he needed a change.*
● After **despite** and **in spite of** we usually use a noun or verb+ing: *In spite of/Despite **his age**, people believed he was a pilot. In spite of/Despite **being** so young, people believed he was a pilot.*
● After **although** and **even though** we usually use a clause: *He moved to Atlanta and got a job as a doctor, although/even though **he didn't have any medical training**.*

TIPS! • *Even though* is usually stronger than *although*.
• We can put *although, even though, despite* and *in spite of* at the beginning or in the middle of a sentence. We usually put *however* at the beginning of a sentence.

V9.4 Health problems, symptoms and treatment
(9D 1 p74)

a runny nose when your nose produces liquid all the time, usually when you have a cold.
a rash a group of small red spots on the skin, often caused by allergies.
wheezy when you breathe noisily and with difficulty, particularly when you have asthma or an allergy.
hay fever an illness with symptoms similar to a cold that is caused by flowers or grass in the spring and summer.
diarrhoea /ˌdaɪə'rɪə/ when you have to go to the toilet all the time.
sneeze when you blow air down through your nose suddenly, for example when you have a cold.
a virus /'vaɪərəs/ a very small living thing which can cause illnesses, disease and infections.
penicillin /ˌpenɪ'sɪlɪn/ a type of antibiotic.
throw up (informal) be sick, vomit.
food poisoning when you eat some food that is bad and makes you ill.
paracetamol /ˌpærə'siːtəmɒl/ a type of painkiller.
a blocked-up nose when you can't breathe through your nose.

Vocabulary

health problems	asthma an allergy hay fever flu a migraine a virus food poisoning an infection
symptoms	a runny nose a rash wheezy be sick diarrhoea a sore throat sneeze a temperature throw up a stomach ache a blocked-up nose
treatment	antibiotics painkillers pills penicillin paracetamol

Grammar

G9.1 **Relative clauses with *who, that, which, whose, where* and *when*** (9A 4 p69)

- We often use relative clauses to say which person, thing, place, etc. we are talking about.

- In relative clauses we use:

  a) *who* or *that* for people: *The person who I was sharing with … . I'm the type of person that eats three meals a day.*

  b) *that* or *which* for things: *The food that we usually eat contains toxins which stay in our bodies.*

  c) *where* for places: *I was taken to the guest house where everyone was staying.*

  d) *whose* for possessives: *The woman whose fasting programme we were following … .*

  e) *when* for times: *This was also when I started getting really hungry.*

TIPS! • We usually use *who* for people (*that* is also correct).
• We usually use *that* for things (*which* is also correct).
• We don't use *what* in relative clauses: ~~The food what we usually eat …~~ . We can use *what* to mean 'the thing/things that': *Now I'm much more careful about what I eat.* (= the things that I eat).

LEAVING OUT *WHO, THAT, WHICH*

- We can leave out *who, that* or *which* when it isn't the subject of the relative clause.

- Compare the relative clauses in these sentences:

  A   I'm the type of person <u>that eats three meals a day</u>.

  In this sentence we must use *that* because it is the subject of the relative clause.

  B   The food <u>(that) we usually eat</u> contains toxins.

  In this sentence we can leave out *that* because it is the object of the relative clause (*we* is the subject).

TIPS! • We never leave out *whose* in relative clauses.
• We can usually leave out *where* if we add a preposition at the end of the relative clause: *That's the café **where** I met my wife.* → *That's the café I met my wife **in**.*
• We can only leave out *when* if the time reference is clear: *Monday's the day (when) I play tennis.*

G9.2 **Present Perfect Simple active and passive for recent events** (9B 4 p70)

- We use the **Present Perfect Simple** for giving news about things that happened in the past, but which are connected to now. We **don't say** exactly when these things happened: *The government has also carried out a survey on the causes of allergies.*

- We make the **Present Perfect Simple active** with: subject + 've (= have)/haven't or 's (= has)/hasn't + past participle.

  The health service **has failed** to meet its targets.
  We **haven't met** our targets yet.

- We make the **Present Perfect Simple passive** with: subject + 've (= have)/haven't or 's (= has)/hasn't + *been* + past participle.

  A new report on allergies **has** just **been published**.
  That survey still **hasn't been published**.

- We often use passive verb forms in news reports and newspaper articles.

- When we say the exact time something happened, we must use the Past Simple active or passive: *She **was taken** to hospital **two days ago**.*

TIPS! • For information about how to use *just, yet* and *already,* see G3.1.
• We only use *still* in negative sentences with the Present Perfect Simple active and passive: *That survey still hasn't been published.* not ~~That survey still has been published~~. We put *still* before the auxiliary.

Real World

RW9.1 **At the doctor's** (9D 4 p74)

I'm not feeling very well.
I haven't been feeling very well recently.
I've got a terrible stomach ache.
My chest hurts.
I keep getting really bad headaches.
I can't stop sneezing.
Do I need some antibiotics?
I'm allergic to penicillin.
How often should I take them?
Do I need to make another appointment?

Now, what seems to be the problem?

I've got a terrible stomach ache.

- We use *I keep …* and *I can't stop …* for things that happen lots of times. We don't want these things to happen: *I keep waking up at night.*

- After *I keep …* and *I can't stop …* we use verb+*ing*: *I can't stop **coughing**.*

Language Summary 10

V10.1 Contacting people (10A ❶ p76)

get hold of sb contact somebody, often with difficulty: *Did you manage to get hold of Mrs Edwards?*

let sb know sth tell somebody some information: *Let me know when you get there.*

be in touch with sb communicate regularly with somebody by phone, email, letter, etc.: *Are you still in touch with any of your old school friends?*

lose touch with sb not be in touch with somebody any more, usually because they have moved house, changed job, etc.: *I lost touch with Tim after he moved to Australia.*

keep in touch with sb or **stay in touch with sb** not lose touch with somebody: *I hope we keep in touch while you're in the USA.*

get in touch with sb contact somebody by writing, emailing or phoning them: *I'm trying to get in touch with somebody from the office.*

TIPS! • We can say *be/keep/lose/get in touch with somebody* or *be/keep/lose/get in contact with somebody*: *I'm still in touch/contact with my old boss.*

• We can also say *get back in touch with somebody*, which means 'communicate with somebody again after a long time'.

V10.2 Describing people (10B ❶ p78)

APPEARANCE

dyed hair   shoulder-   straight hair   curly hair   wavy hair
             length hair

her hair up   a ponytail   going bald   a dark blue   a light blue
                             /bɔːld/   jacket   jacket

a striped tie   a flowery   a plain shirt   glasses   jewellery
                 dress

AGE

• We often use *in his/her teens/early twenties/mid-thirties/late forties*, etc. to talk about someone's approximate age.

TIP! • We use *The person/man/woman/one with* … + (red) hair, glasses, a beard, etc., but *The person/man/woman/one in* … + clothes: *She's the woman with long wavy hair and glasses. He's the one in a blue suit.*

V10.3 Phrasal verbs (3): meanings (10C ❷ p80)

get out of sth avoid doing something you don't want to do: *I tried to get out of the whole thing.*

get over sth feel better after you have been unhappy or ill: *Olivia got over her last three divorces quite quickly.*

go up increase or rise: *The number of divorces in the UK is still going up.*

look sth up find some information in a book or on a computer: *I looked some figures up.*

point sth out tell someone some information you think that they don't know or have forgotten: *I didn't like to point this out to her.*

put sth off decide or arrange to do something at a later time: *She should put the wedding off.*

fall out (with sb) argue with somebody and stop being friendly with them: *You two have never fallen out.*

come up with sth think of an idea or a solution to a problem: *I couldn't come up with a good enough excuse.*

split up (with sb) end a marriage or relationship: *I wondered how long it would be before Olivia and Tony split up.*

come across sth find something by accident: *I came across a newspaper report.*

V10.4 Phrasal verbs (3): grammar (10C ❸ p81)

• Phrasal verbs have two or three words: *wake up, look after, get on with*, etc. Look at the differences between the four types of phrasal verbs.

TYPE 1 phrasal verbs don't have an object (*fall out, split up, go up*, etc.):
You two have never fallen out.

TYPE 2 phrasal verbs always have an object (*get over sth, come across sth*, etc.). The object is always after the phrasal verb:
Olivia got over her divorces quickly.
Olivia got over them quickly.

TYPE 3 phrasal verbs always have an object (*look sth up, put sth off, point sth out*, etc.). If the object is a noun, you can put it in the middle or after the phrasal verb:
I looked some figures up.
I looked up some figures.
If the object is a pronoun, you must put it in the middle of the phrasal verb:
I looked them up. not *I looked up them.*

TYPE 4 phrasal verbs have three words and always have an object (*get out of sth, come up with sth*, etc.). The object is always after the phrasal verb:
I tried to get out of the whole thing.
I tried to get out of it.

TIP! • We can sometimes add a preposition to some type 1 phrasal verbs to make them type 4 phrasal verbs:
I've never fallen out with my brother.
Georgina has just split up with her boyfriend.

Grammar

G10.1 *was/were going to, was/were supposed to* `10A` ❻ p77

- We use *was/were going to* to talk about plans we made in the past which didn't happen, or won't happen in the future. Look at these sentences.
  *We **were going to** visit the Bradleys later that year, but we didn't go for some reason.*
  (They planned to visit the Bradleys, but they didn't visit them.)
  *We **were going to** spend our anniversary in the cottage in Wales where we had our honeymoon, but it was already booked.*
  (They planned to spend their anniversary in the cottage in Wales, but now they aren't going to go there.)

- We use *was/were supposed to* to talk about things we agreed to do, or other people expected us to do, but we didn't do. Look at these sentences.
  *Tom **was supposed to** book the cottage months ago, but he forgot.*
  (Tom agreed to book the cottage, but he didn't book it.)
  *I **was supposed to** call you back, wasn't I? Sorry, Leo, I was out all day.* (Leo expected his mother to call him back, but she didn't.)

- After *was/were going to* and *was/were supposed to* we use the infinitive: *It was going to **be** a surprise party. I was supposed to **call** you back.*

TIP! • We often use *was/were going to* or *was/were supposed to* to apologise for not doing something. We usually give a reason: *Sorry, I was going to call you back last night, but I didn't get home until late.*

G10.2 Modal verbs (2): making deductions
 `10B` ❸ p79

- We often use the modal verbs *must, might, could, may* and *can't* to make deductions in the present.

- We use *must* to talk about something that we believe is true: *He must be talking to some guests in the other room. He must know that speech by now.*

- We use *could, may* or *might* to talk about something that we think is possibly true: *He might be in the bathroom. He could be picking people up from the station. It could be the guy that moved to New York. He may want to be on his own for a bit.*

- We use *can't* to talk about something that we believe isn't true: *That can't be her real hair colour. He can't be having a cigarette.*

- When we know something is definitely true, or is definitely not true, we don't use a modal verb: *He's practising his speech in front of the mirror. No, that isn't Derek Bradley.*

- To make deductions about **states** we use: modal verb + infinitive: *He must know that speech by now.*

- To make deductions about **something happening now** we use: modal verb + *be* + verb+*ing*: *He must be talking to some guests in the other room.*

TIP! • We don't use *can* or *mustn't* to make deductions: *It could be him.* not *It can be him. He can't be a millionaire.* not *He mustn't be a millionaire.*

Real World

RW10.1 Asking for, giving and refusing permission
`10D` ❹ p82

ASKING FOR PERMISSION

- We use the phrases in **bold** to ask for permission to do something:
  Do you think I could (send a few emails)?
  Is it OK if I (borrow a couple of books)?
  May I (download some photos onto your computer)?
  Would you mind if I (gave my girlfriend a call)?
  Can I (make myself a sandwich)?
  Do you mind if I (do some washing)?

- After *Do you think I could … ?, May I … ?* and *Can I … ?* we use the infinitive: *Do you think I could **use** your computer for a few minutes?*

- After *Is it OK if I … ?* and *Do you mind if I … ?* we use the Present Simple: *Is it OK if I **borrow** your bike? Do you mind if I **watch** TV?*

- After *Would you mind if I … ?* we use the Past Simple: *Would you mind if I **watched** TV?*

GIVING PERMISSION

- We usually give permission by saying: *Yes, of course (you can/it is, etc.); Sure, go ahead.; Help yourself.,* etc.

- *Do you mind if I … ?* and *Would you mind if I … ?* mean 'Is it a problem if I do this?'. To give permission for these phrases, we usually say: *No, not at all* (= It's not a problem for me if you do this). Compare these conversations.
  A Can I make myself a sandwich?
  B Yes, of course.
  A Do you mind if I make myself a sandwich?
  B No, not at all.

REFUSING PERMISSION

- We don't usually say *no* to refuse permission because it isn't polite.

- Instead of saying *no*, we usually give a reason to say why we refuse permission: *Sorry, I don't think we have the software for that.*

- When we refuse permission, we often use *Sorry, …* or *Actually, …* at the beginning of the sentence to be polite.

TIPS! • We can also ask permission for other people to do things: *Can John stay the night? Is it OK if Tania uses your computer?*
• *Would you mind if I … ?* is a very polite way to ask for permission.
• We can also use *Could I … ?* or *Is it all right if I … ?* to ask for permission: *Could I borrow your pen? Is it all right if I use your phone?*

My Notes

My Notes

My Notes

Answer Key

4B ❷ b) p30

Who were the first people to ...	fly a plane across the English Channel?	reach both the North and South Poles?	travel in space?
men	Louis Bleriot	Sir Ranulph Fiennes and Charles Burton	Yuri Gagarin
dates	1909	1979 and 1982	1961
women	Harriet Quimby	Ann Daniels and Caroline Hamilton	Valentina Tereshkova
dates	1912	2000 and 2002	1963

6C ❾ p108

HOW LUCKY ARE YOU?

16–18 points:
You're very positive about life and probably think that you're already a very lucky person. When things go badly, you don't worry too much because you know something good is going to happen soon. Why don't you do the lottery next weekend – you might win!

13–15 points:
You're quite a lucky person and tend to look on the bright side of life. You know lots of people and have a very busy social life. Try to do something new every month and make sure you have some time to yourself as well.

9–12 points:
You think you're lucky in some parts of your life, but not in others, and maybe you worry about the past and the future too much. Try to enjoy the present a little more and listen to your heart when you make decisions, not just your head.

6–8 points:
You're not very lucky at the moment and probably expect things to get worse, not better. Why not try to meet some new people and take a few more chances in life? What's the worst that could happen?

7A ❸ c) p52

1 a) 0 points	b) 1 point	c) 2 points
2 a) 2 points	b) 0 points	c) 1 point
3 a) 0 points	b) 1 point	c) 2 points
4 a) 0 points	b) 2 points	c) 1 point
5 a) 2 points	b) 1 point	c) 0 points

9–10 points:
You're very computer literate and you probably spend quite a lot of your free time in front of a computer screen in the evenings. Maybe you should turn your computer off and go out with your friends a bit more often!

5–8 points:
You know how to use a computer and you probably have to use one at work or for your studies. You've learned what you need to know, but that's all. Maybe you should try and learn one or new things that you can do with your computer.

0–4 points:
Obviously computers aren't very important to you. You can probably manage to turn it on and check your email, but not much else! Maybe you should think about doing a course so that you can improve your computer skills.

10B ❾ b) p79

baseball cap: Nick Bradley
wedding photos: Peggy
glasses case: Brenda Bradley
speech: Tom
earrings: Jane Lewis
wedding ring: Sheila Jones

football key ring: Leo
driving test book: Karen
London book: Brenda Bradley
wallet: Derek Bradley
watch: Trevor Jones

Recording Scripts

R1.1

SARAH What makes me happy? Well, I love watching my children when they're sleeping. That makes me feel very happy and peaceful. My days are usually extremely busy – I work for my father's travel company until 3 and pick up the kids from school on the way home. At the moment they're in the other room watching TV so I've got a bit of time to myself. Um, so what else makes me happy? Well, ooh – I really enjoy going to museums and art galleries. Last Saturday I went to an exhibition with a friend from work – oh, it was just wonderful.

GREG Well, I really love travelling and visiting new places, that makes me really happy. I've been to about 20 countries so far, and I've enjoyed visiting every one of them, they're all so different. Um, last year I spent 6 weeks travelling around South America, which was amazing, a different world really. When I'm here in the UK, er, well I really like gardening, that makes me happy too. I only have a small garden, but I spend a few hours working in it every weekend. I love watching things grow, it's very satisfying.

JENNY What makes me happy? Well, having a lie-in makes me *really* happy! I have to get up at 6.30 every morning for work, including Saturdays, so Sunday lie-ins are very important to me. Last Sunday I woke up at about 11, then I made some toast and coffee, got the papers and went back to bed – and I didn't get up until half past one. It was wonderful! But my flatmate is the complete opposite to me. She's happiest when she's doing some exercise – on Sundays she usually gets up early and goes out for a run. Um, what else? Well, dancing makes me happy – I don't go clubbing very often, but when I do I always have a fantastic time.

R1.2

Whereabouts do you /dʒə/ live? | How long have you /həvjə/ lived there? | Who do you /dʒə/ live with? | Who gets up first in your home? | Why are you /əjə/ studying English? | Who told you about this school? | Did you /dɪdʒə/ study here last year? | How many countries have you /həvjə/ been to in your life? | Which of your friends lives closest to you? | What did you /dɪdʒə/ do last New Year?

R1.4

I don't often call my sister. | No one in my family has a mobile. | Miranda hasn't sent me a text. | I don't think I'll buy a new phone. | There's no message for you. | None of my friends have got mobiles. | Neither of my sisters likes texting.

R1.5

AMY Oh, I love it, but I know a lot of people don't like it at all. I can't understand why – it's much safer than driving. I always try to get a window seat, and I, er, love just sitting back and watching the clouds go by. And, um, if I'm on a long flight, I stay up and watch films all night, which is great fun – I hardly ever get time to watch films at home. The food's much better nowadays too – I always eat everything they give me. Yes, it's my favourite way to travel, definitely.

JEREMY Yes, it's the one thing about modern life that really drives me crazy. You have to listen to this terrible music while you're waiting, and then, er, a voice says, "you're a hundred and sixtieth in the queue" or something. Sometimes you can wait an hour just to talk to someone, and you can't put the phone down because you don't want to lose your place. Then, um, when you do finally speak to someone it's usually the wrong department, so you have to start again anyway.

A When I was growing up, it was hardly ever on, maybe once on Saturday night or something. But these days it's on almost every evening, and my husband watches it *all* the time – it doesn't seem to matter who's playing. And for some reason he always thinks it's more important than what *I* want to watch, and, er, that really gets on my nerves. I don't think I've ever watched a whole match because I get so bored – to me it's just a group of millionaires kicking a ball around. No, I can't stand it, sorry.

J Yes, this is, er, one of the things I really enjoy doing, partly because it helps me to stop thinking about work and all the other stressful things in life. When I'm in the kitchen with the music on, I'm in my own little world. I, er, love going to the local fruit and veg market because I always try to use really fresh ingredients. We often have friends round for dinner, and it's very satisfying to see them enjoying what I've prepared for them. My wife, Anne, is the opposite, though – she can't even make toast!

R1.6

SALLY That was wonderful! I haven't had a meal like that for months.

MIKE Yes, I didn't know you were such a good cook, Jeremy.

JEREMY I'm glad you enjoyed it. Do you want some coffee?

S Yes, I'd love some, thanks.

J Milk and sugar are on the table.

M Cheers.

S Oh, it's so nice to relax for a change.

M Yes, I know what you mean. Work's really busy these days. I don't seem to get much time to do anything else.

ANNE So what do you do to relax, Mike?

M I do yoga, actually.

A Really?

M Yes, every morning when I get up. Only for, um, about half an hour, but it really helps me stay calm during the day.

J Well, Anne goes to a health club to relax – very expensive it is too.

A Hey! It doesn't cost *that* much!

S Do you go there a lot?

A No, not really, only two or three times a month. But I always have a massage when I'm there. It's absolutely wonderful. I feel like a new woman afterwards.

M Don't you go swimming or do some proper exercise there as well?

A No, that's too much like hard work.

J What about you, Sally?

S Me? Well, I relax by doing things. I'm not very good at just sitting around doing nothing.

J So what do you do?

S I paint, actually. Watercolours, that kind of thing.

J Really?

A Yes, you should see some of her paintings. She's very good.

S Oh, I'm not really. But you know, I find it very relaxing. I'm in a painting club, and every Sunday we all go into the country and paint.

A Well, Jeremy relaxes by sitting in front of the TV every night, don't you, dear?

J Er, not every night, no. Maybe, um, six nights a week, that's all. It doesn't matter what's on, really, I'm just waiting for my brain to switch off before I go to bed.

S That's not very healthy, you know. You should do something more active.

J Yeah, I know. But I just never have the energy.

A Anyway, one day when we all retire, we can all relax as much as we want.

M Only twenty years to go, then!

R1.7 **R1.8**

A

EVELYN John?

JOHN Yes?

E You work with Dave, don't you?

J Yes, I do. **[end of R1.7]** Er, why do you ask?

E Have you got his email address? I want to invite him to my birthday party.

J Sure, I'll text it to you. So, um ... why do you want him to come to your party?

E I think he's nice, that's all.

J Really ...

B

STEVE Hi, Gary.

GARY Hello, Steve.

S Are Kate and Stuart here?

G No, not yet. They'll be here later, though.

S Kate went to Bristol University, didn't she?

G Yes, she did. **[end of R1.7]**

S Did she like it there?

G Yes, she had a great time, I think. Why?

S Well, my brother wants to go there. To study law.

G Oh, right.

C

JULIET ... and I got back last week.

INGRID It sounds a great trip.

J Yes, it was.

I You haven't been to China, have you?

J No, I haven't. Why? **[end of R1.7]**

I I'm going there next month, and I'm looking for some travel tips.

J Well, do you know my friend, Tom?

I Yes, of course I do.

J He went there last year. Perhaps you could talk to him.

I Yeah, that'd be good. Cheers.

D

BRUCE Hi, Alice. Are you and Jack hungry?

ALICE Yes, that's why I'm here. What have you got?

B Jack's vegetarian, isn't he?

A No, he isn't, actually. **[end of R1.7]** He just doesn't eat red meat.

B Oh, right. So do you think he wants some of this chicken?

A Yes, probably. I'll go and ask him. Jack ... do you want some chicken?

R1.10

A

JOHN ... want him to come to your party?

EVELYN I think he's nice, that's all.

J Really ...

E You're coming to my party, aren't you?

J Yes, of course. I wouldn't miss it for the world.

E Good. Er, Dave hasn't got a girlfriend, has he?

J No, he hasn't.

E Oh, good.

J Actually, he's married.

E Oh ...

B

STEVE ... wants to go there. To study law.

GARY Oh, right.

S Your sister did law too, didn't she?

G Yes, she did. It was a very hard course, I think.

S Yes, so I've heard. She works for a big law firm now, doesn't she?

G No, she doesn't, actually. She left there a couple of months ago. Now she works for Greenpeace, you know, the environmental group.

S Really? Wow!

C

JULIET Perhaps you could talk to him.

INGRID Yeah, that'd be good. Cheers.

J Tom went to school with you, didn't he?

I Yes, that's right. We grew up together. He's my oldest friend.

J Right. He isn't here today, is he?

I Yes, he is, actually. That's him over there.

J Oh, yes, of course. I didn't see him. I'll go and talk to him later.

D

ALICE ... Jack ... do you want some chicken? Yes, he does.

BRUCE You eat meat, don't you?

A Yes, of course. I'll eat anything.

B Right, here you go.

A Thanks. That looks great.

B You've got a drink, haven't you?

A Yes, I have, it's over there.

B OK, enjoy the food.

A Thanks a lot.

R2.1

PRESENTER Welcome to *Cover to Cover*. Today we're talking about Carl Honoré's book *In Praise of Slow*, which tells us that we're all living too fast and should slow down. With me are two journalists, Kim Mayhew and Rob Davis – both workaholics, of course. Kim, what did you think of the book?

KIM Yes, very interesting and extremely funny at times too. Er, for example, I loved the bit about the group in Austria that goes into city centres and tries to stop people hurrying.

P Oh, yes.

K They actually time people with a stopwatch, and if someone hasn't got a good reason for walking fast, then that person has to walk behind a tortoise for 50 metres!

P And what did you think of the book, Rob?

R2.2

PRESENTER ... what did you think of the book, Rob?

ROB Well, after I finished it I decided that I really must take more time off work.

KIM Yes, me too.

R Actually, the whole chapter on work was very interesting. For example, Honoré says people should only work 35 hours a week.

P And do you think that's a good idea?

R Yes, definitely. Most people work too hard, I think. And apparently some French employees are allowed to begin their weekend at 3 p.m. on Thursday. I think we should all do that.

P Kim, what do you think?

K Oh, yes, I agree with Rob, everyone works too hard these days. Honoré definitely believes we ought to spend more time relaxing with our families.

P But that's already happening in some countries, isn't it? For example, Germans spend 15% less time at work now than in 1980.

R Yes, and Honoré also says people can get their best ideas when they're doing nothing. Albert Einstein was famous for just looking into space at his office at Princeton University. And you can't say he didn't have some good ideas!

K Yes, and I was interested to read that Americans work 350 hours a year more than Europeans, but in some American companies, employees can sleep whenever they want. Apparently they have special rooms where people can go and lie down if they're tired.

R That sounds like an excellent idea.

P Yes, I'd be in there every afternoon, I can tell you!

R Actually, by law in the UK people are supposed to have a break every 4 hours, but a lot don't. It's amazing that 20% of British people work more than 60 hours a week. We work the most hours in Europe and it's certainly not making us happier.

K Yes, and then lots of people have to take work home because they're under so much pressure to meet deadlines. Apparently 60% of people in the UK who were interviewed said they didn't take all their paid holiday. That's just crazy!

R And now we've all got mobile phones and laptops, we're able to continue working when we're travelling. You know, when we're on the train going to and from the office.

P Yes, and even illness doesn't stop some people. According to Honoré's book, 20% of Americans don't take time off work when they're ill. It seems that some people can't stop working, even when it's nearly killing them.

R Yes, the Japanese even have a word for it – *karoshi* – which means 'death from working too hard'.

P On that happy note, we'll leave it there.

R2.3

ANSWERS 2 must 3 Are you able to 4 I'm supposed to 5 don't have to 6 Are you allowed to 7 can 8 have to 9 ought to 10 have to 11 mustn't

R2.5

My mother still cooks a three-course meal every evening. | I'm writing a book in my spare time. | People who live in the UK spend a lot on ready meals. | The market is growing rapidly. | Many experts now believe they're bad for our health. | We need to read the labels carefully. | People in the USA also buy a lot of ready meals. | They're becoming more common in Germany.

R2.6

MAN Do people you know have problems sleeping at /ət/ night? Or maybe you just can't get to sleep yourself. For /fə/ many people, insomnia is a way of /əv/ life and /ən/ not being able to /tə/ get to /tə/ sleep isn't just annoying – it can /kən/ also be very dangerous.

WOMAN Yes, and /ən/ with us today is sleep scientist, Doctor Iris Saunders.

IRIS Good afternoon.

W Dr Saunders, how much of /əv/ a problem is this, do /də/ you /jə/ think?

I Well, we know that tiredness can /kən/ cause accidents. More than fifty per cent of /əv/ road accidents in the USA are because of /əv/ people driving when they're tired.

W That's amazing!

I Indeed. And /ən/ when you /jə/ think that thirty per cent of /əv/ people in the UK have problems getting to /tə/ sleep or staying asleep and /ən/ ten per cent of those suffer from serious insomnia – that's a lot of /əv/ accidents waiting to /tə/ happen.

W So how much sleep are people getting these days?

I Well, a hundred years ago, before electricity, people went to /tə/ sleep when it got dark and woke up when it got light. But now in our twenty-four-hour society we sleep about one and /ən/ a half hours less than we did a century ago.

W Well, we have two teenage kids and /ən/ no one can /kən/ say they're sleeping less.

I Ah well, that's interesting. Scientists now think that teenagers really *do* need more sleep than adults. It's because they're still growing. Of course they don't need as much as babies and /ən/ small children – they need the most sleep. It's actually older people who generally need the least amount of /əv/ sleep.

M So why do we need sleep?

I We don't actually know. Scientists used to /tə/ think that sleep was the only time you /jə/ had complete rest, but in fact we use about the same amount of /əv/ energy when we're asleep as when we're sitting on the sofa resting.

M Really? That's surprising.

I Yes, and our brains are very active for some of /əv/ the time we're asleep. Apparently that's when our brains organise information they've collected during the day.

W What about cultures where they have naps in the day; you know, siestas?

I They were unpopular for a while but now they're coming back. In Spain, for example, they now have 'siesta salons'. Because people don't have time to /tə/ go home, they go to /tə/ these places for a quick nap, then go back to /tə/ work.

M Really? What a good idea.

I Yes, apparently a thirty-minute nap in the /ðə/ day can /kən/ improve our performance at /ət/ work for /fə/ three to four hours.

W Well, that's absolutely fascinating. Thank you, Doctor Saunders.

R2.8

1

DIANE So, ... how are things, Lorna?

LORNA Well, Andy and I aren't getting on too well at the moment.

D Oh, dear. What's the matter?

L He's working so hard he's hardly ever home. And when he is, he's absolutely shattered and really moody.

D Hmm, I can see why you're upset. Have you tried talking to him about it?

L Yes, but he says I'm spending too much money and then just gets really angry.

D Oh, how awful!

L But I'm only buying things for the house and the kids. Oh, I'm so miserable, Diane. What do you think I should do?

D Well, maybe you should talk to him again. Tell him you're concerned about him and that you're worried that he's going to make himself ill.

L Well, it's worth a try, I guess. Thanks.

2

ROBIN Hi, Andy. You look a bit fed up. Is everything OK?

ANDY Yeah, I suppose so. Just got a few money worries, that's all.

R Oh, I'm sorry to hear that. What's the problem?

A Well, you know – 2 kids, new house, and Lorna's spending more and more every month. Not on herself, but she buys lots of things for the house and the kids that we don't need.

R Well, why don't you talk to her about it?

A I tried that, but she doesn't listen and then she goes on about me being tired all the time. Which is true, I am.

R Yeah, I see what you mean. But I guess it can't be much fun for her, at home all day with the kids.

A Yes, good point. So what should I do?

R Well, I'd take her out for a really nice meal and talk to her about it.

A Yes, that's a good idea. I might try that. Thanks, Robin.

R No problem.

3

MOTHER Hello?

LORNA Hi, Mum, it's Lorna.

M Oh, hello, darling. How are you?

L Er, well, not bad, I suppose. I'm still not getting on very well with Andy.

M Oh, dear. What a shame. Is he still working all the time?

L Yeah, he is.

M It can't be good for him, working so hard. I think he should look for another job.

L Yes, you could be right.

M And maybe you ought to spend some time together, you know, just the two of you. You both need a night off, dear.

L Actually, I'm so glad you said that.

M Oh, why's that?

L Andy's just phoned. He's asked me to go out to dinner with him tonight and we need a babysitter.

M Er, well, actually ...

L You did say I needed a night off.

M Yes, fine, of course I'll do it. What time do you want me to come round?

L Um, at about 7?

M OK, see you then.

L Thanks a lot, Mum. Bye.

M Goodbye, darling.

R2.9

1 Oh, dear. What's the matter? b)
2 I can see why you're upset. a)
3 Oh, how awful! b)
4 Oh, I'm sorry to hear that. b)
5 Yes, I see what you mean. a)
6 Oh, dear. What a shame. a)

R2.11

ANSWERS 2 need 3 can't 4 have to 5 easy 6 game 7 have to 8 long 9 must 10 find 11 thing 12 almost 13 can 14 break 15 bear 16 call 17 go on 18 words 19 wait 20 long 21 waiting 22 talk 23 arms 24 waiting

R3.1

SAM I work as a guide for a company that organises rainforest holidays here in Costa Rica. I've lived in this country for three years and I love it. I've worked in two other Central American countries and I had a great time in both places, but, er, this country is really special. It's not, um ... It's not an easy job – you have to deal with some very difficult people and most of our guests have never been in a rainforest before. But they always say it's the best experience they've ever had. Of course, I've also had to put up with some idiots. For example, last month two guys set off on their own without telling anyone. They got lost in the rainforest and it took us 2 days to find them. And I've just been to San Isidro to pick up a guest from the hospital. He was bitten by a poisonous spider he found in his room. He's OK now, though, and, you know, at least he'll have a good story to tell people when he gets back home.

MARCIA I started working in the hotel industry 14 years ago, but this is the first time I've run a hotel in a touristy place like Cornwall. My husband and I have had this place since 2001 and I'm a bit, er, fed up with it, to be honest. Managing a hotel is quite stressful, particularly when people complain all the time, which can happen. And I can't stand it when people steal things from the rooms.

I suppose people want to bring back a souvenir of their holiday, but surely they've got enough towels at home! Another problem is that, um, one of us always has to be here. For example, my husband's gone to see some friends off at the station, so I have to stay and look after the hotel. Also it's very hard to get a holiday together. We've been away together a few times, but each time there was a problem at the hotel so we had to come back early. But this winter we're going to close the hotel for 2 weeks and go skiing – we're really looking forward to it.

R3.2

I've worked in two other Central American countries. | We've been away together a few times. | I've lived in this country for three years. | My husband and I have had this place since 2001. | I've just been to San Isidro to pick up a guest. | My husband's gone to see some friends off. | I've also had to put up with some idiots.

R3.4

1 They had their hotel for 10 years.
2 We've opened a restaurant.
3 I've decided to stay here.
4 I lost a lot of money.
5 She's visited some interesting places.
6 He called all his friends.

R3.5

ANSWERS 2 decided 3 've lived 4 've just opened 5 've been 6 was 7 haven't had 8 've visited 9 's just gone

R3.6

I've been /bɪn/ working here for /fə/ two months. | How long have /əv/ you been /bɪn/ travelling on your own? | Scott's been /bɪn/ writing books since he left university. | He's written three books so far. | They haven't been /bɪn/ playing tennis for very long. | I've known my best friend since we were kids. | How long has /əz/ your sister been /bɪn/ an actress? | We haven't had a holiday for three years.

R3.7

JUDITH So let's meet our first holidaymaker. Hello there, can you tell us a bit about yourself?
ALAN Hi, Judith. My name's Alan Marsh. I'm in my fifties and I work in advertising.
J And which of our holidays are you going on?
A Well, I'm flying out to Cape Town in South Africa next week to, er, have a bit of cosmetic surgery.
J Oh, and why have you chosen this holiday?
A Well, I've been working in advertising for more than 30 years. It's a very

competitive business and how you look is important. My face is getting a bit old these days, and I thought I needed to do something about it.
J But the holiday's not just about having a facelift, is it?
A No, not at all. After I've had my operation and, you know, had a bit of time to recover, I'm going on a week's safari, which I think will be quite exciting. I'd love to see a lion up close.
J Hmm, that sounds a bit frightening.
A Well, when I've had my facelift all the lions will probably be scared of me!
J Well, we hope you have a fantastic time, Alan.
A Thanks a lot.
J And our next holidaymaker is Emily.
EMILY Hi, Judith.
J Can you tell us a bit about yourself?
E Well, my name's Emily Ward and I'm an editor for a weekly women's magazine. I'm thirty-one, and, um, I'm not married.
J And which holiday are you going on?
E Well, I'm setting off tomorrow morning to fly to Byron Bay in Australia to work on an organic farm.
J And why did you choose this holiday?
E Er, the main reason is that I'm bored with going on the same old package holidays year after year. This time I just wanted a ... you know, a different kind of holiday.
J Right, I see.
E And I hope I'll learn a bit about organic farming, which I'm interested in.
J Is there anything about the holiday that you're worried about?
E Well, let me think ... I know that I'll have to do quite a lot of physical work and I'm not very fit. But I hope it won't be too bad.
J Well, we look forward to hearing all about it. Have a great time, Emily.
E Thanks very much.
J Right, moving on to our third holidaymaker ...

R3.9

MICHAEL Ellen, you've been to Delhi, haven't you?
ELLEN Yes, I have. Three times, actually. It's an amazing place.
M Oh, good. I'm going there next week. Maybe you can give me some tips.
E Sure. What do you want to know?
M Well, firstly, do you know any good places to stay?
E There are lots of good hotels in Connaught Place – that's right in the centre of New Delhi. The place I always stay in is called The Raj Hotel. I can give you the address if you like.

M Great, thanks. And what's the best way to get around?
E In Delhi it's probably best to use rickshaws. They're quicker than taxis, and quite cheap.
M OK.
E And to travel to other cities I'd recommend the trains. They're a lot safer than the buses, especially at night.
M Hmm, that's good to know. So what are the things I shouldn't miss – any good museums?
E Er no, don't bother going to the museums. There are much better things to see in Delhi. You should definitely see the Red Fort, in Old Delhi – it's absolutely huge.
M Right. Is there anything else worth visiting?
E Well, er, there is a much older fort about half an hour from the centre. But it isn't really worth visiting, I don't think. But there's the Jami Masjid – that's the biggest mosque in India and it's very near the Red Fort. That's well worth seeing.
M Hmm, that sounds good. And what about places outside Delhi?
E Well, you really must go to Agra to see the Taj Mahal. It's only 3 hours away by train. You can do it in a day if you start early.
M Great. And, er, what about the food? Do you know any good places to eat?
E Yes, there are lots of really good restaurants in Connaught Place. I remember one called the Shanti – the food there is delicious. We ate there every night!
M Thanks, that's really useful. Er ... have you got any other tips?
E Like most places, don't drink the water. Buy bottled water instead. And I wouldn't eat anything that's sold in the street. You can get ill quite easily there.
M Yes, I've heard that before. Thanks a lot, Ellen, you've been really helpful.
E No problem. Send me a postcard.
M Yes, I will!

R4.1

ANSWERS 1 Elton John 2 The Rolling Stones 3 Jennifer Lopez 4 Britney Spears 5 Prince 6 Luciano Pavarotti 7 Foreigner

R4.2

he asked for a kitchen in his hotel suite → While he was staying in New York, he asked for a kitchen in his hotel suite. | they threw the pies at each other → While they were having a party, they threw the pies at each other. | everything in her room had to be white → When she was making the video, everything in her room had to be white. | no one could phone her dressing room → When she was on tour, no one could phone her dressing room.

Recording Scripts

R4.3

They used to /juːstə/ take their own furniture. | He always used to /juːstə/ say what size sofa he wanted. | Van Halen didn't use to /juːstə/ like brown M&Ms. | Some promoters didn't use to /juːstə/ read the contracts properly. | What did they use to /juːstə/ put in their contracts? | Did Pavarotti use to /juːstə/ do his own cooking?

R4.4

LUKE What are you working on at the moment, Beth?

BETH I'm making a TV series about famous women in history.

L Hmm, that sounds interesting.

B Yes, it is. I decided to make the series because I'd seen an article in the newspaper about men and women adventurers. I realised that I'd learned about some of the men at school, but I hadn't heard of any of the women before I read the article. But when I read about them I was absolutely amazed by what they'd achieved. They were incredibly brave and adventurous.

L Women like who?

B Harriet Quimby, for example. She's the star of the first programme.

L Never heard of her.

B That's exactly my point. Harriet was a beautiful New York journalist. She was very independent, extremely determined and she wanted to do everything that men could do. For example, she was the first woman in New York to get her driving licence. And in 1911 she became the first woman to get a pilot's licence in the whole of the USA.

L Really? Wow!

B Yes, and she was also very ambitious. She'd only had her licence for a few months when she decided to become the first woman to fly across the English Channel.

L And didn't that make her famous?

B Er no, it didn't. She arrived in England in April 1912, on a Sunday, and the weather was perfect. Unfortunately, by the time she got up the next day, the weather had changed. She waited for it to get better, but it didn't. So she set off on the Tuesday, even though the weather was still really bad.

L And planes in those days were fairly basic.

B Yeah. She couldn't see anything and she got lost. So, when she landed she didn't know which country she was in. But luckily, it was France.

L So why wasn't that front-page news?

B Well, it was the same day the story of the *Titanic* was on the front page of every newspaper in the world.

L Oh no!

B Yes, it's true. Actually, the *Titanic* had sunk on the Monday – the day before Harriet landed in France.

L So, everyone was interested in the *Titanic*, not Harriet's flight?

B Yes, then she died two months later in a flying accident in the USA. She was only 37.

L Oh, how sad! So when's this series going to be on TV … ?

R4.5

I'd seen an article in the newspaper. → I decided to make the series because I'd seen an article in the newspaper. | I'd learned about some of the men at school. → I realised that I'd learned about some of the men at school. | before I read the article → I hadn't heard of any of the women before I read the article. | the weather had changed → By the time she got up the next day the weather had changed. | Harriet landed in France → The *Titanic* had sunk the day before Harriet landed in France.

R4.7

1 I had a bad day. I'd had a bad day.
2 John had arrived early. John arrived early.
3 She made her mistake. She'd made her mistake.
4 Tom had thought it was wrong. Tom thought it was wrong.
5 They asked for a bigger room. They'd asked for a bigger room.
6 We'd told him the news. We told him the news.

R4.8

ANSWERS 2 were 3 'd/had already walked
4 left 5 'd/had trained 6 'd/had put on
7 set off 8 started 9 got 10 had become
11 arrived 12 'd/had walked 13 received
14 had ever walked

R4.9

INTERVIEWER Still on the subject of plants, I'm talking to Monica and Kaz Janowski about an amazing story that happened while they were living in the jungle in Borneo and their daughter, Molly, was badly burned. First of all, why were you living there, Monica?

MONICA Well, I'm an anthropologist and I was studying how the people of Pa'Dalih grow rice.

I Right. And how old was Molly then?

M Erm … about 18 months.

I And can you tell us what happened?

KAZ Well, we were living in one of the village longhouses and we had a place where we could make a small fire. That's where we used to cook all our meals and eat and everything. Well, one day Molly was, er, dancing around, you know, as kids do, and a teapot full of boiling water fell on her.

I So what did you do?

R4.10

INTERVIEWER … So what did you do?

MONICA I immediately took off all her clothes, of course. And then within seconds, people from the longhouse were bringing banana flowers and they started putting the sap from the flowers on Molly's burns.

I So how bad were the burns?

M They covered about one-sixth of her body. It was very serious.

I And how far away were you from a doctor?

KAZ The nearest one was in a village called Bario, about 20 miles away. Fortunately she was a flying doctor – she visited villages in a helicopter. Normally it's a 12-hour walk to Bario, but the helicopter came to pick us up, so it only took us 10 minutes to get there. The doctor wanted us to take Molly to hospital in Marudi, the nearest town.

I Did you take her there?

K No, we didn't, actually. The Pa'Dalih people had told us that the doctors would put purple medicine on the burns and it was no good, it would leave scars on her body.

I So what happened next?

R4.11

INTERVIEWER …So what happened next?

KAZ We decided to go back to /w/ our village. The doctor wasn't happy /j/ about it, but she /j/ agreed in the /j/ end and gave us some antibiotics. Oh /w/ and she /j/ also asked us not to use the remedy that the Pa'Dalih people used.

I But you'd already used their remedy.

K Yes, we had. The Pa'Dalih people have been treating burns this way for /r/ ages. Of course, Molly /j/ often cried while Monica /r/ and I were putting the sap on – it was obviously very painful for her. And we /j/ also had to keep her clean, of course.

I Yes, I can imagine. How /w/ often did you /w/ and Kaz have to do /w/ all of this?

MONICA Every two /w/ hours.

I Right. And how long did you do that for?

M Ten days, more /r/ or less.

I Wow!

M Yes, it was really /j/ exhausting for everyone.

I And what happened to Molly /j/ in the /j/ end? Did the skin heal?

K Yes, completely. It was a bit white at first. But after /r/ a week or two /w/ it changed back to /w/ its normal colour.

I And has Molly got any scars now?

M No, there /r/ isn't a scar /r/ anywhere /r/ on her body. Not one!

I Well, that's a remarkable story. Thanks for /r/ allowing us to hear /r/ about your /r/ experiences, and I hope …

R4.13

MICHELLE Hi, Ewan. Did you see the match last night?

EWAN Er, no, I didn't.

M We lost.

E Yes, I know. I saw it on the TV this morning. Most of the report was about what happened after the match. You know, all the fights. Football fans are all just a bunch of stupid idiots.

M Hey, they're not all like that.

E Yes, they are. Most of them are really rude and noisy and—

M I agree some of them can be quite rude at times and, yes, they tend to get rather loud.

E Rather loud! You're joking. They're … they're really aggressive – most of them are just out looking for a fight.

M OK, I admit, some of them can be quite aggressive at times.

E Didn't you see the news? There was a huge fight in the town centre! It seems to me that most football fans are, you know, just incredibly violent.

M Yes, and I agree that's not very normal behaviour. Generally speaking, most people who go to matches are just loyal fans. OK, you get a few who can be a bit too enthusiastic.

E A bit too enthusiastic! They're just like a bunch of spoilt children.

M Yes, well, some of them are, I admit. On the whole, most fans just want to see a good game and to see their team win.

E Yes, and then have a fight about it afterwards. Seriously, don't you find the behaviour of some football fans offensive?

M Yes, of course I do. But lots of families take their kids to football matches, so it can't be all that bad!

E Yes, and those kids become the next generation of football idiots.

M Oh, I give up!

R5.1

IAN So, what do you think?

LIZ Well, I think they were much better than the ones we saw yesterday. (Yeah, me too.) What did you think of the terraced house in Eccles?

I Well, I thought it was OK – and it's the least expensive place we've seen.

L Yes, that's true.

I The wooden floors were lovely, *and* it had a new kitchen.

L Yes, the floors were nice, I agree.

I Also, it seemed slightly bigger than our house.

L No, I think it was the same size as ours. It just seemed bigger because it had less furniture.

I Yeah, maybe.

L Anyway, I preferred the detached house, to be honest – you know, the one in Monton.

It's one of the oldest houses we've seen so far, anyway. And I like old houses, they've got character.

I Yeah, I see what you mean. But it's on a very busy road; I'm not sure I want that. It was much noisier than the other two.

L Yes, that's true. I noticed that too. That might be a problem, especially at night.

I Also the garden was far smaller than I expected. And it's very similar to this house. We might as well stay here.

L Right. So you didn't like any of them?

I No, I was quite keen on the flat in Salford. It's not as big as the others but it felt a lot more spacious.

L Yes, it did, didn't it? I thought it was very different from anything else we've seen.

I And it had the most amazing view. You know, down the river.

L Yes, that was wonderful, wasn't it?

I But you prefer the house in Monton, don't you?

L Well, I did like the Monton house, yes, mainly because it had a garden and you know how much I enjoy gardening. But it's a little further away from the city centre, isn't it?

I Yes, it is a bit, but it's within walking distance of a station, that's the important thing.

L Yeah, you're right. Oh, I don't want to live in that house in Eccles, though – it's got the worst bathroom I've ever seen.

I Oh, I didn't really notice the bathroom. Anyway, the Salford flat's got that big balcony. We can get some plants and sit out there in the evenings. It'll be as good as having a garden, but a lot less work. *And* it's a bit less expensive than the Monton house.

L Yes, maybe. It *was* nice, wasn't it? Maybe we can look at it again tomorrow.

I Sure. I'll call the estate agent now, and …

R5.2

It seemed slightly bigger than /ðən/ our house. | It was /wəz/ the same size as /əz/ ours. | The garden was /wəz/ far smaller than /ðən/ I expected. | And /ənd/ it's very similar to /tə/ this house. | It's not as /əz/ big as /əz/ the others. It was /wəz/ very different from /frəm/ anything else. | It'll be as /əz/ good as /əz/ having a garden.

R5.3

LIZ Right, what's next?

IAN What about this box of toys? The kids are much too old for them now.

L Actually, I'm going to give those to my sister. Her kids will probably like them. She's picking them up tomorrow evening after work.

I OK, so those go in …

L … the pile with the books.

I Right. And what about all these old letters? I don't know why you've kept them.

You'll never read them again.

L OK, I'll throw those away.

I So, which pile?

L Put them next to those old magazines.

I Right.

L And what shall we do with all these old photos?

I Oh, I'm in the middle of going through those.

L But we never look at them.

I I know, but that's because they're not in order or anything. I'm going to sort out the rest of them at the weekend. Then we can get rid of the ones we don't want.

L OK, so we're keeping these for now.

I Yes. So … that pile.

L Yes, the one with the TV and the pillows. And can we throw out these old records?

I Sorry, you're not getting rid of those. I've had them since I was a teenager.

L But you'll never listen to them again.

I That's not the point. They're probably quite valuable now.

L Fine, put them in the 'keep' pile. And that old tennis racket? You've got to throw *that* out.

I Actually, I'm going to give that to Ricky, next door. His mum asked if I had one. He's going to start taking tennis lessons.

L You're joking! That old thing? It's going to break the first time he uses it!

I Oh, it's fine for a 10-year-old.

L You don't like throwing things out, do you? Right, what's next?

R5.4 R5.5

1 I'm going to /gəʊntə/ finish the report tonight.
2 Look, it's going to /gənə/ rain soon.
3 I'm meeting her after school.
4 I'll call you at about six.
5 I think he'll find another job.
6 What are you doing tonight?

R5.6

ANSWERS 1 it's going to fit 2 I'll throw
3 He's coming 4 I'll put 5 I'm going to start
6 It'll look 7 We're meeting 8 I'll finish

IAN … OK, see you later. Bye.

LIZ Bye, darling. Right, now let's see what I want to throw out. Those old records, for a start – and those horrible running shoes, that broken tennis racket … but I'm definitely going to keep my old letters …

R5.7

GILLIAN Well, I've, er, I've been to IKEA, er, let me think, about 8 or 9 times. And I mean you can't argue with the prices. Everything's … well, like, everything's so cheap compared to other places. But I'm, um, not a fan of the place, I must admit. I love the things they sell, like it's, you know it's good quality and well designed and all that, but I don't like shopping here.

Recording Scripts

I'd prefer to have <u>more</u>, <u>um</u>, more personal service. <u>You can never you know</u> find, <u>um</u>, there's never anyone to help, which I find <u>kind of</u> annoying. And <u>well</u>, on a Saturday the queues they're enormous. <u>You see</u>, <u>I haven't</u>, <u>um</u>, I've got no patience at all, and I just <u>sort of</u> stand there and get angry. And, <u>um</u>, putting the stuff together drives me crazy. All that time standing in the queue and then <u>you</u>, <u>um</u>, you get home, start putting it together and there are always <u>well</u>, <u>you know</u> bits missing – <u>I mean</u>, how frustrating is that?

SUE   Er, well, IKEA's more like a supermarket than a department store. I mean at IKEA you get your trolley or, um, your big blue bag and away you go. You see, there isn't … there aren't many assistants so no one's like asking you if you want any help all the time. I hate that, I just kind of want people to let me walk around on my own. But I, um … I always seem to buy lots of little things, candles and, er, glasses and plants, you know, stuff that I didn't actually plan to buy. But you can furnish an entire house in a day, in fact we did, er … when we lived in Paris. Well, it wasn't a house, actually. We got, um, we rented an unfurnished flat and there was nothing in it, obviously. So, um, we went to IKEA and bought loads of things and you know, just took them home in the back of the car. We were, um, … we were able to put all the furniture together quite easily, and by the evening, we had a furnished flat. And everything was like really cheap. I mean, what more do you want from a store?

R5.8

1

SHOP ASSISTANT   Are you looking for something?

LARS   Yes. I'm sorry, I've forgotten what it's called, but, um, it's a thing for opening bottles of wine.

SA   Do you mean one of these?

L   Yes, that's it. What's it called?

SA   A corkscrew.

L   Corkscrew. Thanks.

2

LARS   Could you help me?

SHOP ASSISTANT   Sure. What do you need?

L   I'm sorry, I don't know the word for it. It's stuff for getting marks off your clothes.

SA   Washing powder?

L   No, it's a type of liquid. You use it when you get coffee on your shirt.

SA   Oh, you mean stain remover. It's er … over there, by the soap.

L   What's it called again?

SA   Stain remover.

L   Thanks very much.

3

SHOP ASSISTANT   Can I help you?

LARS   Yes, I hope so.

SA   What are you looking for?

L   Er … I can't remember what they're called. You use them to put posters up on the wall. They're made of metal and, um, they've got a round top.

SA   Oh, you mean drawing pins? Er, just a minute – these things?

L   Yes, that's right. What are they called again?

SA   Drawing pins.

L   Yes, can I have a box of those, please?

SA   Sure. Anything else?

L   No, that's all, thanks.

4

LARS   Excuse me?

SHOP ASSISTANT   Yes?

L   I'm looking for something for my mobile. I'm sorry, I don't know what it's called in English. It looks like a black box. You use it when the batteries are dead.

SA   Is this what you're looking for?

L   Yes, that's right. What's it called in English?

SA   A charger.

L   Right, a charger. Thanks a lot.

SA   No problem.

R5.10

ANSWERS   2e) 3d) 4f) 5c) 6a) 7i) 8h) 9l) 10g) 11k) 12j) 13q) 14n) 15r) 16p) 17m) 18o) 19t) 20s) 21v) 22u)

R6.1

STEVE   Hello?

KATE   Hi, Steve.

S   Hi, Kate. How are things?

K   Oh, OK, I suppose. But being at home all the time is driving me crazy. Now the kids are all at school, I've been thinking about what to do with the rest of my life.

S   So, what choices do you have?

K   Well, I could just go back to work – you know, teaching French – but I'm thinking of going back to university instead.

S   Really? Wow!

K   The trouble is, if I start teaching again, I'll be exhausted after a year. And then what?

S   What will you study if you go back to university?

K   I'd like to do Business Studies. I've talked to a few universities and I don't think it'll be a problem getting in.

S   Well, that's good. But you might have to wait until next year if you don't apply soon. It's already June.

K   Yes, I know.

S   What does Colin think?

K   Well, he thinks it's a good idea, but he's worried about how much it'll cost. We haven't got much spare money, you see. But unless I do it now, I'll be too old.

S   Well, have you asked Mum and Dad? I'm sure they'll help if they can.

K   Yes, that's a good idea. I'll give them a ring before they go on holiday.

S   I think you should do what will make you happiest.

K   Yes, you're probably right. As soon as I make up my mind, I'll let you know. Anyway, how are things with you?

S   Well, *I'm* trying to decide if I should leave my job and become a writer.

K   Are you serious?! You want to stop being a doctor?

S   Yes, I think so. I might leave after I finish this contract.

K   But what about money?

S   Yes, that's a bit of a problem. I've got some savings, enough to last me two or three months.

K   Well, why don't you work part-time? Then you can earn some money and write on your days off.

S   Yes, maybe. That might work.

K   Have you told Mum and Dad about this?

S   Er, no, not yet.

K   Right …

S   I won't tell them until I decide what to do. You know what they're like. But I think that's what I want to do.

K   Well, I'll believe it when I see it!

S   You laugh all you want. Just wait till I'm famous!

K   Anyway, how's it going with your new girlfriend?

R6.2

I'll be exhausted after a year → If I start teaching again, I'll be exhausted after a year. | if you go back to university → What will you study if you go back to university? | I'll be too old → But unless I do it now, I'll be too old. | I'll let you know → As soon as I make up my mind, I'll let you know. | after I finish this contract → I might leave after I finish this contract. | until I decide what to do → I won't tell them until I decide what to do.

R6.3

you worry about them all the time → If you have children, you worry about them all the time. | they become unfit → If children stay indoors all the time, they become unfit. | they shouldn't protect them so much → If parents want their kids to grow up healthy, they shouldn't protect them so much. | they can't learn to look after themselves. → But if kids never go outside, they can't learn to look after themselves. | give them back their freedom → If you want happy and healthy kids, give them back their freedom.

R6.5

1   If I don't know where my children are, I worry a lot.

2   If they don't do more exercise, they'll get fat.

3   We'll pick up the kids if we have time.

4   If it's a nice day, I take them to the park.

5 If they can't sleep, I'll read them a story.
6 They play computer games all day if they can.

R6.6

EDWARD Charlotte, are you very superstitious?

CHARLOTTE No, not really. Why do you ask?

E I'm reading this absolutely fascinating book about the history of superstitions. Did you know that in the UK, people think that seeing a black cat is good luck, but in nearly every other country it's bad luck? Don't you think that's strange?

C Um, yes, I suppose so.

E And do you know why breaking a mirror is seven years' bad luck?

C No, why?

E Well, um, the Romans believed that life started again every seven years. If a mirror broke, then people thought the last person who looked at it was very ill and would continue to be ill for the next seven years of their life – that is, until they got a "new life".

C OK then – my uncle always carries a rabbit's foot around with him. Why's that lucky?

E Hang on – lucky charms are here somewhere – yes, here it is – er, rabbits were believed to help families grow their crops because they lived in the fields and had lots of babies. So they became a sign of fertility, and therefore good luck.

C Hmm. Not so lucky for the rabbit, though – you know, having its foot cut off.

E Yeah, true. So, what superstitions do you believe in?

C Well, let me think ... Oh, I touch wood – but everyone does that, don't they?

E Ah, that's an interesting one. According to this book, thousands of years ago, people believed that good spirits lived in the trees and that touching wood called on these spirits and protected people from danger.

C That's interesting. I also do that thing with salt, you know, throw it over my shoulder. I've no idea why, though.

E Ah, that's in here too ... Yes, here it is. Apparently hundreds of years ago salt used to be very expensive and valuable, and was mainly used as a medicine, so spilling it was a really bad thing to do. You throw it over your left shoulder – or the right one if you live in Argentina and Italy – into the faces of the evil spirits behind you, to stop them hurting you.

C Hmm, sounds like an interesting book.

E Yes, it is. You can borrow it when I've finished, if you like.

C Yes, please. Thanks a lot.

R6.7

SARAH CLARK Hello, everyone. Welcome to today's meeting. Perhaps we can start by all introducing ourselves. My name's Sarah Clark, from the local government planning department, and I'm chairing today's meeting.

JIM MATTHEWS Hello, everyone. I'm Sergeant Jim Matthews from the Avon and Somerset Police Force.

TERRY GIBSON Hi, my name's Terry Gibson, from the UK Party Network. We organise gigs and festivals all over the country.

FELICITY RICHARDS And I'm Mrs Felicity Richards. I live in Coleford, which as you know is very near the suggested site of the festival.

PAUL DAVIDSON Hello, I'm Paul Davidson, and I'm a local farmer.

SC Thank you all very much. As you all know, we're here to discuss the UK Party Network's application for a music festival on Paul Davidson's farm, near the village of Coleford. Right, Mr Gibson, perhaps you would like to start by telling us a bit more about the festival.

R6.8

SARAH CLARK ...telling us a bit more about the festival.

TERRY GIBSON Please call me Terry. Well, we're planning to put on a 3-day festival at Mr Davidson's farm on the last weekend in August. We're hoping to have a capacity of 30,000 people, and there will be—

FELICITY RICHARDS Sorry, do you mind if I interrupt?

TG Sure, go ahead.

FR Did you say 30,000 people?!

TG Yes, that's right.

FR Well, how do you expect our little village to cope with that many people? It seems to me that you haven't thought about local residents at all.

TG That's not true, actually, Felicity.

FR Mrs Richards.

TG Sorry – Mrs Richards. We've been running festivals for over 10 years and we've always had a very good relationship with local residents. This festival will bring thousands of people to the area, which will help local businesses and provide jobs for local people.

FR Well, I'm not sure about that. The people who go to these festivals aren't the kind of people we want in our village. It seems to me that the only thing you care about is—

PAUL DAVIDSON Can I just say something here?

FR If I could just finish making this point. The only thing you people care about is making money. You don't care about local residents at all.

SC Paul, you had something you wanted to say.

PD Yes, thank you. I just wanted to point out that my farm is over 4 miles from Coleford, so most of the festival-goers won't pass through the village at all. You'll never know it's happening.

SC What's your opinion, Sergeant?

JIM MATTHEWS I'm not sure I agree, actually. Not many people will pass through the village, that's true, but residents will definitely know there's a festival because of the noise.

FR Yes, absolutely.

TG But the noise won't be a problem, I promise you. The live music stops—

FR Won't be a problem?

TG Can I just finish what I was saying?

FR Yes, of course.

TG The live music will stop at midnight, and after that it'll be very quiet, I promise you.

PD Can I make a point here?

SC Yes, of course.

PD Don't forget there's a hill between Coleford and the farm, so that will stop a lot of the noise.

FR That may be true, but what about all the cars? Surely the traffic will be a big problem?

JM Yes, I'd agree with that. The roads around here aren't really big enough for that amount of traffic. That's what worries me most about this idea, to be honest. And there's also the problem of security. We might not have enough police to deal with this festival.

SC What do you think, Mr Gibson?

TG Well, we will be providing our own security staff to check tickets and ...

R6.9

You had something you wanted to say. | What's your opinion? | What do you think? | That may be true, but what about ...? | Yes, absolutely. | Yes, I'd agree with that. | That's not true, actually. | Well, I'm not sure about that. | I'm not sure I agree, actually. | Sorry, do you mind if I interrupt? | Can I just say something here? | Can I make a point here? | Sure, go ahead. | Yes, of course. | Can I just finish what I was saying? | If I could just finish making this point.

R6.10

Listening Test (see Teacher's Book)

R7.1

I was able to /tə/ learn this very quickly. | I'm still useless at /ət/ doing these things. | I could do these things after I read the instructions. | I haven't got a clue how to /tə/ do this. | I usually manage to /tə/ find what I want. | I'm quite good at /ət/ doing this. | I have no idea how to /tə/ do this. | I find this quite easy to /tə/ do. | I think I know how to /tə/ do this. | I'm able to /tə/ use most new stuff. | I find it difficult to /tə/ use anything new. | I'm no good at /ət/ using new stuff.

Recording Scripts

R7.2

ANSWERS 2 to save 3 type 4 to go 5 send 6 search 7 to create 8 working 9 to sort out

R7.3

DON I came here to work for a multinational company about 10 years ago, and I've been here ever since. I love living here, but it can get really hot in the summer months, and I'm no good at all in that kind of weather. Er, which is why air conditioning is so important here. I know for sure, if we didn't have it in the office, I wouldn't get much work done. I just don't know how people managed to do anything here before it was invented. And if we didn't have it at home I wouldn't get any sleep at all.

HOLLY I like straight hair, but mine is really curly and I hate it. So after I wash my hair I always have to use these hair straighteners. I'd never leave the house if I didn't have these. Well, would you go out in public if you looked like a clown? I've had these straighteners for a couple of years now, they're OK but, um, they're not as good as my friend Jane's. But the really good ones are quite expensive. Still, I've got my birthday coming up next month, and Mum says if she has enough money, she'll get me some new ones.

KATHY I've got absolutely no sense of direction and I'm hopeless at finding my way around. My brother-in-law's got a new car and it's got a GPS, and it's just amazing. If my car had one, life would be so much easier. I'd probably never get lost again in my life. I'd get one tomorrow if I had enough money, that's for sure. But, um, they're still quite expensive at the moment so I'll have to wait until they come down in price. But you know, I spend so much on petrol because I get lost all the time, it might be cheaper to buy one now.

R7.4

if I didn't have these → I'd never leave the house if I didn't have these. | life would be so much easier → If my car had one, life would be so much easier. | I wouldn't get much work done → If we didn't have it in the office, I wouldn't get much work done. | if I had enough money → I'd get one tomorrow if I had enough money. | I wouldn't get any sleep at all → if we didn't have it at home, I wouldn't get any sleep at all. | if you looked like a clown? → Would you go out in public if you looked like a clown?

R7.6

1 If he calls, I'll let you know. If he called, I'd let you know.
2 It'd make life easier if we got one of these. It'll make life easier if we get one of these.

3 If they worked harder, they'd pass their exams. If they work harder, they'll pass their exams.
4 You'll enjoy it if you read it. You'd enjoy it if you read it.
5 I'd buy a new TV if I had enough money. I'll buy a new TV if I have enough money.
6 If they need a computer, they'll buy one. If they needed a computer, they'd buy one.

R7.7

ANSWERS 1 I'd 2 didn't 3 see 4 I'll 5 wouldn't 6 knew 7 didn't 8 I'd 9 write 10 I'll

R7.8

These days, computer viruses are /ə/ part of /əv/ everyday life. But as /əz/ early as /əz/ 1940, a man called John von Neumann predicted that /ðət/ computer programmes would be able to /tə/ make copies of /əv/ themselves – and /ənd/ he was /wəz/ right. This ability has /həz/ meant that /ðət/ people have /həv/ been able to /tə/ create viruses which can /kən/ travel from /frəm/ computer to /tə/ computer. As we all know, computer viruses can /kən/ cause a huge amount of /əv/ damage – but what's the history of /əv/ these viruses, and /ən/ what kind of /əv/ people write them?

The word 'virus' was /wəz/ first used by a computer scientist called Frederick Cohen in 1983. He noticed that /ðət/ a computer virus travels from /frəm/ computer to /tə/ computer in the same way as /əz/ a flu virus travels from /frəm/ person to /tə/ person. The first virus to /tə/ travel from /frəm/ PC to /tə/ PC was /wəz/ called Brain in 1986. Its creators, Basit and /ənd/ Amjad Alvi, owned a computer store called Brain Computer Services in Pakistan. They created the virus so they could find out how many people were /wə/ stealing their software, and were /wə/ amazed when their virus spread all over the world and /ən/ became international news.

Fortunately, Brain didn't do any damage and /ən/ was /wəz/ easy to remove, but later viruses were /wə/ much more dangerous. The famous Melissa and /ən/ Love Bug viruses, for /fə/ example, made headline news in 1999 and 2000 and /ən/ caused enormous problems for /fə/ computer systems everywhere. And in 2004 an eighteen-year-old from /frəm/ Germany, Sven Jaschan, created a virus called the Sasser Worm, which he wrote in his bedroom on a home-made computer. It caused tens of /əv/ millions of /əv/ computers to /tə/ crash all around the world and /ənd/ affected banks, airlines, hospitals and /ən/ government buildings worldwide. The Sasser Worm was /wəz/ particularly dangerous because it could infect any computer online and /ən/ didn't need to /tə/ travel via email, unlike earlier viruses.

Of /əv/ course, viruses aren't the only thing computer users have to /tə/ worry about. Trojan Horses, for /fə/ example, are /ə/ often attached to /tə/ software that /ðət/ you can /kən/ download from /frəm/ the Internet, such as /əz/ computer games. When you open the software, the Trojan Horse loads itself onto your hard disk. It can /kən/ then allow other people to /tə/ access your computer without you knowing about it, for /fə/ example to /tə/ steal your passwords and /ən/ credit card details or to /tə/ send junk emails.

So what do /də/ we know about the young men who write these viruses, people like Sven Jaschan? Well, it seems that /ðət/ most of /əv/ them are /ə/ people who ...

R7.11

1

CAROL Come on, you stupid machine. What's wrong with you?

SIMON Hello, Carol. How was the trip?

C Oh, hello, Simon. Er, it went very well, thank you. Some new contracts, I think.

S Good. Er, don't forget we've got a meeting with our new German clients tomorrow afternoon.

C Yes, don't worry, I hadn't forgotten.

S Do you know if we asked Alex Ross to come? He knows a lot about the German market and should be there, I think.

C I'll call him and check.

S Fine. Oh, by the way, we've got a new computer expert. His name's Ken Baxter.

C Right.

S Yes, he put in a new email system while you were away.

C So that's why I can't log on. Do you think he's changed the password?

S No, your old one should still work.

C Well, it doesn't seem to.

S Well, I'd give Ken a ring. I'm sure he can fix it.

C Right. Can you tell me what his number is?

S Um, it's on the side of the computer.

C Oh yes, thanks.

WOMAN Hello, IT, can I help you?

C Oh, hello. Can I speak to Ken Baxter, please?

W He's not here, I'm afraid. He went out about an hour ago.

C Have you any idea where he's gone?

W Yes, he went to meet an estate agent. He's trying to buy a house.

C Oh, dear. Could you tell me whether he'll be back soon?

W Um, he said he'd be back around 3.

C OK, thanks. I'll call again then. Bye. What was wrong with the old system anyway?

2

CAROL Hi darling, sorry I'm so late. Had a few problems at the office.

BEN Don't worry. I'm glad you're back. I need your help.
c Where's Tim?
B He's gone out.
c Where's he gone?
B To the cinema with some friends. He said you knew about it.
c Oh yes, I remember. Will he be back soon?
B He said he'd be home by 9.
c Right. What are you doing?
B I wanted to finish sending out those party invitations, but I can't get into Tim's laptop. Has he changed the password?
c Yes, now it's "keep out". All one word.
B Very funny. OK, that works. Right, about this party. I thought we could go through the address book and see who we haven't invited yet.
c Good idea. Who's first?
B Right. Did we ask Alex Ross to come? You know, your friend from work.
c Yes, I think so ... Oh no, I forgot to call him about a meeting tomorrow. What's his number?
B Hang on ... it's 020 8244 5690.
c Right, I'll be back in a minute ... Sorry.
B Oh well, at least we made a start ... .

R7.12 R7.13

1 Could you tell me whether he'll be back soon? a)
2 Do you know if we asked Alex Ross to come? a)
3 Have you any idea where he's gone? a)
4 Can you tell me what his number is? b)
5 Do you think he's changed the password? b)

R8.1

Heat from the sun is held in the Earth's atmosphere. | More and more heat is being kept in the atmosphere. | More extreme weather conditions have been caused by climate change. | New Orleans was hit by a huge hurricane in two thousand and five. | More and more places are going to be affected by climate change. | Many towns and villages near the coast will be flooded. | Many other useful tips can be found on public information websites.

R8.2

ANSWERS 1 is hit 2 will be hit 3 spend
4 was hit 5 lost 6 happened 7 was taken

R8.3

VAL Hi, James.
JAMES Hello, Val. Hi, Pete. Come in.
PETE Hi.
v Ready to go?
J Not quite. Do you want a coffee? I've just put the kettle on.
v Yes, sure. You get ready, we'll make it.
J OK. Oh, there's a bit of pasta there too if you're hungry.

v Er, no thanks, we've just eaten ... Well, I've found some coffee, but there's no sugar.
P There's some in that jar by the toaster.
v Oh yes.
P Hm. There's enough milk for two cups, but not enough for three, I don't think.
v It's OK, I'll have it black.
J Can someone feed the cat? There are plenty of tins of cat food in the cupboard.
v Sure. Here you go, kitty. James, where's your recycling box?
J Haven't got one. Why?
v Oh, everyone should have a recycling box. Too much rubbish is just thrown away when a lot of it could be recycled.
J Oh, dear, you're probably right. I never recycle anything, I'm sorry to say.
P Well, you're not the only one. Hardly any stuff is recycled in this country. Did you know that Germany recycles over 50% of its rubbish, but in the UK it's only about 15%.
J Hm, that's not much, is it?
v No, and there aren't enough recycling bins in this country. With stuff like ... er, glass, for example, we only recycle 25%, but in Switzerland they recycle about 90%!
J Yes, I see what you mean. I hadn't really thought about it.
v Well, it's never too late to start. And there's a lot of stuff in your bin that could be recycled. Look, there's loads of paper and several plastic bottles. The bottles can be made into supermarket bags and the paper can be made into toilet paper – and, oh, these empty cat food tins can be recycled and the metal could be used for making fridge parts.
J Wow, you know a lot about all this.
P Yes, well, there's plenty of information on it these days, isn't there? But it's hard changing people's habits in this country. People are naturally lazy, I think.
v Yes, too many people just don't bother. But the government should do more too. In Germany people *have* to recycle their rubbish – it's the law. They should do that here too, I think.
J Yes, I suppose you're right. I've only got a few friends who recycle things. But in the future I'll try to recycle what I can.
P Come on, we're late.
J Let me get my coat. Won't be a second.
v We made a little progress there.

R8.4 R8.5

I think there's a bit_of milk_in the fridge. | We haven't got_enough bags_of crisps. | There's hardly /j/ any food in the cupboard. | He's got_a lot_of tins_of cat food. | We need to get_a few packets_of biscuits. | There's lots_of coffee /j/ and plenty /j/ of cups.

R8.6

BEVERLY A British tourist has been_attacked by /j/ a shark_off the coast_of Texas, making it the /j/ eighth shark_attack in the /j/ USA this year. We now go /w/ over live to Freeport for /r/ a special report from_our North_American correspondent, Andrew /w/ Evans. Andrew, /w/ I /j/ understand the man didn't do /w/ anything_unusual to cause this_attack.
ANDREW Yes, that's right, Beverly. Mark Skipper, a 47-year /r/ -old man from_Oxford, was just swimming_on his_own quite close to the beach when he was_attacked.
B How badly was he hurt?
A Well, we don't have much_information yet, but we know his leg was bitten quite badly. He was_immediately taken to hospital_and we're waiting to hear how he /j/ is.
B So /w/ Andrew, why /j/ are the sharks coming_in so close?
A Well, Ryan Williamson, who works for the Texas Parks_and Wildlife Department, believes that the /j/ increase_in shark attacks_is because_of what they call dead zones. These_are /r/ areas_in the /w/ ocean where there /r/ isn't_enough_oxygen, so /w/ all the fish die.
B So there /r/ aren't_any fish for the sharks to /w/ eat.
A Exactly. Many /j/ of these dead zones are /r/ actually quite close to the coast, so the sharks come_in closer /r/ and closer looking for food.
B So what turns_an_area /r/ of the /j/ ocean_into /w/ a dead zone?
A I'm_afraid_it's_us, Beverly, people. There's too much pollution in the sea – and_it's killing_all the fish. And these dead zones cover fairly large_areas – the one we're talking_about here, for /r/ example, covers_about 5,800 square miles.
B And are these dead zones only /j/ around the US coast?
A No, they're not. According to the United Nations, there /r/ are /r/ about_a hundred_and fifty dead zones_around the world – that's twice_as many /j/ as there were 15 years_ago. The largest ones_are /r/ in the /j/ oceans_and seas_around China, Japan, South_America, Australia, and New Zealand. And the number /r/ of shark attacks has_increased_in_all_of those places.
B So /w/ is the wildlife department_in Texas now saying that people shouldn't go swimming?
A No, they /j/ aren't telling people to stay /j/ out_of the water, but they've_advised holidaymakers

Cultura Inglesa

not to go swimming early /j/ in the morning or /r/ in the /j/ evening, because those are the times when sharks feed.

B Thank you, Andrew /w/ Evans, for that report.

R8.7

1

JESSICA You obviously know this area well. Could you give us some advice?

FRANK Well, if I were you, I'd take plenty of warm clothes. The weather can turn bad very quickly.

J Yes, we've got enough, I think.

F And don't forget to check the weather forecast before you set off.

J Yes, we will. Anything else we should know?

F Yes. Watch out for bears.

J Right! What should we do if we see one?

F Make yourself look as big as possible. Open your coat, stand on your toes – anything to make yourself look bigger. With any luck, it'll leave you alone.

J Er ... I hope so!

F And be careful when you're crossing rivers, they can be quite dangerous. Which reminds me – it's a good idea to take a spare map in case you lose one.

J That's a good idea. I hadn't thought of that.

F The last bit of advice – stay together at all times.

2

CLIVE Your car's over there, and here are the keys.

HENRY Thanks a lot.

C No worries. Is this your first trip to the outback?

H Yes, it is actually.

C Well, whatever you do, don't leave without telling people where you're going.

H Oh, good idea. I hadn't thought of that.

C And don't forget to tell them when you expect to be back.

H Right. And what do you think we should take with us?

C Well, make sure you take plenty of water. You'll need it out there. And of course you'll need your own food, sun cream, a hat and a spare can of petrol.

H Right, that's really useful, thanks. And do you think it's a good idea to take some warm clothes? I hear it can get cold at night.

C Yes, that's always a good idea. Oh, and watch out for kangaroos, particularly when it starts to get dark. They move around a lot in the evening and you might hit one. The big ones can cause a lot of damage to your car. I mean, my car!

H Right, thanks. That's very helpful. See you next week!

3

INSTRUCTOR Right, this is your first open water dive, so be careful. Remember, whatever you do, don't lose your partner. Stay together at all times, and watch out for sharks.

DIVER 1 What should we do if we see one?

I Just stay calm. Most of them are harmless and remember, sharks under water look a lot bigger than they really are. So if you see one, don't worry. It'll probably just swim past you.

DIVER 2 And if it doesn't?

I Well, just swim away and come back up. But remember, don't come up too quickly or else you could be in trouble.

D2 Right. OK.

I OK we've got 40 minutes' bottom time. Don't forget to check your air every 2 minutes. And if you start to shiver, that's a bad sign because it means you've lost too much body heat. So if that happens, you'd better come up immediately. OK. Ready everyone?

DIVERS Ready, Yes, Let's go!

I Right, let's have some fun! In we go!

R8.9

ANSWERS 2 blue 3 living 4 down
5 completely 6 There's 7 old 8 very 9 now
10 Just 11 here 12 away 13 probably 14 ever
15 us 16 hot 17 all 18 again 19 on

R9.2

ANSWERS 1 A surgeon 2 An operating theatre
3 Asthma 4 A specialist 5 The A&E
department 6 An allergy

R9.3

AMBER BENSON Hello, I'm Amber Benson, and here is the news this Tuesday lunchtime. The health service has failed to meet its targets to reduce waiting times in A&E departments in NHS hospitals, according to a new survey carried out by the British Medical Council. The survey said that patients were still waiting too long to see a doctor, with some patients waiting up to 9 hours. However, government spokesperson Francis Hall told reporters that the situation was improving.

FRANCIS HALL We haven't met our targets yet, that's true, but we've made a lot of progress. The average waiting time has already been reduced from 3½ hours to nearly 2½ hours, and we expect to see even better figures in the future.

AB A new report on allergies has just been published. The report shows that allergies have become one of the UK's biggest causes of illness, with one in three people now affected. According to the report, the UK also has the highest rate of asthma in Europe, and treatment for this illness cost the NHS over £1 billion last year. Dr Jeff Gordon, from the charity Allergy Action, welcomed the report.

JEFF GORDON We're pleased to see that the government has finally decided to take this issue more seriously. However, we feel they still haven't told us the whole story. For example, the government has also carried out a survey on the causes of allergies, but why haven't we seen those results yet? That survey still hasn't been published, although it was completed 6 months ago. We think they're hiding something.

AB And we've just heard that the actress Tanya Fisher has died. She was taken to hospital two days ago with heart problems. Mrs Fisher was best known as Jennifer Sheldon in the TV comedy series *Over My Dead Body*. She was 79. That's the news this Tuesday lunchtime, now over to Danny Strong for the sport.

R9.5

A new survey has /həz/ just been /bɪn/ published. | The government has /həz/ just published a new survey. | Three people have /həv/ been /bɪn/ taken to hospital. | The police have /həv/ taken three people to hospital. | The government hasn't met its targets yet. | The targets haven't been /bɪn/ met yet. | The workers have /həv/ already rejected the pay offer. | The pay offer has /həz/ already been /bɪn/ rejected.

R9.6

ANSWERS 2 have been arrested 3 has been taken 4 has been called off 5 has accepted
6 have found 7 have been discovered
8 has just arrived 9 has already sold

R9.7

INTERVIEWER With me in the studio is Dr Miriam Richards, who's a lecturer in psychology at the University of Washington.

MIRIAM Hello.

I Now, Dr Richards, I've heard that body language is responsible for 80% of communication. Is that true?

M Well, yes, it can be, in certain situations. For example, when you're meeting new people, at, um, at a party or somewhere, body language is usually more important than what you say.

I And most body language is instinctive, isn't it?

M Of course. And it's much harder to change your body language than it is to control what you say. For example, when someone is lying, they'll often avoid eye contact. However, very good liars might, er, might make more eye contact than usual to try and make you think they're telling the truth.

I Really?

M Yes, and they often smile a lot too – but they won't be real smiles, of course.

I So how can you tell if a smile is real?

M   Well, a real smile uses the muscles around the eyes, but a fake smile doesn't. So if you can't tell if someone's really smiling, then look at their eyes, not their mouth.

I   Are there any other ways you can tell if someone is lying?

M   Oh yes. When we tell the truth, our eyes tend to move to the right, because the left side of the brain, which stores facts, controls the right side of the body.

I   I see.

M   Yes, and when we're lying, the right side of the brain, which controls imagination, makes the eyes go left.

I   Hmm, that's interesting.

M   Yes, and people tend to look up when they're telling the truth, because they're getting information from their brain. If they start lying, they'll look down or straight ahead. When they go back to telling the truth, their eyes will go up again.

I   I've also been told that people put their hands over their mouths when they're lying. Is that true?

M   Yes, it is. People also touch their noses a lot when they're lying, because that covers the mouth too.

I   Fascinating. And what about white lies?

M   Well, of course most people tell white lies when they don't want to hurt people's feelings, for example, er, saying a meal was delicious when it was awful. But some people can also train themselves to become expert liars, like, er, politicians, for example.

I   Thanks for coming in to talk to us today.

M   My pleasure. And I really mean that.

R9.9

1   My aunt is 40 today. a) Br b) Am
2   I saw a girl walking across the park. a) Am b) Br
3   Why can't you ask your mother? a) Am b) Br
4   My brother's got a lot of cars. a) Br b) Am
5   The water isn't very hot. a) Br b) Am
6   This party's better than I thought. a) Am b) Br

R9.10

ANSWERS 2 feeling 3 allergic 4 eaten 5 back 6 taking 7 symptoms 8 look 9 temperature 10 prescription

R9.11

1

DOCTOR   Hello, Mr Philips. Take a seat.

MR PHILIPS   Thanks.

DR   Now what seems to be the problem?

MR P   Well, er, I'm not feeling very well. I've got a terrible stomach ache and I keep throwing up.

DR   Have you had any diarrhoea?

MR P   Yes, I have, actually.

DR   How long have you been feeling like this?

MR P   Since, um, late last night.

DR   Do you know if you're allergic to anything?

MR P   No, not that I know of.

DR   What have you eaten recently?

MR P   Well, let me think … my children cooked dinner for my wife and me last night. It was our wedding anniversary, you see, and they wanted to surprise us.

DR   What did you have?

MR P   Well, I'm not sure what it was, actually. Some sort of, er, seafood and pasta dish. They spent a long time cooking it, so, you know, I felt I had to eat it. It wasn't very nice, to be honest. My wife hardly ate any.

DR   OK, I think you've got food poisoning. The best thing to do is to rest and don't eat anything for the next 24 hours. After that you can eat things like bread or rice, but no milk or cheese.

MR P   Right.

DR   And drink lots of water or black tea with a little sugar in.

MR P   OK. Do I need to make another appointment?

DR   No, I'm sure you'll be fine, but come back if you're not feeling better in two days.

MR P   Thanks a lot.

DR   And maybe tell your kids that you want to go to a restaurant next year.

MR P   Yes, I will. Goodbye.

DR   Goodbye.

2

DOCTOR   Hello. It's Mr Taylor, isn't it?

MR TAYLOR   Yes, that's right.

DR   Please sit down.

MR T   Thanks. Achooo!

DR   What seems to be the problem?

MR T   Well, I haven't been feeling very well recently. My chest hurts and I keep getting really bad headaches.

DR   Have you been taking anything for them?

MR T   Yes, paracetamol, but, er, they don't really help much.

DR   Have you got any other symptoms?

MR T   Yes, I can't stop sneezing. Achoooo!

DR   Yes, I can see that. And how long have you been feeling like this?

MR T   Oh, let me see, it's 3 days now.

DR   Right, let me have a look at you. Say "aaaah".

MR T   Aaaah … .

DR   … That's fine, thanks. I'm just going to take your temperature …Yes, you've got a bit of a temperature, but nothing serious. I think you've got a virus. You need to stay in bed and rest for 2 or 3 days.

MR T   Do I need a … a … a …

DR   A what?

MR T   ACHOOO!

DR   Bless you.

MR T   Thanks. Do I need some antibiotics? I'm allergic to penicillin, by the way.

DR   No, antibiotics don't work with viruses, but I'm going to give you something stronger for the headaches.

MR T   Oh, right.

DR   Here's a prescription for some painkillers.

MR T   How often should I take them?

DR   Every 4 hours. If you're not better in 3 days then come back and we'll do some blood tests.

MR T   Thank you, doctor.

DR   Not at all. Goodbye.

MR T   Bye.

DR   Right, who's the next patient … AchOOO … oh no …

R9.12

I'm not feeling very well. | I haven't been feeling very well recently. | I've got a terrible stomach ache. | My chest hurts. | I keep getting really bad headaches. | I can't stop sneezing. | Do I need some antibiotics? | I'm allergic to penicillin. | How often should I take them? | Do I need to make another appointment?

R10.1

PEGGY   Hello?

LEO   Hi, Mum.

P   Oh, hello darling. How are you?

L   I'm OK, thanks. Did you get the message I left yesterday?

P   Oh, dear, yes I did. I was supposed to call you back, wasn't I? Sorry, Leo, I was out all day. Hope it wasn't important.

L   No, it's OK. It's just that, well, Karen and I wondered if you had any special plans for your wedding anniversary this year. You know, as it's your 25th and all that.

P   Er, well, we were going to spend our anniversary in the cottage in Wales where we had our honeymoon, but it was already booked. Tom was supposed to book it months ago, but he forgot. So the short answer is no, no plans.

L   Right. Karen and I want to organise a party for you. It was going to be a surprise party, but we can't organise it without you.

P   What a lovely idea.

L   Actually, we want to invite all the people who came to your wedding so we borrowed some of your old wedding photos. But we haven't got a clue who most of them are.

P   Well, we've lost touch with most of them. Twenty-five years is a long time.

L   What about the best man?

P   Oh, Derek Bradley. Yes, he and his wife, Brenda, were our closest friends back then. She was my bridesmaid. They moved to New York just after our wedding. We were going to visit them later that year, but we didn't go for some reason. Haven't heard from them in, oh,

153

15 years or so. I've no idea how to get in touch with them.

L Well, if you let me have all the information you've got, I'll try to get hold of as many people as I can.

P Well, let's see. I'm still in touch with Trevor Jones and his wife, Sheila – they met at our wedding, you know. And then there's Jane Lewis. We used to share a flat together. I think I still have a phone number for her somewhere …

R10.2

We were /wə/ going to spend our anniversary in Wales. | It was /wəz/ going to be a surprise party. | We were /wə/ going to visit them later that year. | I was /wəz/ supposed to call you back. | Your father was /wəz/ supposed to book it months ago. | We were /wə/ supposed to leave a message.

R10.3

KAREN You look lovely with your hair up, Mum. And I love that red dress.

PEGGY Thank you, Karen. Have you seen your father?

K Not for a while, no. Anyway, how are you feeling?

P A bit nervous, actually. And where's Leo?

K I'm not sure. He could be picking people up from the station.

P Oh, right.

K Who's that, Mum? The woman in the flowery skirt with wavy hair and glasses.

P That's Brenda Bradley. She was my bridesmaid, remember?

K That's right. That can't be her real hair colour, though, can it? It looks dyed to me.

P Yes, I think it is. She used to be fair, I think. She must be going grey.

K And who's the woman with the blonde hair in the blue suit. Is that Jane Lewis?

P Yes, it might be. Hang on, she's spotted us.

JANE Peggy! Gosh, it must be, what, 15 years since I last saw you.

P Hi, Jane. You look fantastic.

J Thank you. You too. Um, where's Tom?

P Good question. He must be talking to some guests in the other room. So, anyway, what are you doing these days …

LEO Karen!

K Ah, there you are. Have you seen Dad?

L No, why?

K Mum's looking for him.

L Well, he must be around somewhere. He may want to be on his own for a bit. You know, it's a big thing, this party.

K Yes, maybe … Hey, who's that?

L Who?

K Him – the guy in the dark suit with curly hair and the moustache. It could be the guy that moved to New York, er, what's his name, Derek something?

L No, that isn't Derek Bradley. He's the tall guy over there, the one in the grey suit.

K With the beard?

L Yeah.

K Oh, right.

L And that's his son, Nick, next to him, with the flowery tie and glasses.

K Look, the man with the curly hair is coming over.

TREVOR Hi, you must be Peggy's daughter.

K Yes, that's right, I'm Karen. Hi. And this is my brother, Leo.

L Nice to meet you.

T Hi, I'm Trevor Jones. Thanks very much for inviting us, it's a wonderful party.

K Glad you're having a good time.

T Have you met my wife, Sheila?

K Er, no, not yet.

T She's over there – the one with red hair in the dark brown dress. We first met at your parents' wedding, you know…

K Haven't you found him yet, Mum?

P No, I haven't.

K Maybe he's having a secret cigarette somewhere.

P Don't be silly. He can't be having a cigarette. He stopped smoking months ago. Ah, Leo, there you are. Where's your father? He should be here talking to the guests.

L Well, he might be in the bathroom.

P Yes, perhaps. Go and look, will you, Leo?

L Sure, won't be a minute … Yes, he's in there. He's practising his speech in front of the mirror. He says he'll be out in a few minutes.

P Honestly, he must know that speech by now. We spent hours going over it last night. Go and get him, will you? I'm going back to join the party.

L Sure. I'm glad we only have to do this every 25 years!

R10.6

PRESENTER Welcome to *Money Watch*. Today's topic is prenuptial agreements, an[d] with me is Alison Farmer, a lawyer who is an expert_in family law.

ALISON Goo[d] morning.

P Alison, first_of all, we shoul[d] star[t] with the most_obvious question – what_exactly is a prenuptial agreement?

A Well, it's like a divorce contrac[t] couples sign *before* they ge[t] married. They agree how they'll divi**de**_up their property an[d] money if they ever ge[t] divorced.

P Well, don'[t] mos[t] couples jus[t] ge[t] 50 per cent_each of everything they own?

A Er, not usually, no. People don'[t] ge[t] divorce[d] when their marriage is going well, of course, so when people do fall ou[t] they often show their wors[t] side. So a prenuptial agreemen[t] gives people a chance to deci[de] wha[t] to do before they ge[t] themselves into tha[t] situation.

P Right, time for our firs[t] caller, Yolanda Walters from Manchester.

YOLANDA Yes, er, hi. Can you tell me if a prenuptial agreement_is a legal guarantee?

A Not_in the UK, no. People don'**t**_always ge[t] what was written in the prenuptial agreement.

Y Oh, I see. Bu[t] they are in, you know, places like the USA, aren'[t] they?

A Er, well, no, actually they're not. Even in countries where prenuptials are often use**d**_in court, Australia an[d] the USA for example, people can ge[t] more or less than i[t] sai**d**_in the prenuptial agreement.

P Can you give us an example?

A Er, well, Boris Becker, the famous tennis player, an**d**_his wife Barbara Feltus, go[t] marrie**d**_in 1993 an[d] spli**t**_up in the year 2000. When they go[t] marrie[d] Boris was worth 65 million pounds. According to the prenuptial, Barbara was suppose[d] to ge**t**_abou[t] five million pounds, bu[t] she actually go[t] ten million, a one point_eight million pound home in Florida an[d] two thousand five hundred pounds a month for their children.

P Tha[t] probably help**ed**_her ge**t**_over the divorce, I woul[d] think!

A Yes, probably. An[d] Steven Spielberg's ex-wife, Amy Irving, receive**d**_a hundre[d] million dollars when they spli**t**_up after only four years.

P Right, let's go to our nex[t] caller, Marcus Brown from Southampton.

MARCUS Hello. Er, if prenuptials aren'**t**_a guarantee, what's the point_of having one? Isn'**t**_i[t] just_another way for lawyers to make money ou**t**_of people?

A Er, no, no[t] really. If both the husban**d**_an[d] wife agree to follow the prenuptial agreemen[t] when they ge[t] divorce[d] then they don'[t] nee**d**_a lawyer at_all. An[d] when you think you can buy a prenuptial online for £50, it's actually much cheaper than hiring a divorce lawyer.

P OK, over to our nex[t] caller …

R10.7

1

BRENDA Peggy, do you think I could send a few emails? Er, I just want to let people at home know how the party went.

PEGGY Sorry, I'm afraid Tom's using the computer at the moment. He's got to do some stuff for work tomorrow. He probably won't be too long, though.

B No problem, I can do it later. Oh, and is it OK if I borrow a couple of books? I've already read the ones that I brought with me.

P Yes, of course it is. There are some over there you can choose from.

B Thanks.

2

NICK Er, excuse me.

TOM Hi, Nick. What can I do for you?

N May I download some photos onto your computer? When you're not using it, of course. I'd like to send some photos of the party to people back home.

T Sorry, I don't think we have the software for that. Our computer's rather old, you see.

N OK, no problem. Would you mind if I gave my girlfriend a call?

T No, not at all. Go ahead. The code for America is 001, I think.

N Thanks a lot. I won't be too long.

T Oh, don't worry.

N Thanks.

3

DEREK Peggy, Can I make myself a sandwich?

PEGGY Yes, of course you can. Help yourself. You know where everything is.

D Thanks. Do you want one?

P Er, no, thanks, I've just had something to eat.

D Oh, um, do you mind if I do some washing?

P Actually, I'd rather you didn't, if you don't mind. I was just going to do some myself, and I've got rather a lot.

D Sure, no problem. There's no hurry. Oh, by the way, what did you think of …

R10.8

ANSWERS 2b) 3b) 4a) 5a) 6b)

R10.9

Do you think I could send a few emails? | Sorry, I'm afraid Tom's using the computer at the moment. | Is it OK if I borrow a couple of books? | Yes, of course it is. There are some over there you can choose from. | May I download some photos onto your computer? | Sorry, I don't think we have the software for that. | Would you mind if I gave my girlfriend a call? | No, not at all. Go ahead. | Can I make myself a sandwich? | Yes, of course you can. Help yourself. | Do you mind if I do some washing? | Actually, I'd rather you didn't, if you don't mind.

R10.10

ANSWERS 2 going 3 because 4 think 5 see
6 much 7 make 8 two 9 picture 10 hides
11 back 12 much 13 forget 14 going
15 because 16 think

My Notes

My Notes

My Notes

Phonemic Symbols

Vowel sounds

/ə/	/æ/	/ʊ/	/ɒ/	/ɪ/	/i/	/e/	/ʌ/
father ago	apple cat	book could	on got	in swim	happy easy	bed any	cup under

/ɜː/	/ɑː/	/uː/	/ɔː/	/iː/			
her shirt	arm car	blue too	born walk	eat meet			

/eə/	/ɪə/	/ʊə/	/ɔɪ/	/aɪ/	/eɪ/	/əʊ/	/aʊ/
chair where	near we're	tour mature	boy noisy	nine eye	eight day	go over	out brown

Consonant sounds

/p/	/b/	/f/	/v/	/t/	/d/	/k/	/g/
park soup	be rob	face laugh	very live	time white	dog red	cold look	girl bag

/θ/	/ð/	/tʃ/	/dʒ/	/s/	/z/	/ʃ/	/ʒ/
think both	mother the	chips teach	job page	see rice	zoo days	shoe action	television

/m/	/n/	/ŋ/	/h/	/l/	/r/	/w/	/j/
me name	now rain	sing think	hot hand	late hello	marry write	we white	you yes

Irregular Verb List

infinitive	Past Simple	past participle
be	was/were	been
become	became	become
begin	began	begun
bet	bet	bet
bite	bit	bitten
blow	blew	blown
break	broke	broken
bring	brought /brɔːt/	brought /brɔːt/
build /bɪld/	built /bɪlt/	built /bɪlt/
buy	bought /bɔːt/	bought /bɔːt/
can	could /kʊd/	been able
catch	caught /kɔːt/	caught /kɔːt/
choose	chose /tʃəʊz/	chosen
come	came	come
cost	cost	cost
cut	cut	cut
do	did	done /dʌn/
draw /drɔː/	drew /druː/	drawn /drɔːn/
drink	drank	drunk /drʌŋk/
drive	drove	driven
eat	ate	eaten
fall	fell	fallen
feed	fed	fed
feel	felt	felt
find	found	found
fly	flew /fluː/	flown /fləʊn/
forget	forgot	forgotten
get	got	got [US: gotten]
give	gave	given
go	went	been/gone
grow /grəʊ/	grew /gruː/	grown /grəʊn/
hang	hung	hung
have	had	had
hear	heard /hɜːd/	heard /hɜːd/
hide	hid	hidden
hit	hit	hit
hold	held	held
keep	kept	kept
know	knew /njuː/	known /nəʊn/
learn	learned/learnt	learned/learnt
leave	left	left
lend	lent	lent

infinitive	Past Simple	past participle
let	let	let
lie	lay	lain
lose /luːz/	lost	lost
make	made	made
meet	met	met
pay	paid /peɪd/	paid /peɪd/
put	put	put
read /riːd/	read /red/	read /red/
ride	rode	ridden
ring	rang	rung /rʌŋ/
run	ran	run
say	said /sed/	said /sed/
see	saw /sɔː/	seen
sell	sold	sold
send	sent	sent
set	set	set
shake	shook /ʃʊk/	shaken
shoot	shot	shot
show	showed	shown
sing	sang	sung /sʌŋ/
sink	sank	sunk
sit	sat	sat
sleep	slept	slept
speak	spoke	spoken
spell	spelled/spelt	spelt
spend	spent	spent
split	split	split
spread	spread	spread
stand	stood	stood
steal	stole	stolen
strike	struck	struck
swim	swam	swum /swʌm/
take	took /tʊk/	taken
teach	taught /tɔːt/	taught /tɔːt/
tell	told	told
think	thought /θɔːt/	thought /θɔːt/
throw /θrəʊ/	threw /θruː/	thrown /θrəʊn/
understand	understood	understood
wake	woke	woken
wear	wore	worn
win	won /wʌn/	won /wʌn/
write	wrote	written

 **Cultura Inglesa**

My Notes

Cultura Inglesa

face2face

Intermediate Workbook

Nicholas Tims with **Chris Redston & Gillie Cunningham**

Contents

Acknowledgements

Nicholas Tims would like to thank everyone at Cambridge and Pentacor for all their hard work, in particular Sue Ullstein (Commissioning Editor), Rachel Jackson-Stevens, Andrew Reid (Editors) and Linda Matthews (Production Editor) for their invaluable editorial and production skills. He would also like to thank Chris Redston, Gillie Cunningham, Clare Turnbull and Pat Tims for their encouragement and inspiration.

The authors and publishers would like to thank the following teachers for the invaluable feedback which they provided:
Fernando Alba, Spain; Kevin Rutherford, Poland

The authors and publishers are grateful to the following contributors:
pentacor**big**: cover and text design and page make-up
Hilary Luckcock: picture research

The authors and publishers are grateful to the following for permission to reproduce copyright material. All efforts have been made to contact the copyright holders of material reproduced in this book which belongs to third parties, and citations are given for the sources. We welcome approaches from any copyright holders whom we have not been able to trace but who find that their material has been reproduced herein.
For the text on p23: Pascale Harter, adapted from 'Trying the Saharan sand cure', BBC News, www.bbc.news.co.uk; for the text on p43: Sue Flood, adapted from 'Filming killer whales hunting grey whales' *BBC Wildlife Magazine*, April 1999, www.bbc.co.uk/nature.

The publishers are grateful to the following for permission to reproduce copyright photographs and material:
Key: l = left, c = centre, r = right, t = top, b = bottom

Advertising Archives for p33 (t); Ardea/©Francois Gohier for page 43; Bubbles/Angela Hampton for page 15, /Chris Rout for page 32; Camera Press/Stephen Mansfield/TSPL for page 48 (l); Channel 4/RDF Media for page 48 (r); Corbis/©Royalty Free for page 5 (l), /©Bettmann for page 20 (tr), /©Jules Perrier for page 50; Getty Images for pages 10 (t), 17 and 23; Image State/Dave Houser for page 16; Photolibrary.com/ Photononstop for page 5 (r); Punchstock/ Image Source for page 10 (b), /StockDisc for page 13; PhotoDisc for page 31, /Comstock for page 33 (b), /Brand X for page 49, /Digital Vision for page 74; Rex for pages 20 (l), 20 (br), 28 and 63; Science Photo Library/NASA for page 41.

The publishers would like to thank the following illustrators:
Fred Blunt (Joking Apart), Mark Duffin, Joanne Kerr (New Division), Naf (Joking Apart), Jacquie O'Neill

1 How do you feel?

Language Summary 1, Student's Book p114

1A **Be happy!**

Weekend activities V1.1

1

a) Which words/phrases do **not** go with the verbs?

1 go *clubbing/for a walk/exhibitions*
2 have *a quiet night in/the house/a lie-in*
3 visit *friends/relatives/to people online*
4 do *relatives/some gardening/some exercise*

b) Match the incorrect words/phrases in **1a)** to these words/phrases to make four more weekend activities.

~~go to~~ chat visit tidy up

1   *go to exhibitions*

2   ....

3   ....

4   ....

Question forms G1.1

2

Make questions with these words.

a) house / you / at weekends / tidy up / Do / your ?

  Do you tidy up your house at weekends?

b) been / in / the / you / last / clubbing / month / Have ?

  ....

c) quiet / having / you next / When / a / night / in / are ?

  ....

d) round / you / have / How often / do / for dinner / people ?

  ....

e) people / online / ever / Have / chatted / you / to ?

  ....

f) you / a / have / Did / last weekend / lie-in ?

  ....

g) friends / visiting / you / weekend / this / Are / or relatives ?

  ....

h) many / How / last year / go / did / you / exhibitions / to ?

  ....

3 Read the article and write a question from **2** in the correct places 1–5.

Weekends **in** or weekends **out**?

Megan

Karen and Andy

¹*How often do you have people round for dinner?*

MEGAN	Never. But last month I ate out with friends at least five times.
KAREN	About once a month. My husband always cooks. This weekend we're visiting friends for dinner.

2   ....

MEGAN	I haven't had a quiet night in since I was a teenager!
ANDY	Next Friday. We always have a quiet night in on Fridays.

3   ....

MEGAN	Yes, of course. Sunday mornings are perfect for lie-ins!
KAREN	No! Lie-ins are impossible with two young children.

4   ....

MEGAN	Yes, I have. My brother lives abroad and it's cheaper than phoning.
KAREN	The children chat to their friends online, but I haven't tried it yet.

5   ....

MEGAN	No, but I'm looking forward to going next week. It's my best friend's birthday.
ANDY	The last time I went to a club it was called a disco and I was about 18!

4 **a)** Complete the questions with an auxiliary if necessary.

1 How many times __did__ Megan eat out last month?

2 Who _____ cooks when Karen and Andy have friends round for dinner?

3 When _____ Megan last have a quiet night in?

4 How often _____ Karen and Andy have quiet nights in?

5 Why _____ Karen and Andy never have lie-ins?

6 Why _____ Megan going clubbing next week?

7 How many clubs _____ Andy been to in the last year?

8 Who _____ chatted to people online at the weekend?

b) Answer the questions in 4a).

1 _She ate out with friends at least five times._

2 _____

3 _____

4 _____

5 _____

6 _____

7 _____

8 _____

1B Love it or hate it

Likes and dislikes V1.2

1 **a)** Match beginnings of sentences 1–8 to endings a)–h).

1 I'm very interested __e)__
2 I'm quite _____
3 I don't _____
4 I don't like going _____
5 Tidying up my house _____
6 I think lie-ins _____
7 I'm not very keen _____
8 I can't stand _____
9 I enjoy having _____

a) keen on joining my local gym.
b) mind going food shopping.
c) working at weekends.
d) a quiet night in.
e) in working abroad.
f) to the dentist at all.
g) drives me crazy.
h) on takeaway food.
i) at the weekends are wonderful.

b) Match the sentences in 1a) to A–C.

A phrases to say you like something:

__1__ , _____ , _____ , _____

B phrases to say something is OK:

_____

C phrases to say you don't like something:

_____ , _____ , _____ , _____

Positive and negative verb forms, words and phrases G1.2

2 Read Martin's opinion of computers and fill in the gaps. Choose a), b) or c).

There aren't many things I ¹ __don't like__ in life, but computers drive me crazy. Of course, **everyone** ² _____ they are a wonderful invention and we've got one at home for the children. **Both of them** ³ _____ a computer since they ⁴ _____ young and they **hardly ever** ⁵ _____ any problems. But when I ⁶ _____ to send an email or use the Internet, it **never** works properly. I ⁷ _____ excuses – I know it's my problem rather than the computer's. **None of** my friends like computers so maybe it ⁸ _____ something to do with our age. **I don't think** we'll ever understand them.

1 a) 'm not liking   (b) don't like   c) didn't like
2 a) says   b) said   c) is saying
3 a) are using   b) use   c) have used
4 a) have been   b) are   c) were
5 a) have   b) had   c) are having
6 a) tried   b) 'm trying   c) try
7 a) haven't made   b) didn't make   c) 'm not making
8 a) has been   b) was   c) 's

Now read Diane's opinion of computers and fill in the gaps with the correct form of the verbs in brackets. Use the Present Simple, Present Continuous, Past Simple or Present Perfect Simple.

I think computers are amazing. We ¹ _'ve had_ (have) one in our family for almost 20 years – since I ² _____ (be) about 12. At that time we ³ _____ (not use) it for anything serious – **no one** did. My sister and I **usually** played games on it. Then at university I **always** ⁴ _____ (write) my essays on it and I soon realised **there are lots of** things a computer can help with. Since then I ⁵ _____ (not be able to) leave it alone! **All of** my friends ⁶ _____ (call) me with their computer problems. I ⁷ _____ (not get) paid or anything – I just do it as a favour. I ⁸ _____ (help) two of my friends with their computers at the moment – they're broken. **Neither of them** know anything about computers, but they know how to take me out for a meal!

 Match these phrases in bold in 2 with their opposites in bold in 3.

1 There aren't many   _there are lots of_
2 everyone   --------------------
3 Both of them   --------------------
4 hardly ever   --------------------
5 never   --------------------
6 None of   --------------------
7 I don't think   --------------------

 Make these sentences positive or negative by changing the underlined words.

1 I <u>hardly ever</u> send emails from home.
  I usually send emails from home.
2 He <u>thinks</u> the computer's got a virus.
  ----
3 I <u>understood everything</u> he said.
  ----
4 We <u>never used</u> our computer to do serious things.

  ----
5 <u>There aren't many</u> computers at my school.
  ----
6 <u>Joe's repaired</u> my laptop.
  ----
7 <u>None of</u> my colleagues can type quickly.
  ----
8 <u>Neither of</u> our parents can use computers.
  ----
9 He works with computers all day so he <u>doesn't need</u> one at home.

  ----
10 We <u>aren't using</u> the latest software.

Review: verb forms

 Correct the mistake in each sentence.
                        drive
1 My parents ~~drives~~ me crazy at times.
2 I'm going swimming about three times a week.
3 Who does works with you?
4 How many countries have you gone to?
5 In the past I walk to school.
6 I am think you are correct.
7 I'm playing a lot of tennis in my free time.
8 I live in London for three years and I love it.
9 I've been to Brazil last year.
10 Who does they work with?

1C The best medicine

Adjectives to describe feelings V1.3

 Read the sentences. Fill in the puzzle with adjectives to describe how the people are feeling.

1 She works really hard, but she can't get promotion.
2 He's forgotten his best friend's birthday.
3 She's got her driving test this afternoon.
4 He's just come back from a long holiday.
5 He didn't get the birthday present he wanted.
6 They don't understand the exercise.
7 Their son got the job he was applying for.
8 She hasn't got time to do everything she needs to do.

```
↓
1 F R U S T R A T E D
2 E
3 E
4 L
5 I
6 N
7 G
8 S
```

Reading: prepositions with adjectives V1.4

 a) Read the article and choose the correct prepositions.

The funniest jokes in the world?

A recent experiment in the UK attempted to discover the world's funniest jokes. Dr Richard Wiseman from the University of Hertfordshire invited people from all over the world to send in their funniest jokes and rate* the jokes sent in by other people. In the year of the experiment, the website received over 40,000 jokes and 2 million ratings*!

The experiment showed many things about what different nationalities find funny. Many European countries, such as France and Denmark, preferred jokes about things we normally worry ¹about/with/of – for example, death, illness and marriage. Americans and Canadians liked jokes where someone was better ²in/of/at something than someone else. Germans, in particular, seem to be keen ³at/on/about jokes. Overall they gave jokes the highest scores.

Of course, there is a serious reason for the research. Dr Wiseman is interested ⁴in/on/at how we communicate. And humour and laughing are important parts of communication. Dr Wiseman was very pleased ⁵of/with/at the results.

He said the popular jokes seem to have three elements: a stressful situation, we feel superior to someone in the joke and we are surprised ⁶of/by/in something in the joke. Many of the jokes contained all three elements. For example, here is one of the most popular jokes:

> *Two men are playing golf one day. While they are playing they see a funeral procession* passing along the road nearby. One of the golfers stops, takes his cap off his head and closes his eyes. His friend says: "Wow, that is the nicest, sweetest thing I have ever seen. You really are a kind man." The first man answers: "Yeah, well, we were married for 35 years."*

*rate = give something a score (out of ten, for example)
*rating = the score you give something
*funeral procession = the line of people taking a dead body on its last journey

b) Are these sentences true (T), false (F) or the text doesn't say (DS)?

1 [T] The experiment used the Internet.
2 [ ] The experiment lasted 12 months.
3 [ ] The experiment only involved Europeans.
4 [ ] The experiment was just for fun.
5 [ ] French people generally found jokes less funny than Danish people.
6 [ ] German people generally found jokes funnier than other nationalities.
7 [ ] Dr Wiseman felt the experiment was unsuccessful.

1D **At a barbecue**

Question tags [RW1.1]

1 **a)** Fill in the gaps with *not* and the correct form of the auxiliaries *do*, *be* or *have*.

1 You __aren't__ coming tomorrow.

2 I _____ need to bring anything to the barbecue.

3 Clare _____ eat beef.

4 He _____ been here before.

5 They _____ got any children.

6 We _____ see him yesterday.

7 It _____ going to rain.

8 You _____ told him yet.

b) Write the sentences in **1a)** next to the correct question tags a)–h).

a) __You aren't coming tomorrow__ , are you?

b) _____ , is it?

c) _____ , have they?

d) _____ , did we?

e) _____ , has he?

f) _____ , have you?

g) _____ , does she?

h) _____
_____ , do I?

2 Write question tags for these sentences.

1 You eat fish, __don't you__ ?

2 You're vegetarian, _____ ?

3 Children love barbecues, _____ ?

4 They came round for dinner once, _____ ?

5 He's being very sociable, _____ ?

6 Their garden is looking very nice, _____ ?

7 I've cooked too much food, _____ ?

8 We've got a barbecue like yours, _____ ?

3 Change these questions into positive (+) or negative (–) statements with question tags.

1 Is she a teacher? (+) __She's a teacher, isn't she?__

2 Are they married? (–) __They aren't married, are they?__

3 Are we going home soon? (+)
_____

4 Have you met our neighbours? (–)
_____

5 Did you drive here? (–)
_____

6 Is it warm outside? (+)
_____

7 Does he want something to eat? (+)
_____

8 Do you know Sam? (–)
_____

9 Has he got the address? (+)
_____

10 Have you ever tried English sausages? (+)
_____

11 Is he working this weekend? (–)
_____

12 Am I late? (–)
_____

Review: common mistakes

4 Correct the mistake in each sentence.

        interested
1 I'm really ~~interesting~~ in gardening.

2 Everyone want to go clubbing tonight.

3 Their going to have a lie-in tomorrow.

4 I often loose against my brother when we play tennis.

5 He's worked here for the year before last.

6 I've gone to France and I thought it was beautiful.

7 I can't bear Paul and Sallys' dog.

8 Nobody doesn't want to come.

 Reading and Writing Portfolio 1 p64

Cultura Inglesa

9

2 We haven't got time

Language Summary 2, Student's Book p116

2A Slow down!

Work collocations V2.1

1 Put sentences a)–j) in the correct order.

Do you live to work ... or work to live?

a) | 1 | Count the hours! Do you spend more than

b) | | long hours? And weekends? Do you often take

c) | | long hours is an early sign you might be

d) | | work home with you or regularly work

e) | | some time off. It's good for you!

f) | | to meet deadlines and sometimes everyone is

g) | | 50 hours at work every week? Do you work

h) | | a few hours overtime? Of course, everyone has

i) | | a workaholic. Find time to plan a holiday and take

j) | | under pressure at work. But working

Modal verbs (1); *be able to, be allowed to, be supposed to* G2.1

2 Read the conversation and choose the correct verb form.

JAKE I'm really fed up with work.

KAY Why? You ¹*don't have to*/*mustn't* take work home like me.

JAKE I know, but I ²*'m able to*/*have to* work long hours and we're not ³*allowed*/*supposed* to be paid overtime.

KAY You aren't paid overtime! You ⁴*ought*/*'re supposed* to speak to your boss about that.

JAKE I know. I ⁵*should*/*can* ask him about a promotion, too.

KAY Are you ⁶*allowed*/*supposed* to work flexible hours?

JAKE Yes, but we're ⁷*allowed*/*supposed* to be at work between ten and four.

KAY And what about working at home? ⁸*Can*/*Must* you do that?

JAKE We ⁹*'re allowed to*/*must* work at home – but we have to ask our manager first. But I won't ¹⁰*be able to*/*can* work at home until I get my own flat.

KAY Well, you ¹¹*must*/*'re able to* start saving!

JAKE Yes, I know. I think I'm just a bit bored.

KAY Most work isn't interesting, I'm afraid. You ¹²*can*/*ought* to know that by now!

3 Rewrite these sentences with the words in brackets.

1 My advice is to ask for a promotion. (should)

You *should ask for a promotion.*

2 If I were you, I'd take a week off. (ought)

You ....

3 I can't meet you tonight. (not be able to)

I ....

4 It's against the rules to work at weekends. (allowed)

You ....

5 It isn't necessary to wear a tie. (not have to)

You ....

6 It's necessary to arrive before 9 a.m. (must)

You ....

7 The company should give us holiday pay. (be supposed to)

The company ....

8 You aren't allowed to leave work before 4 p.m. (mustn't)

You ....

4 **a) Make questions with these words.**

1 ought / do / we / about / What / to / overtime ?

 What ought we to do about overtime?

2 long hours / you / when you / have a / able / How are / to work / family ?

 ----

3 be / Should / at / of / work / we / pressure / a lot / under ?

 ----

4 we / to / he's / a / tell him that / workaholic / becoming / Ought ?

 ----

5 wear / you / Are / informal / at your / allowed / clothes / to / work ?

 ----

6 Do / to / the summer / time off / in / take / we / have ?

 ----

7 before December / take / all our / Are / supposed / we / holiday / to ?

 ----

b) Match questions 1–7 in 4a) to answers a)–g).

a) ___1___ I'm not sure. Perhaps we should speak to the manager.

b) _____ Yes, we do.

c) _____ No, but sometimes stress is good for your work.

d) _____ Yes, you are.

e) _____ Yes, we should. I don't think he knows.

f) _____ I get up early.

g) _____ Yes, we are.

  # Ready, steady, eat

In the kitchen V2.2

1 Look at pictures a)–t) and find the words in the puzzle.

```
S O P O B R O C C O L I O
A E R E D P E P P E R C A
U L T E P F R E E Z E R U
C O V E N S F R I D G E B
E R U B B I S H B I N C E
P R B L E N D E R G B O R
A R C O O K E R P R A U G
N C A R R O T S E I R R I
R E B E E F U B A L B G N
T O A S T E R U S L E E E
O F R Y I N G P A N J T G
B M I C R O W A V E U T E
B W O K I L A M B P E E K
```

 2 Choose the correct verbs. Sometimes more than one answer is correct.

1 *bake/fry/microwave* food in a frying pan

2 *fry/boil/roast* food in a wok

3 *roast/steam/bake* food in the oven

4 *heat up/fry/microwave* food in a microwave

5 *boil/bake/steam* food in a saucepan

6 *grill/roast/steam* food under the grill

 Cultura Inglesa

Present Continuous and Present Simple `G2.2`

3 **a)** Fill in the gaps with these words/phrases. Use the Present Continuous.

~~become~~	make	not eat	heat up
not help	grow	work	

1 Good cooks _are becoming_ celebrities in the UK.

2 I _____ some soup in the microwave.

3 Ready meals _____ people to eat healthily.

4 That smells good. What _____ you _____ ?

5 I _____ long hours at the moment so I _____ properly.

6 The market for quick, healthy meals _____ .

b) Write sentences or questions. Use the Present Simple.

7 / you often buy ready meals?

Do you often buy ready meals?

8 / he know I'm here?

_____

9 The Spanish and Italians / cook / more than the British.

_____

10 Over 60 million people / live / in the UK.

_____

11 He / not / work / on Fridays.

_____

12 I / not / think so.

_____

c) Match the sentences in **3a)** and **3b)** to these uses of the Present Continuous and Present Simple.

Present Continuous for things that are:

a) happening at the moment of speaking

_2_ , _____

b) temporary and happening around now

_____ , _____

c) changing over a period of time

_____ , _____

Present Simple for:

d) habits, daily routines, things we do every day/week/year, etc. __7__ , _____

e) things we think are permanent or true for a long time _____ , _____

f) verbs that describe states _____ , _____

4 **a)** Read the first part of Alison's email and choose the correct verb form.

From: alisonw@mymail.net
To: kathrynb@mymail.net
Subject: We're making progress

Hi Kate,

I ¹*type/'m typing* this on the laptop while I ²*sit/'m sitting* in our new fitted kitchen! We ³*do/'re doing* a lot of work on the house at the moment and this ⁴*is/is being* our first 'finished' room. It ⁵*always takes/'s always taking* so long to do these things. I ⁶*don't think/'m not thinking* we'll finish the rest of the house before I'm a grandmother! ⁷*Do you remember/Are you remembering* the kitchen in our old house? I think the new people ⁸*still try/are still trying* to finish that!

b) Read the second part of Alison's email. Fill in the gaps with the verbs in brackets. Use the Present Continuous or Present Simple.

Anyway, now we ¹ _have_ (have) a new oven, fridge, freezer – everything. What's more, while I ² _____ (write) to you, Michael ³ _____ (cook)! Surprised? So am I! Usually Michael ⁴ _____ (not understand) recipes unless they ⁵ _____ (use) a microwave. Actually, he ⁶ _____ (do) an Italian cooking course this year. His teacher ⁷ _____ (say) the secret is good quality, fresh ingredients. So we ⁸ _____ (try) to buy organic vegetables from local shops at the moment. ⁹ _____ you _____ (eat) organic food? It all ¹⁰ _____ (taste) the same to me! Dinner's ready! Speak to you soon,

Alison x

2C It's a nightmare

Sleep

1 Replace the phrases in **bold** with the correct form of the phrases in the box.

> take a nap   not sleep a wink   get back to sleep
> have a lie-in   be a light sleeper   be fast asleep
> have nightmares   doze off

take a nap

1 My grandparents often **have a short sleep** after lunch.

2 I **haven't had bad dreams** for a long time.

3 I **didn't sleep at all** last night.

4 My dad often **falls asleep for a short time** in front of the TV.

5 I love **staying in bed** on a Sunday morning.

6 He often wakes up early, but he finds it easy to **go to sleep again**.

7 You won't be able to wake him up. He**'s in a deep sleep**.

8 Shhhh! My brother **wakes up very easily**.

Reading

2 Read the article and write headings a)–c) in the correct places 1–3.

a) How much sleep do we need?

b) Why do we sleep?

c) What happens when we go to sleep?

3 Read the article again and answer the questions.

1 What happens to your heart in stages 1 to 4 of sleep?

   It slows down.

2 Why is stage 5 called REM?

   ----

3 Why do we need stages 1 to 4 of sleep?

   ----

4 What happens during REM sleep?

   ----

5 Why is REM sleep important to babies?

   ----

6 Put these in order of the amount of sleep they need (least to most): babies, adults, bats, giraffes.

The science of sleep

Sleep is one of the body's most mysterious experiences. Scientists don't completely understand the process, but it seems that all living things need some sleep. And some need a lot more than others!

1 --

There are five stages of sleep: stages 1, 2, 3, 4 and REM (rapid* eye movement). In stages 1 to 4 our body becomes more relaxed. Our muscles and heart rate slow down and our brain becomes less active. Stage 5 is called REM sleep. Our heart beats faster and our eyes move quickly in different directions. People dream during this stage and we cannot move at all – probably to stop us from doing the actions in our dreams.

2 --

An average person spends almost a third of their life sleeping! Is it a waste of time? Scientists believe that when the heart and brain slow down, the body is recovering* after the day's work. They also think that REM sleep is important for memory and learning – babies have twice as much REM sleep as adults.

3 --

On average an adult needs about 7–8 hours' sleep every day. A baby needs 12–16. In the animal world, bats sleep for about 20 hours every day. But a giraffe sleeps for only an hour or two every night.

*rapid = very quick
*recover = get back your strength

Gradable and strong adjectives; adverbs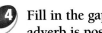

4 Fill in the gaps with these adverbs. More than one adverb is possible.

> really   incredibly   absolutely   extremely

1 *really*   hot   6 ---------------- boiling

2 *absolutely* shattered   7 ---------------- dirty

3 ---------------- beautiful   8 ---------------- tired

4 ---------------- small   9 ---------------- gorgeous

5 ---------------- filthy   10 ---------------- tiny

2D ## What's the matter?

Showing concern, giving and responding to advice **RW2.1**

1 **Choose the best response for each sentence.**

1 Clare's had terrible insomnia.
   a) Oh, dear. What's the matter?
   b) Yes, I see what you mean.
   c) I can see why you're upset.

2 Look at Mike's report. It's terrible!
   a) Oh, how awful!
   b) Oh, dear. What a shame.
   c) Yes, I see what you mean.

3 Mo's in hospital with a broken leg.
   a) Yes, I see what you mean.
   b) Oh, how awful!
   c) Oh, dear. What's the matter?

4 We started at the company at the same time, but he's been promoted.
   a) Oh, dear. What a shame.
   b) I can see why you're upset.
   c) Oh, how awful.

5 Sally lost her job last week.
   a) Oh, I'm sorry to hear that.
   b) I can see why you're upset.
   c) Yes, I see what you mean.

2 **Match problems 1–5 to the advice a)–e).**

1 My children don't eat enough vegetables. _c)_

2 She's angry that I forgot her birthday. _____

3 One of my best students doesn't do his homework. _____

4 I can't sleep! My husband snores so much. _____

5 My sister doesn't go out much because she's got two children. _____

a) You should offer to babysit.
b) Maybe you ought to see the doctor about it.
c) Have you tried giving them a choice of different types?
d) I'd have a chat with him and find out what the problem is.
e) Why don't you send her some flowers?

3 **Complete the conversations with the phrases in the boxes.**

> Oh, dear. What's the matter?   Why don't you
> Yes, I see what you mean   I've tried that
> Have you tried   Well, it's worth a try

1

RITA   Mark seems really fed up at the moment.

DAVID   [1] *Oh, dear. What's the matter?* _____

RITA   I think he's under pressure at work.

DAVID   [2] _____ talk to him about it?

RITA   [3] _____ , but he says I don't understand.

2

SAM   I've got too much work at the moment.

ALEX   [4] _____ .

SAM   I don't know where to start.

ALEX   [5] _____ asking your boss for help?

SAM   [6] _____ , I guess.

> You ought to   I'm sorry to hear that   that's a good idea
> I'd take   I can see why you're upset   might try that

3

CHRIS   Pat and I broke up last week.

SIMON   [7] _____ .

CHRIS   She wants to get back together, but I'm not sure.

SIMON   [8] _____ some time off work and think about it.

CHRIS   Yes, [9] _____ .

4

CHLOE   It was really expensive and it's already broken down twice.

PAUL   [10] _____ .

CHLOE   It's new as well.

PAUL   [11] _____ write to the company.

CHLOE   I [12] _____ . Thanks.

 Reading and Writing Portfolio 2 p66

3 The tourist trade

Language Summary 3, Student's Book p119

 3A # Your holiday, my job

Phrasal verbs (1): travel V3.1

1 Read the conversation. Replace the phrases in **bold** with a phrasal verb from the box in the correct form.

~~look forward to~~	see (somebody) off	get around
put up with	pick (somebody) up	check into
set off	get back	

Are you looking forward to

MUM [1]**Are you excited about** tomorrow?

CASS Of course. We're [2]**leaving** very early, though.

MUM I know. I still want to come to the airport to [3]**say goodbye to you**.

CASS Of course. Thanks, Mum.

MUM And give me a quick call when you[4]**'ve arrived at** the hotel.

CASS Sure. Are you going to miss me?

MUM A bit. But at least I won't have to [5]**tolerate** your loud music.

CASS And you won't have to give me lifts so I can [6]**travel about**.

MUM No. That's true. So what time do you [7]**return**?

CASS At one o'clock in the morning.

MUM That's late!

CASS I know. So I was wondering ... can you [8]**meet me** in the car?

Present Perfect Simple G3.1

2 Fill in the gaps in conversations 1–6 with the verbs in brackets. Use the Present Perfect Simple.

1 A Shirley *hasn't been* (not go) abroad.

 B You're joking! Not even to France?

2 A *Have* you ever *worked* (work) in tourism?

 B Yes, I was a waiter in a hotel a long time ago.

3 A You *have* never *brought* (bring) me back anything from your holidays.

 B Yes, I have! I gave you a picture of Venice once.

4 A Wow! You two have got a good suntan.

 B Yes. We *have* just *got back* (get back) from two weeks in the Caribbean.

5 A Hi, can I speak to Pat or Harry Skilton please?

 B Let's see. I'm afraid they *haven't checked into* (not check into) the hotel yet.

6 A The passengers are angry about the late flights.

 B I know. I *have* already *dealt* (deal) with three complaints today.

3 Are sentences 1–9 correct? Change the incorrect sentences.

've known

1 I ~~knew~~ him since I was young.

2 Wendy and Carl never saw our old house.

 for

3 We've run a bed and breakfast ~~since~~ three years.

 have   d

4 I like your house. How long ~~did you live~~ here?

 gone

5 Mark isn't here. He's ~~been~~ to work.

6 We've set off hours ago, but we're stuck in traffic.

7 We haven't had a holiday this year.

 Have   ed

8 ~~Did~~ you check into the hotel yet?

9 No one has picked me up at the airport.

4 Fill in the gaps with the Past Simple or Present Perfect Simple of the verbs in brackets.

José Guerreiro is a head chef in a restaurant for 1,000 people. But it's not a normal restaurant. It's open for breakfast, lunch and dinner, and it's always full.

José Guerreiro trained as a chef in Goa, India and ¹ _spent_ (spend) seven years working in restaurants in Indian cities. Then he saw an advertisement which changed his life. "I ² _'ve always loved_ (always love) travelling so this seemed perfect," said José. He was offered the job and it ³ _didn't take_ (not take) him long to make his decision. Six months later he started work on a cruise ship, *The Sea Princess*.

15 years later, José is Head Chef on the same ship. "I ⁴ _have worked_ (work) on four ships since I ⁵ _joined_ (join) the company.

But this is the first time I ⁶ _have been_ (be) Head Chef on a cruise. I ⁷ _have never felt_ (never feel) so nervous in my life!"

José shouldn't be nervous. In over 20 years as a chef he guesses he ⁸ _has learned_ (learn) cooking styles from over 20 countries. "I can't think of anything I ⁹ _haven't cooked_ (not cook). I ¹⁰ _have dealt with_ (deal with) every kind of special diet you can think of!" he laughed. "We had one passenger who ¹¹ _couldn't_ (not can) eat meat, fish, milk products or bread!"

I saw José again at the end of the first week. I asked him "What ¹² _have_ we _eaten_ (eat) so far, José?"

"So far, you ¹³ _have drunk_ (drink) 5,000 litres of milk and 150 kg of coffee. We ¹⁴ _have roasted_ (roast) about 1,000 chickens and made over 300 birthday and anniversary cakes. And no one ¹⁵ _have complained_ (complain) yet!"

3B Lonely Planet

Phrases with *travel*, *get* and *go on*

V3.2

1 **a)** Fill in gaps 1–3 with these verbs.

| ~~travel~~ | get | go on |

b) Fill in gaps a)–f) with these words/phrases.

~~together~~	taxi to work
on your own	a journey
a cruise	out of a car

1 _travel_
light
a) _together_
b) _____

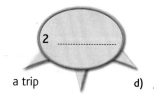

2 _____
a trip
c) _____
d) _____

3 _____
on a bus
e) _____
f) _____

Present Perfect Continuous and Present Perfect Simple `G3.2`

 2 **Make sentences in the Present Perfect Continuous with *for* or *since*.**

1 They started going on cruises three years ago.

   They've been going on cruises for three years.

2 Marta started giving guided tours when she was 16.

   ----

3 I started looking forward to my holiday six months ago.

   ----

4 Cambridge University Press published its first book in 1584.

   ----

5 We started going out together when I was 18.

   ----

6 You moved into this house two months ago.

   ----

 3 **Choose the correct words. Sometimes both verb forms are possible.**

 Philip Martin has never [1](had)/*been having* a permanent home. He's [2]*travelled/been travelling* round the world since he left university. "There are over 190 countries in the world and I've [3]*stayed/ been staying* in about 85 of them," he told me. At the moment he's in the Gambia in Africa. Unfortunately Philip hasn't [4]*felt/been feeling* well for the last week. "I've [5]*tried/been trying* a lot of different foods on my travels and I've never [6]*had/ been having* any problems before. But everyone has [7]*looked after/been looking after* me very well!"

For the last ten years Philip has [8]*kept/been keeping* a diary of his travels and so far he's [9]*published/ been publishing* two books about his adventures. Since he started writing, Philip hasn't [10]*had/been having* to do other work. He's just [11]*finished/been finishing* his third book and he's now planning his journey to South America. "I've [12]*explored/been exploring* this world for over 15 years, but I've got a long way to go!"

 4 **Write questions with these words. Use the Present Perfect Simple or Present Perfect Continuous.**

1 How long / Jane / wait?

   How long has Jane been waiting?

2 How many cruises / you / go / on?

   How many cruises have you been on?

3 How many hotels / you / work / in?

   ----

4 How many times / you / go / on a package holiday?

   ----

5 How long / he / take / work home?

   ----

6 How many times / you / get / a taxi to work?

   ----

7 How long / you / study / English?

   ----

8 How long / Tony and Maureen / be / married?

   ----

5 **Fill in the gaps with the correct form of the verbs in brackets. Use the Present Perfect Continuous if possible.**

1 We *'ve been watching* (watch) a lot of travel programmes recently.

2 Why didn't you call me? How _____ you _____ (get around) with a broken leg?

3 We _____ (not go) on a guided tour of the city before, so we'd like to go.

4 The sun _____ (shine) all weekend. It's wonderful!

5 I _____ (go) on package holidays for years and I've never had any problems.

6 Lindsay _____ (not take) any time off this year. She works so hard.

7 _____ you _____ (know) each other for long?

8 I _____ (not travel) first class before and I'm quite excited about it.

9 Who is he? He _____ (stand) outside for hours.

Word formation (1): suffixes for adjectives and nouns **V3.3**

 1 Complete the table with the adjectives or nouns.

	adjective	noun
1	adventurous	*adventure*
2	dangerous	
3		enormity
4		importance
5	sad	
6		seriousness
7	famous	
8	modest	
9	accidental	

2 Read the article. Choose the best answers.

1 Alan is from …

   a) Nepal. (b) the UK. c) Japan.

2 Alan Hinkes has climbed …

   a) Everest 14 times.

   b) 14 mountains in Nepal and Pakistan.

   c) the 14 tallest mountains in the world.

3 Alan climbs mountains because …

   a) he loves doing it.

   b) he doesn't like teaching any more.

   c) he gets a lot of money for it.

4 Alan hurt his back …

   a) in a snowstorm.

   b) because he sneezed.

   c) when he fell.

5 To pay for his trips, Alan …

   a) speaks about his adventures.

   b) makes films about climbing.

   c) both a) and b).

6 In his country, Alan is …

   a) very well-known.

   b) a hero to some people.

   c) a schoolteacher.

 3 Read the article again and fill in gaps 1–9 with an adjective or noun from **1**.

Climb every mountain …

There is a popular saying in Japanese: "There are two kinds of fool*. Those who never climb Mount Everest and those who do it twice."

So what is Alan Hinkes? An ¹a *dventurous* fool perhaps? This 51-year-old former geography teacher has climbed all 14 of the world's highest mountains. More people have landed on the moon than have tried this extremely ²d_____ achievement.

The world's tallest mountains are all in Nepal and Pakistan. They are over 8,000 metres high. At this height helicopters cannot rescue people and the physical demands are ³e_____ . When you finally reach the top of a mountain, there's no time to celebrate – it's ⁴i_____ to remember that you have to get down the mountain again.

Alan's been climbing mountains since he was teenager. "I'm addicted to it," he says. However, there has been some ⁵s_____ in his adventures. In 1995 he was climbing K2 with his close friend Alison Hargreaves. Near the top, they separated and Alan continued to climb alone. Alison and six other people later died in a snowstorm.

One of Alan's most ⁶s_____ injuries on a mountain was rather unusual. He was eating a chapati – a type of Indian bread – when the flour got up his nose and he sneezed*. He injured his back and had to be rescued by helicopter.

Despite his amazing achievement, Hinkes is not ⁷f_____ . His ⁸m_____ means that people remember him more for the chapati ⁹a_____ than the mountains he's climbed. Each trip costs him about £30,000 and he raises the money by giving talks and selling videos of his climbs. Now, many people want him to receive a knighthood* from the Queen. Perhaps the 'fool' Alan Hinkes will soon be Sir Alan Hinkes …

*fool = stupid person
*sneeze = when you sneeze, air comes out of your nose and mouth in a way you can't control
*knighthood = an award from the Queen of England for doing something special

3D # A trip to India

Review: prepositions with adjectives

 1 **Choose the correct preposition. Sometimes more than one answer is possible.**

1 I'm feeling very nervous (of)/(about)/at the flight next week. I'm really scared *with/of/at* flying.

2 I'm fed up *by/with/on* my husband's snoring and he gets annoyed *about/with/of* me when I wake him up.

3 The manager didn't seem concerned *with/about/by* our worries and we were so angry *at/on/with* him that we checked out early.

4 Nikki was very upset *of/by/about* splitting up with Mark, but she told me she was fed up *of/at/with* him going out every night.

Asking for and making recommendations `RW3.1`

 2 **a) Make questions with these words.**

1 know / Do / any good / stay / places / to / you ?

   Do you know any good places to stay?

2 anything / worth / Is / seeing here / there ?

   _____

3 tips / got / other / Have / you / any ?

   _____

4 near / about / sea / places / What / the ?

   _____

5 place / a / the / to / What's / best / car / hire ?

   _____

b) Complete the conversations with the sentences in 1a).

1 A   *Do you know any good places to stay?*
  B   Sorry, no. But I wouldn't recommend anywhere near the station.

2 A   _____
  B   I'd recommend one of the companies at the airport.

3 A   _____
  B   Yes. You should definitely visit the cathedral.

4 A   _____
  B   It isn't really worth going there. The beaches are quite dirty.

5 A   _____
  B   Yes. You should learn a bit of the language. It really helps.

 3 **Fill in the gaps in the conversations with the phrases in the boxes.**

> ~~are the best~~   's the best   'd recommend
> sounds wonderful   wouldn't go   really useful

1

ANN   You've been to India, Louise. What
      ¹ *are the best* places to visit?

LOUISE   I ² _____ Kerala – in the south. Beautiful lakes, canals ... it's like paradise.

ANN   That ³ _____ . What
      ⁴ _____ time of year to visit?

LOUISE   Well, I ⁵ _____ between September and January. It can be really wet then.

ANN   That's ⁶ _____ .

> to know   bother   should go to
> Do you know any   And is there

2

ANN   ⁷ _____ good places to stay?

LOUISE   Yes, but don't ⁸ _____ booking in advance. It's cheaper to get a hotel there.

ANN   That's good ⁹ _____ .
      ¹⁰ _____ anything else worth visiting in the south?

LOUISE   Of course. India's a big place. If you like beaches, you ¹¹ _____ Goa.

> I've heard   And what about   You really must
> It's probably best   Have you got any

3

ANN   ¹² _____ money?

LOUISE   ¹³ _____ to take cash. Credit cards aren't very useful outside big cities.

ANN   Right. ¹⁴ _____ ' other tips?

LOUISE   Lots. ¹⁵ _____ visit one big city. Indian cities are just incredible.

ANN   Yes, ¹⁶ _____ that.

 Reading and Writing Portfolio 3 p68

Cultura Inglesa   **19**

4 Born to be wild

Language Summary 4, Student's Book p122

4A Riders

Music collocations V4.1

1 Fill in the gaps with the correct form of these verbs.

> ~~release~~   see   go (x 2)
> play   appear   have

Nowadays the business of selling music is a little more complicated than simply
¹ _releasing_ a new album. Groups also have to promote their records so they have to ² .... on TV and talk about the new album. What's more, fans like ³ .... their favourite group play live so groups also have to ⁴ .... on tour. ⁵ .... onstage and ⁶ .... concerts every night is exhausting, but if you want to ⁷ .... an album in the charts, you have to promote it!

Past Simple and Past Continuous

G4.1

2 Fill in the gaps with the verbs in brackets. Use the Past Simple or Past Continuous.

Seven things you didn't know about ... Rock and Pop

◆ In 1958, while Elvis ¹ ___was earning___ (earn) $400,000 a month, he had to go into the army. His salary ² .... (go) down to $78 a month.

◆ In 1959, a teacher ³ .... (throw) a 16-year-old Jimi Hendrix out of school because he ⁴ .... (hold) the hand of a white girl in his class.

◆ In April 1964, while the Beatles ⁵ .... (finish) their second album, they ⁶ .... (have) hit records in all of the top 5 positions in the US charts.

◆ In 1963, Roy Orbison ⁷ .... (be) on tour with the Beatles. He ⁸ .... (wear) sunglasses because he couldn't find his glasses. He liked the look so much that for the rest of his career he only ⁹ .... (wear) sunglasses.

◆ In 1970, while the rock group Pink Floyd ¹⁰ .... (playing) in front of a large lake in London, the music ¹¹ .... (be) so loud that some of the fish in the lake ¹² .... (die).

◆ Sheryl Crowe ¹³ .... (lose) her two front teeth when she ¹⁴ .... (be) eight. Over 15 years later she ¹⁵ .... (sing) in a bar when a waitress accidentally ¹⁶ .... (hit) her with a glass. The same two front teeth ¹⁷ .... (fall) out.

◆ In 2000, while Madonna ¹⁸ .... (stay) in Sweden for the MTV Music Awards, she ¹⁹ .... (ask) the hotel to change the colour of the room. She ²⁰ .... (want) a 'calm colour' to help her meditate. Madonna ²¹ .... (not joke) and the hotel immediately ²² .... (paint) the room.

used to `G4.2`

3 Fill in the gaps with *used to* or the Past Simple of the verb in brackets. Use *used to* where possible.

Before they were famous ...

1 Madonna ___used to work___ (work) at Dunkin' Donuts. She ___got___ (get) sacked for spilling jam on a customer.

2 When the rap singer P Diddy _____ (be) a teenager, he _____ (wash) cars and make tea at a record company.

3 Ricky Martin _____ (be) an actor on the American TV soap, *General Hospital*. After two years, Ricky decided he _____ (prefer) music to acting.

4 Elvis _____ (lose) his first job in a factory because he _____ (be) only 15. He _____ (earn) $30 a week there.

5 Britney Spears and Justin Timberlake _____ _____ (present) a children's TV programme called the *Mickey Mouse Club*.

6 Elton John _____ (not be) called 'Elton John'. In 1971, he _____ (change) his name because he wanted to be famous. What _____ his name _____ (be)? Reginald Dwight!

4B Adventurers

Character adjectives `V4.2`

1 Choose the correct word.

1 He works long hours and never takes time off.
   a) ambitious   b) generous   c) (reliable)

2 They often go on holiday to places I've never heard of!
   a) organised   b) adventurous   c) ambitious

3 Tim gets embarrassed quite easily.
   a) sensitive   b) sensible   c) brave

4 My sister always brings me back a present from her holidays.
   a) reliable   b) practical   c) generous

5 I think he prefers to travel on his own.
   a) determined   b) independent   c) confident

6 Kathy will know what time the meeting is.
   a) practical   b) talented   c) organised

7 My boss always makes good decisions.
   a) sensitive   b) mean   c) sensible

8 They won't give up until they find the answer.
   a) determined   b) reliable   c) adventurous

Past Perfect `G4.3`

2 Fill in the gaps with the verbs in brackets in the Past Perfect. Use contractions if possible.

1 Connor ___had arranged___ (arrange) to meet up with some friends so he couldn't come with us.

2 I really wanted to see the concert, but it _____ (sell out).

3 Simon _____ (not drive) abroad before, so he wasn't very confident.

4 I _____ (not hear) any of their music before, but I thought the gig was excellent.

5 By the time I arrived, everyone _____ (leave).

6 He failed the test because he _____ (not do) any revision.

7 When Jade arrived at the restaurant, she realised she _____ (go) there before.

8 They _____ (not know) each other for long when they decided to get engaged.

3 a) Read the first part of Charlie's story and choose the correct words.

By the time I was 18, I ¹*stopped/* (had stopped) going on holiday with my parents. The first year I ²*stayed/ had stayed* at home, my parents asked me to pick them up at the airport. The night before they ³*got back/had got back*, I realised the house was a mess. I ⁴*didn't tidy up/ hadn't tidied up* for two weeks. I finally went to bed about 3 a.m. and a few minutes later I ⁵*was/ had been* fast asleep. I woke up suddenly at 7 a.m. I ⁶*arranged/ had arranged* to meet them at the airport at 6.30 a.m. and I ⁷*didn't set/ hadn't set* the alarm! I quickly set off for Heathrow airport, but there are four terminals at Heathrow airport and it's one of the biggest airports in the world! I had no idea which terminal they ⁸*arrived/ had arrived* at! And this ⁹*was/had been* before the days of mobile phones ...

b) Tick three more events that happen in the story.

a) [✓] Charlie's parents asked him to pick them up at the airport.

b) [ ] Charlie tidied up the house.

c) [ ] Charlie set his alarm.

d) [ ] Charlie's parents arrived at the airport.

e) [ ] Charlie woke up.

f) [ ] Charlie phoned his parents.

 4 a) Read the second part of the story and put the verbs in brackets in the Past Perfect or Past Simple.

When I arrived at Terminal 1, I was an hour late. When I eventually found my parents at Terminal 3, they ¹ __had spent__ (spend) two hours waiting for me. They ² _____ (not be) pleased. They ³ _____ (be) on a flight for 12 hours and they were exhausted. But things were getting worse ... when we ⁴ _____ (get back) to the car, I realised I ⁵ _____ (lose) my car keys somewhere at the airport. We phoned my elder brother and he came and took my parents home.

About three hours later, I ⁶ _____ (get) home. Fortunately someone ⁷ _____ (find) my keys at the airport. The first thing I ⁸ _____ (see) was my father repairing a broken window. What had happened?

When my parents and my brother ⁹ _____ (get) home, they realised they hadn't got any house keys. They ¹⁰ _____ (have to) break a window to get into the house!

b) Put events a)–f) in the correct order 1–6.

a) [1] Charlie lost his keys.

b) [ ] Charlie's parents got home.

c) [ ] Charlie's parents broke a window.

d) [ ] Charlie met his parents.

e) [ ] Charlie got home.

f) [ ] Charlie's brother arrived at the airport.

Review: apostrophes

5 Write the full form of *'s* and *'d* if possible.

1 It**'s** taken three hours to get here. __has__

2 I**'d** always thought he was sensible. __had__

3 He**'s** been living in London three years. _____

4 We**'d** recommend practical clothes for the journey. _____

5 It**'s** published by Cambridge University Press. _____

6 She**'d** never been skiing before. _____

7 They**'d** get home earlier if they didn't always drive. _____

8 It**'s** the first time Simon**'s** been to Scotland. _____ , _____

9 I thought I**'d** enjoy the film because I**'d** loved the book. _____ , _____

10 Paul**'s** brother**'s** always been ambitious. _____ , _____

4C Natural medicines

Reading: guessing meaning from context V4.3

1 Read the article quickly. Complete the sentence. Choose a), b) or c).

The writer tried the sand cure ...

a) because he had health problems.

b) but didn't enjoy the experience.

c) and thought it was a positive experience.

2 a) Look at the words in **bold** in the article. Are they nouns, verbs or adjectives?

1 tribe   ...noun...

2 gaining   ....

3 alleviates   ....

4 backs up   ....

5 peak   ....

6 scorching   ....

7 crunching   ....

8 measly   ....

b) Choose the correct meanings of the words in **2a)**.

1 **tribe**	a) (group of people)	b) group of animals
2 **gaining**	a) increasing	b) decreasing
3 **alleviates**	a) doesn't help	b) helps
4 **backs up**	a) supports	b) doesn't support
5 **peak**	a) lowest point	b) highest point
6 **scorching**	a) very hot	b) very cold
7 **crunching**	a) chewing	b) drinking
8 **measly**	a) very large	b) very small

3 Read the article again. Are these sentences true (T), false (F) or the article doesn't say (DS)?

1 [F] The sand cure is a modern natural cure.

2 [ ] The sand cure is only practised in the Saharan desert.

3 [ ] Tourists have been trying the sand cure.

4 [ ] The sand cure can help with stomach problems.

5 [ ] Local doctors don't think the sand cure is useful.

6 [ ] The writer tried the sand cure because he had had too much tea.

7 [ ] It's good to try the sand cure on windy days.

8 [ ] The writer spent less time in the sand than the Saharawi usually do.

Trying the Sahara sand cure

The Sahara Desert is one of the driest regions on earth. Very little grows in temperatures that can reach 57°C. So what could be healthy about this place? According to the Saharawi, a **tribe** who live in the desert in the Western Sahara, it has more than enough of what is needed: heat and sand*.

The Saharawi have been using the sand cure* for hundreds of years. And recently this treatment has been **gaining** popularity with tourists. My guide explained the technique: "We make a big hole, cover ourselves in lotion*, get in the hole and stay in the sun for a few hours."

The Saharawi believe the cure **alleviates** skin and back problems. And a local doctor **backs up** their claims. Dr Coulon has been a doctor in Morocco for more than 30 years and has tried the sand cure herself. "It's very good for your bones, muscles and circulation," she says.

So, after several cups of mint tea, I agreed to try the cure myself. At midday the heat is at its **peak** and you can hardly walk on the **scorching** sand. I started wishing for a cooling wind. Bad idea. The experience of being buried in sand is not unpleasant – it's a bit like a hot, dry bath. But the experience of **crunching** on sand in your mouth is not pleasant at all.

After 20 minutes I was so relaxed I felt I could stay there for ever. The desert is so quiet. But ten minutes later, my guides starting helping me out. I had spent a **measly** half an hour in the sand. The Saharawis spend two hours. My conclusions? Well, I certainly felt more relaxed and very clean – when I'd got all the sand out of my ears, nose and mouth, of course.

*sand = something found on beaches and in deserts
*cure = something that makes someone with an illness healthy again
*lotion = a liquid that you put on your skin to protect it

Cultura Inglesa

4D It's just a game!

Adjectives to describe behaviour V4.4

1 Complete the puzzle with character adjectives.

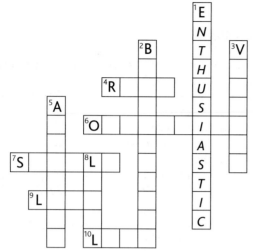

People who ...
1 are very interested and involved in an activity.
2 become angry easily.
3 hurt or attack others.
4 aren't polite.
5 always think they are the best.
6 upset other people by their behaviour.
7 are selfish because they're allowed to do what they want.
8 will always support their friends.
9 don't like working.
10 make a lot of noise.

Softening opinions and making generalisations RW4.1

2 Match sentences 1–5 to the softer opinions in sentences a)–e) about professional football players.

1 They are selfish towards their younger team-mates.
   _d)_

2 They're often a bit stupid.
   ....

3 They train a lot. ....

4 They usually aren't violent people. ....

5 They think they know everything. ....

a) Some of them can be quite arrogant at times.
b) They tend to be rather hard-working.
c) On the whole, most of them aren't very intelligent.
d) They can be a bit inconsiderate towards young players.
e) Generally speaking, they aren't aggressive.

3 Correct the mistakes in the phrases in **bold**.
   quite helpful
1 She can be **helpful quite** at times.
2 **He tends being** rather noisy in class.
3 **On whole** most of our students are hard-working.
4 **General speaking,** my children are quite polite.
5 Some modern films can be a bit **violence**.
6 My teenage son can be **arrogant a bit**.
7 They can be rather **inpolite** at times.
8 A few football fans can be a bit **agressive**.

4 Use the words/phrases in brackets to soften these opinions about men and women.

MEN

1 They snore.
   (Some of them / can / at times)

   Some of them can snore at times.

2 They are considerate.
   (not very / at times)

   ....
   ....

3 They are untidy.
   (Some of them / can / rather)

   ....
   ....

WOMEN

4 They are better with money.
   (tend to / a bit)

   ....
   ....

5 Women like shopping.
   (Generally speaking / most)

   ....
   ....

6 They are more organised than men.
   (On the whole / tend to)

   ....
   ....

 Reading and Writing Portfolio 4 p70

5 Home truths

Language Summary 5, Student's Book p125

5A Moving house

Homes V5.1

 Look at the pictures. Write the names.

Who lives in a …

1 semi-detached house? *Lisa and Mike*

2 detached house? ....

3 bungalow? ....

4 terraced house? ....

Sam

Lisa and Mike

The Stephens family

James and Mel

 Do the puzzle. Find the type of house (↓).

A room or place …
1 outside the house.
2 at the top of the house.
3 where you work.
4 where you cook.
5 where you wash.
6 where the car is parked.
7 at the bottom of the house.

↓

¹B	A	L	C	O	N	Y

Making comparisons G5.1

 Look at the advertisements and match the places to sentences 1–8. Write P (Poplar), H (Hackney) or B (Bow).

Poplar	Hackney	Bow
3-bedroom semi-detached house (needs work) 120 square metres Built in 1910 **£230,000** Distance to underground: 10 mins	2-bedroom spacious terraced house 150 square metres Built in 1920 **£280,000** Distance to underground: 5 mins	NEW 3-bedroom flat 100 square metres **£250,000** Distance to underground: 7 mins

1 [H] It's far more spacious than the other two.
2 [ ] It's slightly cheaper than the Hackney house.
3 [ ] It isn't as big as the others.
4 [ ] It needs a lot more work than the other two.
5 [ ] It's a bit more expensive than the Bow flat.
6 [ ] It's a little older than the Hackney house.
7 [ ] It's slightly further from the underground than the Hackney house.
8 [ ] It's slightly closer to the underground than the Poplar house.

 Glen and Bev went to see the three places. Fill in their comments with these words.

smallest	little	much less	similar
most	best	the least	far	as close

The Poplar house has got the ¹ *smallest* garden I've ever seen.

It isn't ² .... to the underground as they said.

It's very ³ .... to our house.

The Bow flat is ⁴ .... interesting than the others.

It's ⁵ .... more modern than the other two.

It needs ⁶ .... work of the three.

The Hackney house feels a ⁷ .... lighter than the other three.

It's in the ⁸ .... neighbourhood.

It seems to be the ⁹ .... popular of the three.

(5) Glen and Bev are making their decision. Fill in the gaps with the correct form of the adjectives.

GLEN I hate doing this. Everything is so expensive.

BEV Yes ... and then next year they'll be a bit
¹ _more expensive_ (expensive)!

GLEN OK. Well let's start with the flat. I know it's your
² .... (favourite) place.

BEV Yes. But it's just not as ³ .... (interesting) as the other two.

GLEN So, what about the house in Poplar? It's £50,000
⁴ .... (cheap).

BEV And it's probably got the ⁵ .... (character) of the three.

GLEN But could we do all that work?

BEV Well, you're one of the ⁶ .... (determined) people I know.

GLEN Yes, but I'm no ⁷ .... (good) at DIY than you.

BEV So, the Hackney house. I know you thought this was the ⁸ .... (light) of the three.

GLEN But it's in the ⁹ .... (busy) area.

BEV And £280,000 is such a lot of money ...

GLEN Yes, well it's a lot ¹⁰ .... (fashionable) round there than it used to be.

BEV So are we any ¹¹ .... (far) towards making a decision?

GLEN Not really. Let's sleep on it.

5B A load of old junk

Phrasal verbs (2) V5.2

(1) Fill in the gaps with the correct form of these verbs.

~~clear~~	throw (x 2)	come	take
sort	give	tidy	put	go

1 I've been _clearing_ out the junk in the loft.

2 Have you .... out which clothes you want to keep?

3 .... your toys away – it's time for bed!

4 I'm .... out these old CDs! Do you want any of them?

5 Don't forget to .... through the pockets before you wash those trousers.

6 I don't want any money for the old sofa – I'm happy to .... it away for nothing.

7 When are you going to .... away those old newspapers?

8 Are you .... back tonight or are you staying at your friend's house?

9 Have you .... up the living room? It was a mess earlier.

10 The dentist said he'd have to .... a tooth out.

The future G5.2

(2) **a)** Match questions 1–5 to the best responses a)–e).

1 Why are you watching me? _b)_

2 Have you asked your boss about promotion? ....

3 Is Tim there, please? ....

4 Have you decided what you want? ....

5 Why won't you lend him your laptop? ....

a) Wait a minute. I'll just check.
b) Because you're going to cut yourself.
c) Because he'll break it.
d) Yes. I'm going to have some lamb.
e) Not yet. I'm seeing him this afternoon.

b) Match sentences a)–e) in 2a) to these uses of the future.

1 a prediction _c)_

2 a prediction based on present evidence ....

3 a decision made at the time of speaking ....

4 a plan to do something ....

5 an arrangement ....

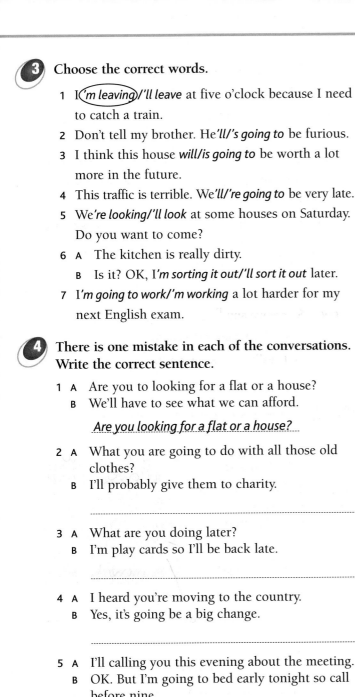

3 Choose the correct words.

1 I *'m leaving*/*'ll leave* at five o'clock because I need to catch a train.

2 Don't tell my brother. He *'ll*/*'s going to* be furious.

3 I think this house *will*/*is going to* be worth a lot more in the future.

4 This traffic is terrible. We *'ll*/*'re going to* be very late.

5 We *'re looking*/*'ll look* at some houses on Saturday. Do you want to come?

6 A The kitchen is really dirty.
  B Is it? OK, I *'m sorting it out*/*'ll sort it out* later.

7 I *'m going to work*/*'m working* a lot harder for my next English exam.

4 There is one mistake in each of the conversations. Write the correct sentence.

1 A Are you to looking for a flat or a house?
  B We'll have to see what we can afford.

  Are you looking for a flat or a house?

2 A What you are going to do with all those old clothes?
  B I'll probably give them to charity.

  ----

3 A What are you doing later?
  B I'm play cards so I'll be back late.

  ----

4 A I heard you're moving to the country.
  B Yes, it's going be a big change.

  ----

5 A I'll calling you this evening about the meeting.
  B OK. But I'm going to bed early tonight so call before nine.

  ----

6 A Mum and Dad will be furious when they see this!
  B I'll to tidy it up before they come back.

  ----

5 Put the verbs in brackets in the correct form. Use the Present Continuous, *be going to* or *'ll* + infinitive. Sometimes more than one answer is possible.

1

RUTH Simon [1] *'s having* (have) a birthday lunch on Sunday.

MEL I know. [2] .... you .... (buy) him a present?

RUTH Yes. That's why I wanted to come to the market.

MEL Well, maybe we [3] .... (find) something here.

RUTH It [4] .... (be) hard. It's mainly a load of old junk.

2

ELLEN Do you think we [5] .... (need) any of this stuff again?

JERRY Well, I [6] .... definitely .... (not listen) to any of these CDs.

ELLEN [7] .... you .... (give) them to charity?

JERRY Maybe. They cost me hundreds of pounds, though.
  Wait. I've got an idea. I [8] .... (sell) them on the Internet!

ELLEN Good idea. People [9] .... (buy) anything on eBay.

3

BEN I [10] .... (tidy) the flat this weekend. It's a mess.

PETE You're right. I [11] .... (not do) anything on Saturday. I [12] .... (help) you.

BEN Ah. I can't do it tomorrow. I'm really sorry. I [13] .... (meet) Amy.

PETE OK. I [14] .... (give) you a hand on Sunday then.

BEN Hmm. I [15] .... (take) Amy to my parents on Sunday.

PETE So when [16] .... you .... (tidy) the flat then?

BEN OK. Maybe I [17] .... (do) it next weekend. Are you free then?

5C Flatpack world

Reading

1 Read the article quickly and decide which paragraph 1–5 is about these things.

a) IKEA's newest product in the UK. __1__

b) The history of BoKlok housing. _____

c) The advantages of prefabs. _____

d) The history of prefabs in general. _____

e) How BoKlok housing is built. _____

2 Read the article again and complete the sentences with the meaning of these names and numbers.

1 IKEA _One of the companies working with BoKlok UK._

2 12

The minimum number _____

3 1998

The year _____

4 Over 2,000

The number of _____

5 Japan and the UK

The countries where _____

_____

Verb patterns (1) V5.3

3 Complete sentence b) so it has the same meaning as sentence a).

1 a) BoKlok makes it possible for low-income people to buy their own home.

   b) BoKlok allows _low-income people to buy their own home._

2 a) It looks like prefabs are more popular nowadays.

   b) Prefabs seem _____

3 a) Over 2,000 people in Scandinavia have bought a BoKlok home.

   b) Over 2,000 people in Scandinavia have decided

   _____

4 a) In the future perhaps more people will live in prefabs.

   b) In the future more people might _____

5 a) Many people want to buy their own home.

   b) Many people would like _____

6 a) It doesn't bother me that I live with my parents.

   b) I don't mind _____

PREFABULOUS!

1 IKEA is working with BoKlok UK to be part of a revolution in housing in the UK. BoKlok means 'Live Smart' and is a project to provide affordable homes to people on average incomes. It aims to build small communities of BoKlok housing with at least 12 flats, 6 in each block.

2 So will you soon be able to go to IKEA and drive away with a new home? Well, no, you won't. BoKlok finds the land, gets permission to build, and the low-cost housing will only be available to people who can't afford their own home. The flats are built in a factory and delivered to the site – IKEA supply the kitchens and the bathrooms. Buyers can then choose furniture and get advice on interior design from IKEA.

3 BoKlok has been selling housing in Scandinavia since 1998 and the flats cost about 30% less than a normal flat. So far, BoKlok has sold over 2,000 homes – all of them in communities with shared facilities, such as gardens, to make neighbours socialise as much as possible.

4 Houses of this type are called prefabs* in the UK and the USA. And they're not a new idea. In the early 20th century, the large American shop, Sears, offered prefabs. In Japan and the UK after World War II, prefabs were a popular way of building new houses quickly and cheaply.

5 Nowadays the price of housing in many countries makes it very difficult for a lot of people to buy or even rent. Prefabs offer home-buyers modern, quality homes which are designed by architects and are often very environmentally efficient. In the USA the popularity of prefabs is growing rapidly with young people who want a 21st century-designed house.

*prefabs = short for prefabricated houses

Is this what you mean?

Materials V5.4

 1 What is the main material usually used in these items?

~~rubber~~	plastic	metal	paper	wool
cardboard	wood	glass	cotton	leather

1 a tyre _rubber_   6 a ballpoint pen _____

2 a mirror _____   7 a microwave oven _____

3 shoes _____   8 a jumper _____

4 socks _____   9 a bookshelf _____

5 boxes _____   10 a magazine _____

Explaining what you need RW5.1

 a) Match sentences 1–6 to pictures a)–f).

1 You use them to put rubbish in. __b)__

2 They're things for cleaning your mouth or hands when you're eating. _____

3 You use it when you want to cut vegetables. _____

4 They're things for cutting paper. _____

5 You use it to join two things when they are broken.

  _____

6 I'm looking for something for my computer. You use it under a mouse. _____

b) Match sentences 1–6 to pictures a)–f) in 2a).

1 They're made of metal. __e)__

2 It's a type of liquid. _____

3 They're made of paper or cotton. _____

4 It's made of wood or sometimes plastic. _____

5 They're made of plastic. _____

6 It's made of rubber. _____

 3 Fill in the gaps in the conversations with the phrases in the boxes.

~~You use them~~	Do you mean	it's made of
You mean	the word for	what they're called
They're usually	It's stuff for	

JUAN ¹ _You use them_ to start a barbecue.

MAN ² _____

  matches?

JUAN No, I'm sorry. I can't remember

  ³ _____ in

  English. ⁴ _____ white.

MAN Oh, you mean firelighters.

BIBI ⁵ _____ putting on food.

  I'm sorry, I don't know

  ⁶ _____ it.

MAN Do you mean salt?

BIBI No, ⁷ _____ plastic.

MAN Ah! ⁸ _____ clingfilm.

~~You use~~	You use them	they're made of
What's it called	you're looking for	
I'm looking for	It's a type of	for cleaning

MARIA ⁹ _You use_ it when you make a mistake.

  ¹⁰ _____ liquid.

WOMAN Is this what ¹¹ _____ ?

MARIA Yes, that's it. ¹² _____

  in English?

WOMAN Tippex or correction fluid.

HUGO ¹³ _____

  something for my shoes.

WOMAN Is it something

  ¹⁴ _____ them?

HUGO No, ¹⁵ _____ cotton.

  ¹⁶ _____ to tie your shoes.

WOMAN Oh, you mean shoelaces!

6 Decisions and choices

Language Summary 6, Student's Book p128

Make up your mind

make and *do* V6.1

1 Choose the correct word.

1 You are lazy! You've (done)/made nothing all weekend!

2 Have you *done*/made a decision yet?

3 I've *done*/made a lot of progress in English since I started.

4 Did you *do*/make a degree?

5 He's *done*/made me lots of favours.

6 Look at the mess you've *done*/made!

7 He often *does*/makes excuses about being late.

8 Have you *done*/made any work today?

2 Replace the phrase in **bold** with the correct form of *do* or *make* and a phrase in the box.

| ~~mistake~~ | the washing | me laugh |
| a course | the washing-up | up your mind |

made a mistake

1 I've **done something wrong** in this exercise.

2 I like him because he's **funny**.   *makes me laugh*

3 Have you **cleaned the clothes**?   *done the washing*

4 I'm **studying** at an evening school at the moment.   *doing a course*

5 Do you want more time to **decide**?   *make up your mind*

6 Would you mind **cleaning the dishes** with your brother?   *doing the washing-up*

First conditional G6.1

3 Write first conditional sentences.

1 If you / make dinner, I / do / the washing-up.

   If you make dinner, I'll do the washing-up.

2 / you / do / me a favour if I / help / you do your homework?

   Will you do me a favour if I help you do your homework?

3 You / not / pass if you / not do / any work.

   You won't pass if you don't do any work.

4 What / you / say / if she / not make up / her mind soon?

   What will you say if she doesn't make up her mind soon?

5 They / never learn / if they / be allowed to / behave so badly.

   They will never learn if they are allowed to behave so badly.

Future time clauses G6.2

4 Match beginnings 1–8 to endings a)–h).

1 I won't be able to cook dinner until
2 They'll be exhausted tomorrow unless
3 We'll write to you as soon as
4 She'll do a degree unless
5 After we get your letter,
6 When I finish the housework
7 Before she does a degree,
8 As soon as they start making a noise,

a) they go to bed early.
b) she'll have to pass her exams.
c) I might do the shopping.
d) they'll have to go to bed.
e) we make a decision.
f) we'll make a decision.
g) I've done the shopping.
h) she fails her exams.

5 Fill in the gaps with the correct form of these verbs. Use the Present Simple or *will*.

| ~~do~~ | make | put | get | release | check |

1 I *'ll do* the cleaning when you've tided up this mess.

2 As soon as she *releases* her new album, I'll buy it.

3 After I've sorted this stuff out, I *will put* everything away.

4 I won't phone him until we *check* into a hotel.

5 Unless he *makes* some progress, he won't pass.

6 *Will* we *get* there before they do?

6 Read the conversation and choose the correct words.

VIC OK. I'm leaving now.

DAD Where will you stay ¹(when)/if you get there?

VIC At the youth hostel ²if/unless we find a good hotel.

DAD And if the youth hostel is full?

VIC We'll worry about that ³before/when we get there.

DAD Well, ⁴(as soon as)/until you've left, we'll probably start worrying.

MUM And we'll worry ⁵until/as soon as you ring tomorrow.

VIC I'll only call you ⁶after/unless I find a place to stay.

DAD But don't call ⁷before/after ten. I'm looking forward to having a lie-in tomorrow.

MUM A lie-in? But ⁸unless/if Vic's away, we can decorate his room.

VIC No way! Promise me you won't do anything ⁹until/after I get back.

DAD OK. We won't touch your room … ¹⁰if/unless you forget to phone us.

7 Rewrite the sentences with *unless*.

1 If the weather isn't bad, we'll meet in the park.
   Unless the weather's bad, we'll meet in the park.

2 If you don't tell me about the problem, I won't be able to help. _Unless you tell me about the problem, I won't be able to help._

3 If your employees don't have time to relax, they won't work well. _Unless your employees have time to relax, they won't work well._

4 She should be here later if she doesn't make another excuse! _She should be here later unless she makes another excuse._

5 We'll have to get a loan if you don't start making more money. _We'll have to get a loan unless you start making more money_

6 He'll continue to make the same mistakes if we don't do anything. _He'll continue to make the same mistakes unless we do anything_

6B Protective parents

Reflexive pronouns V6.2

1 Fill in the gaps with a reflexive pronoun.

1 My daughter made the decision __herself__ .

2 The washing-up isn't going to do _itself_ you know!

3 We really enjoyed _ourselves_ last night. Thanks very much.

4 My son made dinner for the whole family by _himself_ last night!

5 Dave and Polly designed their cottage _themselves_.

6 Simon! If you don't like the way I've done it, do it _yourself_ !

7 Promise me that you will both look after _yourselves._

8 I didn't need any help – I made up my mind _myself_ .

Zero conditional; conditionals with modal verbs and imperatives; *in case* G6.3

2 Fill in the gaps in the conversation with the correct form of these verbs.

~~buy~~	go (x 2)	book	call	send	get	be

PAT My son's just gone on holiday to Italy with his friends. They didn't book a hotel or anything.

MARY Don't worry. My daughter only ¹ _buys_ a flight when she ² _goes_ away.

PAT But when we ³ _go_ on holiday, we always ⁴ _book_ a room in advance!

MARY Yes. And when we ⁵ _get_ there, I still ⁶ _call_ my parents. Nowadays I ⁷ _am_ lucky if my daughter ⁸ _sends_ me a postcard.

a) Fill in the gaps in these clauses with *If* or *When*.

1 __If__ you don't like the present,

2 _When_ I finish an exercise,

3 __If__ you live to be 100 in the UK,

4 _When_ I'm older,

5 _When_ this bus stops,

6 __If__ he doesn't feel better soon,

7 _When_ you get up in the morning,

8 _When_ you finish a meal,

b) Write zero or first conditional sentences. Use the *if/when* clauses in 3a) and these words.

1 you / not / have to / keep it.

If you don't like the present,

you don't have to keep it.

2 I / check / the answers immediately.

When I finish an exercise,
I check the answers
immediately.

3 you / get / a letter from the Queen.

If you live to be 100 in the UK,
you get a letter from the
Queen.

4 I / start / saving some money.

When I'm older, I'll
start saving some money

5 you / help / me with these bags?

When this bus stops, do you
help me with these bags?

6 we / have to / call the doctor.

If he doesn't feel better soon,
we'll have to call the doctor.

7 you / listen / to the radio?

When you get up in the morning,
do you listen to the radio?

8 you / always do the washing-up?

When you finish a meal
do you always do the washing
up?

 Read Lucy's tips and fill in the gaps. Use a modal and the verb in brackets or the imperative of the verb. Sometimes more than one answer is possible.

Lucy Samuel has been helping parents for over 20 years with their teenage children. She shares a few of her tips with us.

• If you want to show your children you love them, [1] _spend_ (spend) time with them. And when you haven't got time, you [2] _shouldn't make_ (not make) excuses. Explain to them why you're busy.

• If you want your children to talk to you, you [3] _shouldn' tell_ (not tell) anyone their secrets. Teenagers need to trust you and if they can't do that, why [4] _should_ they _tell_ (tell) you anything?

• Teenagers see everything you do. Unless you can stop doing something yourself, for example smoking, how [5] _can_ you _expect_ (expect) your children to stop?

• If you remember anything at all about your younger days, you [6] _must remember_ (remember) being a teenager. It's a confusing time. When children come to you for advice, [7] _listen !_ (listen). Their problems may be different from those you had.

• Teenagers will argue with you – it's part of growing up. But if you argue with them, [8] _don't expect_ (not expect) things to get better.

⑤ Fill in the gaps with *if* or *in case*.

1 I'll read the instructions __in case__ they say anything useful.

2 We should make some extra food now _in case_ he changes his mind.

3 I'm not making him dinner __if__ he won't help me with the washing-up.

4 We don't buy travel insurance __if__ we aren't going abroad.

5 We always buy travel insurance _in case_ we have an accident.

6 I ring my brother __if__ my car breaks down.

7 Take a mobile phone with you _in case_ the car breaks down.

8 Read the instructions first __if__ you don't want to break it.

6C Touch wood

Reading

1 Read the article and fill in the gaps with these sentences.

a) ~~In fact, many successful people simply got a 'lucky break'~~

b) But the pieces of paper he used kept falling out

c) A young, relatively unknown singer was asked to take over

d) He decided to move the family to Australia

e) A week later she had a part in a film

2 Are these sentences true (T), false (F) or the article doesn't say (DS)?

1 | **F** | The article says that people become successful because they work hard.

2 | T | Aretha Franklin used to sing in her church.

3 | F | Sarah Michelle Gellar's acting career started slowly at first.

4 | DS | Luciano Pavarotti became world-famous in 1963.

5 | DS | Mel Gibson's parents were millionaires.

6 | F | Mel Gibson had a fight at the audition for *Mad Max*.

7 | T | Post-It™ notes were invented in 1974.

8 | F | Spencer Silver invented Post-It™ notes by himself.

Synonyms V6.3

3 Read the article again and match words 1–6 to synonyms a)–f).

1 break   a) role
2 legendary   b) opportunity
3 part   c) discovery
4 unknown   d) trying
5 invention   e) unheard of
6 attempting   f) very famous

Serendipity

We tend to think that successful people deserve their success. They probably studied hard at school, they worked hard every day or they took a lot of risks. ¹*In fact, many successful people simply got a 'lucky break'* : something happened that gave them a chance to be successful; they took the opportunity and the rest, as they say, is history.

Some people just fell into fame. Aretha Franklin, the legendary Queen of Soul, was singing in her church choir* when a record company executive heard her voice. Sarah Michelle Gellar, star of *Buffy the Vampire Slayer*, was in a restaurant when a TV executive saw her. She was four. ² *A week later she had a part in a film* .

A month later she was in an advert for Burger King.

Other people were lucky because someone else was unlucky. In 1963 the very famous Italian opera singer Giuseppe di Stefano had a throat problem while he was singing in the opera *La Bohème*. ³ *A young, relatively unknown singer was asked to take over*

His name? Luciano Pavarotti.

Some people are just very lucky. Mel Gibson was born in New York. In 1968 his dad won a lot of money on a quiz show. ⁴ *He decided to move the family to Australia*

In Sydney Mel studied drama because his sister sent off his application form. Then the night before one of his first auditions, Mel had a fight at a party. And when the unheard-of actor arrived at the audition, he looked awful – but perfect for the role of Mad Max. He got the part.

Sometimes lucky breaks lead to a new invention. When that happens, it's called serendipity. The discovery of Post-It™ notes were an accident. In 1970 Spencer Silver was attempting to make a strong type of glue. He failed. Then four years later, Spencer's colleague was trying to mark the songs in a hymn book at his local church. ⁵ *But the pieces of paper he used kept falling out*

He remembered Spencer's glue and the Post-It™ was born. Last year 3M sold over $100 million worth of the notes.

In life, it seems, sometimes you need a little luck. But while you're waiting, it's probably safer to keep working hard.

choir = a group of people who sing together in a church, school, etc.

6D # What's your opinion?

Discussion language RW6.1

1 **You are at a meeting. Choose the best response for each situation.**

1 You are speaking and someone interrupts you.

   a) Be quiet!

   b) Can I just finish what I was saying? *(circled)*

   c) Sorry, do you mind if I interrupt?

2 Someone is speaking. You want to say something.

   a) Can I make a point here? *(circled)*

   b) If I could just finish making this point.

   c) What's the point of this?

3 You know Jason has an opinion, but he hasn't said anything yet.

   a) That may be true, but what about Paul?

   b) Jason, you had something you wanted to say. *(circled)*

   c) Sorry, do you mind if Paul interrupts?

4 Someone is speaking and you have the same opinion as him/her.

   a) Yes, I'd agree with that. *(circled)*

   b) Sure, go ahead.

   c) I'm sure I agree, actually.

2 **Complete the conversations with these phrases.**

> What's your opinion   Go ahead   Can I just
> That may be   You had something   I'm not sure
> Yes, I'd agree with   Can I just finish

1

TIM ¹ *What's your opinion* of teenage behaviour?

ANN It's simple. Firstly, parents should be stricter.

TIM ² *Yes, I'd agree with* that. But the reasons …

ANN ³ *Can I just finish* what I was saying?

TIM Sure. ⁴ *go ahead* .

2

PAM ⁵ *You had something* you wanted to say about superstitions.

CARL Yes, statistics show that Friday 13th isn't unluckier than any other day.

PAM ⁶ *That may be* true, but the worst days for accidents last year were all Fridays.

AL ⁷ *Can I just* say something here?

   ⁸ *I'm not sure* about Fridays in general, but the idea that Friday 13th is actually an 'unlucky day' is ridiculous.

> of course   I agree actually   make a point here
> That's not   If I could just finish   What do you think
> Yes, sure   I interrupt

3

KIM Can I ⁹ *make a point here*?

MEL Yes, ¹⁰ *of course* .

KIM Mel, you must agree that tourism is good for the country.

MEL ¹¹ *Yes, sure* .

KIM And that we need more hotels.

MEL I'm not sure ¹² *I agree actually*.

4

JAN ¹³ *What do you think* about prefabs?

ELLA I hate them. They're ugly and poor quality …

JAN Sorry, do you mind if ¹⁴ *I interrupt* ?

   ¹⁵ *that's not* true actually. In Sweden …

ELLA ¹⁶ *If I could just finish* making this point.

JAN Yes, sorry. Go ahead.

Review: gradable and strong adjectives

3 **Change the words in bold to make these sentences more positive. Use *absolutely* and an adjective in the box.**

> fascinated   delighted   fantastic   furious
> tiny   gorgeous   delicious   filthy

1 I was **quite interested**. *absolutely fascinated*

2 The room was **quite small**. *absolutely tiny*

3 The weather was **good**. *absol. fantastic*

4 His house was **fairly dirty**. *absol. filthy*

5 My husband was **angry**. *absol. furious*

6 The food was **quite tasty**. *absol. delicious*

7 She looks **beautiful**. *absol. gorgeous*

8 We were **very pleased**. *absol. delighted*

 Reading and Writing Portfolio 6 p74

7 Technology

Language Summary 7, Student's Book p130

7A Save, copy, delete

Computers (1) and (2) [V7.1] [V7.2]

1 Find seven more pieces of computer equipment in the puzzle (→, ↓ or ↘).

```
M C M P R I N T E S S
P E S C A N N E R S P
K R M C A M S C A C E
E R I O R S O E U A A
Y S E N R O R U E N K
B C R M T Y O I S N E
O R U O I E S S R E R
B E S U E E R T P A S
K E Y B O A R D I O Y
O S S C R E E N E C O
M O N I T O R I S D K
```

2 Cross out the incorrect words.

1 save *a document/an email/a hard disk*

2 delete *a document/a link/a folder*

3 make a back-up copy of your *icons/hard disk/documents*

4 print *an email/a folder/a document*

5 log on to *the Internet/online/ your computer*

6 click on *an icon/a website address/ a password*

Ability [G7.1]

3 **a)** Read the advertisement for a computing course and choose the correct words.

http://www.surfdirect.co.uk/courses/

Surf direct

In the 21st century, you [1] *can't/couldn't* ignore computers or the Internet. They're a necessary part of life and they [2] *can/are brilliant at* save you time and money. This two-day course is suitable for beginners who have used a computer, but find email and the Internet difficult [3] *understand/to understand*. You should have some experience of computers and [4] *can/be able* to use a mouse and a keyboard. And if you haven't got a clue how [5] *start/to start*, then don't worry! Click here for details of our basic computing course.

At the end of our **Surf direct** course, you will:

• know how [6] *to set up/setting up* an email account, and read and send emails.

• [7] *can/be able to* search the Internet accurately.

• [8] *could/be able to* buy something on the Internet safely.

b) Read about the experiences of three people who went on the course. Fill in the gaps with the correct form of the verb in brackets (infinitive, infinitive with *to* or verb+*ing*).

I can't [1] ___thank___ (thank) you enough for this course. I hadn't got a clue how [2] _to use_ (use) email before I did **Surf direct**. If I ever managed [3] _to send_ (send) anything, I'd always ring the person to check it had arrived! **Robert, Newcastle**

We're addicted! We're still useless at [4] _sending_ (send) emails, but we're brilliant at [5] _searching_ (search) the Internet for the lowest prices. My husband was able to [6] _find_ (find) a book I wanted for half the price it is in the shops. Unfortunately we also managed [7] _to order_ (order) two copies, but never mind! Great course. Thanks. **Pat, Sunderland**

My children use the Internet for their homework every night. I was always hopeless at [8] _helping_ (help) them and I hadn't found anyone who could [9] _help_ (help) me. Now I'm better at [10] _understanding_ (understand) search results than they are. And I find the Internet easy [11] _to use_ (use). Of course, I still have no idea how [12] _to work_ (work) the video recorder! **Diane, Sheffield**

4 Rewrite these sentences using the words in brackets.

1 My daughter can use a computer much better than me. (know how)

  My daughter knows how to use a computer much
  better than me.

2 I never remember passwords. (hopeless at)

  I am hopeless at remembering passwords.

3 My parents don't have a clue how to get broadband. (no idea)

  My parents have no idea how...

4 I was able to send an email, but I don't know if it arrived. (manage)

  I managed to send an email.

5 I could get emails, but I couldn't send any. (be able to; not be able to)

  I was able to get emails, but I
  wasn't able to send any.

Review: verb patterns

5 Complete sentence b) so it has the same meaning as sentence a).

1 a) She doesn't let her sister borrow her clothes.

  b) She doesn't allow _her sister to borrow her clothes._

2 a) I'd rather stay at home.

  b) I'd prefer _to stay at home._

3 a) He continues to phone me every night.

  b) He keeps _phoning me every night._

4 a) They said to me, "Buy a house with a garden."

  b) They told _me to "Buy a house with a_
  garden."

5 a) It looked like it was closed.

  b) It seemed _to be closed._

Want it, need it!

Electrical equipment `V7.3`

1 Look at the pictures. Write the names of the electrical equipment needed.

a) _hand-held computer_

b) _GPS sat/nav_

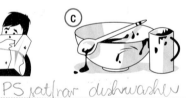
c) _dishwasher_

d) _washing machine_

e) _hair dryer_

f) _hair straighteners_

g) _a hands-free phone_

h) _air conditioning_

i) _central heating_

j) _MP3 player_

k) _DVD recorder_

l) _web cam_

Second conditional `G7.2`

2 Choose the correct words.

1 She *did/*would check her email more often if she had/*has broadband.

2 If it *wouldn't/didn't cost so much, I'll/*'d get one tomorrow.

3 We *spent/would spend less time on the Internet if there *was/were more things to do.

4 If they saved/*are saved their documents more regularly, they *lost/wouldn't lose them.

5 You *didn't/wouldn't have this problem if you made/*make back-up copies of your hard disk.

6 Do/*Would you get air conditioning if you *would be able to/could afford it?

7 If he weren't/*wouldn't be so arrogant, more people would ask/*will ask for his advice.

8 If I *give/gave you a hand-held computer, *do/would you use it?

3 Complete sentence b) so it has the same meaning as sentence a).

1 a) I might do a computer course. Then I'd use the computer more.

   b) I'd use the computer more if _I did a computer course._

2 a) Our central heating doesn't work and I'm freezing.

   b) If our heating _worked_ , I wouldn't feel so cold.

3 a) We don't have a GPS and we're lost!

   b) We _wouldn't be lost_ if we had a GPS.

4 a) He can't record it on DVD. He doesn't have a DVD recorder.

   b) If he had a DVD recorder, he _would be able to_ record it on DVD.

5 a) I can't remember my password so I can't use my computer.

   b) If I _could remember_ my password, I could use my computer.

6 a) I have no idea how to do this or I would help you.

   b) I would help you if I _had any idea_ how to do this.

First conditional G6.1 Second conditional G7.2

4 Choose the correct ending for each sentence.

1 Will you lend me yours if ...
  a) I promise to look after it?
  b) I promised to look after it?

2 If it cost about half as much, ...
  a) we'll be able to buy one.
  b) we'd be able to buy one.

3 The program will start automatically if ...
  a) you click on the document icon.
  b) you clicked on the document icon.

4 If I were you, ...
  a) I'll get an MP3 player
  b) I'd get an MP3 player.

5 If you forget your password, ...
  a) we'll send you a reminder.
  b) we'd send you a reminder.

6 Would it be more comfortable if ...
  a) it has air conditioning?
  b) it had air conditioning?

5 **a)** Read about a competition and fill in the gaps with the correct form of the verbs in brackets.

What You Want competition

These people answered the question: If you ¹ _could_ (can) buy any piece of electronic equipment, what ² _would_ it _be_ (be)?

Read the descriptions and guess the answers! If you ³ _answer_ (answer) all four questions correctly, you ⁴ _'ll have_ (have) a chance of winning this month's What You Want competition.

a) It ⁵ _is be_ (be) absolutely freezing when I ⁶ _get_ (get) home. This house was built over 200 years ago and it simply didn't exist then.

b) If I ⁷ _don't do_ (not do) it tonight, I ⁸ _will find_ (find) it all in the kitchen tomorrow morning. If we ⁹ _got_ (get) one, we ¹⁰ _would have_ (have) a lot more time in the evenings and we definitely ¹¹ _wouldn't argue_ (not argue) so much!

c) I go jogging a lot and the one that I have is useless and I keep having to change the CDs. If I ¹² _had_ (have) one of these, the music wouldn't finish all the time and I ¹³ _would be able to_ (be able to) carry a lot more music.

d) You aren't allowed to use mobiles in the car without one now. The trouble is I spend a lot of time driving. If I ¹⁴ _didn't speak_ (not speak) to people, I won't get anything done. Anyway, I'll just have to buy one. If I ¹⁵ _don't do_ (not do) it soon, I ¹⁶ _will get_ (get) a fine.

b) What is each person talking about in **5a)**? Write the names of the electrical equipment.

a) _central heating_

b) _dishwasher_

c) _MP3 player_

d) _hands-free phone_

7C Virus alert!

Reading

1 Read the article and write questions a)–e) in the correct places 1–5.

a) ~~What is spyware?~~
b) How do I get rid of it?
c) What can it do?
d) How does it get on to my computer?
e) Is spyware a common problem?

Spyware

Nobody likes a computer virus, but at least you can get rid of it. And there is a lot of anti-virus software these days. It can find a virus, fix it and you can forget about it. Unfortunately the same isn't true for spyware.

1 _What is spyware?_

Spyware is software that hides somewhere on your computer. It collects information about what you do on the Internet and passes this information to companies without your permission. If you shop on the Internet and use your credit card, you should know that some spyware can record this information!

2 _How does it get on to my computer?_

Your computer can catch spyware in lots of ways. If you open the wrong email, or even visit the wrong website, spyware can download itself onto your computer. And spyware often comes with free software.

3 _What can it do?_

Most spyware just collects information about your surfing habits for advertising reasons. But some spyware can be more powerful and will often make your computer slower. Adware is a type of spyware which is advertising software. It makes 'pop-up' advertisements appear while you are connected to the Internet. Not dangerous … but very annoying.

4 _Is spyware a common problem?_

If this is the first time you've heard of spyware, you've probably got some on your PC. Surveys have found that 90% of computers have several pieces of spyware on them. And spyware will stay on your computer for a long time, quietly collecting information and sending it back to its authors.

5 _How do I get rid of it?_

There is some anti-spyware software that will remove most of your problems. However, some anti-spyware software is spyware itself, so be careful! For a complete list of software, go to spywarewarrior.com.

2 Read the article again and answer these questions.

1 Why can it be difficult to find spyware?
   Because it hides on your computer.

2 Why is spyware important if you buy things online?
   Because it records your habits.

3 Can you get spyware if you're not using the Internet?
   Yes, by email or free software.

4 What kind of information can spyware collect?
   Your habits and sometimes your informations like your creditcard.

5 Why does most spyware want this information?
   To advertise products.

6 How might you know your computer has spyware on it?
   If it get slower.

7 What percentage of computers are not infected with spyware?
   Around 10%

8 What advice is given about removing spyware?
   To install a anti-spyware software.

Use of articles: *a, an, the,* no article V7.4

3 Read these comments on the article and fill in the gaps with *a, an, the* or – (no article).

Frankie

There are now laws against spyware in ¹ _the_ USA. Criminals behind ² _the_ most serious software can be sent to ³ _a_ prison for five years and get ⁴ _a_ fines of over ⁵ _a_ million dollars!

Rory

Thanks for ⁶ _the_ article. I get 'pop-up' advertisements all ⁷ _the_ time and I had no ⁸ _____ idea that there was ⁹ _a_ reason for them all. I'll visit ¹⁰ _the_ site.

Tess

¹¹ _An_ expert in ¹² _____ California estimates that spyware writers are making up to $2 billion dollars ¹³ _a_ year. ¹⁴ _The_ fine for writing this annoying stuff should be ¹⁵ _____ higher!

7D What's the password?

Indirect and direct questions RW7.1

 1 Which question in each pair is more polite? Choose a), b) or both if you think they are both polite.

1 (a) What's the time, please?
   b) Do you know what the time is?

2 a) Can you tell me what happened?
   (b) Have you any idea what happened?

3 (a) Do you think you could send it to me?
   (b) Please could you send it to me?

4 a) Is he coming later?
   (b) Do you know whether he is coming later?

5 (a) Could you tell me what the password is?
   b) What's the password?

2 Match beginnings 1–6 to endings a)–f) in these indirect questions.

1 Do you know whether broadband
2 Have you any idea whether
3 Could you tell
4 Do you know
5 Can you tell me if there
6 Do you think he

a) will be able to help me?
b) is a password for this?
c) how this scanner works?
d) he's made a back-up?
e) is available here?
f) me how I save a document?

3 Correct the mistakes in the phrases in **bold** in these indirect questions.

a webcam is
1 Do you know **what is a webcam**?
2 Could you tell me **how do I download software**?
3 Can you tell them **what are the passwords**? _are_
4 Do you know how much **does air conditioning cost**?
5 **Do you think if we can** log on without a password? _could_
6 Have you any idea **where could I buy** a GPS?

4 Rewrite direct questions 1–8 in the conversations using the phrases in brackets.

1

JACK Hi. I'm Jack. I need to use this PC. ¹What's Sean's password? (Can you tell me) _Can you tell me what Sean's password is?_

ISABELLA Sorry, I don't know.

JACK ²Is he at home today? (Do you know) _Do you know if he is at home today?_

ISABELLA Yes, he is. He isn't well.

JACK ³What's his phone number? (Have you any idea) _Have you any idea what his phone number is?_

ISABELLA No, I'm sorry. I'll ask the secretary.

2

JACK Sean, it's Jack Ross from accounts. I need to use your PC. ⁴Can I get your password? (Could you tell me) _Could you tell me your password?_

SEAN Er ... ⁵Could you use another PC? (Do you think) _Do you think you could use another PC?_

JACK Sorry. There aren't any.

SEAN ⁶Is there a girl with dark hair opposite you? (Can you tell me) _Can you tell me if there is a girl with dark hair opposite you?_

JACK Yes, long dark hair.

SEAN Er ... OK. My password is I–S–A B–E–L–L–A. It's er ... a place in Italy.

JACK Very interesting. Isa Bella. I've never heard of it.

SEAN ⁷Could you speak more quietly, please? (Do you think) _Do you think you could speak more quietly, please?_

JACK Are you OK, Sean?

 Reading and Writing Portfolio 7 p76

 Cultura Inglesa

39

8 One world

Language Summary 8, Student's Book p132

8A Changing weather

Weather V8.1

1 Correct the **bold** words/phrases.

1 A tornado is a type of **snow**. — *wind*

2 A shower is a **long** period of rain. — *short*

3 **Lightning** makes a noise. — *Thunder*

4 When it's humid, the air is **dry**. — *wet*

5 A gale is a type of **rain**. — *wind*

6 A gale is **more** violent than a hurricane. — *less*

7 Fog makes it difficult to **hear** things. — *see*

8 A heat wave is a period of **cool** weather. — *hot*

9 Floods happen where there is too **little** water. — *much*

2 Cross out four letters from each word and label the thermometer.

1 b̶r̶oyil̶l̶ings
2 t̶c̶hiel̶l̶iey
3 k̶cewool̶t̶
4 v̶w̶e̶oawrm̶n̶
5 hau̶o̶gh̶t̶
6 fr̶i̶eaezzin̶n̶g

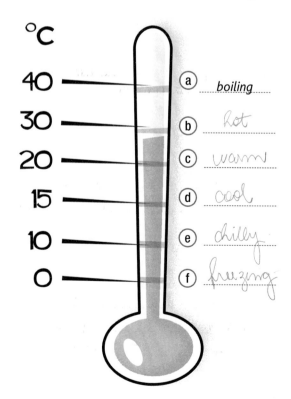

°C

40 — a boiling
30 — b hot
20 — c warm
15 — d cool
10 — e chilly
0 — f freezing

The passive G8.1

3 Choose the correct active or passive verb form.

1 The UK *(gets)/is got* some of its gas from the North Sea.

2 Several agreements *have made/(have been made)* to try and reduce greenhouse gases.

3 The full environmental effects won't *understand/(be understood)* for many years.

4 Wear something warm – I heard the weather will *(change)/be changed* later.

5 Thousands of people *kill/(are killed)* every year in storms and hurricanes.

6 Climate change *(is affecting)/is being affected* the weather all over the world.

7 It *(felt)/was felt* a lot chillier yesterday.

8 Many simple things can *do/(be done)* to prevent climate change.

4 Read sentences 1–4. Then choose sentence a) or b) to continue.

1 I recycle as much rubbish as possible.
   (a) I use three rubbish bins for different materials.
   b) Three rubbish bins are used by me for different materials.

2 My car is environmentally friendly.
   a) Someone designed it to use petrol and electricity.
   (b) It was designed to use petrol and electricity.

3 Deserts are getting larger.
   (a) They can only be stopped by planting new trees.
   b) People can stop them by planting new trees.

4 We use over 18 billion tins and cans every year in the UK.
   (a) We recycle about 4 billion of them.
   b) About 4 billion are recycled by us.

5 Fill in the gaps with the passive form of the verbs. Use the Present Simple, Past Simple, Present Perfect Simple or *will*.

The hurricane season in 2005 was one of the worst on record. Two of the worst hurricanes [1] _were reported_ (report) in North America: Hurricanes Katrina and Rita.

Since 1953, Atlantic hurricanes [2] _have been given_ (give) names from lists written by the National Hurricane Centre. Only women's names [3] _were used_ (use) at first, but in 1979 men's names [4] _were added_ (add). Now there are six lists of names and hurricanes [5] _are named_ (name) in alphabetical order from the lists. So the list that [6] _was used_ (use) in 2004 [7] _won't be used_ (not use) again until 2010. For example, the first hurricane of 2004 was Hurricane Alex. And the first hurricane in 2010 [8] _will be called_ (call) Hurricane Alex. The names of serious hurricanes [9] _aren't repeated_ (not repeat). For example, in 2005, Katrina and Rita [10] _were removed_ (remove) from the list. Since 1954, 62 names [11] _have been retired_ (retire) from the list.

8B Recycle your rubbish

Containers V8.2

1 Which container can we use for each group of things? Use the containers in the box.

| ~~bottle~~ tin box can |
| bag jar packet carton |

1 _a bottle of_ milk, orange juice, wine
2 _a bag of_ sweets, chips [US], shopping
3 _a tin of_ tuna, beans, cat food
4 _a box of_ tissues, chocolates
5 _a can of_ cola, lemonade, beer
6 _a carton of_ orange juice, milk, soup
7 _a jar of_ coffee, marmalade, honey
8 _a packet of_ tissues, crisps, sweets

2 Read the shopping list. Tick the usual containers. Correct the unusual containers.

Shopping

1 a ~~can~~ _bottle_ of olive oil
2 a box ✓ of washing powder
3 a box _bag_ of potatoes
4 a tube _carton_ of soup
5 a packet ✓ of biscuits
6 a ~~tin~~ _jar_ of honey
7 a carton ✓ of milk
8 a ~~bag~~ _packet_ of butter

Quantifiers G8.2

3 Look at the picture and complete the sentences. Use *There's/There are* and *not any, not much, not many* or *a lot of.*

1 *There isn't much* food.
2 *There aren't any* boxes.
3 *There is a lot of* paper.
4 *There aren't many* tins.
5 *There is a lot of* rubbish.
6 *There are a lot of* bottles.
7 *There aren't many* jars.
8 *There isn't much* bread.
9 *There aren't any* cans.
10 *There are a lot of* cartons.

4 Fill in the gaps with *a few* or *a little.*

1 I've got ___*a few*___ chocolates.
2 The weather is ___*a little*___ warm today, isn't it?
3 Would you like ___*a little*___ more coffee?
4 There are ___*a few*___ empty bottles for recycling.
5 Could you buy ___*a few*___ tins of cat food?
6 I'll give you ___*a little*___ help if you wait ___*a few*___ minutes.
7 He knows ___*a few*___ words of French and he speaks ___*a little*___ English.

5 Rewrite the sentences using the words/phrases in brackets. Make other changes if necessary.

1 There's a bit of soup in the fridge. (much)
   There isn't much soup in the fridge.

2 We've got more than enough time to get there. (plenty)
   We've got plenty of time.

3 Hardly any people I know recycle plastic. (few)
   Only *a few people that I know...*

4 I'm a little too tired to go out tonight. (bit)
   I'm a bit too tired.

5 Oliver hasn't got many teeth, but he's only six months old. (hardly)
   Oliver has got hardly any teeth...

6 A lot of children recycle things at school. (loads)
   Loads of children...

7 There's hardly any olive oil in the cupboard. (only a little)
   There's only a little olive oil...

8 There isn't any time left. (no)
   There's no time left.

6 Choose the correct words.

ROSE   Adam. If you've got [1]*a few/* **enough** time, can you put the recycling bin out?

ADAM   There's [2]hardly *any/much* rubbish in it.

ROSE   That's strange. Adam! Look in the other bin! [3]*Much/* **Lots of** this stuff can be recycled.

ADAM   But there isn't [4] **any**/*no* paper in there. I checked.

ROSE   What about glass? There are [5]*a lot/* **loads of** bottles in here.

ADAM   Sorry. You're right. Actually, I can see [6]*a little/* **a few** tins too.

ROSE   And there's more than [7]*a little/* **a few** plastic.

ADAM   Plastic? Can [8] **much**/*many* plastic be recycled?

ROSE   Yes, I think so. You know, [9] **a bit of**/*hardly any* care could save our planet.

ADAM   I know. Sorry. Look, there's [10]*a few/* **hardly any** room in the recycling bin now.

ROSE   Stop making excuses! There's [11] **plenty**/*several* of room.

8C Dangers at sea

Word formation (2): prefixes and opposites,
other prefixes and suffixes **V8.3** **V8.4**

1 **a)** Read the first part of the article. Fill in gaps 1–6 with the correct word, a), b) or c).

1 a) (sleepless)   b) oversleep   c) sleepy
2 a) unaccurate   b) disaccurate   c) (inaccurate)
3 a) (unfair)   b) underfair   c) fairless
4 a) harmful   b) (harmless)   c) unharmful
5 a) replay   b) implay   c) (playful)
6 a) incommon   b) (uncommon)   c) overcommon

The Orca

If you think you have a ¹ _sleepless_ baby, consider this: baby killer whales don't sleep for the first month of their life so their mothers have to stay awake too!

In fact, the name 'killer whale' is a little ² _____ and also ³ _____ . Firstly, killer whales (or orcas) are not really whales. They're in fact the largest member of the dolphin family. Secondly, they are usually ⁴ _____ to humans. There are no records of any orca attacks on humans in the wild.

Instead, these animals are highly sociable and even quite ⁵ _____ They live in groups called 'pods', with between 5 and 30 orcas, for their whole lives. And it is very ⁶ _____ to see one swimming alone.

b) Read the second part of the article and add the correct suffix or prefix to words 7–16. Use these suffixes and prefixes.

Suffixes: -ful, -less
Prefixes: re-, im-, under-, over-, ir-, dis-, un- (x 2)

The orcas' friendly and cooperative nature is very ⁷use _ful_ for finding food. Orcas hunt in their pods and then work together to kill. In 1999 a BBC team filmed a pod hunting a grey whale and its calf. The journalist described the event:

"The desperate calf* was fighting for its life and I wanted the orcas to finish their job quickly. But the mother was ⁸tire _less_ in her attempts to protect her calf. Her job was an ⁹ _im_ possible one."

The total worldwide population of orcas is ¹⁰ _un_ known, but is thought to be around 100,000. It is likely that we have ¹¹ _under_ estimated how many there are because they live in all of the world's oceans. Although they haven't been hunted since 1981, scientists believe their numbers are decreasing. In particular, ¹² _over_ fishing and oil accidents are reducing their food supplies.

There are about 40 orcas in aquariums all over the world, but many people ¹³ _dis_ agree with keeping them in these conditions and believe it's ¹⁴ _ir_ responsible. The most famous orca, Keiko, who appeared in the 1993 film *Free Willy*, was in an aquarium until scientists attempted to ¹⁵ _re_ introduce him into a pod in the wild. The $20 million attempt was ¹⁶ _un_ successful, however, and Keiko swam 1,400 kilometres on his own to Norway where he spent the last two years of his life.

*calf = a young whale

2 Read both parts of the article again. Are these sentences true (T), false (F) or the article doesn't say (DS)?

1 [T] Killer whales are not a type of whale.
2 [T] A human has never been killed by an orca.
3 [DS] Orcas hunt alone.
4 [F] In the description, the young grey whale survives.
5 [T] There are probably more than 100,000 orcas in the world.
6 [DS] In 1981 hunting whales was made illegal.
7 [T] Pollution is a problem for orcas.
8 [DS] Keiko was found in an aquarium in Mexico.
9 [F] Keiko became part of a pod when he was released.

Cultura Inglesa

43

8D Be careful!

Warnings and advice RW8.1

1 a) Make sentences with these words.

a) think / should / we / visit / do you / Which ?

Which do you think we should visit?

b) the streets / you / Make sure / the stadium / around / avoid .

Make sure you avoid the streets around the stadium

c) careful / in / Vine Street / you're / Be / when .

Be careful when you're in Vine Street

d) heard / hadn't / before / that / I .

I hadn't heard that before

e) you / advice / give / Could / some / me ?

Could you give me some advice?

f) I wouldn't / were you / I / him / listen to / if .

I wouldn't listen to him if I were you

g) make the / same mistake / or else you'll / in summer / Don't go / as I did .

Don't go in summer or else you'll make the same mistake as I did

h) really / thanks / That's / useful .

That's really useful thanks

b) Complete the conversation with sentences a)–d) from **1a)**.

JON We're looking for a house in your area, Clare. Here's some information about a few places.
¹ *Which do you think we should visit?*

CLARE Hmm. ² C
It's a bit of a bad neighbourhood.

JON Vine Street? ³ D
Thanks. Anything else?

CLARE ⁴ B

Image: House4U brochure — Terraced House Price £200,000, Vine Street

JON The football stadium? Is it noisy?

CLARE Yes, it can be.

c) Complete the conversation with sentences e)–h) from **1a)**.

NINA Mike, you've been to the Caribbean, haven't you?
⁵ E

When is it a good time to go?
⁶ F

LIZ He spent his Caribbean holiday in his hotel room!

MIKE That was because it was the start of their hurricane season. ⁷ G

My holiday was a disaster, so I <u>would</u> listen to my advice!

NINA ⁸ H

I had no idea. So you went in the summer?

MIKE Yes, in August.

Review: indirect and direct questions

2 Rewrite these direct questions as indirect questions. Use the words/phrases in brackets.

1 Did you reply to his email? (Could you tell)

Could you tell me if you replied to his email?

2 Is Argentina hot at this time of year? (Do you know)

Do you know if Argentina is...

3 Who sells maps around here? (Can you tell)

Can you tell me who...

4 Should I book a hotel before I go? (Do you think)

Do you think I should book...

5 Why is it so expensive? (Have you any idea)

Have you any idea why it is...

Reading and Writing Portfolio 8 p78

REAL WORLD • REAL WORLD • REAL WORLD • REAL WORLD • REAL WORLD • REAL WORLD • REAL WORLD

9 Look after yourself

9A Get healthy!

Health V9.1

1 Fill in the gaps in the vocabulary notebook with these words.

surgeon	GP	doctor	operating	specialist
A&E	asthma	prescription	ward	attack
allergy	migraine	chemist's		

(surgeon, A&E, ward, chemist's crossed out)

Relative clauses with *who, that, which, whose, where* and *when* G9.1

2 Fill in the gaps with *which, that, who, whose, where* or *when*. Sometimes more than one answer is possible.

1 He eats a lot of stuff __which/that__ is really unhealthy.

2 She's the woman __whose__ juice diet I tried.

3 After the accident they took her to the A&E department __where__ she works.

4 Do you know anyone __who__ suffers from migraines?

5 There was a guy on my ward __whose__ operation was cancelled.

6 Is there a good time __when__ I can come and visit you in hospital?

7 There are over 20 hospitals __which__ carry out major surgery in London.

8 I know several people __that__ don't eat meat, but eat fish.

9 The ward __where__ I got the infection was really dirty.

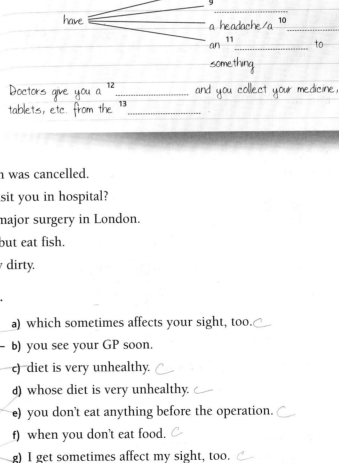

Health

doctors		place of work
people	¹ __surgeon__	in an ² __operating__ theatre
	hospital ³ __specialist__	in a hospital department, for example ⁴ __chemist's__
	⁵ _____	in a hospital department
	⁶ _____	in a surgery
	other	
	nurse	on a ⁷ _____

illness		
serious	have	cancer
		a heart ⁸ _____
not serious	have	an infection
		⁹ _____
		a headache / a ¹⁰ _____
		an ¹¹ _____ to something

Doctors give you a ¹² _____ and you collect your medicine, tablets, etc. from the ¹³ _____

3 Match beginnings of sentences 1–10 to endings a)–j).

1 I think it's a good idea

2 A migraine is a painful headache

3 It's important

4 He gave me some juice

5 It's likely his

6 The headaches

7 A surgery is

8 A fast is a period

9 The juice I tried

10 He's the type of person

a) which sometimes affects your sight, too.

b) you see your GP soon.

c) diet is very unhealthy.

d) whose diet is very unhealthy.

e) you don't eat anything before the operation.

f) when you don't eat food.

g) I get sometimes affect my sight, too.

h) that tasted like dirty water.

i) where you see your GP.

j) tasted like dirty water.

a) Is *who*, *that* or *which* the subject (S) or the object (O) of the relative clause?

1 The GP who Mike has seen ... _O_

2 A hospital that doesn't have an A&E department ... _S_

3 The people that the allergy affects ... _O_

4 The specialist that is going to speak to you ... _S_

5 The patient who the surgeon operated on ... _O_

6 The ward which I stayed in ... _O_

7 An operation which lasted eight hours ... _S_

8 The migraines that he gets ... _O_

b) In which phrases in 4a) can we leave out *who*, *that* or *which*?

___1___ (The GP Mike has seen ...), _6_ , _8_ , _3_ , _5_

 5 Join the sentences. Use *which*, *that*, *who*, *whose*, *where* or *when* if necessary. Make any other changes you need to.

1 I'm on a diet. It doesn't allow me to eat bread or pasta.

I'm on a diet which doesn't allow me to eat bread or pasta.

2 I'm going on a retreat. I think you've been on it.

I'm going on a retreat where I think, you've been.

3 She's the woman. She runs an organic fruit and vegetable shop.

She's the woman, who runs an organic fruit and vegetable shop.

4 I think it's very interesting. You decided to become a surgeon.

I think it's very interesting that you decided to become a surgeon.

5 I regularly get migraines. They're really painful.

I regularly get migraines which are really painfull.

6 He's got a disease. I had never heard of it.

He's got a disease which I had never heard of.

 Good news, bad news

News collocations V9.2

1 Put the news stories in the correct order.

A
a) Paris, France. French surgeons refused to call off — _1_
b) offer of a shorter working week. They are protesting — _3_
c) illness that requires an operation, union leaders — _7_
d) in a demonstration next Monday. If someone is taken — _5_
e) their strike yesterday and rejected the government's — _2_
f) promised that there would be no shortage of surgeons. — _8_
g) against long hours and over 2,000 surgeons will take part — _4_
h) to hospital in an emergency or is suffering from an — _6_

B
a) London, England. A government report that was — _1_
b) a target of employing 20% more nurses by 2010. — _8_
c) the offer of a job in the private sector if they made — _4_
d) carried out in ten hospitals all over the UK. These — _6_
e) published yesterday has discovered something — _2_
f) the same money. The report comes from a survey — _5_
g) worrying about nurses. Over 25% would accept — _3_
h) results are a problem for a government trying to meet — _7_

Present Perfect Simple active and passive for recent events G9.2

 2 Correct the mistakes in these sentences.

1 Anyone injured ~~have~~ *has* already been taken to hospital.

2 I've just been offer~~ed~~ another job.

3 You ~~have~~ *Have* just changed the TV channel?

4 Her new record still hasn't *been* released.

5 The prime minister hasn't said ~~yet~~ anything. *yet*

6 Scientists ~~already~~ have *already* discovered some causes of migraines.

7 Have you ~~being~~ *been* paid for that survey yet?

8 You haven't ~~still~~ told anyone. *still*

3 Make sentences with these words.

1 strike again / have / Underground drivers / on / gone .

Underground drivers have gone on strike again.

2 been / The reports / yet / published / haven't .

The reports haven't been published yet.

3 in / part / never / I've / a demonstration / taken .

I've never taken part in a demonstration.

4 has / been / The offer / just / government / by the / rejected .

The offer has just been rejected by the government.

5 already / called / have / off the / The unions / strike .

The unions have already called off the strike.

6 last year's / government / The / yet / met / hasn't / targets .

The government hasn't met last year's target yet.

7 been / Four / have / so far / surveys / carried / out .

Four surveys have been carried out so far.

8 him / already / they / Have / to hospital / taken ?

Have they already taken him to hospital?

4 Rewrite the sentences using the words in brackets.

1 I believe you should take plenty of water. (good idea)

It's a good idea to take plenty of water.

2 My advice is to get bottled water. (were)

If *I were you I would get bottled water.*

3 I advise you to see a dentist soon. (had better)

You'd better see a dentist soon.

4 Is booking ahead sensible? (good idea)

Is *it a good idea to book ahead* ? *sensible*

5 The worst thing to do is feed the animals. (Whatever)

Whatever you do don't feed the animals.

6 You should take all your valuables out of your car. (Don't)

Don't leave any valuables in your car.

5 Fill in the gaps in these news stories with the verbs in the boxes. Use the Present Perfect Simple active or passive.

~~not find~~	~~have~~	not see

A missing teenager from West London [1] *has* still *not been found* and police say they [2] *have had* little information about where he could be. Damian Urwin [3] *hasn't been seen* since last Tuesday when he left his friend's house in Notting Hill.

shock	be	publish

Cleanliness in hospital wards [4] *has been* in the news recently. The government [5] *has* just *published* a report about it and the results [6] *have shocked* many people.

charge	not give	release

Two men [7] *have* just *been charged* with the murder of a local businessmen. A third suspect [8] *has been released* from Paddington police station, but police [9] *haven't given* the names of the arrested men yet.

suffer	see	go

Lucy [10] *has suffered* from severe asthma for four years. She [11] *has been* to several hospitals and [12] *has been seen* by some of the best specialists.

receive	finish	release

It [13] *has been finished* for over a year, but Tom Cruise's new film [14] *has* only just *been released* at cinemas in London and it [15] *has* already *received* excellent reviews.

9C Faking it

Reading

1 Read the article quickly and write the correct names.

1 Who learned to cook professionally? ....

2 Whose experience involved a sport? ....

3 Who learned how to interview famous people? ....

2 Read the article again and answer the questions.

1 Which people successfully 'faked it'?

Ed Devlin and Jatinder Sumal successfully 'faked it'.

2 What skill does Ed think he has improved?

....

3 What did Maximillian think he did wrong?

....

....

4 Why did Jatinder decide to go on the programme?

....

....

5 Where did Jatinder meet Robbie Williams?

....

6 What happened?

....

....

7 What has Jatinder decided to do after her experience?

....

....

Connecting words: *although, even though, despite, in spite of, however* V9.3

3 Rewrite sentences 1–6 in the article using the words in brackets.

1 (even though) *Even though Ed Devlin had never cooked anything more than a burger, he beat three other professional chefs.*

2 (despite) ....

....

3 (however) ....

....

4 (however) ....

....

5 (although) ....

....

6 (in spite of) ....

....

Are you fed up with your job? Have you ever wanted to do something completely different? A top chef perhaps? Or maybe a racing driver or even a nightclub DJ? *Faking It* is a reality TV programme that does exactly that. The programme trains people to 'fake it' in a totally different job. They are given four weeks to learn the skills of their new jobs. Then they have to convince a group of experts that they aren't faking it.

Previous shows have taken a fast food worker and trained him as a top chef. **¹Ed Devlin had never cooked anything more than a burger, but he beat three other professional chefs.** At the moment Ed is still doing the job he was doing before. However, he says he is much better at cutting up onions now!

Maximillian Devereaux, a professional chess player, learned how to be a football manager. **²He didn't manage to persuade* the experts, but he enjoyed the experience.** He thinks his body language at football matches wasn't good enough. "I never managed to look comfortable," he says.

Jatinder Sumal works in her family's newsagent's in Scotland. She learned to be a show business reporter! When a TV researcher phoned her and offered her the chance, Jatinder thought it was a joke. **³Although she had never heard of *Faking It*, her friends said it was a really good show.** So Jatinder thought she would have a go. Jatinder said the worst moment of her experience was at a film premiere. **⁴She tried to interview Robbie Williams, but she couldn't think of anything to ask him!** "I was very nervous," she said. "I couldn't stop shaking." **⁵It was a terrible experience, but Jatinder quickly recovered.** And at the end of her month's training, when she interviewed a pop group in front of the experts, they thought she was a genuine showbiz* reporter. **⁶Despite her success at 'faking it', Jatinder doesn't plan to leave her job.** "I wouldn't give up my life here in Glasgow for anything," she said. "I'm just glad to be back to my old life."

*persuade = make someone believe something
*showbiz = showbusiness

9D At the doctor's

Health problems, symptoms and treatment `V9.4`
At the doctor's `RW9.1`

1 Fill in the gaps with the words in brackets.

1 _Hay fever_ gives you a _runny_ nose and makes you _sneeze_ . (hay fever; sneeze; runny)

2 Food _poisoning_ can often make you _sick_ and give you _diarrhoea_ (diarrhoea; poisoning; sick)

3 _Paracetamol_ is a type of _painkiller_ and is usually a _pill_ . (pill; painkiller; paracetamol)

4 A _symptom_ of _asthma_ is that you feel _wheezy_ . (wheezy; asthma; symptom)

5 If you have an _infection_ , a doctor will probably prescribe _antibiotics_ However, they don't work with a _virus_ . (infection; virus; antibiotics)

2 Put the conversation in the correct order.

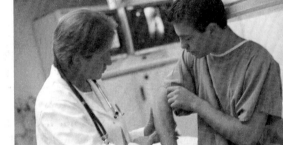

a) DOCTOR Now, what seems to be the problem? _1_

b) DOCTOR Doesn't it? It's very red. Do you know if you're allergic to anything? _5_

c) PATIENT It doesn't hurt. _4_

d) PATIENT I keep getting a rash on my arm. _2_

e) DOCTOR Right, let me have a look at you. _3_

f) PATIENT I'm allergic to cats, but we haven't got one. _6_

3 **a)** Fill in the gaps with the words in the boxes.

| ~~feeling~~ suffering getting (x 2) taking |

a) I haven't been _feeling_ very well recently, doctor.

b) I keep _getting_ migraines in the morning.

c) Have you been _taking_ anything for them?

d) How long have you been _suffering_ from them?

e) I'm _getting_ a sore throat.

| a prescription some antibiotics take them another appointment a week |

f) Come back if you're not feeling better in _a week_

g) How often should I _take them_ ?

h) Here's a prescription for _some antibiotics_

i) Do I need to make _another appointment_ ?

j) Do I need _a prescription_ , doctor?

b) Complete the conversation with sentences a)–e) in 3a).

CASS   1 _a)_
          2 _b_

DOCTOR I see. 3 _d_

CASS   About a month or two.

DOCTOR Right. That's quite a long time. 4 _c_

CASS   Paracetamol and aspirin.

DOCTOR OK. Painkillers are fine. Any other problems?

CASS   Well … 5 _e_ today, but it's not serious.

c) Complete the conversation with sentences f)–j) in 3a).

BOB   So you think it might be an infection.
          6 _j_

DOCTOR Yes, I'm going to write one. 7 _h_

BOB   Thanks a lot. 8 _g_

DOCTOR Twice a day, after meals.

BOB   9 _i_

DOCTOR No. 10 _f_

Reading and Writing Portfolio 9 p80

10 Happy ever after?

Language Summary 10, Student's Book p136

10A The anniversary

Contacting people V10.1

1 Look at the photo. Choose the correct words in Bill and Jilly's conversation.

BILL Hello! It's Jilly, isn't it?

JILLY Bill! I haven't seen you since university!

BILL That's right. ¹*Are you/Do you get* in touch with people from then?

JILLY Not really. I've ²*kept in/lost* touch with almost everybody I think. And you?

BILL Last year I ³*got/got in* touch with someone who was on my course – I found her email address on the Internet. I even ⁴*phoned/gave* her a call and ⁵*left/posted* her a message.

JILLY A girlfriend from the past?

BILL You guessed it. She never ⁶*called/called in* back.

JILLY Oh, well. And your brother? You've ⁷*kept in/lost* touch with him I hope!

BILL Matt? He's here in London. You two went out once, didn't you?

JILLY A long time ago ... when I used to hang about with that girl Susie.

BILL Susie? Susie James?

JILLY Yes, I'd love to ⁸*find/get* hold of her. But I haven't a clue where she is now. I haven't heard ⁹*of/from* her since she went to work in Spain.

BILL Well, I ¹⁰*got/'m* in touch with her – she's my sister-in-law!

JILLY What?

BILL Yes, in fact it's Matt and Susie's tenth wedding anniversary tomorrow.

JILLY You're joking! Well, let them ¹¹*know/hear* I'm living in London now. Here's my card.

BILL You're a divorce lawyer! Sounds fun!

was/were going to, was/were supposed to G10.1

2 Read sentence a). Then decide if statement b) is true (T) or false (F).

1 a) We weren't going to phone.
   b) [T] We phoned.

2 a) They weren't supposed to be here until seven.
   b) [ ] They arrived before seven.

3 a) We were supposed to pick up Carl, but we overslept.
   b) [ ] Carl was picked up.

4 a) Mike was going to get hold of the manager, but he forgot.
   b) [ ] Mike didn't get in touch with the manager.

5 a) We were going to catch the early train, but we missed it by a few minutes.
   b) [ ] They didn't catch the early train.

3 Choose the correct ending to the sentences. Sometimes both endings are possible.

1 I was going to give you a call,
   a) but I didn't have enough time.
   b) and I left a message.

2 You were supposed to let them know
   a) and now they won't worry.
   b) that you weren't going to go.

3 He was supposed to give you my message,
   a) but you didn't call me back.
   b) but I guess he forgot.

4 Sandy and I weren't going to come
   a) but we're glad we did.
   b) because we didn't think we were invited.

5 It was supposed to be sunny today,
   a) however, it looks like it's going to rain.
   b) so perhaps this rain will stop soon.

4 **a)** Match beginnings of sentences 1–8 to endings a)–h).

1 We had planned to go to bed early, but ____c)____

2 I didn't ask for a big room, but _____

3 I'd thought about having a party that weekend, but _____

4 Someone had asked me to invite him, but _____

5 We had expected the concert to end at nine, but _____

6 No one had planned to give them anything, but _____

7 We had arranged to meet in the morning, but _____

8 I was told to get in touch with Diana, but _____

a) then they heard it was for charity.

b) it's already half past.

c) Mike gave us free tickets to a concert.

d) it's good that it is.

e) Cath rang earlier and made an excuse.

f) I didn't know you were going to be on holiday.

g) her phone number had changed.

h) I knew he wouldn't come.

b) Rewrite beginnings of sentences 1–8 in **4a)** using the correct form of *was/were going to* or *was/were supposed to*.

1 We *were going to go to bed early, but …*

2 The room _____

3 I _____

4 I _____

5 The concert _____

6 No one _____

7 We _____

8 I _____

10B Who's that?

Describing people V10.2

1 **a)** Correct the two mistakes in each description.

          in

1 Oscar is ~~on~~ his late fifties. He's got glasses and he's going to bald.

2 Chris is in his mid-thirties. He's got dark short hair and striped shirt.

3 Erin is Maisie's twin. She's got straight blonde hairs and a dress flowery.

4 Alice is in her mid-fifties. She's got some length-shoulder hair and a light jacket.

b) Read the descriptions in **1a)** again. Write the names of people a)–d) on the picture.

Phoebe   Leo   Maisie **a**   Jamie   Fern   Kian   Jay   **b**   **c**   **d**

2 Look at the picture. Write full sentences.

1 Describe these people's hair.

  a) Kian's hair *is short and curly.*

  b) Jay's hair _____

  _____

  c) Fern's hair _____

  _____

2 Describe the differences between what these people are wearing.

  a) Fern has got *dark trousers.*

    Alice has got _____

  b) Chris has got _____

    Oscar has got _____

 Cultura Inglesa

Modal verbs (2): making deductions G10.2

3 **a) Make sentences with these words.**

1 use / must / hair straighteners / Eve .

   Eve must use hair straighteners.

2 with / Ruby / be / ponytail/ could / the / The girl .

   ----

3 stuck / be / Jo / in traffic / could .

   ----

4 be / later / party / might / Joel / to the / coming .

   ----

5 must / leaving / in a / Stephen / minute / be .

   ----

6 may / at home / stay / The children / to / prefer .

   ----

7 can't / any worse / weather / The / get .

   ----

8 working / be / Simon / there any more / can't .

   ----

b) Read the sentences in 3a) again. Are these sentences true (T) or false (F)?

The speaker ...

1 [T] believes Eve uses hair straighteners.
2 [ ] knows who Ruby is.
3 [ ] thinks Jo is possibly stuck in traffic.
4 [ ] doesn't know if Joel is coming to the party.
5 [ ] is sure that Stephen is leaving soon.
6 [ ] thinks the children definitely want to stay at home.
7 [ ] thinks the weather isn't very good.
8 [ ] isn't sure whether Simon has left his old job.

4 **a) Look at the picture on page 51 again and fill in the gaps with the words in the boxes.**

~~can't~~   must   may

PHOEBE Chris looks absolutely exhausted. Jamie [1] *can't* be sleeping very well.

LEO Yes. And Jamie's crying a lot. He [2] _____ need something to eat.

PHOEBE Or he [3] _____ be tired, perhaps?

LEO You're probably right. But I don't think I'll point that out to Chris!

must   could   can't

LEO I'm not sure, but Oscar's new girlfriend [4] _____ be the woman with sunglasses.

PHOEBE Well she [5] _____ be the one with curly hair. She's my age!

LEO No. She [6] _____ have lots of money. Look at all that jewellery!

can't   must   might

PHOEBE Kian came with his parents. I'm not sure but he [7] _____ be working with his dad again. Who's the girl near him?

LEO I think her name's Fern.

PHOEBE Oh, she [8] _____ be Kian's girlfriend. I've heard him speak about her.

LEO Then Kian [9] _____ be working with his dad. She said she works in the same office as her boyfriend.

b) Write sentences using *must*, *could*, *may*, *might* or *can't*. Sometimes more than one verb is possible.

1 Jamie / be / feel / hungry or tired.

   Jamie might be feeling hungry or tired.

2 Jamie / be Chris's son.

   Jamie must be Chris's son.

3 Phoebe / be / have / a baby soon.

   ----

4 Leo / be Phoebe's grandfather.

   ----

5 Chris / be / stay / at the party until late.

   ----

6 Phoebe and Leo / get on well.

   ----

7 Erin and Maisie / be / chat / about Oscar.

   ----

8 Jay / be retired yet.

10C # The party's over

 Phrasal verbs (3): meanings and grammar V10.3 V10.4

1 Read the article. Then fill in the gaps with sentences a)–e).

a) he was younger
b) I had hardly eaten anything
c) you don't tend to worry about things for long
d) I was still surprised
e) my brother was actually going to get married

Being a **best man** by Oliver Pedoe

"I'd like you to be my best man," said my brother.

Even though my brother and I had always got on well and rarely ᵃ⁾**argued**, ¹ _I was still surprised_ . I was only just 18. I had only been to a few weddings in my life and I was already going to be a best man. I accepted immediately – it was more evidence that I was becoming an adult. At last.

During dinner that evening, my mother ᵇ⁾**told me** that best men were, of course, supposed to make speeches.

"Supposed to or have to?" I asked, feeling my heart rate* ᶜ⁾**increasing** a little.

"Well, have to," she said.

Suddenly I didn't feel hungry any more.

There wasn't any point in trying to ᵈ⁾**avoid doing it**. And of course when you're young, ² ....
I started making excuses to myself so I could ᵉ⁾**do it later**: after all, my brother and his fiancée might ᶠ⁾**end their relationship** and the wedding would be cancelled.

A week before the wedding it was clear that ³ .... I needed a speech. Quickly.

I ᵍ⁾**searched for** wedding speeches in the place which seems to have the answers to everything: the Internet. After a few minutes I ʰ⁾**found** a website with tips on making speeches. It suggested finding photos of the groom when ⁴ ....

Perfect! There were hundreds of photos of my brother when he was young: my brother as a baby, my brother with his first 'girlfriend', my brother with long hair, my brother with short hair and a beard. Easy.

When the moment finally arrived, I can't say I wasn't nervous. Wedding speeches are made after a meal and ⁵ .... However, within a few minutes of standing up to make my speech, I started to ⁱ⁾**feel better about it**. The photos were a huge success and everyone was asking how I ʲ⁾**had thought of** such an original idea. Of course I lied. More evidence I was becoming an adult. At last.

heart rate = the speed at which your heart beats

VOCABULARY AND READING

2 Rewrite words/phrases a)–j) in **bold** in the article using the correct form of these phrasal verbs.

point out	get out of it
come up with	look up
come across	go up
split up	get over it
~~fall out~~	put it off

a) _fell out_
b) ....
c) ....
d) ....
e) ....
f) ....
g) ....
h) ....
i) ....
j) ....

3 Are these sentences true (T) or false (F)?

1 [T] Oliver was 18 when his brother asked him to be his best man.

2 [ ] He had been a best man before.

3 [ ] He knew a best man had to make a speech when he accepted.

4 [ ] He didn't try to avoid having to make a speech.

5 [ ] He was sure his brother was going to split up with his fiancée.

6 [ ] It was Oliver's own idea to use photos for his speech.

7 [ ] At the wedding, Oliver was nervous at first.

8 [ ] Oliver told everyone where he got the idea for his speech.

 Cultura Inglesa

53

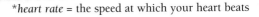

10D Do you mind?

Asking for, giving and refusing permission RW10.1

1 Read the situations. Then choose the correct questions and sentences.

1 Your teacher has forgotten her pen. She asks:
   a) Is it OK if you use a pen?
   b) Would you mind if I used my pen?
   c) Do you think I could use your pen?

2 You give her permission. You say:
   a) Yes, I'd rather you didn't.
   b) Yes, of course you can. Go ahead.
   c) Yes, of course it is.

3 You want to borrow some money from a friend. You ask:
   a) Would you mind if I borrowed some money from you?
   b) Is it OK if I lend you some money?
   c) Would you like to borrow some money?

4 Your friend gives you permission. Your friend says:
   a) Yes, I'd rather you didn't.
   b) No, not at all.
   c) Yes, of course.

2 Read the short conversations and choose the correct words. Sometimes more than one answer is correct.

1 A *Do you mind if/Do you think* I do the washing-up later?
   B *Yes, go ahead./No, do whatever you like.*

2 A *May/Can* I borrow your bike?
   B *No, take whatever you like./Yes, help yourself.*

3 A *Is it OK if/Do you think* I change the channel?
   B *Of course./I'm afraid I'm watching this.*

4 A *Is it OK/Would you mind if* Mike stayed here this evening?
   B *I'd rather he didn't./Go ahead!*

5 A *Could/May* I put our meeting off for a week?
   B *I'd rather you didn't./Yes, sure.*

6 A *Do you think/Do you mind* I could use your bathroom?
   B *Yes, of course./No, not at all.*

3 a) You are staying at a friend's house. Write questions with these words to ask for permission.

1 May / borrow / a towel?
   May I borrow a towel?

2 Do you think / have / a glass?
   ----

3 Is it OK / make / some coffee?
   ----

4 Can / look round / your garden?
   ----

5 Would / mind / check / my email?
   ----

6 Do / mind / have / a shower?
   ----

b) Use one of these phrases to complete the replies to the questions in 3a).

| ~~Yes, of course~~   Yes, of course it is   Sorry, you can't |
| No, not at all   Go ahead   Yes, of course you can |

1 *Yes, of course* . I'll just get one.

2 ----------------------------------- . I'll just wash one up.

3 ----------------------------------- . Help yourself to anything you want.

4 ----------------------------------- . It's a bit of a mess, though.

5 ----------------------------------- . There's something wrong with the laptop at the moment.

6 ----------------------------------- . Use my hair dryer if you want.

 Reading and Writing Portfolio 10 p82

My Notes

My Notes

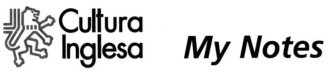

My Notes

My Notes

My Notes

My Notes

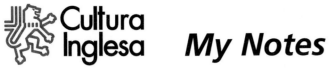

My Notes

My Notes

My Notes

Describing a holiday

Reading a letter about a holiday
Writing informal letters: ellipsis of words
Review Past Simple; likes and dislikes

 Read the letter quickly.

a) Who is the letter to?

----

b) Who is the letter from?

----

c) What is the writer doing?

 Read the letter and choose the best answers.

1 Who is Anna travelling with?
   a) David and her children.
   b) David's grandparents.
   c) Her parents.

2 Which places have they been to so far?
   a) New York.
   b) New York and Boston.
   c) New York, Boston and Province Town.

3 What annoys David?
   a) He prefers cities.
   b) His grandparents have dinner very early.
   c) The traffic in New York.

4 When did they stay in New Hampshire?
   a) Between Boston and Cape Cod.
   b) Between New York and Boston.
   c) Between Boston and Cambridge.

5 What have they done on holiday so far?
   a) Had friends round for dinner.
   b) Visited friends and relatives.
   c) Both a) and b).

6 Why did the children stop exploring the woods?
   a) Because there were bears in there.
   b) Because their father told them to.
   c) Because they were scared.

De

¹Writing this in the car. We're driving to Province Town, a beach town near Cape Cod in Massachusetts. We're in the second week of our two weeks away. And so far, Mum, it's been really special. We spent two days in New York. **²Hotel was a bit basic but it was safe and clean.** We went to a few exhibitions and Simon and Ailsa had us round for lunch – you remember our neighbours from Oxford, don't you? NY is a wonderful place – really exciting. The traffic got on my nerves after a while – **³worse than Cambridge!**

⁴Tuesday we drove up to New Hampshire. On the way, we said a quick 'hello' to David's grandparents near Boston. And we're going to go back and stay with them later in the week. They're well. They have dinner at about 4 p.m. these days – **⁵drives David crazy!**

I can't normally bear the country, Mum. You know me – I'm a city girl. But New Hampshire is so quiet and so green – I fell in love with it. We stayed in a beautiful house there – some friend of David's grandmother owns it. Eve and Harry had a lot of fun exploring the woods at the back of the house – until David told them there might be some bears in there! Then they wouldn't go back again!

⁶Will write again before we come home.

Love,

Anna, David, Eve and Harry

3

a) We sometimes miss out words in informal writing when it is clear what or who we are talking about. Look at this sentence from the letter.

I'm Writing this in the car.

b) What types of words are missed out in sentences 1–6 in **bold** in the letter?

1 *pronoun and auxiliary verb*

2 ....

3 ....

4 ....

5 ....

6 ....

c) Match words a)–f) to answers 1–6 in **3b)**.

a) I'm ..... *1* .....

b) I ....

c) it's ....

d) The ....

e) it ....

f) On ....

 4 Cross out the words you can miss out in these sentences.

1 ~~The~~ queue is so long. (1 word)
2 In August Sally and I are going to Washington. (1 word)
3 I can't find the map. (2 words)
4 I have not got any money! (2 words)
5 Have you had a lie-in today? (2 words)
6 We have been out for dinner. (2 words)
7 It is going to be sunny tomorrow. (2 words)
8 We are going to Al's tonight. (2 words)

 5 **a)** Imagine you are on holiday for two weeks. Make notes on your own ideas in the diary.

Mon 1	Leave home. Fly to	Mon 8	
Tue 2	Stay with	Tue 9	Go to ....
Wed 3		Wed 10	
Thur 4	Leave for .... by	Thur 11	
Fri 5		Fri 12	
Sat 6	Visit	Sat 13	Go back to .... by ....
Sun 7		Sun 14	....

b) Write a letter to a family member on Monday 8th.

- Use your notes from **5a)**.
- Add information about what you liked and didn't like during the first week of your holiday.
- Organise your letter into paragraphs.
- Use ellipsis of words where possible.
- Read and check for mistakes.
- Give your letter to your teacher next class.

....
Tick the things you can do in English in the
Reading and Writing Progress Portfolio, p88.
....

Notices at work

Reading notices
Writing notices: abbreviations
Review modal verbs

1 Read notices A–F and sentences a)–e). Which notice or notices would each person be interested in?

a) TOM   I ought to do more exercise. ___*A*___ , _____

b) EVA   I have to get a part-time job. _____

c) MARK   I found something in a classroom recently. _____

d) SALLY   I lost something recently. _____

e) VICTORIA   I have to find some accommodation before university starts. _____

A

Man's bike for sale
6 months old – vgc
£150 ono (for quick sale!)
Call Mike on
07912 004121

B

Cleaner needed

Private house in Percy St.

No experience necessary.

£7 **p/h**, 3 hours **p/w**

nancy@ukmail.net

C

Lost

Red bag in class 7B on Wednesday.

Pls. help! It's got all my notes in it.

Carla 07980 545618

D

Room to let

In friendly shared house near college. Available from 1st October.

£90 **p/w** + bills

n/s only

room_for_rent@ukmail.net

E

Yoga class

8-week beginners' course in sports centre.

7–8.30 p.m.
Mondays and Thursdays.

Call Sue
Tel. no. 01222 641813
(**eves.** only)

F

FOUND

Mobile phone in room 4A.

Nokia 332 (black).

Last **Tue.** at about 7 p.m.

07232 412119 (Paul)

2 Are these sentences true (T), (F) or the notices don't say (DS)?

1 [*F*] Mike wants more than £150 for his bike.

2 [   ] Anyone can apply for the job in Percy Street.

3 [   ] Carla is worried about losing all her notes.

4 [   ] This room will cost at least £90 every week.

5 [   ] The yoga class has eight lessons every two months.

6 [   ] The mobile phone was found by Paul.

Help with Writing Notices: abbreviations

 a) We use some common abbreviations in notices. What do you think the abbreviations in **bold** mean in notices A–F?

Pls. = Please

b) Write the **bold** abbreviations in notices A–F next to their meaning.

1 per hour .... *p/h* ....
2 non-smokers ....
3 very good condition ....
4 or near offer ....
5 per week ....
6 evenings ....
7 Tuesday ....
8 telephone number ....

c) Which other abbreviations do you know? Write these words/phrases next to their abbreviation.

| ~~Street~~ | for example | Avenue | including |
| Thanks | April | as soon as possible | Road |

1 St. .... *Street* ....
2 Ave. ....
3 Apr. ....
4 e.g. ....
5 asap ....
6 incl. ....
7 Rd. ....
8 Thx. ....

 4 Write notices for information a)–c). Use the abbreviations in **3** where possible.

a) Alex is offering a cookery course. There are 3-hour classes every week – on Saturday mornings. You can call him after 7 o'clock in the evening on 01923 434325.

Cookery course

b) Margie wants to rent out a double room in her house. It's £140 a week but that includes bills. She doesn't want anyone that smokes and you can email her on mjparks@ukmail.net.

c) Tom is selling his television. It's nearly new – he won it in a competition two months ago. He wants about £120 for it. The buyer will have to pick it up. He lives in Carston Avenue. His phone number is 07986 304207.

 5 **a)** Think of something you would like to sell. Answer these questions and make notes.

What is it?

....

Is it in good condition?

....

How much is it? Will you take a near offer?

....

How should a buyer contact you?

....

When can they contact you?

....

b) Write a notice.

- Use your notes from **5a)**.
- Organise your notice and make it interesting.
- Use abbreviations.
- Read and check for mistakes.
- Give your notice to your teacher next class.

> Tick the things you can do in English in the Reading and Writing Progress Portfolio, p88.

Holiday arrangements

Reading formal letters
Writing formal letters: American and British English
Review phrasal verbs (1): travel

 a) Are these sentences about formal letters true (T) or false (F)? Correct the false sentences.

1 [T] You should put your address first, before the address of the person you are writing to.

2 [ ] A letter which starts *Dear Sir* should end *Yours faithfully*. A letter which starts *Dear Mr/Mrs*, etc. + surname should end *Yours sincerely*.

3 [ ] The first paragraph of the letter should explain your reason for writing.

4 [ ] You should start a new paragraph for each sentence.

5 [ ] You should use contractions (*I'm*, *He's*, etc.).

6 [ ] You should write your signature above your name.

b) Read letter A quickly. Which rule about formal letters in **1a)** <u>isn't</u> used in this letter?

 Read letter A again and choose the correct answer.

1 Where is Mr Turnbull's holiday?
   a) Italy
   b) the USA
   c) The letter doesn't say.

2 Mr Turnbull will now set off …
   a) earlier.
   b) later.
   c) at the same time.

3 Mr Turnbull is now staying at the hotel for …
   a) seven nights.
   b) more nights than before.
   c) fewer nights than before.

4 They will now check out of the hotel on …
   a) Friday.
   b) Saturday.
   c) Sunday.

5 Why has the hotel changed?
   a) The original hotel is full.
   b) The original hotel is closed for redecoration.
   c) The letter doesn't say.

6 What is different about the new hotel?
   a) It's not as good.
   b) It's better.
   c) It's nearer the airport.

7 How should Mr Turnbull get from the airport to the hotel?
   a) Someone will pick him up.
   b) He should get a taxi.
   c) He should get a coach.

Color Blue Travel
14–18 Summer Street
MA 00105

12/17/06

15 Shaw Ave.
Bedford
MK40 2JA

Dear Mr Turnbull,

I am writing to inform you of some changes to your holiday arrangements in March 2007.

The flight will now leave at 10.15 a.m. on Saturday March 14th (03/14/07) not Friday March 13th (03/13/07). The hotel booking is still for 7 days and is therefore Saturday through Friday. The return flight is now Saturday March 21st (03/21/07). However, the hotel will now be Hotel Atlas. This hotel is a five-star hotel rather than the original three-star hotel offered.

Please note that all travelers will be taken from the airport to their hotel by a coach or taxi service.

We hope you are looking forward to your holiday with Color Blue Travel. We are very grateful for your cooperation with these changes and apologize for any inconvenience caused. Please contact us at the above address with any queries.

Sincerely,

Terry Samuels

Terry Samuels

Help with Writing Formal letters: American and British English

3 **a)** Look at formal letter A in American English (US) and formal letter B in British English (UK). Starting formal letters in American and British English is the same. Complete the table for ending formal letters with *US* or *UK*.

ending a letter if you:

know the person's name	1 _____ : Yours sincerely
	2 _____ : Sincerely (yours)
don't know the person's name	3 _____ : Yours faithfully
	4 __US__ : Yours truly

b) Complete the table with examples of American English from letter A.

	British English	American English
dates	14th March 14/03/07	1 _March 14th_ 2 _____
spelling	apologise colour traveller	3 _____ 4 _____ 5 _____
prepositions	Saturday to Friday	Saturday 6 _____ Friday

(B)

Colour Blue Travel
14–18 Summer Street
MA 00105

21/12/06

15 Shaw Ave.
Bedford
MK40 2JA

Dear Mr Samuels,

Thank you for your letter with details of our changed holiday arrangements. We realise holiday arrangements sometimes have to change but the current flight times and hotel make our situation difficult. Firstly, we booked our original hotel to be near friends. Hotel Atlas is nearly 50 miles away from our original hotel. Secondly, we've got a relative's wedding on 14th March (14/03/07). We've been booking holidays with your company for over ten years and this is the first time we've been in this situation. I'd appreciate it if you could contact me on 00 44 1234 324732 to discuss this problem.

Yours sincerely,

Richard Turnbull

Richard Turnbull

4 **a)** Read letter B. Richard Turnbull makes four common formal letter writing mistakes in his reply. What are they?

1 *You should put your address first.* _____
2 _____
3 _____
4 _____

b) Richard uses British English in his letter. Find four examples of British English and change them to American English. Use the tables in **3** to help you.

1 *Colour (UK) → Color (US)*   3 _____
2 _____   4 _____

5 **a)** Look at the following holiday arrangements. Make notes on your own ideas in the table.

	original	new
flight	04/10/07	
hotel	Hotel Luxor (***)	
other	pick-up service from airport	

b) Write either letter a) or letter b).

a) A letter from a travel company explaining the change in holiday arrangements.
b) A letter from a customer who has received these new arrangements but has a problem.

- Use your notes from **5a)**.
- Organise your letter correctly.
- Use either American English or British English.
- Read and check for mistakes.
- Give your letter to your teacher next class.

Tick the things you can do in English in the Reading and Writing Progress Portfolio, p88.

A book review

 Read these reviews quickly. What connects the two books?

They are both:
a) written by journalists.   b) based on true stories.   c) about real people.

Reading book reviews
Writing book reviews: organisation, useful phrases
Review character adjectives; verb forms

books:reading:literature

REVIEWS

Cameron Crowe was once a teenage reporter for *Rolling Stone* – the famous American music magazine. He uses his experiences in his novel *Almost Famous* (Faber and Faber, £6.99). The main character is William Miller, a 15-year-old kid who is hired by *Rolling Stone* magazine to go on tour with an unknown band, Stillwater. Their adventures take place all over the USA as William learns about life and love. Crowe's writing is both interesting and believable.

The book also includes an interview with Cameron Crowe about his adventurous life and he explains some of the more confusing parts of the story.

You will not be disappointed by this book. The ending is thoughtful and emotional and I'm going to remember it for a long time.

In 1915 Henry James, the famous author, was seriously ill in his home in London. He was waiting to die. And this is where David Lodge's historical novel *Author! Author!* (Secker & Warburg, £6.99) begins. Lodge tells the story of Henry James' successes and failures in his novels and plays from *Portrait of a Lady* (recently a film with Nicole Kidman) to his disaster of a play *Guy Domville*. And *Author! Author!* would make an interesting historical film. The title itself is fantastic and refers to what audiences used to shout if they liked a play.

Lodge's novel is a sensitive story of an author who was never confident of his talent. And Henry James will get many more fans from people who read this book. I'm going to take a couple of his novels on holiday myself!

 Read the reviews again and choose the best answer.

1 Cameron Crowe …
   a) was a journalist.
   b) was in a band.
   c) owned a magazine.

2 William goes on tour with …
   a) a famous group.
   b) The Rolling Stones.
   c) a new group.

3 The reviewer of *Almost Famous* particularly liked …
   a) the end of the story.
   b) the interview with Cameron Crowe.
   c) the title.

4 Henry James wrote …
   a) *Author! Author!*
   b) *Portrait of a Lady*.
   c) a book about Nicole Kidman.

5 The reviewer thinks *Author! Author!*
   a) is a good play.
   b) should be made into a film.
   c) has a strange title.

6 On holiday the reviewer is going to read …
   a) *Author! Author!* again.
   b) some more David Lodge books.
   c) some more Henry James books.

Help with Writing Book reviews: organisation, useful phrases

3 Both reviews in **1** contain four parts, which each have a different function. Put parts a)–d) in the order 1–4 in which they occur in the reviews.

a) Recommendation: ___4___

b) Plot: _____

c) Introduction to the story: _____

d) General comments: _____

4 The reviews use different verb forms for the different parts. Match parts a)–d) in **3** to 1–3.

1 past verb forms: ___c)___

2 present verb forms: _____ , _____

3 *will/be going to*: _____

5 The reviews contain some useful phrases for reviewing books. Match parts of the phrases 1–6 to a)–f) and then check your answers in the reviews.

1 The book tells ⎯⎯⎯⎯⎯   a) character …
2 The main   b) really good and refers to …
3 The title is   c) a good film because …
4 The story takes   d) is amazing/disappointing …
5 The ending   e) the story of …
6 It would make   f) place in …

6 Complete this review with the correct verb forms. Remember the four parts of a review in **3** and the different verb forms in **4**.

About 10 years ago I ¹ _went_ (go) skiing in Lahti, Finland. And this was the reason that *The Lahti File* by Richard MacAndrew (CUP, £3.50) ² _____ (attract) my attention. I ³ _____ also _____ (learn) English at the moment and this book is written especially for students. The novel ⁴ _____ (take) place in Finland and MacAndrew ⁵ _____ (describe) the town of Lahti very well. The main character ⁶ _____ (be) a spy called Ian Munro. He's sent to Lahti to investigate several strange deaths.

The book ⁷ _____ (be) also available on CD and if you want to practise your English more, there ⁸ _____ (be) worksheets on CUP's website.

If you like a good thriller, you ⁹ _____ (love) *The Lahti File*. The ending is very exciting and I have a feeling there are going to be more novels with Ian Munro. I ¹⁰ _____ (read) them all!

7 Rewrite these sentences using the word in brackets.

1 At the end the story is amazing. (ending)
   The ending is amazing. _____

2 The book is about a young boy who has no parents. (tells) _____
   _____

3 The most important person in the book is Jack. (main) _____
   _____

4 The story happens in Buenos Aires, Argentina. (place) _____
   _____

5 I think a film version would be good because the book is so exciting. (make) _____
   _____

6 The name of the book is *Loyal* because of the relationship between the man and his dog (title; refer) _____
   _____

8 **a)** Think about a book you have read recently and make notes in the table.

title of the book	
some background information	
takes place	
main character	
general comments	
recommendation	

b) Write a review of your book.

- Use your notes from **8a)**.
- Organise your review and use the verb forms in **4**.
- Use the phrases in **5**.
- Read and check for mistakes.
- Give your review to your teacher next class.

Tick the things you can do in English in the Reading and Writing Progress Portfolio, p88.

Emails with news

Reading an informal email
Writing short emails and notes: useful phrases
Review verb patterns; homes

 1 Read the email and fill in gaps 1–8 with the correct words.

1 a) **absolutely**
  b) very
  c) fairly

2 a) more far
  b) more further
  c) further

3 a) read
  b) 'd read
  c) 've read

4 a) to pack
  b) packing
  c) pack

5 a) enough big
  b) big enough
  c) enough room

6 a) B&Bs
  b) airports
  c) stations

7 a) flights
  b) planes
  c) flying

8 a) thinks
  b) thinking
  c) think

 2 Read the email again. Are these sentences true (T) or false (F)?

1 [T] Alex and Lucien's cat had never been outside before.

2 [ ] Alex wants to find out where Pat Austin lives.

3 [ ] They didn't go to the party because they were tired.

4 [ ] They're having a party at their new house next year.

5 [ ] Their new house has enough space for some guests to stay.

6 [ ] It's a good idea to book train or plane tickets to Edinburgh in advance.

7 [ ] Alex and Lucien moved because Lucien has got a new job.

From: alex@rousso.co.uk
To: huwprice@medaid.com; arvind@24-7work.com; (plus 10 others...)
Subject: Greetings from Scotland!

Hi everyone,

We've finally moved! The house is ¹ _absolutely_ gorgeous – better than I remember it. And the cat's fascinated by the garden – she was born in our old flat and she's never been ² _____ than the balcony!

We're so grateful for all your cards and presents. I ³ _____ the cards again this morning and they made me cry! (Can anyone tell me what Pat Austin's email is? She sent some flowers to our new address.)

We're so sorry that we didn't come to Jackie and Bill's party on Saturday afternoon. What happened was that we were supposed to finish ⁴ _____ in the afternoon. But we quickly realised the lorry wasn't ⁵ _____ . So in the end we had to hire another van and Mike had to drive to Edinburgh in the evening.

Talking of parties, we're going to have a house-warming party on 3rd February. Would you all like to come? I know it'll be a long time after we've moved in but we might have a chance to decorate first. We'd rather get organised before you come! I'm telling you about this more than three months in advance so there are no excuses. There are lots of ⁶ _____ nearby and some of you can sleep here. Don't forget to book train or plane tickets soon if you're going to come! Superflights (www.superflights.com) are offering ⁷ _____ to Edinburgh for £30 at the moment but they'll get more expensive soon.

Everything's still in boxes of course, but I don't start work for a week. Lucien's got an interview next week so ⁸ _____ of him on Wednesday.

Anyway, more news soon. Hope you all have a lovely break during the holiday!

Much love,

Alex (and Lucien)

Help with Writing
Short emails and notes: useful phrases

 3 **a)** Find phrases 1–8 in the letter and <u>underline</u> them.

1 We'd rather …
2 We're so sorry that …
3 Don't forget …
4 Can anyone tell me … ?
5 Hope you have …
6 We're so grateful for …
7 What happened was that …
8 Would you like … ?

b) Match phrases 1–8 in **3a)** with meanings a)–h).

a) [2] apologising
b) [ ] reminding
c) [ ] wishing someone a good thing
d) [ ] thanking
e) [ ] inviting someone
f) [ ] saying your preference
g) [ ] explaining what happened
h) [ ] asking for information

c) Which phrase or phrases in **3a)** are often followed by:

a) an infinitive _____
b) an infinitive with _to_ _____ , _____

4 **a)** Complete these sentences with phrases 1–8 in **3a)**.

1 *We're so sorry that* we didn't do the washing-up. I promise I'll do it when I get home.

2 ------------------------------------ a good time at the gig. I'd love to come but I've got to work tonight.

3 ------------------------------------ if this is rubbish? I'd like to get rid of it.

4 A Have you decided how you're getting to Alex's party?

   B ------------------------------ fly than get the train.

5 ------------------------------------ your help last Saturday. You must be as tired as we are today.

6 ------------------------------------ to meet me for lunch tomorrow? I've got a meeting near your office and it finishes at about one o'clock.

7 I didn't tell you why we left early on Friday, did I? ------------------------------ I got a phone call from the babysitter.

8 ------------------------------------ to ring your mum. She called yesterday.

b) Read the situations and write sentences using the correct form of the phrases in **3a)**.

1 You have just arrived at the cinema. You are meeting a friend and you are late because you couldn't find your keys. **Apologise** to your friend and **explain** what happened.

   I'm so sorry that I'm late. What happened was that I couldn't find my keys.

2 It's your parents' wedding anniversary tomorrow. **Remind** your brother.

   ----

3 You are looking for the station but you are lost. **Ask** a group of people.

   ----

4 You received a birthday present from friends who are going on holiday tomorrow. **Thank** them for the present and **wish** them a good time on holiday.

   ----

5 You want to go to a pop concert on Friday. **Invite** your friend and say you **prefer** going with someone rather than going alone.

   ----

5 **a)** Match situations 1–3 to plans a)–c) for a short email.

1 You borrowed a friend's CD and broke it.

   ----

2 You had dinner at a friend's house on Friday.

   ----

3 Your boss is going on holiday next week.

   ----

a) • thank your friend.
   • invite your friend to go out next week.
   • remind your friend to bring your jacket you left at his/her house.

b) • say you'd prefer to work at home on Friday.
   • ask him/her for his mobile number in case of emergency.
   • wish him/her a good time.

c) • apologise for the accident.
   • explain what happened.
   • say what you're going to do.

b) Write three short emails for situations 1–3 in **5a)**.

• Use the plans in **5a)**.
• Use the phrases in **3a)**.
• Read and check for mistakes.
• Give your emails to your teacher next class.

Tick the things you can do in English in the Reading and Writing Progress Portfolio, p88.

Cultura Inglesa

Letters to a newspaper

> **Reading** an article and two letters about pocket money
> **Writing** giving an opinion
> **Review** conditionals; *make* and *do*

1 Read the article and letters quickly. Who:

a) thinks children should work for their pocket money? ....

b) isn't sure if children should work for their pocket money? ....

c) disagrees with a)? ....

Househusband

By Phil Marsden

Pocket money – do your kids earn it?

I have three children who are 8, 10 and 12. They get pocket money every Saturday of between £3 and £5. This is about the national British average but according to a recent survey, British children receive the highest pocket money in Europe. And of course, <u>they're absolutely convinced that</u> their friends get at least twice as much as they do.

I've always felt that pocket money is a good idea. I have no doubt that it teaches children to think about money and to save up for things they want –

appropriate training for adult life. However, recently we've started to ask our kids to earn their pocket money. They do the washing-up, for example, or do some cleaning. Or sometimes we pay them not to make noise!

They're not happy about it! They say that they don't have time. They say their friends don't have to do anything for their pocket money. My twelve-year-old makes me laugh. As far as he's concerned, we pay less than the government's minimum wage! When he refused to help my wife do the shopping recently, we didn't give him his pocket money for a week. He was so upset that we had to have a family meeting to discuss the situation. (And then later I saw our eight-year-old gave him half of *her* pocket money!)

So what do you think readers? We're not being unfair, are we?

We've got two children. They started getting pocket money when they were about four. But it was always for helping or doing some work. Now, they're 14 and 16 and they volunteer to make dinner and do the housework. As they see it, they have to earn their pocket money.

I'm positive that your own children will soon learn the same thing. And if they refuse, don't give them their pocket money!

Children who are old enough – and yours are – have to learn that home is not a hotel!

Barry, North London

To me, children are becoming obsessed by money – just like their parents! If you give children money for helping at home, then they start thinking they should make money out of anything and everything they do.

We have four boys (2, 7, 9 and 13). The three who receive pocket money get it every week on Saturday morning. It doesn't matter how much work they have done or what they have done at school. Of course, we ask them to help at home. And *usually* they do everything we ask them to do. And if they don't do it, there is usually a good reason. If there isn't one, we'll tell them that we're disappointed. We strongly believe that this is a much better idea than the threat of no pocket money.

Nicole, Glasgow

2 Read the article and letters again. Are these sentences true (T), false (F) or the text doesn't say (DS)?

1 [F] Phil has always asked his children to help around the house.

2 [ ] Phil thinks pocket money is important because children learn about saving money.

3 [ ] Phil's eldest child never helps with the housework.

4 [ ] Phil gives his children extra money for doing things in the house.

5 [ ] Barry's children expect to help at home.

6 [ ] Barry thinks Phil's children should help at home.

7 [ ] Nicole gives pocket money to her four children.

8 [ ] Nicole's children always help her when they can.

9 [ ] Nicole's children don't mind doing the housework.

Help with Writing Giving an opinion

3 a) Read the article and letters again. Fill in the gaps in these phrases for giving an opinion.

1 I'm *absolutely* convinced *that* ...

2 .... felt ....

3 .... doubt that ...

4 .... far .... I'm .... , ...

5 .... I see .... , ...

6 .... positive ....

7 .... me, ...

8 I strongly ....

b) Four phrases in **3a)** are used to give stronger opinions. Which phrases are they?

........*1*........ , ... , ... , ...

c) Notice how you can change the phrases in **3a)**. <u>Underline</u> the four phrases in the article and letters that don't use the subject pronoun *I*.

4 a) Rewrite these sentences using the words in brackets and the phrases in **3a)**.

1 We really think that he stole the money. (strongly)

   We strongly believe that he stole the money.

2 She really believes she will win. (convinced)

   ....

3 I believe everyone should be able to afford a house. (felt)

   ....

   ....

4 He thinks we will find life on other planets. (doubt)

   ....

5 I'm sure I saw him earlier. (positive)

   ....

6 She thinks that housework is a waste of time. (sees)

   ....

7 I think that children spend too much time watching TV. (me)

   ....

8 My brother thinks that children shouldn't get pocket money. (concerned)

   ....

   ....

b) Write one sentence giving your opinion on these subjects.

1 Tax

....

....

2 Protective parents

....

....

3 Superstitions

....

....

4 Learning languages

....

....

5 Pocket money

....

....

5 a) Choose one of the subjects in **4b)**. What are your opinions on the subject? Make notes in the table.

opinion	reasons
I think all children should have a mobile phone.	It's safer when they go out.

b) Write a short article giving your opinion on one of the subjects in **4b)**.

- Use your notes in **5a)**.
- Use the phrases in **3a)**.
- Read and check for mistakes.
- Give your article to your teacher next class.

Tick the things you can do in English in the Reading and Writing Progress Portfolio, p88.

Instructions

Reading instructions
Writing instructions: connecting words (1), useful phrases
Review imperatives; computers

1 Read instructions A–D quickly. Which is probably:

1 an email to a friend? ___C___

2 written on a food packet? ___D___

3 connected with computer software? ___B___

4 a note to a new flatmate? ___A___

A

The washing machine looks old but it still works. Use these instructions and you should be fine.

1 Put some washing powder or liquid in section A of the tray.

2 <u>Make sure</u> you don't put too much powder in the tray.

3 Choose a washing programme – I always use 3!

4 Press 'Start'.

5 It takes about 40 minutes on programme 3. Don't forget to switch the machine off when it's finished!

2 Are these sentences true (T), false (F) or the instructions don't say (DS)?

1 [F] The washing machine is unreliable.

2 [T] You shouldn't put too much washing powder in the machine.

3 [F] The **face2face** CD-ROM always starts automatically.

4 [T] You need a mouse to start the CD-ROM.

5 [DS] Thomas often forgets to put the rubbish outside.

6 [T] Thomas shouldn't use the sink in the upstairs bathroom.

7 [F] The dish in the recipe is suitable for vegetarians.

8 [F] The recipe takes less than an hour.

B

- First insert the **face2face** CD-ROM into your CD-ROM drive.
- If Autorun is enabled, the CD-ROM will start automatically.
- If the CD-ROM doesn't start, double-click on '**My Computer**'. Then double-click on **D:**. Finally double-click on the **face2face** icon.

Help with Writing Instructions: connecting words (1), useful phrases

3 Tick the ideas that are useful when writing instructions.

1 [✓] Use numbers or bullet points to organise your instructions.

2 [ ] Add some jokes.

3 [✓] Use imperatives.

4 [✓] Write the stages in the order they should happen.

5 [ ] Give detailed technical information about something.

6 [ ] Use the passive more than the active.

7 [✓] Use illustrations.

4 a) Instructions also use connecting words. Look at the recipe (instructions D). Which five connecting words does it use?

___First___ , _____ , _____ ,

_____ , _____

b) Which word or words in **4a)** would you use:

1 in the middle of your instructions?
___then___ , _next_

2 at the end of your instructions? _finally_

3 meaning 'at the same time'? _meanwhile_

4 at the beginning of your instructions? _first_

5 a) Look at these useful phrases for instructions. <u>Underline</u> them in instructions A–D.

1 *Make sure ...*   4 *You will need ...*

2 *Don't forget ...*   5 *Whatever you do, ...*

3 *Remember that ...*   6 *Try to avoid ...*

b) Which phrase or phrases in **5a)** are:

a) followed by the infinitive with *to*? ___2___ ,
You will need

b) followed by the verb+*ing*? _try to avoid_

c) a positive or negative imperative? _whatever you do_

d) a clause? _make sure , remember that_

C

Hi Thomas,

Thanks very much for looking after the house and the dogs while I'm away. I left instructions on the kitchen table but here are a couple of things I forgot.

Remember that the rubbish is collected early on Monday mornings. You will need to put the bins outside on Sunday night.

Whatever you do, don't use the sink in the upstairs bathroom. It's broken! Sorry.

See you in a couple of weeks. Call me if there are any problems.

Anya

D

1 First chop up the onions and garlic.

2 Then heat a little butter in a frying pan and cook the onions and garlic slowly for about 10 minutes. Try to avoid using too much heat otherwise you will burn the onions.

3 Next add the beef and cook for 10 minutes or until the meat is brown.

4 Meanwhile boil 1.5 litres of water in a saucepan with a little olive oil. Add the spaghetti and cook for about 10 minutes.

5 Add the tomato sauce, salt and pepper to the meat, onions and garlic. Leave on a low heat for 30 minutes.

6 Finally, you can mix the sauce and spaghetti or serve them separately.

6 **a)** Read these instructions. Which of the useful ideas in **3** does the writer <u>not</u> use?

___1___ , ___4___ , ___3___ , ___7___

Dad. This time we're going to get it right! We don't want to miss Big Brother again! You need to put a DVD in the DVD recorder and then you should press the record button. Of course, you'll probably need to change the channel first. I think Big Brother is on Channel Four but you can check. The record button is red, by the way, – you can't miss it. And remember to use a blank DVD!

b) Write the instructions in **6a)** again as clearly as possible. Use the connecting words in **4a)** when possible.

Dad,
Here are some instructions for the DVD recorder. Follow them carefully!

1 Put a blank DVD in the DVD recorder.

_____

_____

_____

_____

7 Complete sentence b) so it has the same meaning as sentence a). You can use one, two or three words. You must use the word in brackets.

1 a) If you want to eat there on Saturday, I think it's a good idea to book a table. (need)

   b) If you want to eat there on Saturday, you ___need to___ book a table.

2 a) Don't forget to lock all doors and windows. (sure)

   b) ___make sure___ you lock all doors and windows.

3 a) Don't forget that the oven will stay hot for up to 30 minutes. (remember)

   b) ___Remember that___ the oven will stay hot for up to 30 minutes.

4 a) Don't use the hand-held computer in heavy rain. (avoid)

   b) ___avoid using___ the hand-held computer in heavy rain.

5 a) Remember to take your suit to the dry cleaner's. (forget)

   b) ___Don't forget to___ take your suit to the dry cleaner's.

6 a) The only thing you shouldn't do is press the button on the left. (whatever)

   b) ___Whatever you do___ don't press the button on the left.

8 **a)** Choose one of the ideas below. Make notes on your instructions in the table.

- You are going on holiday and a friend is going to feed your cats. Write instructions on how often he/she should feed them, where the food is, etc.
- Write instructions for using a computer programme you know.
- You have a new flatmate. He/She is moving in while you are on holiday. Write some instructions for him/her about general things he/she needs to know.

stages of instructions	1- why you are writing e-mail
useful phrases	2- Description of the steps
other useful points, for example illustrations	3- further details 4 - Reminder and final comment 100 - 120 words

b) Write instructions for one of the ideas in **8a)**.

- Use your notes in **8a)**.
- Use the useful ideas for writing instructions in **3**.
- Use connecting words and phrases in **4** and **5**.
- Read and check for mistakes.
- Give your instructions to your teacher next class.

> **Tick the things you can do in English in the Reading and Writing Progress Portfolio, p88.**

Problems and solutions

1 a) Put paragraphs A–F in the correct order to make two letters.

Letter 1: ___E___ , _____ , _____

Letter 2: _____ , _____ , _____

b) Which letter is about:

a) a pollution problem? _____

b) a safety problem? _____

B

I work in the town centre and, like many other people, live on the other side of the park. My journey home is about 15 minutes shorter if I cycle through the park but in the future I will be cycling on the road. It is simply too dangerous.

C

It is time that both the school and the council take some action about this problem. For example, students should be told that it can take up to 12 years for a cigarette stub to decompose*. **In addition** just three or four bins, that are emptied regularly, would help the problem enormously. Brighton is a beautiful town. We should keep it like that.

A

Although I feel that children should understand that the street (or my garden) is not a litter bin, I do not think we help them. There are no bins in front of Brighton High. And I have never seen any of the teachers, who drive down the road on their way home, speak to any students about their behaviour.

decompose = gradually become worse in condition

D

It would be simple and inexpensive to repair the path and replace some of the lights. Furthermore it would encourage people to walk or cycle to work rather than drive on our already busy roads. If the council do not want to do this, the park should be closed at night and they should lock the gates. It would be very inconvenient for everyone who lives in my area but at the moment it is simply not safe.

E

I enjoyed the article about the environment and our town last week. **However**, you failed to mention the most obvious problem in Brighton: litter. I live opposite Brighton High Secondary School. Every evening when I come home from work, I pick up a collection of crisp and sweet packets that <u>have been left</u> in my front garden. **Furthermore**, I am not alone. My neighbours have to do the same thing. In the street, it is even worse with old cigarette stubs and chewing gum stuck to the pavement.

F

There are only about two working lights and it is impossible to see anything at night. **Moreover**, when I am not worrying about hitting a pedestrian or being attacked, I am worrying about falling off my bike. The path is in a terrible condition, with several dangerous potholes. Nothing has been done about this **even though** I have phoned the council several times.

2 Read the letters again. Are these sentences true (T), false (F) or the letters don't say (DS)?

In letter 1 the writer ...

1 | DS | is a teacher.

2 | ☐ | thinks children should be more responsible about litter.

3 | ☐ | believes teachers could help more with the problem.

4 | ☐ | thinks that some more bins would completely solve the problem.

In letter 2 the writer ...

5 | ☐ | often cycles through the park.

6 | ☐ | has fallen off his/her bike before.

7 | ☐ | has tried contacting the council about the lights.

8 | ☐ | thinks the park should be closed at night.

The writers of both letters ...

9 | ☐ | live in the same town.

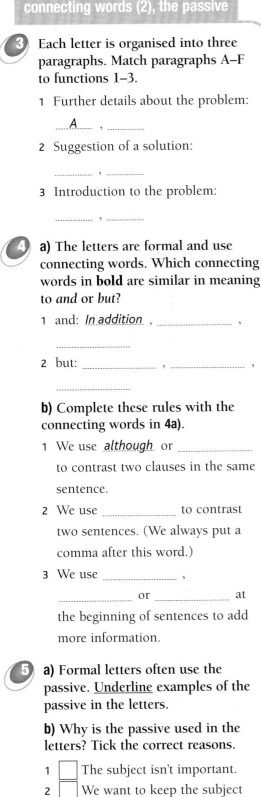

Help with Writing Letters to
a newspaper: organisation,
connecting words (2), the passive

3 Each letter is organised into three
paragraphs. Match paragraphs A–F
to functions 1–3.

1 Further details about the problem:

___A___ , _____

2 Suggestion of a solution:

_____ , _____

3 Introduction to the problem:

_____ , _____

4 **a)** The letters are formal and use
connecting words. Which connecting
words in **bold** are similar in meaning
to *and* or *but*?

1 and: *In addition* , _____ ,

_____

2 but: _____ , _____ ,

_____

b) Complete these rules with the
connecting words in **4a)**.

1 We use *although* or _____
to contrast two clauses in the same
sentence.

2 We use _____ to contrast
two sentences. (We always put a
comma after this word.)

3 We use _____ ,
_____ or _____ at
the beginning of sentences to add
more information.

5 **a)** Formal letters often use the
passive. Underline examples of the
passive in the letters.

b) Why is the passive used in the
letters? Tick the correct reasons.

1 ☐ The subject isn't important.

2 ☐ We want to keep the subject
secret.

3 ☐ The subject is obvious.

4 ☐ We don't know the subject.

6 Choose the correct words. Sometimes both answers are possible.

1 The park is empty in the week. *Moreover*/*However*, it is quite
crowded at weekends.

2 *Even though*/*However*, there is a lot of traffic, I love where I live.

3 Schools are not teaching students about recycling. *Furthermore*/
Even though there are very few recycling bins in our town.

4 *Even though*/*Although* I recycle a lot of rubbish, I know I could
do more.

5 There is nothing to do in our town at weekends. *Moreover*/
However, there are very few places to go at night.

6 There aren't many places to park here. *In addition*/*Furthermore* the
car parks we have are incredibly expensive.

7 The British recycle about 12% of their rubbish. *Furthermore*/
However, the Japanese recycle over 40% of theirs.

7 Write these sentences in the passive.

1 They've put in more cycle lanes. *More cycle lanes have been put in.*

2 They must repair the road. _____

3 People don't use recycling bins regularly.

_____

4 No one ever empties the bins. _____

5 They recycle a lot of glass. _____

6 They told me that they would replace the lights.

_____

8 **a)** Think about a problem in your town or city. Make notes in
the table.

describe the problem	
further details about the problem	
possible solutions	
possible results	

b) Write a formal letter to a local newspaper about the problem
you chose in **8a)**.

● Use your notes from **8a)**.
● Use the organisation of the letter in **3**.
● Use the connecting words in **4** where possible.
● Use the passive if appropriate.
● Read and check for mistakes.
● Give your letter to your teacher next class.

Tick the things you can do in English in the
Reading and Writing Progress Portfolio, p88.

A letter of application

1 Read the advertisement. Tick four more qualities you think an applicant for this job should have.

a) organised ✓
b) speaks foreign languages
c) gets on well with people
d) ability to work overtime
e) good computer skills
f) non-smoker
g) ability to make quick decisions
h) ability to drive

2 Read the letter of application and answer the questions.

1 Where did Christine see the advertisement?

   In the Guardian newspaper.

2 Does Christine ever teach at the Black Lion? ....

3 What information in the advertisement does Christine talk about in her letter? ....
   ....
   ....

4 Why does she want a new job?
   ....
   ....
   ....
   ....

5 How do we know Christine likes doing sport? ....
   ....

6 What has Christine sent with her application letter? ....

7 What kind of person do you think Christine is? ....
   ....
   ....

Fitness Trainer

We require an experienced fitness trainer for the Well Retreat Centre. As part of a team, you will develop training programmes for our customers. You will travel to several of our centres and give advice and training to other Well Retreat Centre instructors. This position is based at our centre in North London but involves extensive travel and flexible working hours.

Please apply in writing with a recent CV to:

Dear Sir/Madam,

A   [1]I am writing in reply to your advertisement in the *Guardian* for a fitness trainer at the Well Retreat Centre.

B   [2]At the moment, I am working as the Health and Fitness assistant manager at the Black Lion Sports Centre in Kent. [3]My responsibilities range from organising timetables and managing instructors to giving classes. I also offer specialised fitness training advice for several gyms in London and in the Southeast. This role involves working with instructors and customers to plan diets, fitness and lifestyle programmes, according to their needs. I work long hours, but I enjoy my work.

C   I have been working at the Black Lion and for other gyms for three years and both jobs have taught me a wide range of skills that are valuable in my work. However, I would now like the opportunity to develop these skills in a full-time position with more responsibility. Furthermore, I would also like to work in more of a team environment. For these reasons [4]I am very interested in working for the Well Retreat Centre.

D   [5]As you will see from my CV, fitness is also one of my main interests. When I have time to relax, I go running. I recently participated in this year's London Marathon. I have also written several articles for fitness training magazines in the UK and the USA.

E   I would be pleased to discuss this letter and my enclosed CV, and [6]I look forward to hearing from you.

Yours faithfully,

Christine Paine

Christine Paine

Help with Writing   Letters of application: organisation

3 Read the letter again. Match paragraphs A–E to functions 1–5.

1 Further information about yourself: *D*
2 What you are doing at the moment: ......
3 Conclusion: ......
4 Why you are writing: ......
5 Why you are applying: ......

Help with Writing Letters of application: useful phrases

4 **a)** Look at the formal phrases 1–6 in **bold** in the letter. Match them to informal sentences a)–f).

a) There is some information about this on my CV. __5__

b) I saw your advert in the paper so I thought I'd write. _____

c) I really want to work for your company. _____

d) These are the things I have to do at work. _____

e) Please write soon. _____

f) This is what I do now. _____

b) Complete phrases 1–6 from the letter with these words.

~~in~~   at   as (x 2)   from (x 3)   in (x 2)   to (x 3)   for (x 2)

1 I am writing __in__ reply _____ your advertisement _____ the *Guardian* _____ a ...

2 _____ the moment, I am working _____ a/the ...

3 My responsibilities range _____ ... _____ ...

4 I am very interested _____ working _____ ...

5 _____ you will see _____ my CV, ...

6 I look forward _____ hearing _____ you.

5 **a)** Read this letter of application. Put paragraphs A–E in the correct order.

__D__ , _____ , _____ , _____ , _____

A At the moment I am working full-time at a receptionist for a large American bank in London. My responsibilities range of meeting visitors to answering phones and taking messages.

B I look forward to hearing of you.
Yours sincerely,
Elizabeth West
Elizabeth West

C I am interested of medical issues and three years ago, I had a temporary position with a secretary on the Wellington Hospital. I believe my experience, interest and enthusiasm would be excellent for your position.

D Dear Mrs Crouch,
I am writing the reply to your advertisement on *The Times* of a receptionist at St John's Wood Surgery.

E As you will see on my CV, I have over nine years of experience. In this time, I have learned a wide variety of skills connected with my work. I have also realised that I particularly enjoy the personal contact that receptionists have with people. Therefore I would like the opportunity to work in a smaller office environment.

b) Read the letter of application again. Find ten mistakes and correct them.

6 **a)** Choose one of these advertisements or your own idea. Make notes on a letter of application in the table.

Personal trainers

Our agency has a personal trainer position available. You will be working with musicians on tours all over the world. You should have at least 5 years of experience of fitness training and diet planning.

Santé Health Centre

We are looking for a cook for our health centre in Wallingford, near Oxford. We run courses for people who are following special diets as part of a health programme. You should have experience and lots of ideas about cooking for special diets.

where you saw the advertisement	
what you are doing at the moment	
why you are applying	
further information about yourself	

b) Write a letter of application.

- Use your notes from **6a)**.
- Use the organisation of the letter in **3**.
- Use the formal phrases in **4**.
- Read and check for mistakes.
- Give your letter to your teacher next class.

Tick the things you can do in English in the Reading and Writing Progress Portfolio, p88.

Describing people

1 Read the description quickly. Tick the things 1–5 that Fiona mentions.

1. ☐ Kate's boyfriend.
2. ☐ How Fiona met Kate.
3. ☐ Kate's personality.
4. ☐ Kate's appearance.
5. ☐ Kate's favourite hobbies.

Reading a description of a good friend
Writing descriptions of people: organisation, useful phrases
Review describing people; character adjectives; adjectives to describe behaviour

About six years ago I was invited to an old school friend's wedding. We had been really good friends at school but I hadn't seen her for a few years. So I was a bit surprised to get an invitation. When I realised I knew no one else at the wedding, I thought it was going to be a long day ... But then I met Kate. And, well, I guess she's my best friend now.

The first thing I noticed about Kate was her shoes. In fact it was difficult to miss them! They were bright red and they were the only thing I could see – she was under a table looking for her contact lens! As I walked by I said, "Nice shoes!" and I heard her say, "Thanks!" Then, when she came out from under the table we looked at each other and laughed! We had exactly the same dress on! We have very similar taste in clothes in fact - we like bright clothes – striped and flowery dresses and tops. But we look completely different. She is tanned and looks Spanish or Italian. I look typically English! We're both in our mid-twenties but my hair is short and blonde and hers is long and dark. I'm not very tall but she's taller than most men I know. In fact, she looks like a model and I ... well, I don't!

Our personalities are very different, too. She's much more confident than I am. But she can be so disorganised at times. I can't remember the number of times we've missed the start of a film, play or concert because Kate was late! However, she's funny, warm and the most considerate and unselfish person I know. She's always ready with a cup of tea and some good advice when I have a problem.

I've learned so much from Kate. And I was so lucky to meet her. I'm sure we'll be friends for life. And all because of those lovely red shoes and her great taste in clothes!

2 Read the description again and answer these questions.

1. Where did Fiona meet Kate?

   ....

2. Why did they start talking?

   ....

3. What kind of things do they both like?

   ....

4. How are they different in appearance?

   ....

   ....

   ....

   ....

   ....

5. How are they different in personality?

   ....

   ....

6. Why does Fiona think Kate is kind?

   ....

   ....

Reading and Writing Portfolio 10

Help with Writing Descriptions of people: organisation, useful phrases

3 Fiona's story contains four parts, which each have a different function. Put parts a)–d) in the order 1–4 in which they occur in the description.

a) Her feelings now: ___4___

b) Character: _____

c) Introduction/How they met: _____

d) Physical appearance/Clothes: _____

4 a) Read the description again. <u>Underline</u> these useful phrases for describing people.

1 We have similar taste in …
2 I/We look …
3 She looks like a …
4 She's the … (person) I know.

b) Which phrase or phrases in **4a**:

a) are followed by a noun? ___1___ , _____

b) contains a superlative? _____

c) is followed by an adjective? _____

5 a) Complete sentence b) so it has the same meaning as sentence a). Use the phrases in **4a**.

1 a) She has a worried expression on her face.

b) _She looks worried._

2 a) People think I'm intelligent because I wear glasses!

b) I _____ because I wear glasses!

3 a) We like the same kind of music.

b) We have _____ music.

4 a) Can you tell me about her appearance?

b) Can you tell me what she _____ ?

5 a) I don't know anyone more talented than Paul.

b) Paul is _____ person I know.

6 a) Jean and Kate enjoy the same type of films.

b) Jean and Kate have _____ films.

7 a) I have a similar face to my sister.

b) I look _____ sister.

8 a) I don't know anyone worse at driving than him.

b) He _____ driver I know.

b) Correct the mistakes in these sentences.

1 They look ~~angrily~~ *angry*, don't they?

2 My brother and I have similar taste on cars.

3 People think I look like Swedish but I'm actually Brazilian!

4 My dad is one of the most funny people I know.

5 He looks likes his father, doesn't he?

6 She looks well in that dress.

6 a) Think about someone you know well. Make notes in the table.

how you met	
physical appearance	
personality	
what you think of the person now	

b) Write a description.

- Use your notes from **6a**.
- Use the organisation of the description in **3**.
- Use the phrases in **4**.
- Read and check for mistakes.
- Give your description to your teacher next class.

Tick the things you can do in English in the Reading and Writing Progress Portfolio, p88.

83

My Notes

My Notes

My Notes

Intermediate Reading and Writing Progress Portfolio

🖎 Tick the things you can do in English.

Portfolio	Reading	Writing
1 p64	☐ I can understand a simple personal letter talking about a holiday. ☐ I can understand descriptions of events in private letters.	☐ I can write a letter expressing my experiences and feelings about a holiday. ☐ I can use and understand ellipsis of words in informal writing.
2 p66	☐ I can understand notices and common abbreviations used in them.	☐ I can write a detailed notice using appropriate abbreviations.
3 p68	☐ I can understand formal letters and detailed information given in them.	☐ I can write a formal letter and use simple British or American English appropriately.
4 p70	☐ I can read a book review and understand the main information and the reviewer's opinion.	☐ I can write a book review that is clearly organised and uses appropriate language.
5 p72	☐ I can read emails which talk about everyday life, and understand the facts and the reasons why people are writing.	☐ I can write a detailed personal letter describing experiences, feelings and events. ☐ I can use appropriate language for a wide variety of functions, including apologising, thanking and asking for information.
6 p74	☐ I can read columns in newspapers in which someone has an opinion on a topic.	☐ I can write an article which expresses my opinion on a subject using appropriate language.
7 p76	☐ I can understand simple technical instructions for everyday equipment.	☐ I can write clear, organised instructions and use appropriate connecting words.
8 p78	☐ I can understand the main points in short letters to a newspaper about current and familiar topics.	☐ I can write a letter on a problem in my local area. ☐ I can use appropriate connecting words for linking sentences and paragraphs.
9 p80	☐ I can read and understand the most important points in a job advertisement.	☐ I can reply in written form to job advertisements using appropriate language and style.
10 p82	☐ I can understand a detailed description of a person's appearance and personality.	☐ I can write a description of a friend using appropriate language and phrases.

Answer Key

1A Be happy!

1a) 2 the house 3 to people online
4 relatives

b) 2 tidy up the house 3 chat to people
online 4 visit relatives

2 b) Have you been clubbing in the last
month? c) When are you next having
a quiet night in? d) How often do
you have people round for dinner?
e) Have you ever chatted to people
online? f) Did you have a lie-in last
weekend? g) Are you visiting friends
or relatives this weekend? h) How
many exhibitions did you go to
last year?

3 2 When are you next having a quiet
night in? 3 Did you have a lie-in last
weekend? 4 Have you ever chatted
to people online? 5 Have you been
clubbing in the last month?

4a) 2 – 3 did 4 do 5 do 6 is 7 has 8 –

b) 2 Andy (always cooks). 3 When she
was a teenager. 4 Every Friday.
5 Because they've got two young
children. 6 Because it's her best
friend's birthday. 7 None. 8 Megan
(did).

1B Love it or hate it

1a) 2a) 3b) 4f) 5g) 6i) 7h) 8c) 9d)

b) A2; 6; 9 B3 C4; 5; 7; 8

2 2a) says 3c) have used 4c) were
5a) have 6c) try 7c) 'm not making
8c) 's

3 2 was 3 didn't use 4 wrote 5 haven't
been able to 6 call 7 don't get
8 'm helping

4 2 no one 3 Neither of them
4 usually 5 always 6 All of 7 I think

5 2 He doesn't think the computer's
got a virus. 3 I didn't understand
anything he said. 4 We always used
our computer to do serious things.
5 There are lots of computers at my
school. 6 Joe hasn't repaired my
laptop. 7 All of my colleagues can
type quickly. 8 Both of our parents
can use computers. 9 He works with
computers all day so he needs one at
home. 10 We are using the latest
software.

6 2 **I go** swimming … 3 Who **works**
with … 4 … have you **been** to?

---

5 … I **walked** to … 6 **I think** you
are correct. 7 **I play** a lot …
8 **I've lived** in … 9 **I went** to …
10 Who **do** they work with?/Who
does **he/she** work with?

1C The best medicine

1 2 embarrassed 3 nervous 4 relaxed
5 disappointed 6 confused 7 glad
8 stressed

2a) 2 at 3 on 4 in 5 with 6 by

b) 2T 3F 4F 5DS 6T 7F

1D At a barbecue

1a) 2 don't 3 doesn't 4 hasn't 5 haven't
6 didn't 7 isn't 8 haven't

b) b) It isn't going to rain c) They
haven't got any children d) We didn't
see him yesterday e) He hasn't been
here before f) You haven't told him
yet g) Clare doesn't eat beef h) I
don't need to bring anything to the
barbecue

2 2 aren't you 3 don't they 4 didn't
they 5 isn't he 6 isn't it 7 haven't I
8 haven't we?

3 3 We're going home soon, aren't we?
4 You haven't met our neighbours,
have you? 5 You didn't drive here,
did you? 6 It's warm outside, isn't it?
7 He wants something to eat, doesn't
he? 8 You don't know Sam, do you?
9 He's got the address, hasn't he?
10 You've tried English sausages,
haven't you? 11 He isn't working
this weekend, is he? 12 I'm not late,
am I?

4 2 Everyone **wants** to … 3 **They're**
going to … 4 I often **lose** against …
5 He's worked here **since** the …
6 I've **been** to … 7 … Paul and
Sally's dog. 8 Nobody **wants** to …

2A Slow down!

1 2g) 3b) 4d) 5h) 6f) 7j) 8c) 9i)
10e)

2 2 have to 3 allowed 4 ought
5 should 6 allowed 7 supposed
8 Can 9 're allowed to 10 be able to
11 must 12 ought

3 2 You ought to take a week off.
3 I'm not able to meet you tonight.

---

4 You aren't/You're not allowed to
work at weekends. 5 You don't have
to wear a tie. 6 You must arrive
before 9 a.m. 7 The company is
supposed to give us holiday pay.
8 You mustn't leave work before
4 p.m.

4a) 2 How are you able to work long
hours when you have a family?
3 Should we be under a lot of
pressure at work? 4 Ought we
to tell him that he's becoming a
workaholic? 5 Are you allowed to
wear informal clothes at your work?
6 Do we have to take time off in the
summer? 7 Are we supposed to take
all our holiday before December?

b) b)6 c)3 d)5 e)4 f)2 g)7

2B Ready, steady, eat

1 a) broccoli b) fridge c) grill d) peas
e) freezer f) aubergine g) beef
h) frying pan i) courgette
j) microwave k) lamb l) red pepper
m) oven n) toaster o) cooker
p) blender q) rubbish bin r) wok
s) carrots t) saucepan

2 2 fry 3 roast; bake 4 heat up;
microwave 5 boil; steam 6 grill

3a) 2 'm heating up 3 aren't helping
4 are … making 5 'm working;
'm not eating 6 is growing

b) 8 Does he know I'm here? 9 The
Spanish and Italians cook more than
the British. 10 Over 60 million
people live in the UK. 11 He doesn't
work on Fridays. 12 I don't think so.

c) a)4 b)1; 5 c)3; 6 d)11 e)9; 10 f)8; 12

4a) 2 'm sitting 3 're doing 4 is
5 always takes 6 don't think
7 Do you remember 8 are still trying

Answer Key

b) 2 'm writing 3 's cooking 4 doesn't understand 5 use 6 's doing 7 says 8 're trying 9 Do … eat 10 tastes

2C It's a nightmare

1 2 haven't had nightmares 3 didn't sleep a wink 4 dozes off 5 having a lie-in 6 get back to sleep 7 's fast asleep 8 is a light sleeper

2 1c) 2b) 3a)

3 2 Because our eyes move quickly in different directions. 3 Because our body becomes more relaxed. 4 We dream and we cannot move at all. 5 Because scientists think that REM sleep is important for memory and learning. 6 Giraffes, adults, babies, bats.

4 3 really/incredibly/extremely 4 really/incredibly/extremely 5 really/absolutely 6 really/absolutely 7 really/incredibly/extremely 8 really/incredibly/extremely 9 really/absolutely 10 really/absolutely

2D What's the matter?

1 2c) 3b) 4b) 5a)

2 2e) 3d) 4b) 5a)

3 2 Why don't you 3 I've tried that 4 Yes, I see what you mean 5 Have you tried 6 Well, it's worth a try 7 I'm sorry to hear that 8 I'd take 9 that's a good idea 10 I can see why you're upset 11 You ought to 12 might try that

3A Your holiday, my job

1 2 setting off 3 see you off 4 've checked into 5 put up with 6 get around 7 get back 8 pick me up

2 2 Have … worked 3 've … brought 4 've … got back 5 haven't checked into 6 've … dealt

3 2 ✓ 3 We've run a bed and breakfast **for** three years. 4 I like your house. How long **have you lived** here? 5 Mark isn't here. **He's gone** to work. 6 **We set off** hours ago, but we're stuck in traffic. 7 ✓ 8 **Have you checked** into the hotel yet? 9 ✓

4 2 've always loved 3 didn't take 4 've worked 5 joined 6 've been 7 've never felt 8 's learned 9 haven't cooked 10 've dealt with 11 couldn't 12 have … eaten 13 've drunk 14 've roasted 15 has complained

3B Lonely Planet

1a) 2 go on 3 get

b) b) on your own c) a journey/a cruise d) a cruise/a journey e) a taxi to work/out of a car f) out of a car/a taxi to work

2 2 Marta has been giving guided tours since she was 16. 3 I've been looking forward to my holiday for six months. 4 Cambridge University Press has been publishing books since 1584. 5 We've been going out together since I was 18. 6 You've been living in this house for two months.

3 2 been travelling 3 stayed 4 been feeling 5 tried 6 had 7 been looking after 8 kept/been keeping 9 published 10 had 11 finished 12 explored/been exploring

4 3 How many hotels have you worked in? 4 How many times have you been on a package holiday? 5 How long has he been taking work home? 6 How many times have you got a taxi to work? 7 How long have you been studying English? 8 How long have Tony and Maureen been married?

5 2 have … been getting around 3 haven't been 4 's been shining 5 've been going 6 hasn't taken 7 Have … known 8 haven't travelled 9 's been standing

3C Call that a holiday?

1 2 danger 3 enormous 4 important 5 sadness 6 serious 7 fame 8 modesty 9 accident

2 2c) 3a) 4b) 5c) 6b)

3 2 dangerous 3 enormous 4 important 5 sadness 6 serious 7 famous 8 modesty 9 accident

3D A trip to India

1 1 of 2 with; with 3 about/by; with 4 about; with

2a) 2 Is there anything worth seeing here? 3 Have you got any other tips? 4 What about places near the sea? 5 What's the best place to hire a car?

b) 2 What's the best place to hire a car? 3 Is there anything worth seeing here? 4 What about places near the sea? 5 Have you got any other tips?

3 2 'd recommend 3 sounds wonderful 4 's the best 5 wouldn't go

6 really useful 7 Do you know any 8 bother 9 to know 10 And is there 11 should go to 12 And what about 13 It's probably best 14 Have you got any 15 You really must 16 I've heard

4A Riders

1 2 appear 3 seeing 4 go 5 Going 6 playing 7 have

2 2 went 3 threw 4 was holding 5 were finishing 6 had 7 was 8 was wearing 9 wore 10 were playing 11 was 12 died 13 lost 14 was 15 was singing 16 hit 17 fell 18 was staying 19 asked 20 wanted 21 wasn't joking 22 painted

3 2 was; used to wash 3 used to be; preferred 4 lost; was; used to earn 5 used to present 6 didn't use to be; changed; did … use to be

4B Adventures

1 2b) 3a) 4c) 5b) 6c) 7c) 8a)

2 2 'd sold out 3 hadn't driven 4 hadn't heard 5 had left 6 hadn't done 7 'd been 8 hadn't known

3a) 2 stayed 3 got back 4 hadn't tidied up 5 was 6 had arranged 7 hadn't set 8 had arrived 9 was

b) b); d); e)

4a) 2 weren't 3 'd been 4 got back 5 'd lost 6 got 7 had found 8 saw 9 had got 10 had had to

b) 2d) 3f) 4b) 5c) 6e)

5 3 has 4 would 5 is 6 had 7 would 8 is; has 9 would; had 10 –; has

4C Natural medicines

1 c)

2a) 2 verb 3 verb 4 verb 5 noun 6 adjective 7 verb 8 adjective

b) 2a) 3b) 4a) 5b) 6a) 7a) 8b)

3 2DS 3T 4F 5F 6F 7F 8T

4D It's just a game!

1 2 bad-tempered 3 violent 4 rude 5 arrogant 6 offensive 7 spoilt 8 loyal 9 lazy 10 loud

2 2c) 3b) 4e) 5a)

3 2 He tends to be 3 On the whole 4 Generally speaking 5 violent 6 a bit arrogant 7 impolite 8 aggressive

4 2 They aren't very considerate at times. 3 Some of them can be rather untidy. 4 They tend to be a bit better with money. 5 Generally speaking, most women like shopping. 6 On the whole, they tend to be more organised than men.

5A Moving house

1 2 The Stephens Family 3 James and Mel 4 Sam

2 2 loft 3 study 4 kitchen 5 bathroom 6 garage 7 cellar
↓ cottage

3 2B 3B 4P 5H 6P 7B 8B

4 2 as close 3 similar 4 much less 5 far 6 the least 7 little 8 best 9 most

5 2 favourite 3 interesting 4 cheaper 5 most character 6 most determined 7 better 8 lightest 9 busiest 10 more fashionable 11 further

5B A load of old junk

1 2 sorted 3 Put 4 throwing 5 go 6 give 7 throw 8 coming 9 tidied 10 take

2a) 2e) 3a) 4d) 5c)
  b) 2b) 3a) 4d) 5e)

3 2 'll 3 will 4 're going to 5 're looking 6 'll sort it out 7 'm going to work

4 2 What **are you** going to do with all those old clothes? 3 I'm **playing** cards so I'll be back late. 4 Yes, it's going **to** be a big change. 5 I'll **call** you this evening about the meeting. 6 **I'll tidy** it up before they come back.

5 2 Are … going to buy 3 'll find 4 'll be 5 'll need 6 I'm … not going to listen 7 Will … give/Are … going to give 8 I'll sell 9 will buy 10 'll tidy 11 'm not doing 12 'll help 13 'm meeting 14 'll give 15 'm taking 16 are … going to tidy/will … tidy 17 'll do

5C Flatpack world

1 b)3 c)5 d)4 e)2

2 2 The minimum number of flats in each BoKlok community. 3 The year BoKlok began selling housing. 4 The number of homes BoKlok has sold. 5 The countries where prefabs were popular after World War II.

3 2 Prefabs seem to be more popular nowadays. 3 Over 2,000 people in Scandinavia have decided to buy a BoKlok home. 4 In the future more people might live in prefabs. 5 Many people would like to buy their own home. 6 I don't mind living with my parents.

5D Is this what you mean?

1 2 glass 3 leather 4 cotton 5 cardboard 6 plastic 7 metal 8 wool 9 wood 10 paper

2a) 2a) 3d) 4e) 5c) 6f)
  b) 2c) 3a) 4d) 5b) 6f)

3 2 Do you mean 3 what they're called 4 They're usually 5 It's stuff for 6 the word for 7 it's made of 8 You mean 10 It's a type of 11 you're looking for 12 What's it called 13 I'm looking for 14 for cleaning 15 they're made of 16 You use them

6A Make up your mind

1 2 made 3 made 4 do 5 done 6 made 7 makes 8 done

2 2 makes me laugh 3 done the washing 4 doing a course 5 make up your mind 6 doing the washing-up

3 2 Will you do me a favour if I help you do your homework? 3 You won't pass if you don't do any work. 4 What will you say if she doesn't make up her mind soon? 5 They'll never learn if they're allowed to behave so badly.

4 2a) 3e) 4h) 5f) 6c) 7b) 8d)

5 2 releases 3 'll put 4 check 5 makes 6 Will … get

6 2 unless 3 when 4 as soon as 5 until 6 after 7 before 8 if 9 until 10 unless

7 2 Unless you tell me about the problem, I won't be able to help. 3 Unless your employees have time to relax, they won't work well. 4 She should be here later unless she makes another excuse! 5 We'll have to get a loan unless you start making more money. 6 He'll continue to make the same mistakes unless we do something.

6B Protective parents

1 2 itself 3 ourselves 4 himself 5 themselves 6 yourself 7 yourselves 8 myself

2 2 goes 3 go 4 book 5 get 6 call 7 'm 8 sends

3a) 3 If 4 When 5 When 6 If 7 When 8 When

  b) 2 When I finish an exercise, I check the answers immediately. 3 If you live to be 100 in the UK, you get a letter from the Queen. 4 When I'm older, I'll start saving some money. 5 When this bus stops, will you help me with these bags? 6 If he doesn't feel better soon, we'll have to call the doctor. 7 When you get up in the morning, do you listen to the radio? 8 When you finish a meal, do you always do the washing-up?

4 3 shouldn't tell 4 should; tell 5 can; expect 6 must remember 7 listen 8 don't expect

5 2 in case 3 if 4 if 5 in case 6 if 7 in case 8 if

6C Touch wood

1 2e) 3c) 4d) 5b)

2 2T 3F 4DS 5DS 6F 7T 8F

3 2f) 3a) 4e) 5c) 6d)

6D What's your opinion?

1 2a) 3b) 4a)

2 2 Yes, I'd agree with 3 Can I just finish 4 Go ahead 5 You had something 6 That may be 7 Can I just 8 I'm not sure 9 make a point here 10 of course 11 Yes, sure 12 I agree actually 13 What do you think 14 I interrupt 15 That's not 16 If I could just finish

3 2 absolutely tiny 3 absolutely fantastic 4 absolutely filthy 5 absolutely furious 6 absolutely delicious 7 absolutely gorgeous 8 absolutely delighted

7A Save, copy, delete

1

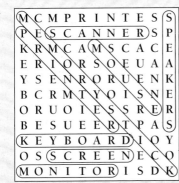

Answer Key

2   2 a link   3 icons   4 a folder   5 online
  6 a password

3a)   2 can   3 to understand   4 be able
  5 to start   6 to set up   7 be able to
  8 be able to

b)   2 to use   3 to send   4 sending
  5 searching   6 find   7 to order
  8 helping   9 help   10 understanding
  11 to use   12 to work

4   2 I'm hopeless at remembering
passwords.   3 My parents have
no idea how to get broadband.
  4 I managed to send an email,
but I don't know if it arrived.
  5 I was able to get emails, but I
wasn't able to send any.

5   2 I'd prefer to stay at home.   3 He
keeps phoning me every night.
  4 They told me "Buy a house with a
garden."   5 It seemed to be closed.

7B Want it, need it!

1   b) GPS/sat nav   c) dishwasher
  d) washing machine   e) hair dryer
  f) hair straighteners   g) hands-free
phone   h) air conditioning   i) central
heating   j) MP3 player   k) DVD
recorder   l) webcam

2   2 didn't; 'd   3 would spend; were
  4 saved; wouldn't lose   5 wouldn't;
made   6 Would; could   7 weren't;
would ask   8 gave; would

3   2 worked   3 wouldn't be lost   4 would
be able to   5 could remember   6 had
any idea

4   2b)   3a)   4b)   5a)   6b)

5a)   5 's/is   6 get   7 don't do   8 'll find   9 got
  10 'd/would have   11 wouldn't argue
  12 had   13 'd/would be able   14 don't
speak   15 don't do   16 'll/will get

b)   b) dishwasher   c) MP3 player
  d) hands-free phone

7C Virus alert!

1   2d)   3c)   4e)   5b)

2   2 It can record your credit card
information.   3 Yes, it often comes
with free software.   4 Information
about your surfing habits.   5 For
advertising reasons.   6 Your computer
is slower or you are getting a lot of
'pop-up' advertisements.   7 10%.
  8 Use some anti-spyware software or
visit spywarewarrior.com.

3   2 the   3 –   4 –   5 a   6 the   7 the   8 –   9 a
  10 the   11 An   12 –   13 a   14 The   15 –

7D What's the password?

1   2b)   3a)   4a) and b)   5a)

2   2d)   3f)   4c)   5b)   6a)

3   2 how I download software   3 what
the passwords are   4 air conditioning
costs   5 Do you think we can
  6 where I could buy

4   2 Do you know if he's at home today?
  3 Have you any idea what his phone
number is?   4 Could you tell me your
password?   5 Do you think you could
use another PC?   6 Can you tell me if
there's a girl with dark hair opposite
you?   7 Do you think you could
speak more quietly, please?

8A Changing weather

1   2 short   3 Thunder   4 wet   5 wind
  6 less   7 see   8 hot   9 much

2   b)5 hot   c)4 warm   d)3 cool
  e)2 chilly   f)6 freezing

3   2 have been made   3 be understood
  4 change   5 are killed   6 is affecting
  7 felt   8 be done

4   2b)   3a)   4a)

5   2 have been given   3 were used
  4 were added   5 are named   6 was
used   7 won't/will not be used   8 will
be called   9 aren't/are not repeated
  10 were removed   11 have been retired

8B Recycle your rubbish

1   2 a bag of   3 a tin of   4 a box of
  5 a can of   6 a carton of   7 a jar of
  8 a packet of

2   3 bag   4 packet/tin/carton   5 ✓   6 jar
  7 ✓   8 packet

3   2 There aren't any boxes.   3 There's
a lot of paper.   4 There aren't many
tins.   5 There's a lot of rubbish.
  6 There are a lot of bottles.   7 There
aren't many jars.   8 There isn't much
bread.   9 There aren't any cans.
  10 There are a lot of cartons.

4   2 a little   3 a little   4 a few   5 a few
  6 a little; a few   7 a few; a little

5   2 We've got plenty of time to get
there.   3 Only a few people I know
recycle plastic.   4 I'm a bit too tired
to go out tonight.   5 Oliver has got
hardly any teeth, but he's only six
months old.   6 Loads of children
recycle things at school.   7 There's
only a little olive oil in the cupboard.
  8 There's no time left.

6   2 any   3 Lots of   4 any   5 loads of
  6 a few   7 a little   8 much   9 a bit of
  10 hardly any   11 plenty

8C Dangers at sea

1a)   2c)   3a)   4b)   5c)   6b)

b)   8 tire**less**   9 **im**possible   10 **un**known
  11 **under**estimated   12 **over**fishing
  13 **dis**agree   14 **ir**responsible
  15 **re**introduce   16 **un**successful

2   2T   3DS   4F   5T   6DS   7T   8DS   9F

8D Be careful!

1a)   b) Make sure you avoid the streets
around the stadium.   c) Be careful
when you're in Vine Street.   d) I
hadn't heard that before.   e) Could
you give me some advice?   f) I
wouldn't listen to him if I were you.
  g) Don't go in summer or else you'll
make the same mistake as I did.
  h) That's really useful thanks.

b)   2 Be careful when you're in Vine
Street.   3 I hadn't heard that before.
  4 Make sure you avoid the streets
around the stadium.

c)   5 Could you give me some advice?
  6 I wouldn't listen to him if I were
you.   7 Don't go in the summer or
else you'll make the same mistake as
I did.   8 That's really useful thanks.

2   2 Do you know if Argentina is hot at
this time of year?   3 Can you tell me
who sells maps around here?   4 Do
you think I should book a hotel
before I go?   5 Have you any idea
why it's so expensive?

9A Get healthy!

1   2 operating   3 doctor   4 A&E
  5 specialist   6 GP   7 ward   8 attack
  9 asthma   10 migraine   11 allergy
  12 prescription   13 chemist's

2   2 whose   3 where   4 who/that
  5 whose   6 when   7 which/that
  8 who/that   9 where

3   2a)   3e)   4h)   5c)   6g)   7i)   8f)   9j)   10d)

4a)   3O   4S   5O   6O   7S   8O

b)   3 (The people the allergy affects ...);
  5 (The patient the surgeon operated
on ...);   6 (The ward I stayed in ...);
  8 (The migraines he gets ...)

5 2 I'm going on a retreat I think you've been on. 3 She's the woman who/that runs an organic fruit and vegetable shop. 4 I think it's very interesting you decided to become a surgeon. 5 I regularly get migraines which/that are really painful. 6 He's got a disease I'd never heard of.

9B Good news, bad news

1 **News story A**
2e) 3b) 4g) 5d) 6h) 7c) 8f)
News story B
2e) 3g) 4c) 5f) 6d) 7h) 8b)

2 2 I've just been **offered** another job. 3 **Have you** just changed the TV channel? 4 Her new record still hasn't **been** released. 5 The prime minister hasn't said **anything yet.** 6 Scientists **have already** discovered some causes of migraines. 7 Have you **been** paid for that survey yet? 8 You **still haven't** told anyone.

3 2 The reports haven't been published yet. 3 I've never taken part in a demonstration. 4 The offer has just been rejected by the government. 5 The unions have already called off the strike. 6 The government hasn't met last year's targets yet. 7 Four surveys have been carried out so far. 8 Have they already taken him to hospital?

4 2 If I were you, I'd get bottled water. 3 You'd better see a dentist soon. 4 Is it a good idea to book ahead? 5 Whatever you do, don't feed the animals. 6 Don't leave any valuables in your car.

5 3 hasn't been seen 4 has been 5 has … published 6 have shocked 7 have … been charged 8 has been released 9 haven't given 10 has suffered 11 has been 12 has been seen 13 has been finished 14 has … been released 15 has … received

9C Faking it

1 1 Ed Devlin 2 Maximillian Devereaux 3 Jatinder Sumal

2 2 Cutting up onions. 3 He thinks his body language at football matches wasn't good enough. 4 Her friends said it was a really good show. 5 At a film premiere. 6 She couldn't think of anything to ask him. 7 She doesn't plan to leave her job.

3 2 Despite not managing to persuade the experts, he enjoyed the experience. 3 She had never heard of *Faking It*. However, her friends said it was a really good show. 4 She tried to interview Robbie Williams. However, she couldn't think of anything to ask him! 5 Although it was a terrible experience, Jatinder quickly recovered. 6 In spite of her success at 'faking it', Jatinder doesn't plan to leave her job.

9D At the doctor's

1 1 runny; sneeze 2 poisoning, sick; diarrhoea 3 Paracetamol; painkiller; pill 4 symptom; asthma; wheezy 5 infection; antibiotics; virus

2 2d) 3e) 4c) 5b) 6f)

3a) b) getting c) taking d) suffering e) getting f) a week g) take them h) some antibiotics i) another appointment j) a prescription

b) 2b) 3d) 4c) 5e)

c) 6j) 7h) 8g) 9i) 10f)

10A The anniversary

1 2 lost 3 got in 4 gave 5 left 6 called 7 kept in 8 get 9 from 10 'm 11 know

2 2T 3F 4T 5T

3 2b) 3b) 4a) and b) 5a) and b)

4a) 2d) 3f) 4h) 5b) 6a) 7e) 8g)

b) 2 The room wasn't supposed to be big, but … 3 I was going to have a party that weekend, but … 4 I was supposed to invite him, but … 5 The concert was supposed to end at nine, but … 6 No one was going to give them anything, but … 7 We were going to meet in the morning, but … 8 I was supposed to get in touch with Diana, but …

10B Who's that?

1a) 1 … he's **going** bald. 2 He's got **short dark** hair and **a** striped shirt. 3 She's got straight blonde **hair** and a **flowery dress**. 4 She's got **shoulder-length** hair and a light jacket.

b) a) Erin b) Alice c) Chris d) Oscar

2 1b) Jay's hair is shoulder-length and wavy. c) Fern's hair is long and curly. 2a) Alice has got light trousers. b) Chris has got a plain jacket. Oscar has got a striped jacket.

3a) 2 The girl with the ponytail could be Ruby. 3 Jo could be stuck in traffic. 4 Joel might be coming to the party later. 5 Stephen must be leaving in a minute. 6 The children may prefer to stay at home. 7 The weather can't get any worse. 8 Simon can't be working there any more.

b) 2F 3T 4T 5T 6F 7T 8F

4a) 2 must 3 may 4 could 5 can't 6 must 7 might 8 must 9 can't

b) 3 Phoebe must be having a baby soon. 4 Leo could/may/might be Phoebe's grandfather. 5 Chris can't be staying at the party until late. 6 Phoebe and Leo must get on well. 7 Erin and Maisie could/may/might be chatting about Oscar. 8 Jay can't be retired yet.

10C The party's over

1 2c) 3e) 4a) 5b)

2 b) pointed out c) going up d) get out of it e) put it off f) split up g) looked up h) came across i) get over it j) had come up with

3 2F 3F 4T 5F 6F 7T 8F

10D Do you mind?

1 2b) 3a) 4b)

2 1 No, do whatever you like. 2 May/ Can; Yes, help yourself. 3 Is it OK if; Of course./I'm afraid I'm watching this. 4 Would you mind if; I'd rather he didn't. 5 Could/May; I'd rather you didn't./Yes, sure. 6 Do you think; Yes, of course.

3a) 2 Do you think I could have a glass? 3 Is it OK if I make some coffee? 4 Can I look round your garden? 5 Would you mind if I checked my email? 6 Do you mind if I have a shower?

b) 2 Yes, of course you can 3 Yes, of course it is 4 Go ahead 5 Sorry, you can't 6 No, not at all

Answer Key

Reading and Writing Portfolio 1

1 a) Anna's mum. b) Anna, David, Eve and Harry. c) She's on holiday.

2 2b) 3b) 4a) 5b) 6c)

3b) 2 article 3 pronoun and auxiliary verb 4 preposition 5 pronoun 6 pronoun

  c) b)6 c)3 d)2 e)5 f)4

4 2 In 3 I; the 4 I; have 5 Have; you 6 We; have 7 It; is 8 We; are

Reading and Writing Portfolio 2

1 a)E b)B c)C d)F e)D

2 2T 3T 4T 5F 6DS

3b) 2 n/s 3 vgc 4 ono 5 p/w 6 eves. 7 Tue. 8 Tel. no.

  c) 2 Avenue 3 April 4 for example 5 as soon as possible 6 including 7 Road 8 Thanks

4 Possible answers
  a) 3 hours p/w on Sat. morning.
    Call Alex
    Tel. no. 01923 434325
    (after 7 eves.)
  b) Double room to let
    £140 p/w incl. bills
    n/s only
    mjparks@ukmail.net
  c) Television for sale
    2 months old – vgc
    £120 ono
    Pick up only from Carston Ave.
    Call Tom
    Tel. no. 07986 304207

Reading and Writing Portfolio 3

1a) 2T 3T 4F You should start a new paragraph for each new subject. 5F You should use full forms. 6T

  b) 2

2 2b) 3a) 4b) 5c) 6b) 7a)

3a) 1 UK 2 US 3 UK

  b) 2 03/14/07 3 apologize 4 color 5 traveler 6 through

4a) 2 You should start a new paragraph for each new subject. 3 You should use full forms. 4 You should write your signature above your name.

b) Possible answers
21/12/06 → 12/21/06
realise → realize
14th March (14/03/07) → March 14th (03/14/07)
Yours sincerely → Sincerely (yours)

Reading and Writing Portfolio 4

1 b)

2 2c) 3a) 4b) 5b) 6c)

3 b)2 c)1 d)3

4 2b); d) 3a)

5 2a) 3b) 4f) 5d) 6c)

6 2 attracted 3 'm … learning 4 takes 5 describes 6 is 7 is 8 are 9 'll love 10 'm going to read

7 2 The book tells the story of a young boy who has no parents. 3 The main character in the book is Jack. 4 The story takes place in Buenos Aires, Argentina. 5 I think the book would make a good film because it's so exciting. 6 The title of the book is *Loyal* because it refers to the relationship between the man and his dog.

Reading and Writing Portfolio 5

1 2c) 3a) 4b) 5b) 6a) 7a) 8c)

2 2F 3F 4T 5T 6T 7F

3a) 2 We're so sorry that we didn't come to Jackie and Bill's party on Saturday afternoon. 3 Don't forget to book train or plane tickets soon if you're going to come! 4 Can anyone tell me what Pat Austin's email is? 5 Hope you all have a lovely break during the holiday! 6 We're so grateful for all your cards and presents. 7 What happened was that we were supposed to finish packing in the afternoon. 8 Would you all like to come?

  b) b)3 c)5 d)6 e)8 f)1 g)7 h)4

  c) a)1 b)3; 8

4a) 2 Hope you have 3 Can anyone tell me 4 We'd rather 5 We are so grateful for 6 Would you like 7 What happened was that 8 Don't forget

b) Possible answers
  2 **Don't forget** that it's Mum and Dad's wedding anniversary tomorrow. 3 **Can anyone tell me** where the station is, please? 4 **I'm so grateful for** my birthday present. **Hope you have** a good time on holiday. 5 **Would you like** to come to a pop concert on Friday? **I'd rather** go with someone than go alone.

5a) 1c) 2a) 3b)

Reading and Writing Portfolio 6

1 a) Barry b) Phil c) Nicole

2 2T 3F 4DS 5T 6T 7F 8F 9DS

3a) 2 **I've always** felt **that** … 3 **I have no** doubt that … 4 **As** far **as** I'm **concerned**, … 5 **As I see it**, … 6 **I'm** positive **that** … 7 **To me**, … 8 I strongly **believe that** …

  b) 3; 6; 8

  c) 2 **As far as he's concerned**, we pay less than the government's minimum wage! 3 **As they see it**, they have to earn their pocket money. 4 **We strongly believe that** this is a much better idea than the threat of no pocket money.

4a) 2 She's absolutely convinced that she will win. 3 I've always felt that everyone should be able to afford a house. 4 He has no doubt that we will find life on other planets. 5 I'm positive that I saw him earlier. 6 As she sees it, housework is a waste of time. 7 To me, children spend too much time watching TV. 8 As far as my brother is concerned, children shouldn't get pocket money.

Reading and Writing Portfolio 7

1 2D 3B 4A

2 2T 3F 4T 5DS 6T 7F 8F

3 3; 4; 7

4a) Then; Next; Meanwhile; Finally

  b) 1 next 2 finally 3 meanwhile 4 first

5a) 2 **Don't forget** to switch the machine off when it's finished! 3 **Remember that** the rubbish is collected early on Monday mornings. 4 **You will need** to put the bins outside on Sunday night. 5 **Whatever you do**, don't use

the sink in the upstairs bathroom.
6 Try to avoid using too much heat otherwise you will burn the onions.

b) a)4 b)6 c)5 d)1; 3

6a) 3; 4; 7

b) Possible answers
2 Check the channel for Big Brother. (I think it's Channel Four.) 3 Change the channel on the DVD recorder. 4 Press the red record button.

7 1 need to/will need to 2 Make sure 3 Remember that 4 Avoid using 5 Don't forget to 6 Whatever you do

Reading and Writing Portfolio 8

1a) Letter 1: A; C Letter 2: B; F; D

b) a)1 b)2

2 2T 3T 4F 5T 6DS 7T 8F 9DS

3 1F 2C; D; 3B; E

4a) 1 Furthermore; Moreover
2 Although; However; even though

b) 1 even though 2 however 3 in addition; furthermore; moreover

5a) C For example, students should **be told** ...; ... three or four bins, that **are emptied** regularly, ... D ... the park should **be closed** ... F When I am not worrying about hitting a pedestrian or **being attacked** ...; Nothing **has been done** about this ...

b) 1; 3

6 2 Even though 3 Furthermore 4 Even though/Although 5 Moreover 6 In addition/Furthermore 7 However

7 2 The road must be repaired 3 Recycling bins aren't used regularly. 4 The bins are never emptied. 5 A lot of glass is recycled 6 I was told that the lights would be replaced.

Reading and Writing Portfolio 9

1 c); d); f); h)

2 2 Yes, she does. 3 Developing training programmes, giving advice and training to instructors. 4 To develop her skills in a full-time position with more responsibility and work as part of a team. 5 She ran in this year's London Marathon. 6 Her CV. 7 Probably hard-working, organised and quite ambitious.

3 2B 3E 4A 5C

4a) b)1 c)4 d)3 e)6 f)2

b) 1 to; in; for 2 At; as 3 from; to 4 in; for 5 As; from 6 to; from

5a) A; C; E; B

b) I am writing **in** reply to your advertisement **in** The Times **for** a receptionist at St John's Wood Surgery.

At the moment I am working full-time **as** a receptionist for a large American bank in London. My responsibilities range **from** meeting visitors to answering phones and taking messages.

I am interested **in** medical issues and three years ago, I had a temporary position **as** a secretary **at** the Wellington Hospital. I believe my experience, interest and enthusiasm would be excellent for your position.

As you will see **from** my CV, I have over nine years of experience. In this time, I have learned a wide variety of skills connected with my work. I have also realised that I particularly enjoy the personal contact that receptionists have with people. Therefore I would like the opportunity to work in a smaller office environment.

I look forward to hearing **from** you.

Reading and Writing Portfolio 10

1 2; 3; 4

2 1 At an old school friend's wedding. 2 Because Fiona liked Kate's shoes. 3 Bright clothes. 4 Kate is tanned and looks Spanish or Italian. She has long, dark hair, is very tall and looks like a model. Fiona looks English, she has short, blonde hair, isn't very tall and doesn't look like a model. 5 Kate is much more confident but she is more disorganised than Fiona. 6 She's always ready with a cup of tea and some good advice when Fiona has a problem.

3 b)3 c)1 d)2

4a) 2 ... **we look** completely different ... **I look** typically English! 3 In fact, **she looks like a** model and ... 4 ... she's ... **the** most considerate and unselfish **person I know**.

b) a)3 b)4 c)2

5a) 2b) look intelligent 3b) similar taste in 4b) looks like 5b) the most talented 6b) similar taste in 7b) like my 8b) 's the worst

b) 2 My brother and I have similar taste **in** cars. 3 People think I look ~~like~~ Swedish ... 4 My dad is one of the **funniest** people I know. 5 He looks **like** his father, doesn't he? 6 She looks **good** in that dress.

CD-ROM/Audio CD Instructions

Start the CD-ROM

- Insert the *face2face* CD-ROM into your CD-ROM drive.
- If Autorun is enabled, the CD-ROM will start automatically.
- If Autorun is not enabled, open **My Computer** and then **D:** (where D is the letter of your CD-ROM drive). Then double-click on the *face2face* icon.

Install the CD-ROM to your hard disk (recommended)

- Go to **My Computer** and then **D:** (where D is the letter of your CD-ROM drive).
- Right-click on *Explore*.
- Double-click on *Install face2face to hard disk*.
- Follow the installation instructions on your screen.

Listen and practise on your CD player

You can listen to and practise language from the Student's Book Real World lessons on your CD player at home or in the car:

R1.9	R2.9	R3.10	R4.14	R5.8	R6.9
R7.13	R8.7	R9.12	R10.9	R11.11	

What's on the CD-ROM?

• Interactive practice activities

Extra practice of Grammar, Vocabulary, Real World situations and English pronunciation. Click on one of the unit numbers (1–12) at the top of the screen. Then choose an activity and click on it to start.

• My Activities

Create your own lesson. Click on *My Activities* at the top of the screen. Drag activities from the unit menus into the *My Activities* panel on the right of the screen. Then click on *Start*.

• My Portfolio

This is a unique and customisable reference tool. Click on *Grammar*, *Word List*, *Real World* or *Phonemes* at any time for extra help and information. You can also add your own notes, check your progress and create your own English tests!

Practice activities   My Activities

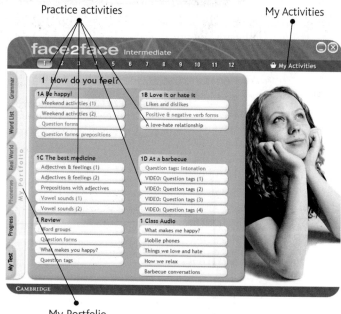

My Portfolio

System specification
- Windows 98, NT4 with Service Pack 6, ME, 2000 or XP
- 128Mb RAM
- 500Mb hard disk space (if installing to hard disk)

Support

If you experience difficulties with this CD-ROM, please visit: www.cambridge.org/elt/cdrom

---

Acknowledgements

The authors would like to thank all the team at Cambridge University Press for their continuing support, enthusiasm and energy, in particular: Sue Ullstein (Senior Commissioning Editor); Laurie Harrison (Electronic Project Manager); Dilys Silva, Rachel Jackson-Stevens, Andrew Reid and Keith Sands (Editorial team); Ruth Atkinson, Brigit Viney and Diane Winkleby (Freelance editors); Alison Greenwood, Nicholas Murgatroyd and Nicholas Tims (CD-ROM team) and all the team at Pentacor (Book design).

Chris Redston would like to thank Adela Pickles for all her encouragement, patience and love, and for all the fun they have had together since Pacha. He would also like to thank the following people for keeping him cheerful: Mark Skipper, Laura Skipper, Will Ord, Heidi Sowter, Karen Thomas, Kari Matchett, Dylan Evans, Katy Wimhurst, Margie Fisher, Emma Murphy, Natasha Muñoz, Joss Whedon, his two wonderful sisters, Anne and Carol, and his dear father, Bill Redston. This book is dedicated to his mother, Maeve Redston – she'd have been proud!

Gillie Cunningham would like to thank Richard Gibb for being such an enormous help and for always delivering humour just when she most needs it. Continued love and thanks to Amybeth for being such a loving, patient and fun daughter. Love and thanks also to Sue Mohamed for her amazing friendship and professional help. And to all her wonderful friends, she offers eternal thanks for their patience and for reminding her she needs to get out more! Very special thanks also go to Monica, Kaz and Molly Janowski for supplying the longhouse photo and information about life in the Borneo jungle.

The authors and publishers would like to thank the following teachers for the invaluable feedback which they provided:

Alejandro Zarzalejos, Spain; David Barnes, Italy; Colin Barnet, Belgium; Julia Blackwell, Germany; Helen Coward, UK; Mike Delaney, Brazil; Josie Dent, UK; Elizabeth Downey, New Zealand; Nick Godfrey, Colombia; Alison Greenwood, Italy; David Hill, Turkey; Maria Helena Iema, Brazil; Gema Mazón, Spain; Darragh O'Grady, Mexico; Marcus Paiva, Brazil; Angela Pitt, Germany; Wayne Rimmer, Russia; Kevin Rutherford, Poland; Ana Carmen Sánchez, Spain; Andrea Sweeney, Mexico; Dave Tucker, Portugal; Yüksel Tuna, Turkey; Luiza Wójtowicz, Poland.

The authors and publishers are grateful to the following contributors:

pentacor**big**: cover and text design and page make-up
Hilary Luckcock: picture research, commissioned photography
Trevor Clifford: photography
Anne Rosenfeld: audio recordings

The authors and publishers are grateful to the following for permission to reproduce copyright material. All efforts have been made to contact the copyright holders of material reproduced in this book which belongs to third parties, and citations are given for the sources. We welcome approaches from any copyright holders whom we have not been able to trace but who find that their material has been reproduced herein.

For the jacket cover in 2A: *In Praise of Slow* by Carl Honoré, © *The Orion* Publishing Group Ltd, 2004; for the text in 2C: adapted from 'Help! I just can't sleep' by Victoria Young, *Evening Standard*, 3rd December 2002, with permission of